Bach's Chorals

(Part II)
The Hymns and Hymn Melodies
of the Cantatas and Motetts

Charles Sanford Terry

Alpha Editions

This edition published in 2019

ISBN : 9789353897208

Design and Setting By
Alpha Editions
email - alphaedis@gmail.com

As per information held with us this book is in Public Domain.
This book is a reproduction of an important historical work. Alpha Editions uses the best technology to reproduce historical work in the same manner it was first published to preserve its original nature. Any marks or number seen are left intentionally to preserve its true form.

BACH'S CHORALS

BY
CHARLES SANFORD TERRY

PART II

THE HYMNS AND HYMN
MELODIES
OF THE
CANTATAS AND MOTETTS

Cambridge:
at the University Press
1917

PREFATORY NOTE

IN Part I of this work the Hymns and Hymn melodies of the "Passions" and Oratorios have been dealt with. In the present volume those of the Cantatas and Motetts are considered. The Hymn melodies of the Organ Works are reserved for Part III.

The author approaches the Chorals from the historical rather than an aesthetic standpoint. His object is to reveal the origin and authorship of the Hymns and Hymn melodies which, like jewels, decorate Bach's concerted Church music. The melodies are printed here in their earliest form and, where possible, Bach's variations of them are traced to an earlier tradition or attributed to himself. In similar manner, the text of his Hymn stanzas, as printed by the Bachgesellschaft, has been collated with the originals in Philipp Wackernagel's *Das deutsche Kirchenlied von der ältesten Zeit bis zu Anfang des XVII Jahrhunderts* (Leipzig, 5 vols.

1864–77) or Albert Fischer and W. Tümpel's *Das deutsche evangelische Kirchenlied des siebzehnten Jahrhunderts* (Gütersloh, 1904–16). The few Hymns which are not in those collections are marked with an asterisk in the following pages. The author has not had the opportunity to examine their original texts elsewhere.

For the help of students and others the author, on the first occurrence of every Choral melody, states where Bach uses it elsewhere in his concerted Church music and Organ works[1]. Thus, Bach's treatment of a particular tune can be studied exhaustively.

Since all but a few of the Cantatas are published only with German texts, it has seemed advisable to provide an Appendix of translations of the Hymn stanzas, upwards of two hundred and fifty in number, which Bach uses in the Cantatas and Motetts. Wherever it is available, the text of Novello & Co.'s and Messrs J. & W. Chester's Editions has been used, with the permission of the two firms.

Six melodies that occur in the "Passions" and Oratorios are not found in the Cantatas or Motetts. They are printed in an Appendix. This volume therefore contains all the Choral tunes used by Bach in his concerted Church music.

[1] The references throughout are to Novello's Edition of Bach's Organ Works, Books xv–xix.

In the Introduction, besides other topics relative to the subject of this work, there will be found a section on Bach's original Hymn tunes. The subject is one which hitherto has not received adequate attention. Schweitzer does not deal with it, and Spitta's chapter is unreliable.

The author thanks the Rev. James Mearns, Mr Herbert Thompson, Mr Ernest Newman, and especially Mr Ivor Atkins, for the valuable help they have given him. He also acknowledges material aid from the Carnegie Trust for the Universities of Scotland towards the publication of this work.

C. S. T.

KING'S COLLEGE,
   OLD ABERDEEN.
      January, 1917.

CONTENTS

	PAGE
PREFATORY NOTE	v
INTRODUCTION	1
The Cantatas	1
The Choral Cantatas	26
The Choral Fantasia	35
The Simple Choral	37
The Embellished Choral	38
The Extended Choral	40
The Unison Choral	41
The Aria *Choral*	41
The Dialogus *Choral*	42
The Motetts	44
The Hymns of the "Passions," Oratorios, Cantatas, and Motetts	46
The Hymn Tunes used by Bach	56
Bach's original Hymn Tunes	67
THE CANTATAS	129
THE UNFINISHED CANTATAS	477
THE CANTATAS OF DOUBTFUL AUTHENTICITY	479
THE MOTETTS	483
APPENDIX I. Hymn Melodies that occur in the "Passions" and Oratorios, but are not found in the Cantatas and Motetts	491
APPENDIX II. Translations	497
APPENDIX III. The Original Texts of Bach's Oratorios, "Passions," Masses, Cantatas, and Motetts	573

MELODIES

	PAGE
A solis ortus cardine (1537)	367
Ach Gott und Herr (1625 & 1655)	237
Ach Gott, vom Himmel sieh darein (1524)	132
Ach wie flüchtig (1652 & 1661)	193
Ainsi qu'on oit le cerf bruire (1542)	164
Alle Menschen müssen sterben (1652 & 1715)	434, 435
Allein Gott in der Höh' sei Ehr' (1539)	305
Allein zu dir, Herr Jesu Christ (c. 1541 & 1545)	205
Also hat Gott die Welt geliebt (1682)	269
Auf meinen lieben Gott (1609)	142
Aus tiefer Noth schrei ich zu dir (1524)	213
Bleiches Antlitz, sei gegrüsset (1686)	218
Christ ist erstanden (1535)	265
Christ lag in Todesbanden (1524)	137, 138
Christ unser Herr zum Jordan kam (1524)	149
Christe, du Lamm Gottes (1557)	188
Christum wir sollen loben schon (1524)	368
Christus, der ist mein Leben (1609)	326
Christus, der uns selig macht (1531 & 1598)	491
Da Christus geboren war (1544)	465
Danket dem Herrn, heut und allzeit (1594)	145
Das neugebor'ne Kindelein (1609)	369
Die Wollust dieser Welt (1679)	231
Dies sind die heil'gen zehn Gebot' (1524)	287
Du Friedefürst, Herr Jesu Christ (1601)	268
Du, O schönes Weltgebäude (1649)	245
Durch Adams Fall ist ganz verderbt (1535)	178
Ein Kind geborn zu Bethlehem (1543 & 1553)	261, 262
Ein' feste Burg (1535)	297
Einen guten Kampf hab' ich (1713)	218
Erhalt' uns, Herr, bei deinem Wort (1543)	147

	PAGE
Ermuntre dich, mein schwacher Geist (1641)	158
Erschienen ist der herrlich' Tag (1560)	266
Erstanden ist der heil'ge Christ (1555)	267
Es ist das Heil uns kommen her (1524)	154
Es ist genug (1662)	253
Es sind doch selig alle (1525)	492
Es woll' uns Gott genädig sein (1525)	271
Freuet euch, ihr Christen alle (1646)	220
Gelobet seist du, Jesu Christ (1524)	257
Gieb unsern Fürsten (1566)	226
Gloria in excelsis Deo (1545)	305
Gott des Himmels und der Erden (1642 & 1687)	493
Grates nunc omnes reddamus (1524)	257
Hast du denn, Liebster, dein Angesicht (1665)	247
Helft mir Gott's Güte preisen (1575 [1569])	160
Herr Christ, der einig' Gott's Sohn (1524)	186
Herr Gott dich loben wir (1535)	173, 365, 366
Herr, ich habe missgehandelt (1649)	435
Herr Jesu Christ, du höchstes Gut (1593)	239
Herr, wie du willt, so schick's mit mir (1525)	426
Herzlich lieb hab' ich dich, O Herr (1577)	417
Herzlich thut mich verlangen (1601)	395
Herzliebster Jesu, was hast du verbrochen (1640)	494
Hilf mir, Herr Jesu, weil ich leb' (1602)	134
Ich dank' dir, lieber Herre (1662)	212
Ich freue mich in dir (c. 1735)	391, 392
Ich hab' mein Sach' Gott heimgestellt (1609)	344
Ich hört ein Fräulein klagen (1549)	186
Ich ruf' zu dir, Herr Jesu Christ (1535)	451
Ich weiss mir ein Röslein hübsch und fein (1589)	343
Il n'y a icy celluy (c. 1551)	385
In dich hab' ich gehoffet, Herr (1581)	242
In Gottes Namen fahren wir (1536)	287
Ist Gott mein Schild und Helfersmann (1694)	307
Jesu, der du meine Seele (1641)	434

	PAGE
Jesu Kreuz, Leiden und Pein (1609)	431
Jesu, meine Freude (1653)	260
Jesu, nun sei gepreiset (1591)	222
Jesus, meine Zuversicht (1653)	412
Komm, Gott Schöpfer, heiliger Geist (1524 & 1535)	479
Komm, heiliger Geist, Herre Gott (1535)	250
Komm, Jesu, komm	489
Kommt her zu mir, spricht Gottes Sohn (1530)	283
Liebster Gott, wann werd' ich sterben (1713)	151
Liebster Immanuel, Herzog der Frommen (1679)	372
Lob' Gott getrost mit Singen (1544)	211
Lobt Gott, ihr Christen alle gleich (1554)	419
Mach's mit mir, Gott, nach deiner Güt' (1628)	402
Meine Hoffnung stehet feste (1680)	218
Meinen Jesum lass' ich nicht (1659)	274
Mit Fried' und Freud' ich fahr' dahin (1524)	302
Nun bitten wir den heiligen Geist (1524)	445
Nun danket alle Gott (1648)	293
Nun freut euch, lieben Christen g'mein (1535)	277
Nun komm, der Heiden Heiland (1524)	208
Nun lasst uns Gott dem Herren (1575 & 1587)	295
Nun lob', mein' Seel', den Herren (1540)	175
O Ewigkeit, du Donnerwort (1653)	181
O Gott, du frommer Gott (1693)	190
O grosser Gott von Macht (1632)	233
O Herre Gott, dein göttlich Wort (1527)	462
O Jesu Christ, mein's Lebens Licht (1625)	134
O Lamm Gottes unschuldig (1542 & 1545)	495
O stilles Gottes Lamm (1738)	392
O Welt, ich muss dich lassen (1539)	167
On a beau son maison bastir (1551)	379
Or sus, serviteurs du Seigneur (1551)	385
Puer natus in Bethlehem (1543 & 1553)	261, 262
Schmücke dich, O liebe Seele (1649)	457
Schönster Immanuel, Herzog der Frommen (1698)	372

xiii

	PAGE
Singen wir aus Herzensgrund (1589)	466
Straf mich nicht in deinem Zorn (1694)	359
Valet will ich dir geben (1614)	328
Vater unser im Himmelreich (1539)	312
Veni Redemptor gentium (1531)	208
Venus du und dein Kind (1574)	142
Verleih' uns Frieden gnädiglich (1535)	226
Vom Himmel hoch da komm ich her (1539)	496
Von Gott will ich nicht lassen (1572 [1571])	159
Wach auf, mein Geist (1642)	181
Wachet auf, ruft uns die Stimme (1599)	404
Wachet doch, erwacht, ihr Schläfer (1662)	290
Wär' Gott nicht mit uns diese Zeit (1524)	169
Warum betrübst du dich, mein Herz (1565)	235
Warum sollt' ich mich denn grämen (1666 & 1713)	487
Was Gott thut, das ist wohlgethan (1690)	162
Was mein Gott will, das g'scheh' allzeit (1572 [1571])	263
Was willst du dich betrüben (1704)	346
Welt, ade! ich bin dein müde (1682)	196
Wenn mein Stündlein vorhanden ist (1569)	171
Wer nur den lieben Gott lässt walten (1657)	184
Werde munter, mein Gemüthe (1642)	244
Wie schön leuchtet der Morgenstern (1599)	129
Wir Christenleut' (1593)	216
Wo Gott der Herr nicht bei uns hält (1535)	280
Wo soll ich fliehen hin (1679)	438
INDEX	585

PART I

ADDENDA AND ERRATA

PAGE

vi ll. 10–11.   *Delete* which...century.

    l. 13.   *For* Johann Crüger *read* Paul Wagner.

viii l. 10.   The melody "In dich hab' ich gehoffet, Herr," in the *Orgelbüchlein* is not the one used by Bach elsewhere.

11 n. 1, 2.   Bach's lines are found in the 1644 edition of Heermann's *Devoti Musica Cordis*.

13 l. 8.   *For* of *read* in.

18 n. 2 }   Bach's line conforms to the 1653 edition of the *Praxis Pietatis Melica*.
27 n. 1 }

22 n. 1.   *For* Weltgenrichte *read* Weltgewichte. In the second line of the second stanza of Gerhardt's Hymn the edition of 1656 *has* Dafür *for* Vor dem.

31 No. 15.   In the second line of the eighth stanza of Heermann's Hymn the original (1630) text *has* solche *for* diese. The third line, as Bach sets it, follows the 1644 text of Heermann's Hymns more closely. In the ninth stanza, line 2, the original (1630) text *has* Erbarmung *for* Erbarmen.

42 No. 7.   The melody, "Gelobet seist du, Jesu Christ," is derived from that of the Latin sequence, "Grates nunc omnes reddamus."

43 ll. 1.   *For* nun *read* in.

52.   In the second line of Runge's stanza the original (1653) text *has* Itzt *for* Dass.

55.   In the last line of Rist's stanza the original (1642) text *has* Jesus *for* Jesu.

58.   In the last line but one of Franck's stanza the original (1674) text *has* denselben *for* dieselbe, and in the last line es *for* sie.

62 l. 12.   *For* Eucharistic *read* Ascensiontide.

INTRODUCTION

The Cantatas

THERE is early and adequate authority for the belief that Bach wrote five complete "year books" of Church Cantatas, i.e. five Cantatas for every one of the Sundays and Festivals of the ecclesiastical year. At Leipzig fifty-nine Cantatas were required annually[1]. Consequently, Bach must have written two hundred and ninety-five Cantatas. Of that number certainly thirty were written before he was inducted at Leipzig as successor to Johann Kuhnau (1667-1722) on May 31, 1723. Bach did not write Cantatas during the last years of his life: the latest that can be dated is "Du Friedefürst, Herr Jesu Christ" (No. 116), written for the Twenty-fifth Sunday after Trinity, November 15, 1744[2]. It is therefore reasonable to limit his

---

[1] Concerted music was not sung at Leipzig during the six Sundays of Lent and the last three of Advent. Cantatas were required on forty-three Sundays and sixteen weekday Festivals.

[2] *Johann Sebastian Bach: His Work and Influence on the Music of Germany*, 1685-1750. By Philipp Spitta. Translated from the German by Clara Bell and J. A. Fuller Maitland (3 vols., London, 1897-99), III. 91.

INTRODUCTION

activity as a composer at Leipzig to twenty-one years. On that hypothesis, he must have written twelve or thirteen Church Cantatas every year, or at the rate of one every month[1]. If it be remembered that during the same period Bach's genius was exceedingly productive in other forms of musical expression, the conclusion that he was a rapid writer hardly can be challenged, though Spitta disputes it[2].

Less than seventy *per cent.* of Bach's Church Cantatas survive. The set of five is complete only for Christmas Day, New Year's Day (Feast of the Circumcision), Whit Sunday (though one of the five is of doubtful authenticity), Feast of the Purification of the B. V. M., and the Feast of St Michael the Archangel (one of which is of doubtful authenticity). There are four Cantatas in every case for the Third Sunday after Epiphany, Quinquagesima, Easter Day, Ascension Day, Sixteenth Sunday

---

[1] During his first eighteen months at Leipzig Bach wrote more than twenty Sunday Cantatas, besides two sacred Cantatas for special occasions. See Albert Schweitzer, *J. S. Bach* (translated by Ernest Newman, 2 vols., London, 1911), II. 164. Bach wrote about seventy Cantatas after 1734 (see list *infra*, p. 4), very nearly half of which are assigned to the years 1735–36 (Schweitzer, II. 328). In 1735 alone no less than twenty Cantatas were composed by him (Spitta, III. 68). With the exception, perhaps, of a single Sunday, he wrote a new Cantata for every Sunday and Festival between Easter and Whitsuntide in that year (*Ibid.* III. 70).

[2] *Ibid.* II. 349.

after Trinity, and the Twenty-first Sunday after Trinity. For no other Festival or Sunday have more than three Cantatas survived, and most of them have less[1].

Without reckoning the six Cantatas which form the "Christmas Oratorio[2]," there survive two hundred and six Church Cantatas composed by Bach, or attributed to him, all of which are published by the Bachgesellschaft. Nos. 1-190 bear the numbers assigned to them in the volumes of the Bachgesellschaft. Nos. 191-198, which are not grouped in a single volume of the B. G. edition, bear the distinguishing numbers attached to them in vol. XX of Breitkopf & Haertel's vocal scores of the Church Cantatas. No. 199 is published by the Neue Bachgesellschaft. There remain three Cantatas which are incomplete: in the following pages they are designated U 1, U 2, U 3. Finally, there are four Cantatas of doubtful authenticity (B. G. xli): they are here indicated as D 1, D 2, D 3, D 4.

Four of the Church Cantatas (Nos. D 1, D 2, D 3, D 4) were written at dates which are not ascertained.

[1] See *infra*, p. 5.
[2] The Oratorio consists of six Cantatas designed respectively for (i) Christmas Day, (ii) Feast of St Stephen, (iii) Feast of St John the Evangelist, (iv) New Year's Day (Circumcision), (v) Sunday after New Year's Day, (vi) Feast of the Epiphany.

The remaining 202 Cantatas are distributed between the five periods of Bach's career:

I. (1704-1708.) ARNSTADT AND MÜHLHAUSEN CANTATAS (3). Nos. 15, 71, 131.

II. (1708-1717.) WEIMAR CANTATAS (23). Nos. 18, 21, 31, 59, 61, 70, 106, 132, 142, 147, 150, 152, 155, 158, 160, 161, 162, 163, 182, 185, 189, 196, 199.

III. (1718-1722.) CÖTHEN CANTATAS (4). Nos. 47, 134, 141, 173¹.

IV. (1723-1734.) LEIPZIG CANTATAS (100). Nos. 4, 8, 9, 12, 16, 19, 20, 22, 23², 24, 25, 27, 28³, 29, 35, 36, 37, 40, 42, 44, 46, 49, 51, 52, 55, 56, 58, 60, 63, 64, 65, 66, 67, 69, 72⁴, 73, 75, 76, 77, 80, 81, 82, 83, 84, 86, 88, 89, 93, 95, 97, 98, 99, 102, 104, 105, 107, 109, 112, 117, 119, 120, 129, 136, 137, 140, 144, 145, 148, 149, 153, 154, 156, 157, 159, 164, 165, 166, 167, 168, 169, 170, 171, 172, 174, 177, 179, 181, 184, 186, 187, 188, 190, 191, 192, 194, 195, 198, U 1, U 2, U 3⁵.

V. (1735-1750.) LEIPZIG CANTATAS (72). Nos. 1, 2, 3, 5, 6, 7, 10, 11, 13, 14, 17, 26, 30, 32, 33, 34, 38, 39, 41, 43, 45, 48, 50, 53, 54, 57, 62, 68, 74⁶, 78, 79, 85, 87, 90, 91, 92, 94, 96, 100, 101, 103,

---

¹ As a Cantata c. 1730.
² Or late Cöthen period. See Wustmann (*infra*, p. 5, note 1), p. 279.
³ But see *Ibid.* p. 275.   ⁴ But see *Ibid.* p. 277.
⁵ But see *Ibid.* p. 298.   ⁶ But see *Ibid.* p. 284.

INTRODUCTION 5

108, 110, 111, 113, 114, 115, 116, 118, 121, 122, 123, 124, 125, 126, 127, 128, 130, 133, 135, 138, 139, 143, 146, 151, 175, 176, 178, 180, 183, 193, 197.

It will be convenient to group the Church Cantatas according to the seasons of the Church's year[1]:

SUNDAYS IN ADVENT.

First (*Epistle* Rom. xiii. 11-14. *Gospel* St Matt. xxi. 1-11).

36 Schwingt freudig euch empor[2, 3].

[1] A useful publication is Rudolf Wustmann's *Joh. Seb. Bachs Kantatentexte im Auftrage der Neuen Bachgesellschaft* (Leipzig, 1913).

[2] The text of the Cantata is suggested by the Epistle for the Day.

[3] The text of the Arias and first Chorus is by Christian Friedrich Henrici. He was born at Stolpe in 1700, and, about the time of Bach's appointment as organist, settled in Leipzig, where he held a position in the Post Office, and later in the Excise. He died in 1764. In 1725 he published a "Collection of profitable thoughts for and upon the ordinary Sundays and Holy Days" (*Sammlung Erbaulicher Gedancken, Bey und über die gewöhnlichen Sonn- und Festtags-Evangelien*, Leipzig). To avoid the ridicule which his religious reflexions might arouse, Henrici adopted the pseudonym "Picander." In 1728 he published a collection of texts for Cantatas, the only one of the kind which he brought out: *Cantaten auf die Sonn- und Fest-Tage durch das gantze Jahr* (Leipzig). In the Preface to the volume he declares that he had been impelled to write by the prospect of his work's deficiencies being made good "by the loveliness of the music of our incomparable Kapellmeister Bach." He must be regarded as the author of most of the Cantatas Bach composed at Leipzig. But it is difficult to point absolutely to the texts which are by him, since he published none but those in the

61 Nun komm, der Heiland[1, 2, 3].
62 Nun komm, der Heiland[1, 2].

Second. See No. 70. (*E*. Rom. xv. 4–13. *G*. St Luke xxi. 25–36.)

Third (*E*. 1 Cor. iv. 1–5. *G*. St Matt. xi. 2–10).
141 Das ist je gewisslich wahr[4].

Fourth[5] (*E*. Phil. iv. 4–7. *G*. St John i. 19–28).
132 Bereitet die Wege, bereitet die Bahn[6, 7].

collection of 1728. His Cantata libretti show facility rather than sincerity and poetic expression. His power of pictorial representation commended him to Bach, and there can be little doubt that he put his texts together in the form in which Bach required them. Though the list is necessarily incomplete, the following Cantatas were either positively or probably composed to Picander's texts: Nos. 6, 30, 36, 42, 67, 73, 84, 93, 144, 145, 148, 156, 157, 159, 171, 174, 188, U 1. See Spitta, II. 340 *et seq.* on Picander.

[1] The text of the Cantata is suggested by the Epistle for the Day.

[2] The Cantata bears the title of the first stanza of a congregational Hymn. See *infra* the section on the Cantata.

[3] Text by Erdmann Neumeister. He was born at Uechtritz, near Weissenfels, in 1671, was educated at Leipzig University, and, after holding Court appointments at Weissenfels and Sorau, was appointed in 1715 pastor of St James' Church, Hamburg. He died at Hamburg in 1756. He was a very prolific Hymn writer; over 650 are attributed to him. Of his Cantata texts Bach set eight. They are Nos. 18, 24, 27, 28, 59, 61, 142, 160. On Neumeister see Spitta, I. 470 *et seq.*

[4] The text is from a cycle of Church Cantata texts published by the State Secretary, Johann F. Helbig, at Eisenach, in 1720.

[5] See also No. 147.

[6] The text is provided or suggested by the Gospel for the Day.

[7] The libretto is one of Salomo Franck's Cantata texts. He was born at Weimar in 1659, and, after holding public appointments at Arnstadt and Jena, was appointed Curator of the Ducal collection

INTRODUCTION 7

CHRISTMAS DAY (*E.* Titus ii. 11–14 or Isaiah ix. 2–7.
G. St Luke ii. 1–14).
  63 Christen ätzet diesen Tag[1].
  91 Gelobet seist du, Jesu Christ[2].
 110 Unser Mund sei voll Lachens[3, 8].
 142 Uns ist ein Kind geboren[4, 5, 6].
 191 Gloria in excelsis Deo[7, 8].
 U 1 Ehre sei Gott in der Höhe[8, 9].

FEAST OF ST STEPHEN (*E.* Titus iii. 4–7 or Acts vi. 8–15, vii. 51–59. *G.* St Luke ii. 15–20).
  40 Dazu ist erschienen der Sohn Gottes[10].

of coins and medals at Weimar in 1702. He died at Weimar in 1725. He was a prolific Hymn writer, but none of his Hymns appears among the 154 which Bach used for his choral works. On the other hand, during his residence at Weimar Bach made use of Franck's Cantata texts, two series of which were published, the first in his *Evangelisches Andachts-Opffer* (Weimar, 1715), and the second in his *Evangelische Sonn- und Fest-Tages Andachten* (Weimar & Jena, 1717) (see Spitta, I. 526 *et seq.*, 569 *et seq.*). The texts of the following Cantatas are by Franck: Nos. 31, 70, 72, 80, 132, 147, 152, 155, 161, 162, 163, 164, 165, 168, 185, 186, and perhaps 12, 21, 53, 172, 182. Of these twenty-one Cantatas nine (Nos. 12, 53, 72, 80, 164, 165, 168, 172, 186) fall within the first Leipzig period.

[1] The text, Wustmann (p. 273) holds, is wrongly attributed to Picander.
[2] The Cantata bears the title of the first stanza of a congregational Hymn. See *infra* the section on the Cantata.
[3] Psalm cxxvi. 2. The author of the libretto is not known (Wustmann, p. 274). Schweitzer (II. 343) attributes it to Picander.
[4] Isaiah ix. 6.   [5] Text by Neumeister.
[6] Bach's authorship is contested. See *Bachjahrbuch*, 1912, p. 132.
[7] The "Gloria" of the B mi. Mass.
[8] The text is provided or suggested by the Gospel for the Day.
[9] Text by Picander.   [10] 1 St John iii. 8. Text by Bach?

8   INTRODUCTION

  57 Selig ist der Mann[1].
121 Christum wir sollen loben schon[2].

FEAST OF ST JOHN THE EVANGELIST (*E*. Heb. i. 1–12 or 1 John. *G*. St John i. 1–14).

  64 Sehet, welch' eine Liebe[3].
133 Ich freue mich in dir[2].
151 Süsser Trost, mein Jesus kommt[4].

SUNDAY AFTER CHRISTMAS (*E*. Gal. iv. 1–7. *G*. St Luke ii. 33–40).

  28 Gottlob! nun geht das Jahr zu Ende[5].
122 Das neugebor'ne Kindelein[2, 4].
152 Tritt auf die Glaubensbahn[6].

FEAST OF THE CIRCUMCISION (NEW YEAR'S DAY) (*E*. Gal. iii. 23–29. *G*. St Luke ii. 21).

  16 Herr Gott dich loben wir[2, 4].
  41 Jesu, nun sei gepreiset[2].
143 Lobe den Herrn, meine Seele[4, 7].
171 Gott, wie dein Name, so ist auch dein Ruhm[8].
190 Singet dem Herrn ein neues Lied[9, 10].

[1] St James i. 12.
[2] The Cantata bears the title of the first stanza of a congregational Hymn. See *infra* the section on the Cantata.
[3] 1 St John iii. 1.
[4] Text probably by Bach.
[5] Text by Neumeister.
[6] Text by Salomo Franck. The subject of the Cantata is remotely suggested by the Gospel for the Day. See Spitta, 1. 560.
[7] Psalm cxlvi. 1, 5, 10.
[8] Psalm xlviii. 10. Text by Picander.
[9] Psalm cxlix.
[10] Text wrongly attributed to Picander. See Wustmann, p. 297.

SUNDAY AFTER THE CIRCUMCISION (*E.* 1 Peter
iv. 12-19. *G.* St Matt. ii. 13-23).
   58 Ach Gott, wie manches Herzeleid[1, 2, 5, 9].
 153 Schau', lieber Gott, wie meine Feind'[1, 5, 9].

FEAST OF THE EPIPHANY (*E.* Isaiah lx. 1-6. *G.*
St Matt. ii. 1-12).
  65 Sie werden aus Saba Alle kommen[3, 5].
 123 Liebster Immanuel, Herzog der Frommen[1].

SUNDAYS AFTER THE EPIPHANY.
First (*E.* Rom. xii. 1-6. *G.* St Luke ii. 41-52).
  32 Liebster Jesu, mein Verlangen[4, 5].
 124 Meinen Jesum lass' ich nicht[1, 9].
 154 Mein liebster Jesus ist verloren[5, 6].

Second (*E.* Rom. xii. 7-16. *G.* St John ii. 1-11).
   3 Ach Gott, wie manches Herzeleid[1, 7].
  13 Meine Seufzer, meine Thränen[7].
 155 Mein Gott, wie lang', ach lange[7, 8].

Third (*E.* Rom. xii. 17-21. *G.* St Matt. viii.
1-13).
  72 Alles nur nach Gottes Willen[5, 8].

[1] The Cantata bears the title of the first stanza of a congregational Hymn. See *infra* the section on the Cantata.
[2] Wustmann (p. 276) attributes the text to Bach.
[3] Isaiah lx. 6. See the Epistle for the Day.
[4] The author is unknown. Perhaps Picander.
[5] The text is provided or suggested by the Gospel for the Day.
[6] Wustmann (p. 277) supposes the authors of Nos. 81 and 154 to be identical.
[7] Cf. Spitta, III. 84, on Bach's conventional treatment of the Gospel subject in these Cantatas.
[8] Text by Salomo Franck.   [9] Text perhaps by Bach.

73 Herr, wie du willt, so schick's mit mir[1, 2, 4].
111 Was mein Gott will, das g'scheh' allzeit[1, 4].
156 Ich steh' mit einem Fuss im Grabe[3, 2].

Fourth (*E*. Rom. xiii. 8–10. *G*. St Matt. viii. 23–27).

14 Wär' Gott nicht mit uns diese Zeit[1, 4].
81 Jesus schläft, was soll ich hoffen?[4, 5]

SEPTUAGESIMA SUNDAY (*E*. 1 Cor. ix. 24—x. 5. *G*. St Matt. xx. 1–16).

84 Ich bin vergnügt mit meinem Glücke[3, 4, 8].
92 Ich hab' in Gottes Herz und Sinn[1, 3, 4].
144 Nimm, was dein ist, und gehe hin[4, 9].

SEXAGESIMA SUNDAY (*E*. 2 Cor. xi. 19—xii. 9. *G*. St Luke viii. 4–15).

18 Gleich wie der Regen und Schnee[4, 6, 7].
126 Erhalt' uns, Herr, bei deinem Wort[1, 4].
181 Leichtgesinnte Flattergeiste[4].

QUINQUAGESIMA ("ESTO MIHI") (*E*. 1 Cor. xiii. *G*. St Luke xviii. 31–43).

22 Jesus nahm zu sich die Zwölfe[4].

---

[1] The Cantata bears the title of the first stanza of a congregational Hymn. See *infra* the section on the Cantata.
[2] Picander's asserted authorship is challenged. See Spitta, II. 414; Wustmann, p. 277.
[3] Text by Picander.
[4] The text is provided or suggested by the Gospel for the Day.
[5] Wustmann (p. 277) supposes the authors of Nos. 81 and 154 to be identical.
[6] Text by Neumeister.   [7] Isaiah lv. 10.
[8] A revision of Picander's text, perhaps by Bach.
[9] Text probably by Picander.

INTRODUCTION 11

23 Du wahrer Gott und Davids Sohn[1,2,13].
127 Herr Jesu Christ, wahr'r Mensch und Gott[1,3,10].
159 Sehet, wir geh'n hinauf gen Jerusalem[1,4].

PALM SUNDAY (*E.* Phil. ii. 5–11 or 1 Cor. xi. 23–32. *G.* St Matt. xxi. 1–9).

182 Himmelskönig, sei willkommen[1,5].

EASTER DAY (*E.* 1 Cor. v. 6–8. *G.* St Mark xvi. 1–8).

4 Christ lag in Todesbanden[1,3].
15 Denn du wirst meine Seele nicht in der Hölle lassen[1,6].
31 Der Himmel lacht, die Erde jubiliret[1,7].
160 Ich weiss, dass mein Erlöser lebt[1,8,9].

EASTER MONDAY (*E.* Acts x. 34–41. *G.* St Luke xxiv. 13–35).

6 Bleib' bei uns, denn es will Abend werden[1,10].
66 Erfreut euch, ihr Herzen[11,13].

EASTER TUESDAY (*E.* Acts xiii. 26–33. *G.* St Luke xxiv. 36–47).

134 Ein Herz, das seinen Jesum lebend weiss[1,12].

[1] The text is provided or suggested by the Gospel for the Day.
[2] The text follows rather the version in St Matt. xx. 30–34.
[3] The Cantata bears the title of the first stanza of a congregational Hymn. See *infra* the section on the Cantata.
[4] Text by Picander.   [5] Text probably by Salomo Franck.
[6] Psalm xvi. 10.   [7] Text by Salomo Franck.
[8] Text by Neumeister.   [9] Job xix. 25.
[10] Text perhaps by Picander.
[11] See Wustmann, p. 280, on the text.
[12] Wustmann (p. 281) regards the text as a reconstruction by Bach of an earlier secular Cantata.
[13] Text perhaps by Bach.

145 So du mit deinem Munde bekennest Jesum[1, 2, 3].
158 Der Friede sei mit dir.

SUNDAYS AFTER EASTER.

First ("Quasimodo geniti") (*E.* 1 John v. 4–10. *G.* St John xx. 19–31).

42 Am Abend aber desselbigen Sabbaths[1, 4].
67 Halt' im Gedächtniss Jesum Christ[1, 4, 5].

Second ("Misericordias Domini") (*E.* 1 Peter ii. 21–25. *G.* St John x. 12–16).

85 Ich bin ein guter Hirt[1, 6].
104 Du Hirte Israel, höre[1, 7].
112 Der Herr ist mein getreuer Hirt[1, 8].

Third ("Jubilate") (*E.* 1 Peter ii. 11–20. *G.* St John xvi. 16–23).

12 Weinen, Klagen, Sorgen, Zagen[1, 9].
103 Ihr werdet weinen und heulen[1, 10].

[1] The text is provided or suggested by the Gospel for the Day.
[2] Text by Picander.
[3] Rom. x. 9.
[4] Text perhaps by Picander.
[5] 2 Timothy ii. 8.
[6] Wustmann (p. 281) questions Spitta's attribution of the text to Marianne von Ziegler.
[7] Psalm lxxx. 1.
[8] The Cantata bears the title of the first stanza of a congregational Hymn. See *infra* the section on the Cantata.
[9] Text probably by Salomo Franck.
[10] Text by Marianne von Ziegler, published, with her other Cantata texts set by Bach, in her *Versuch in gebundener Schreibart* (1728). The authoress was the widow of an officer and resident in Leipzig. There is no evidence that Bach frequented her society, though Professor Gottsched, who wrote the text of the

146 Wir müssen durch viel Trübsal in das Reich Gottes eingehen[1, 2].

Fourth ("Cantate") (*E.* James i. 16–21. *G.* St John xvi. 5–15).
108 Es ist euch gut, dass ich hingehe[3, 5].
166 Wo gehest du hin?[3, 4]

Fifth ("Rogate") (*E.* James i. 22–27. *G.* St John xvi. 23–30 or 33).
86 Wahrlich, wahrlich, ich sage euch[3, 4].
87 Bisher habt ihr nichts gebeten in meinem Namen[3, 5].

Sixth ("Exaudi[6]") (*E.* 1 Peter iv. 8–11. *G.* St John xv. 26—xvi. 4).
44 Sie werden euch in den Bann thun[3, 4].
183 Sie werden euch in den Bann thun[3, 5].

ASCENSION DAY (*E.* Acts i. 1–11. *G.* St Mark xvi. 14–20).
11 Lobet Gott in seinen Reichen[3].
37 Wer da glaubet und getauft wird[3, 4].

"Trauerode," was known to both of them. Spitta (III. 70) detected the hand of "a new poet" in certain of Bach's works, but it was not until his accidental discovery of the volume of 1728 that he was able, in 1892, to identify the authoress. The following are the Cantatas for which she wrote the texts: Nos. 68, 74, 87, 103, 108, 128, 175, 176, 183. See the Cantatas discussed in Spitta, III. 70–73, and Schweitzer, II. 332–338.

[1] Bach's authorship is questioned. [2] Acts xiv. 22.
[3] The text is provided or suggested by the Gospel for the Day.
[4] Wustmann, p. 282, conjectures that the texts of Cantatas 37, 44, 86, 166, are by the same author.
[5] Text by Marianne von Ziegler.
[6] The Sixth Sunday after Easter is the Sunday after Ascension Day.

43 Gott fähret auf mit Jauchzen[1, 5, 10].
128 Auf Christi Himmelfahrt allein[2, 3, 5].

WHIT SUNDAY (*E*. Acts ii. 1–13. *G*. St John xiv. 23–31).

34 O ewiges Feuer, O Ursprung der Liebe[4, 5, 10].
59 Wer mich liebet, der wird mein Wort halten[5, 6].
74 Wer mich liebet, der wird mein Wort halten[2, 5].
172 Erschallet, ihr Lieder[5, 7].
D 2 Gott der Hoffnung erfülle euch.

WHIT MONDAY (*E*. Acts x. 42–48. *G*. St John iii. 16–21).

68 Also hat Gott die Welt geliebt[2, 3, 5].
173 Erhötes Fleisch und Blut[5, 8].
174 Ich liebe den Höchsten von ganzem Gemüthe[9].

WHIT TUESDAY (*E*. Acts viii. 14–17 or ii. 29–36. *G*. St John x. 1–11).

175 Er rufet seinen Schafen mit Namen[2, 5].
184 Erwünschtes Freudenlicht[5, 10].

[1] Psalm xlvii. 5.
[2] Text by Marianne von Ziegler.
[3] The Cantata bears the title of the first stanza of a congregational Hymn. See *infra* the section on the Cantata.
[4] Wustmann, p. 284, states that Bach adapted an older text for Whit Sunday use.
[5] The text is provided or suggested by the Gospel for the Day.
[6] Text by Neumeister.
[7] Text perhaps by Franck.
[8] See Wustmann, p. 284.
[9] Text by Picander.
[10] Text probably by Bach.

INTRODUCTION 15

TRINITY SUNDAY[1] (*E.* Rom. xi. 33–36. *G.* St John iii. 1–15).
   129 Gelobet sei der Herr[2].
   165 O heil'ges Geist- und Wasserbad[3, 4].
   176 Es ist ein trotzig und verzagt Ding[3, 5, 6].

SUNDAYS AFTER TRINITY.
  First (*E.* 1 John iv. 16–21. *G.* St Luke xvi. 19–31).
   20 O Ewigkeit, du Donnerwort[2].
   39 Brich dem Hungrigen dein Brod[3, 7].
   75 Die Elenden sollen essen[3, 8].

  Second (*E.* 1 John iii. 13–18. *G.* St Luke xiv. 16–24).
   2 Ach Gott, vom Himmel sieh' darein[2].
   76 Die Himmel erzählen die Ehre Gottes[3, 9, 10].

  Third[11] (*E.* 1 Peter v. 6–11. *G.* St Luke xv. 1–10).
   135 Ach Herr, mich armen Sünder[2, 3].

---

[1] See also No. 194.
[2] The Cantata bears the title of the first stanza of a congregational Hymn. See *infra* the section on the Cantata.
[3] The text is provided or suggested by the Gospel for the Day.
[4] Text by Salomo Franck.
[5] Text by Marianne von Ziegler.
[6] Jeremiah xvii. 9. A commentary on the conduct of Nicodemus in the Gospel for the Day.
[7] Isaiah lviii. 7.
[8] Psalm xxii. 26.
[9] Psalm xix. 1, 3.
[10] Relative to the Epistle for the Day.
[11] See also No. 21.

Fourth (*E.* Rom. viii. 18-23.   *G.* St Luke vi. 36-42).
    24 Ein ungefärbt Gemüthe[1, 2].
  177 Ich ruf' zu dir, Herr Jesu Christ[1, 3].
  185 Barmherziges Herze der ewigen Liebe[1, 4].

Fifth (*E.* 1 Peter iii. 8-15.   *G.* St Luke v. 1-11).
    88 Siehe, ich will viel Fischer aussenden[1, 5].
    93 Wer nur den lieben Gott lässt walten[3, 6, 7].

Sixth (*E.* Rom. vi. 3-11.   *G.* St Matt. v. 20-26).
    9 Es ist das Heil uns kommen her[1, 3, 7].
  170 Vergnügte Ruh', beliebte Seelenlust[1, 7, 8].

Seventh (*E.* Rom. vi. 19-23.   *G.* St Mark viii. 1-9).
  107 Was willst du dich betrüben[3].
  186 Ärgre dich, O Seele, nicht[1, 4, 9].
  187 Es wartet Alles auf dich[1, 10].

Eighth (*E.* Rom. viii. 12-17.   *G.* St Matt. vii. 15-23).
    45 Es ist dir gesagt, Mensch, was gut ist[1, 11].

[1] The text is provided or suggested by the Gospel for the Day.
[2] Text by Neumeister.
[3] The Cantata bears the title of the first stanza of a congregational Hymn. See *infra* the section on the Cantata.
[4] Text by Salomo Franck.
[5] Jeremiah xvi. 16.
[6] Text by Picander.
[7] Relative to the Epistle for the Day.
[8] See Wustmann, p. 287.
[9] See Wustmann, p. 287, on the text.
[10] Psalm civ. 27.
[11] Micah vi. 8.

136 Erforsche mich, Gott, und erfahre mein Herz[1, 2].
178 Wo Gott der Herr nicht bei uns hält[3].

Ninth (*E*. 1 Cor. x. 6–13. *G*. St Luke xvi. 1–9).

94 Was frag ich nach der Welt[1, 3].
105 Herr, gehe nicht in's Gericht[1, 4].
168 Thue Rechnung! Donnerwort[1, 5].

Tenth (*E*. 1 Cor. xii. 1–11. *G*. St Luke xix. 41–48).

46 Schauet doch und sehet, ob irgend ein Schmerz[1, 6].
101 Nimm von uns, Herr, du treuer Gott[1, 3].
102 Herr, deine Augen sehen nach dem Glauben[1, 7, 8].

Eleventh (*E*. 1 Cor. xv. 1–10. *G*. St Luke xviii. 9–14).

113 Herr Jesu Christ, du höchstes Gut[1, 3].
179 Siehe zu, dass deine Gottesfurcht nicht Heuchelei sei[1, 9].
199 Mein Herze schwimmt im Blut[1, 10].

Twelfth (*E*. 2 Cor. iii. 4–11. *G*. St Mark vii. 31–37).

35 Geist und Seele wird verwirret[1, 11].

[1] The text is provided or suggested by the Gospel for the Day.
[2] Psalm cxxxix. 23.
[3] The Cantata bears the title of the first stanza of a congregational Hymn. See *infra* the section on the Cantata.
[4] Psalm cxliii. 2.   [5] Text by Salomo Franck.
[6] Lamentations i. 12.
[7] Jeremiah v. 3.
[8] Text improbably by Picander. See Wustmann, p. 288.
[9] Ecclesiasticus i. 28.
[10] The title is that of one of Neumeister's Cantata texts. Bach himself arranged the latter part of it.
[11] Text perhaps by Bach. See Wustmann, p. 289.

69 Lobe den Herrn, meine Seele[1].
137 Lobe den Herren, den mächtigen König der Ehren[2].

Thirteenth (*E.* Gal. iii. 15–22. *G.* St Luke x. 23–37).

33 Allein zu dir, Herr Jesu Christ[2, 3].
77 Du sollst Gott, deinen Herren, lieben[4, 5].
164 Ihr, die ihr euch von Christo nennet[4, 6].

Fourteenth (*E.* Gal. v. 16–24. *G.* St Luke xvii. 11–19).

17 Wer Dank opfert, der preiset mich[4, 7].
25 Es ist nichts gesundes an meinem Leibe[4, 8].
78 Jesu, der du meine Seele[2, 4].

Fifteenth[9] (*E.* Gal. v. 25–26, x. *G.* St Matt. vi. 24–34).

51 Jauchzet Gott in allen Landen[4, 10, 11].
99 Was Gott thut, das ist wohlgethan[2, 4].
138 Warum betrübst du dich, mein Herz[2, 4].

Sixteenth (*E.* Eph. iii. 13–21. *G.* St Luke vii. 11–17)[12]

8 Liebster Gott, wann werd' ich sterben[2, 4].

[1] Psalm ciii. 2. Also for Rathswahl use.
[2] The Cantata bears the title of the first stanza of a congregational Hymn. See *infra* the section on the Cantata.
[3] Text relative to the Epistle.
[4] The text is provided or suggested by the Gospel for the Day.
[5] Bach follows the Gospel version in St Matt. xxii. 35–40.
[6] Text by Salomo Franck.
[7] Psalm l. 23. The text perhaps is by Bach.
[8] Psalm xxxviii. 3.   [9] See also No. 100.
[10] Also for general use.
[11] The text may be attributed to Bach himself.
[12] See also No. 161.

27 Wer weiss, wie nahe mir mein Ende[1, 2, 3].
95 Christus, der ist mein Leben[1, 2].
161 Komm, du süsse Todesstunde[1, 4].

Seventeenth (*E.* Eph. iv. 1–6. *G.* St Luke xiv. 1–11).

47 Wer sich selbst erhöhet, der soll erniedriget werden[1, 5].
114 Ach, lieben Christen, seid getrost[1, 2].
148 Bringet dem Herrn Ehre seines Namens[1, 6, 7].

Eighteenth (*E.* 1 Cor. i. 4–9. *G.* St Matt. xxii. 34–46).

96 Herr Christ, der ein'ge Gottes-Sohn[1, 2].
169 Gott soll allein mein Herze haben[1].

Nineteenth (*E.* Eph. iv. 22–28. *G.* St Matt. ix. 1–8).

5 Wo soll ich fliehen hin[1, 2].
48 Ich elender Mensch, wer wird mich erlösen[1, 8].
56 Ich will den Kreuzstab gerne tragen[1, 9].

[1] The text is provided or suggested by the Gospel for the Day.

[2] The Cantata bears the title of the first stanza of a congregational Hymn. See *infra* the section on the Cantata.

[3] Text by Neumeister and Bach. See Wustmann, p. 290.

[4] Text by Salomo Franck.

[5] The text is from a set of Cantata texts published at Eisenach in 1720 by State Secretary Johann F. Helbig.

[6] Text founded on Picander.

[7] Psalm xxix. 2.

[8] Romans vii. 24.

[9] The first *Recitativo* of the Cantata is based on a text of Neumeister's. Bach's arrangement of the text may be inferred. See Wustmann, p. 291.

Twentieth (*E*. Eph. v. 15–21. *G*. St Matt. xxii. 1–14).

49   Ich geh' und suche mit Verlangen[1].
162 Ach, ich sehe, jetzt da ich zur Hochzeit gehe[1,2].
180 Schmücke dich, O liebe Seele[1,3].

Twenty-first (*E*. Eph. vi. 10–17. *G*. St John iv. 47–54).

38   Aus tiefer Noth schrei ich zu dir[1,3].
98   Was Gott thut, das ist wohlgethan[1,3].
109 Ich glaube, lieber Herr, hilf meinem Unglauben[1,4].
188 Ich habe meine Zuversicht[5,6].

Twenty-second (*E*. Phil. i. 3–11. *G*. St Matt. xviii. 23–35).

55   Ich armer Mensch, ich Sündenknecht[1].
89   Was soll ich aus dir machen, Ephraim[1,7]?
115 Mache dich, mein Geist, bereit[1,3].

Twenty-third (*E*. Phil. iii. 17–21. *G*. St Matt. xxii. 15–22).

52   Falsche Welt, dir trau ich nicht[1].
139 Wohl dem, der sich auf seinen Gott[1,3].
163 Nur Jedem das seine[1,2].

---

[1] The text is provided or suggested by the Gospel for the Day.
[2] Text by Salomo Franck.
[3] The Cantata bears the title of the first stanza of a congregational Hymn. See *infra* the section on the Cantata.
[4] St Mark ix. 24.   [5] Text by Picander.
[6] The larger part of this Cantata has been attributed to Bach's eldest son, Friedemann. See Wustmann, p. 298.
[7] Hosea xi. 8.

INTRODUCTION 21

Twenty-fourth (*E.* Coloss. i. 9–14. *G.* St Matt. ix. 18–26).
  26 Ach wie flüchtig[1, 2].
  60 O Ewigkeit, du Donnerwort[1, 2].

Twenty-fifth (*E.* 1 Thess. iv. 13–18. *G.* St Matt. xxiv. 15–28).
  90 Es reifet euch ein schrecklich Ende[2].
  116 Du Friedefürst, Herr Jesu Christ[1].

Twenty-sixth (*E.* 2 Peter iii. 3–14 or 2 Thess. i. 3–10. *G.* St Matt. xxv. 31–46).
  70 Wachet, betet, betet, wachet[3, 4].

Twenty-seventh (*E.* 1 Thess. v. 1–11, or one of the two Epistles for the Twenty-sixth Sunday. *G.* St Matt. xxv. 1–13 or xxiv. 37–51 or v. 1–12).
  140 Wachet auf, ruft uns die Stimme[1, 4].

FEAST OF THE PURIFICATION OF THE B.V.M. (*E.* Mal. iii. 1–4. *G.* St Luke ii. 22–32).
  82 Ich habe genug[2].
  83 Erfreute Zeit im neuen Bunde[2].
  125 Mit Fried' und Freud' ich fahr' dahin[1, 2].
  157 Ich lasse dich nicht, du segnest mich denn[5, 6].

[1] The Cantata bears the title of the first stanza of a congregational Hymn. See *infra* the section on the Cantata.
[2] The text is provided or suggested by the Gospel for the Day.
[3] Text by Salomo Franck.
[4] The subject of the Cantatas for the Twenty-sixth and Twenty-seventh Sundays after Trinity was suggested by their Advent context. No. 70 originally was for the Second Sunday in Advent.
[5] Text by Picander.
[6] Genesis xxxii. 26. Also for a funeral.

158 Der Friede sei mit dir[1, 2].
161 Komm, du süsse Todesstunde[3, 4].

FEAST OF THE ANNUNCIATION OF THE B.V.M.
(*E.* Is. vii. 10–16. *G.* St Luke i. 26–38).
 1 Wie schön leuchtet der Morgenstern[1, 5].

FEAST OF THE VISITATION OF THE B.V.M.
(*E.* Rom. xii. 9–16 or Is. xi. 1–5 or Song of Solomon ii. 8–17. *G.* St Luke i. 39–56).
 10 Meine Seel' erhebt den Herren[1, 5].
147 Herz und Mund und That und Leben[6, 10].
189 Meine Seele rühmt und preist[1, 7].

FEAST OF ST JOHN BAPTIST (*E.* Is. xl. 1–5. *G.* St Luke i. 57–80).
 7 Christ unser Herr zum Jordan kam[5].
 30 Freue dich, erlöste Schaar[1, 8, 9].
167 Ihr Menschen, rühmet Gottes Liebe[1, 8].

[1] The text is provided or suggested by the Gospel for the Day.

[2] The text is from the Gospel for Easter Tuesday, for which occasion Bach also used the Cantata. In the form in which the Cantata has come down to us it is not exactly congruous to either occasion.

[3] Text by Salomo Franck.

[4] Also for the Sixteenth Sunday after Trinity.

[5] The Cantata bears the title of the first stanza of a congregational Hymn. See *infra* the section on the Cantata.

[6] Originally for the Fourth Sunday in Advent (? 1716).

[7] Schweitzer (II. 140) assigns this Cantata to the Fourth Sunday after Easter. The score does not indicate the occasion for which it was composed.

[8] The Feast of St John Baptist was also Midsummer Day.

[9] Probably a reconstruction by Picander of his own original secular text.

[10] Text by Franck and, probably, Bach.

INTRODUCTION 23

FEAST OF ST MICHAEL THE ARCHANGEL[1]
(*E*. Rev. xii. 7-12. *G*. St Matt. xviii. 1-11).
19   Es erhub sich ein Streit[2, 3].
50   Nun ist das Heil und die Kraft[4, 5].
130 Herr Gott, dich loben alle wir[4, 6].
149 Man singet mit Freuden vom Sieg[7].
D 3 Siehe, es hat überwunden der Löwe.

FOR GENERAL OR UNSPECIFIED USE[8].
21   Ich hatte viel Bekümmerniss[9, 10].
*54 Widerstehe doch der Sünde.
*97 In allen meinen Thaten[6, 12].
*100 Was Gott thut, das ist wohlgethan[6, 12].
*117 Sei Lob und Ehr' dem höchsten Gut[6].
*131 Aus der Tiefe rufe ich, Herr, zu dir[11].

* The occasion for which this Cantata was composed is not stated in the score.
[1] See also No. 51, and Spitta, II. 473.
[2] Jude 9. See the Epistle for the Day.
[3] Spitta, II. 344, attributes the text to Picander, inaccurately in Wustmann's (p. 294) opinion.
[4] See the Epistle for the Day.
[5] Revelation xii. 10. The occasion for which the Cantata was composed is not stated in the score. Spitta, III. 83, suggests that it was intended for Michaelmas, from whose Epistle the text is taken.
[6] The Cantata bears the title of the first stanza of a congregational Hymn. See *infra* the section on the Cantata.
[7] Psalm cxviii. 15, 16. See the Epistle for the Day.
[8] See also Nos. 50 and 51.
[9] Text perhaps by Salomo Franck. But see Wustmann, p. 286.
[10] Psalm xciv. 19. See the Epistle for the Third Sunday after Trinity, for which occasion probably Bach composed it.
[11] Psalm cxxx. Wustmann, p. 297, suggests that the text is by Georg Christian Eilmar, at whose request Bach composed the Cantata.
[12] Perhaps used for a wedding.

*150 Nach dir, Herr, verlanget mich[1].
*192 Nun danket alle Gott[2].
*D 4 Lobt ihn mit Herz und Munde.

For a Wedding[3].

195 Dem Gerechten muss das Licht[4].
196 Der Herr denket an uns[5].
197 Gott ist uns're Zuversicht[6].
U 2 O ewiges Feuer, O Ursprung der Liebe.
U 3 Herr Gott, Beherrscher aller Dinge[6].

For a Funeral[7].

53 Schlage doch, gewünschte Stunde[8].
106 Gottes Zeit ist die allerbeste Zeit[9].
118 O Jesu Christ, mein's Lebens Licht[2].
198 The "Trauerode[10]."

* The occasion for which this Cantata was composed is not stated in the score.

[1] Psalm xxv. 1, 2.

[2] The Cantata bears the title of the first stanza of a congregational Hymn. See *infra* the section on the Cantata.

[3] See Spitta, II. 632–637, for three secular Wedding Cantatas by Bach. See also Nos. 97, 100.

[4] Psalm xcvii. 11, 12. The occasion for which the Cantata was composed is not stated in the score.

[5] Psalm cxv. 12–15. See Spitta, I. 370.

[6] Not improbably the text is by Bach himself.

[7] See also No. 157, and Spitta, II. 412.

[8] Text probably by Salomo Franck. The occasion for which the Cantata was composed is not stated in the score. It is strictly a "mourning aria." See Spitta, II. 476; Schweitzer, II. 253; Wustmann, p. 261.

[9] The text is formed from various portions of Scripture discerningly pieced together, perhaps by Bach himself.

[10] Text by Professor J. C. Gottsched.

FOR A PUBLIC FAST.

D 1 Gedenke, Herr, wie es uns gehet[1].

FOR THE REFORMATION FESTIVAL.

   79 Gott, der Herr, ist Sonn' und Schild[2].
   80 Ein' feste Burg ist unser Gott[3, 4].

FOR THE INAUGURATION OF THE TOWN COUNCIL[5].

   29 Wir danken dir, Gott[6].
   71 Gott ist mein König[7].
 119 Preise, Jerusalem, den Herrn[8].
 120 Gott, man lobet dich in der Stille[9].
 193 Ihr Pforten [Tore] zu Zion[10].

FOR THE OPENING OF AN ORGAN.

 194 Höchsterwünschtes Freudenfest[11].

---

[1] The Preface (p. xxxi) to B.G. xli quotes Winterfeld's opinion that this was the occasion of the Cantata, and draws attention to the relation of the text of the first chorus to Jeremiah v. 1, 15, 16.

[2] Psalm lxxxiv. 11. See Spitta, III. 74, on the text.

[3] The Cantata bears the title of the first stanza of a congregational Hymn. See *infra* the section on the Cantata.

[4] Text by Salomo Franck. See also No. 76.

[5] For a secular Cantata in praise of the Leipzig Town Council, see Spitta, II. 634. See also No. 69.

[6] Psalm lxxv. 1.

[7] Psalm lxxiv. 12. The text probably is Bach's arrangement. See Wustmann, p. 295.

[8] Psalm cxlvii. 12.

[9] Psalm lxv. 1.

[10] See Spitta, III. 83 n. The score does not state the occasion for which the Cantata was composed.

[11] As its text shows, the Cantata was adapted by Bach for use on Trinity Sunday.

The Choral Cantatas

So intimate is the association between the Cantata, as it developed in Bach's hands, and the congregational Hymns and Hymn melodies of the Lutheran Church, that the latter are absent only from twenty-two of the two hundred and six Cantatas[1]. The one hundred and eighty-four Cantatas that include Hymn stanzas or melodies fall into three groups. The largest, containing one hundred and eighteen Cantatas, includes those in which Bach introduces Chorals, almost invariably as the concluding movement[2], occasionally in the middle movements, very rarely in the opening movement[3], but always without permitting them to dominate the Cantata[4]. The second, and smallest,

---

[1] They are the following: Nos. 34, 35, 50, 53, 54, 63, 82, 134, 141, 150, 152, 160, 170, 173, 181, 189, 191, 193, 196, 198, U 2, D 1.

[2] The only exceptions to the rule are Nos. 21, 30, 51, 59, 71, 182, 184, 186 (?), 199.

[3] See Nos. 77, 106, 131, 145, 153, D 4. They are the only exceptions.

[4] The complete list of this group is as follows: Nos. 6, 11, 12, 13, 15, 17, 18, 19, 21, 22, 23, 24, 25, 28, 29, 30, 31, 32, 36, 37, 39, 40, 42, 43, 44, 45, 46, 47, 48, 49, 51, 52, 55, 56, 57, 59, 64, 65, 66, 67, 69, 70, 71, 72, 74, 75, 76, 77, 79, 81, 83, 84, 85, 86, 87, 88, 89, 90, 102, 103, 104, 105, 106, 108, 109, 110, 119, 120, 131, 132, 136, 142, 143, 144, 145, 146, 147, 148, 149, 151, 154, 155, 156, 157, 158, 159, 161, 162, 163, 164, 165, 166, 167, 168, 169, 171, 172, 174, 175, 176, 179, 182, 183, 184, 185, 186, 187, 188, 190, 194, 195, 197, 199, U 1, U 3, D 2, D 3, D 4.

group consists of twelve Cantatas which bear the name of a congregational Hymn, whose text and melody are introduced into their opening movements, but are not permitted to close the Cantata, and therefore do not leave a vivid impression of the Choral as the key to the whole composition[1].

The third category contains the Cantatas which are distinguished preeminently as "Choral Cantatas." They number fifty-four and fall into two divisions, the first, which contains fifteen Cantatas, coinciding with the Leipzig period 1723-34; the second, which contains thirty-nine, coinciding with the later Leipzig period 1735-50.

CHORAL CANTATAS, 1723-34 (15).

- 4 Christ lag in Todesbanden.
- 8 Liebster Gott, wann werd' ich sterben?
- 9 Es ist das Heil uns kommen her.
- 20 O Ewigkeit, du Donnerwort.
- 80 Ein' feste Burg ist unser Gott.
- 93 Wer nur den lieben Gott lässt walten.
- 97 In allen meinen Thaten.
- 99 Was Gott thut, das ist wohlgethan.
- 112 Der Herr ist mein getreuer Hirt.
- 117 Sei Lob und Ehr' dem höchsten Gut.
- 129 Gelobet sei der Herr.
- 137 Lobe den Herren, den mächtigen König der Ehren.
- 140 Wachet auf, ruft uns die Stimme.
- 177 Ich ruf' zu dir, Herr Jesu Christ.
- 192 Nun danket alle Gott.

[1] The following Cantatas form this group: Nos. 16, 27, 58, 60, 61, 68, 73, 95, 98, 118, 128, 153.

CHORAL CANTATAS, 1735–50 (39).

1. Wie schön leuchtet der Morgenstern.
2. Ach Gott, vom Himmel sieh' darein.
3. Ach Gott, wie manches Herzeleid.
5. Wo soll ich fliehen hin.
7. Christ unser Herr zum Jordan kam.
10. Meine Seel' erhebt den Herren.
14. Wär Gott nicht mit uns diese Zeit.
26. Ach wie flüchtig.
33. Allein zu dir, Herr Jesu Christ.
38. Aus tiefer Noth schrei ich zu dir.
41. Jesu, nun sei gepreiset.
62. Nun komm, der Heiden Heiland.
78. Jesu, der du meine Seele.
91. Gelobet seist du, Jesu Christ.
92. Ich hab' in Gottes Herz und Sinn.
94. Was frag ich nach der Welt.
96. Herr Christ, der ein'ge Gottes-Sohn.
100. Was Gott thut, das ist wohlgethan.
101. Nimm von uns, Herr, du treuer Gott.
107. Was willst du dich betrüben.
111. Was mein Gott will, das g'scheh' allzeit.
113. Herr Jesu Christ, du höchstes Gut.
114. Ach, lieben Christen, seid getrost.
115. Mache dich, mein Geist, bereit.
116. Du Friedefürst, Herr Jesu Christ.
121. Christum wir sollen loben schon.
122. Das neugebor'ne Kindelein.
123. Liebster Immanuel, Herzog der Frommen.
124. Meinen Jesum lass' ich nicht.
125. Mit Fried' und Freud' ich fahr' dahin.
126. Erhalt' uns, Herr, bei deinem Wort.
127. Herr Jesu Christ, wahr'r Mensch und Gott.
130. Herr Gott, dich loben alle wir.
133. Ich freue mich in dir.

135 Ach Herr, mich armen Sünder.
138 Warum betrübst du dich, mein Herz.
139 Wohl dem, der sich auf seinen Gott.
178 Wo Gott der Herr nicht bei uns hält.
180 Schmücke dich, O liebe Seele.

The Choral Cantata as we have it after 1734 is the supreme expression of Bach's art in that form. He was led to it by the inadequacy of the texts with which Picander provided him, and by the failure of his earlier experiments in building a Cantata upon a congregational Hymn. The Choral Cantata united the best features of both forms. Briefly its essentials are these: (1) The text of the Cantata is based upon that of a congregational Hymn, the Cantata in effect being an elaborate setting of its stanzas. (2) The middle movements are not necessarily set to actual words of the Hymn, all of whose stanzas are not invariably used. If the Hymn is too short, as for instance No. 140, additional stanzas are inserted. But whether the stanzas be reconstructed or extended, the spirit of the original Hymn is preserved, and in the case of reconstructed stanzas the actual words of the original text are preserved so far as is convenient. (3) Whatever liberties are taken with the intermediate stanzas, the words of the first and last movements of the Cantata *invariably*[1] are stanzas

---

[1] But see No. 107.

of the original Hymn, and are, in both movements, wedded to its proper or customary tune[1].

As Spitta comments, the Choral Cantatas assume that the hearer held constantly in mind the Hymn in its original form. "The church-goer of those days could compare the printed text of the Cantata with the version in his Hymn book; or he could even dispense with this material aid, since those Hymns were in every heart as a possession common to all. He had sung them times without number in church, had taken them as his guide in daily life, and had drawn consolation and edification from isolated verses under various experiences. This was the audience to which Bach addressed himself, and such an audience do these compositions still require, for to such alone will they reveal all their meaning and fulness[2]."

It was in the early thirties, or after 1728, that Bach, dissatisfied with the Cantata texts which he had used for so many years, turned to the Hymns of the sixteenth and seventeenth centuries.

[1] Particular care has been taken to discover, in all cases in which a Hymn is set to a tune other than its proper melody, whether the association was usual in the Hymn books of Bach's period. Clearly the devotional purpose Bach had in view would not be served by severing a Hymn from the tune to which it usually was sung. In the Choral Cantatas it is possible to state positively of all, that Bach always associated the Hymn with the tune by which it was known.

[2] *Op. cit.* III. 107.

At Weimar he had been so fortunate as to find in Salomo Franck a man of his own temperament. Erdmann Neumeister also provided him with texts, though in lesser number. Later, at Leipzig, Bach used the Cantata texts of Marianne von Ziegler[1]. But almost from the moment of his arrival at Leipzig, he entered into a literary partnership with Christian Friedrich Henrici, or Picander[2], which lasted for twenty years. Bach's exclusive dependence on Picander is proved, perhaps, by the fact that, excepting Marianne von Ziegler, he seems to have made no effort to secure another librettist. Yet Picander hardly can have satisfied Bach, though he accepted from him and set many texts which are wanting in taste and fine feeling. Picander began his literary career as a lampoonist, a form of expression for which he was better fitted. Cantata work was quite foreign to his character, and he seems to have attempted it at Bach's instigation, under his direction, and subject to his suggestion and correction. It is probable that the texts of the Choral Cantatas also were arranged by Picander under similar conditions. It is to be assumed, therefore, that Bach originated the Choral Cantata, and guided it to its final form in the Cantatas of the *post* 1734 period.

An examination of the earlier group of Choral

See notes pp. 6, 12 *supra*.   [2] See p. 5, note 4, *supra*.

Cantatas, while it reveals contrast, brings out their essential agreement with the later. The first and last movements are stanzas of the same Hymn, set to its proper or customary melody. In every case the first movement is in the form of a Choral Fantasia. In every case the final movement is a simple Hymn setting, except in Nos. 97, 112, 137, where the simple setting is embellished by orchestral detail[1], and Nos. 129, 192, where it is Extended or a Fantasia in form. In eight of the fifteen Cantatas (1723-34) the Hymn and its melody are associated only in the first and last movements. They are Nos. 8, 9, 97, 99, 112, 129, 177, 192.

Of greater importance is the structure of the early Choral Cantata libretti. More than half (eight) are the unaltered text of a congregational Hymn: they are Nos. 4, 97, 112, 117, 129, 137, 177, 192. The text of four Cantatas consists partly of actual and partly of paraphrased Hymn stanzas: they are Nos. 8, 9, 20, 99. In two Cantatas movements are included which are neither actual nor paraphrased stanzas of the Hymn: they

[1] Chorals of this kind are here designated "Embellished." It is very rare for any of the instruments to receive an independent part in the final Simple Chorals. Where it does occur it usually is for the purpose of bringing out the melody prominently and so of emphasising the idea which the melody represented to the congregation. See *infra* for a list of the Embellished Chorals.

are Nos. 80, 140. In a single Cantata, No. 93, in addition to actual and paraphrased stanzas of the Hymn, the libretto adds to the former a commentary of *Recitativo*. As a whole, therefore, the early Choral Cantata group exhibits no uniform treatment of the Hymn libretto. The composer is generally content with the actual text of the Hymn without attempting to mould it to a more plastic form.

But Bach soon discovered that a uniform stanza, particularly a stanza lavishly rhymed, was not as appropriate to *Recitativo* and *Aria* as it was, for instance, to the Simple Choral and more elaborate Fantasia. Rhythmical uniformity impeded his musical utterance. He therefore invented the *paraphrase* of the Hymn stanza, of which he had made trial already in Cantata No. 93. Hence, the libretti of the later Choral Cantatas display a textual uniformity that is lacking in the earlier ones. Only two of them, Nos. 100, 107, are set to the unaltered text of the Hymn. In all the others the libretto is made up of actual and paraphrased Hymn stanzas. Twelve of the thirty-nine Cantatas, however, contain paragraphs foreign to the original Hymn text. Nos. 3, 91, 92, 94, 101, 113, 125, 126, 138, and 178 include movements described as "Recitativ und Choral" which associate actual stanzas of the Hymn with a concurrent commentary. In No. 122 a similar form is found in the fourth movement, "Choral und Arie." The preceding *Recitativo* of that Cantata (No. 122) is not a stanza of the Hymn, and the penultimate number of No. 38 is based upon the Gospel for the Day.

The Choral Cantatas of the *post* 1734 period, written for the most part, as Spitta shows[1], on paper having the same watermark, exhibit the final and perfected type of libretto. In all, the first and last movements are Choruses upon the words and melody of the Hymn. In all, the opening movement is a Choral Fantasia[2]. In all but eight, the last movement is a Simple Choral—Nos. 41, 100, 107 are Extended, Nos. 1, 91, 101, 130 are Embellished, and No. 138 is a Choral of the Fantasia type. As in the Choral Cantatas of the earlier group, Bach comparatively rarely brings the Hymn and melody together between the first and last Choruses, the two "pillars" of the Choral Cantata. He does so only in Nos. 3, 91, 92, 94, 101, 113, 114, 122, 125, 126, 138, 178, and 180[3].

[1] *Op. cit.* III. 285.
[2] Nos. 2, 14, 38, and 121 are in Motett form. The only other Motett Choral Choruses in the Cantatas are Nos. 4 d, 21, 28 a, and 118. Motett Choruses are also found in Cantatas 64, 68, and 108.
[3] It must be remembered that this analysis is directed only upon the movements in which a Hymn text or paraphrase and its melody are associated, or where the melody is introduced by itself to suggest or recall the spirit of the Hymn.

The Choral forms which Bach employs in the Cantatas must now be considered.

The Choral Fantasia

The Leipzig Cantatas are distinguished generally from those of the earlier periods of Bach's activity by the magnificent Choral Fantasias which he introduced into them, generally as their opening movement. With the exceptions to which attention already has been drawn, the Choral Cantatas invariably are opened by a Chorus of this type.

The Choral Fantasia, the logical outcome of Bach's experiments in organ and orchestral form, was essential to the structure of the Church Cantata, as he conceived it. The Choral Fantasia was evolved from the Organ Choral Prelude, a fact which is patent when Bach's treatment of the tune " Ach wie flüchtig" in the *Orgelbüchlein* is compared with his Choral Fantasia on the melody in Cantata 26. The Organ Choral Prelude did not merely evolve the form of the Choral Fantasia itself. Bach's orchestral sense ordained, upon the analogy of the Concerto, the relation of the Choral Fantasia to the Choral Cantata, of which it is at once a part and the key. Like the first movement of the Concerto, the Choral Fantasia colours and defines the whole Cantata. Its grand purpose was, in Spitta's

36   INTRODUCTION

words¹, "the perfect poetic and musical developement of a particular Hymn by means of all the artistic material which Bach had assimilated by a thorough study of the art of his own and former times." In the Choral Fantasia the Hymn, words and melody, is presented with all the technique of Bach's mature genius. It is perfect and complete in itself, and yet a detail in an ordered whole.

The Cantatas contain seventy-eight movements of the Choral Fantasia form². They are as follows: Nos. 1 a, 2 a³, 3 a, 4 a, 4 d³, 5 a, 7 a, 8 a, 9 a, 10 a, 11 b, 14 a, 16 a, 20 a, 21³, 23, 26 a, 27 a⁴, 28 a³, 33 a, 38 a³, 41 a, 61 a, 61 b, 62 a, 68, 73 a⁴, 77 a, 78 a, 80 a, 80 c⁵, 91 a, 92 a, 93 a, 94 a, 95 a⁶, 96 a, 97 a, 98, 99 a, 100 a, 101 a, 106 c, 107 a, 109, 111 a, 112 a, 113 a, 114 a, 115 a, 116 a, 117 a, 118⁷, 121 a⁷, 122 a, 123 a, 124 a, 125 a, 126 a, 127 a, 128 a, 129 a, 130 a, 133 a, 135 a, 137 a, 138 a⁶,⁸, 138 b⁶, 138 c, 139 a, 140 a, 143 b, 177 a, 178 a, 180 a, 182, 192 a, 192 b. With few exceptions all the foregoing are the opening movement of a Cantata. The exceptions are: No. 28 a, which is the second movement; No. 138 b, which is the third movement; No. 4 d, which is the fourth

---

¹ *Op. cit.* III. 104.   ² See also No. 186.
³ A Choral Motett.   ⁴ See also the *Dialogus* group.
⁵ Also under Unison Choral.
⁶ See also the *Dialogus* group.   ⁷ A Choral Motett.
⁸ See note on this movement in Cantata 138.

movement; No. 80 c, which is the fifth movement; No. 182, which is the seventh movement; No. 21, which is the ninth movement; Nos. 11 b, 23, 61 b, 106 c, 109, 138 c, 143 b, 192 b, which are the concluding movement[1].

The Simple Choral

The majority of the Choral movements in the Cantatas, as in the "Passions" and Oratorios, are in simple Hymn form, i.e. suitable for congregational use, but not necessarily so used. While a Choral Fantasia as a general rule begins a Cantata, a Simple Choral, almost invariably, brings it to a close. Only in three instances—Nos. 145 a, 153 a, D 4—does a Simple Choral begin a Cantata[2].

It is remarkable that Bach generally preferred to bring his Cantatas to an end in a simple and unpretentious form. That he did so with the

[1] Spitta, III. 101, regards the following movements as transitional towards the perfect Choral Fantasia: Nos. 1 a, 5 a, 41 a, 61 a, 94 a, 126 a, 127 a, 135 a, 139 a. The following Extended Chorals approach the dimensions of a Choral Fantasia: Nos. 100 b, 129 b, 147 a, 147 b, 167, 186.

[2] With the rarest exceptions, the Simple and Embellished Chorals are printed in Bernhard Friedrich Richter's edition of Bach's *Choralgesänge* (Breitkopf & Haertel, 1898). Some of the Extended and more elaborate movements are given by Ludwig Erk in his *Johann Sebastian Bach's Choralgesänge und geistliche Arien* (2 vols., Peters, 1850-65). The Chorals which are thus rendered accessible are indicated in the following pages.

reverent purpose of rivetting a last impression of the Hymn in its most arresting form cannot be doubted. The following are the one hundred and thirty-four Simple Chorals in the Cantatas: Nos. 2 b, 3 c, 4 g, 5 b, 6 b, 7 b, 8 b, 9 b, 10 b, 11 a, 13 b, 14 b, 16 b, 17, 18, 20 b, 20 c, 25, 26 b, 27 b, 28 b, 30, 32, 33 b, 36 b, 36 d, 37 b, 38 b, 39, 40 a, 40 b, 40 c, 42 b, 43, 44 b, 45, 47, 48 a, 48 b, 55, 56, 57, 60 b, 62 b, 64 a, 64 c, 65 b, 66, 67 a, 67 b, 70 a, 72, 73 b, 74, 77 b, 78 b, 80 d, 81, 83, 84, 85 b, 86 b, 87, 88, 89, 90, 92 e, 93 g, 94 d, 96 b, 99 b, 102, 103, 108, 110, 111 b, 113 e, 114 c, 115 b, 116 b, 117 b, 117 c, 119, 120, 121 b, 122 c, 123 b, 124 b, 125 c, 126 c, 127 b, 132, 133 b, 135 b, 139 b, 140 c, 144 a, 144 b, 145 a, 145 b, 146, 148, 151, 153 a, 153 b, 153 c, 154 a, 154 b, 155, 156 b, 157, 158 b, 159 b, 162, 163, 164, 165, 166 b, 168, 169, 176, 177 b, 178 e, 179, 180 c, 183, 184, 187, 188, 194 a, 197 a, 197 b, U 1, D 4.

The Embellished Choral

Closely related to the Simple Choral is the Embellished, or decorated Simple, form, of which there are thirty-five examples in the Cantatas: Nos. 1 b, 12, 19, 29, 31, 52, 59, 64 b, 65 a, 69 a, 69 b, 70 b, 79 b, 91 c, 95 c, 97 b, 101 f, 104, 112 b, 128 b, 130 b, 136, 137 d, 149, 161, 172, 174, 175, 185, 190 b, 194 b, 195, U 3, D 2, D 3. Excepting

Nos. 59, 64 b, 65 a, these Chorals conclude the Cantata. Bach's purpose in regard to them therefore is obvious. In form they are identical with the Simple Choral. They differ in that, while in the Simple Choral the orchestra merely doubles the voice parts, in the Embellished form certain instruments have independent parts, giving brilliance or adding an ornament to the final statement of the tune. In Nos. 19, 29, 69 a, 130 b, 137 e, 149, 190 b, and U 3, Bach secures an impressive ending by adding Trumpets and Timpani. In No. D 3 he uses two Trumpets *obbligati*[1]. In Nos. 79 b, 91 c, and 195, Horns and Timpani are employed in a similar manner, while in Nos. 1 b, 52, 112 b, 128 b, D 2, Horns emphasise or support the melody[2]. In No. 65 a the Flutes in octave accentuate, and in No. 161 weave an arabesque round the melody[3]. In No. 175 the Strings and Flutes are in unison[4]. In Nos. 59, 70 b, 95 c, 97 b, 136, 172, 185, the Violins are *obbligati* or the Strings support the inner parts of the vocal harmony[5]. In No. 31 the First Violins and Trumpet are *obbligati*, and No. 12

[1] The Trumpet and Timpani group of Embellished Chorals will be found in Richter's *Choralgesänge*, in the order in which their numbers are stated above, as Nos. 99, 272, 97, 131, 230, 155, 205, 230, 387.

[2] For this group see the *Choralgesänge*, Nos. 267, 109, 236, 378, 212, 14, 279, 219.

[3] *Choralgesänge*, Nos. 302, 161.   [4] *Ibid*. No. 220.

[5] *Ibid*. Nos. 220, 243, 356, 297, 27, 376, 184.

provides a similar part for the Oboe *or* Trumpet[1]. In No. 64 b Bach adds an Organ pedal[2]. Nos. 69 b, 101 f, 104, 174, and 194 b contain unimportant additions to the inner vocal parts[3].

In a large number of cases a Simple Choral is strengthened by the addition of octaves in the Continuo.

The Extended Choral

The Extended Choral, familiar in the "Christmas Oratorio[4]," presents the melody in Simple four-part form, but the lines of the Hymn are separated by orchestral interludes which, with the addition of an introduction, give the movement in some cases almost the proportions and character of a Choral Fantasia[5]. There are twenty-three Chorals of this kind in the Cantatas: Nos. 3 b[6], 15, 22, 24, 41 b, 46, 75 a (c), 76 a, 76 b, 79 a, 92 d[6], 100 b, 105, 107 b, 129 b, 142, 147 a, 147 b, 167, 171, 178 d[6], 186, 190 a[6]. All of them are the final movements of a Cantata, or of the first Part of a Cantata, except Nos. 3 b, 79 a, 92 d, 147 a, 178 d, and 190 a.

[1] *Choralgesänge*, Nos. 357, 340.   [2] *Ibid.* No. 280.
[3] Erk, No. 301; *Choralgesänge*, Nos. 318, 13, 153, 268.
[4] Nos. 9, 23, 42, 64. Spitta, II. 457, finds this type of Choral reminiscent of Georg Böhm (1661–1733), whose influence upon Bach was considerable. See Schweitzer, I. 45.
[5] The following movements approach the dimensions of a Choral Fantasia: Nos. 100 b, 129 b, 147 a, 147 b, 167, 186.
[6] The Choral is also included in the *Dialogus* group.

INTRODUCTION 41

In the Cantatas, therefore, as in the "Christmas Oratorio," Bach's purpose in regard to the Extended Choral is clear.

The Unison Choral

Among the Choral movements for individual voices the Unison Chorals are the most numerous. They number twenty-one, and are as follows, the voice to which the melody is given being stated in the bracket: Nos. 4 c (T.), 4 e (B.), 6 a (S.), 13 a (A.), 36 c (T.), 44 a (T.), 51 (S.), 85 a (S.), 86 a (S.), 92 c (A.), 95 b (S.), 113 b (A.), 114 b (S.), 137 b (A.), 140 b (T.), 143 a (S.), 166 a (S.), 178 c (T.), 180 b (S.)[1], 199 (S.). In this group also must be included No. 80 c, which is a Unison Choral Fantasia for S.A.T.B.

As Schweitzer points out[2], most of these Unison Chorals are exceedingly appropriate for use in liturgical services; the Soprano Chorals especially would be effective with instrumental or Organ accompaniment.

The Aria Choral

The term *Aria*, as Bach used it, connotes a song in rhythmical proportions for one *or more* voices. In the Cantatas the term is applied to

[1] The movement actually is marked "Recitatif." See Cantata 180.
[2] *Op. cit.* II. 465.

movements for one, two, and three voices. It will be convenient to set them out in three categories under the designations *Solo, Duetto, Terzetto.*

There are three *Solo Arias*, Nos. 93 c, 93 f, and 101 c, the first for Tenor, the second for Soprano, the third for Bass. In all of them only snatches of the Choral melody are introduced.

The *Duetto* movements are variously described in Bach's score as "Choral," "Arie," "Arie und Choral," "Arie (Duett)." The following are the fifteen examples of this form: Nos. 4 f (S.T.), 36 a (S.A.), 37 a (S.A.), treat the *cantus* in canon. In Nos. 4 b (S.A.), 71 (S.T.), 80 b (S.B.), 131 a (S.B.), 131 b (A.T.), 156 a (S.T.), 158 a (S.B.), and 159 a (S.A.), the *cantus* is given in every case to one of two voices, the first stated in the bracket. In No. 93 d (S.A.), marked "Arie (Duett) und Choral," the *cantus* is played by the Strings; in No. 137 c (T.) by the Tromba. In Nos. 101 e (S.A.) and 113 d (S.A.), the *cantus* is only suggested.

The single example of the *Terzetto* form is No. 122 b (S.A.T.), where the Alto, with the Violins and Viola, has the *cantus*.

The Dialogus *Choral*

Into the Cantata "Ach Gott, wie manches Herzeleid" (No. 58), for the Sunday after the Circumcision, 1733, Bach introduced two numbers

INTRODUCTION

in which Soprano and Bass voices converse, the former to the melody of the Choral, the latter in *Recitativo*. At about the same time, in "O Ewigkeit, du Donnerwort" (No. 60), for the Twenty-fourth Sunday after Trinity, Bach wrote another Cantata which is also in the form of a conversation between two characters. Hence their designation as a "Dialogus" in the score.

Besides these two "Dialogus" Cantatas, there are twenty-six movements in the Cantatas which are in the nature of a conversation between the Choral *cantus* and a voice or voices speaking in *Recitativo*[1]. Bach marks them indifferently, "Recitativ," or "Recitativ und Choral." But they can be sub-divided into three classes. In the first, the conversation is between two voices of contrasted calibre: their numbers are Nos. 49 (S.B.), 58 a (S.B.), 58 b (S.B.), 60 a (A.T.), 106 b (A.B.), 126 b (A.T.), the Choral *cantus* in every case being allotted to the first of the two voices stated in the bracket, except in the case of the last, where both voices share the *cantus*. A larger number are movements for a single voice, though improbably for the same individual voice. They are Nos. 91 b (S.),

---

[1] The term does not imply that the literary text invariably is a dialogue, but that the movement is cast in the form of a musical conversation between the *cantus* and *Recitativo*. Frequently the latter is a commentary rather than a reply.

92 b (B.), 93 b (B.), 93 e (T.), 94 b (T.), 94 c (B.), 101 b (S.), 101 d (T.), 113 c (B.), 125 b (B.), and 178 b (A.). The third class of Dialogue Chorals consists of Choruses which have been classified already, but belong also to the class under discussion. They exhibit the same determining characteristic, in that they consist of alternating periods of the Choral (S.A.T.B.) and *Recitativo* for one or more voices of the chorus. They are Nos. 3 b, 27 a, 73 a, 92 d, 95 a, 138 a, 138 b, 178 d, and 190 a.

The Motetts

It was the custom at Leipzig, both in St Thomas' and St Nicholas' Churches, for Motetts to be sung, usually in Latin, at the morning and evening service; also, during the communion office, occasionally on the high festivals, and always on Palm Sunday and Holy Thursday. Special occasions, and particularly funerals, also were marked by their performance. Hence Bach had large opportunity to write in this form. Yet, no Latin Motetts of his are extant, though there is evidence suggesting the conclusion that he wrote one. Of the Motetts with German texts that have come to us under Bach's name only six are by him. His barrenness in this form is explained by the fact that, in common with the musicians of his period, he held

the Motett of little importance beside the Cantata, the "principal music" of the Church service, and in general was content to perform other composers' works[1].
The following six Motetts indubitably are Bach's :

1. Singet dem Herrn ein neues Lied[2].
2. Der Geist hilft unsrer Schwachheit auf[3].
3. Jesu, meine Freude[4].
4. Fürchte dich nicht, ich bin bei dir[5].
5. Komm, Jesu, komm, mein Leib ist müde[6].

[1] See Spitta, II. chap. ix; Schweitzer, II. chap. xxxi; Parry, *J. S. Bach* (New York, 1909), ch. vii.

[2] Psalms cxlix. 1-3; cl. 2, 6. Spitta, II. 603, suggests that the Motett was composed for New Year's Day.

[3] Romans viii. 26, 27. The Motett was composed for and performed at the funeral of the Leipzig Professor and Rector, Johann Heinrich Ernesti, October 16, 1729. The concluding Whitsuntide Choral is an addition and suggests that Bach made use of the Motett for that season, to which the original words are congruous.

[4] The text of the Motett is Johann Franck's Hymn, "Jesu, meine Freude" (see Cantata 64), and Romans viii. 1, 2, 9, 10, 11. The work was composed for and performed at the funeral of Frau Reese in 1723. She probably was the wife of a member of the Prince's Court band at Cöthen. As the Bible text is relative to and in context with the Epistle for the Eighth Sunday after Trinity, it is possible that Bach used the Motett for that Sunday.

[5] Isaiah xli. 10, and xliii. 1. The date of the Motett is not ascertained. It was composed for the funeral of Frau Winkler, wife of the deputy Mayor of Leipzig.

[6] The Motett consists of two stanzas of an *Aria* text. Neither the date nor the occasion of the Motett is ascertained.

6. Lobet den Herrn, alle Heiden[1].

Of the six Motetts only the last is without Choral movements. In form the latter for the most part are Simple (Motetts 2, 3, 5). A single example of the Extended form is found in Motett 1, and of the Choral Fantasia or Motett form in Motett 3 (verse 5) and Motett 4[2].

The Hymns of the "Passions," Oratorios, Cantatas, and Motetts

Bach employs 154 congregational Hymns in his choral works, of which two ("O Gott, der du aus Herzensgrund," and "Komm, Gott Schöpfer, heiliger Geist") occur in Cantatas of doubtful authenticity, and one ("Wenn einer alle Ding verstünd") cannot be regarded positively as Bach's selection. The source whence Bach drew so large a supply of Hymn texts can be indicated readily. Spitta prints[3] a "Specification of the property belonging to and left by Herr Johann Sebastian Bach, deceased July 28, 1750, late Cantor to the school of

---

[1] Psalm cxvii. Neither the date nor the occasion of the Motett is ascertained.

[2] In Motetts for single chorus the sections or lines of the thematic text were worked out *fugato*. For examples of this form in the Cantatas see note, p. 34 *supra*. The so-called Motett, "Sei Lob und Preis mit Ehren" (B. G. xxxix. 167), is, with slight alterations, the second movement of Cantata 28.

[3] *Op. cit.* III. 351–356.

St Thomas, in Leipzig." Under the heading "Theological books in octavo," there is the entry, "Wagner, Leipziger Gesangbuch, 8 vols." It was valued at one thaler, and was the only Hymn book in Bach's possession at the time of his death. Paul Wagner's "Andächtiger Seelen geistliches Brand- und Gantz-Opfer. Das ist: vollständiges Gesangbuch in acht unterschiedlichen Theilen" was published at Leipzig in 1697. Of the 154 Hymns used by Bach all but eleven are found there[1]. Of the eleven, all but two (Neander's "Lobe den Herren, den mächtigen König der Ehren" and Neumann's "Auf, mein Herz") are found in the 1708 edition of Crüger's *Praxis Pietatis Melica*. The choice of Hymn texts therefore need not have occasioned Bach much research. The following are the 154 Hymns, tabulated under the names of their authors:

JOHANNES AGRICOLA (1492–1566).
    Ich ruf' zu dir, Herr Jesu Christ.

JOHANN GEORG ALBINUS (1624–79).
    Alle Menschen müssen sterben.
    Welt, ade! ich bin dein müde.

ALBRECHT MARGRAVE OF BRANDENBURG-CULMBACH (1522–57).
    Was mein Gott will, das g'scheh' allzeit.

---

[1] It contains no tunes.

JOHANN MICHAEL ALTENBURG (1584-1640).
Verzage nicht, du Häuflein klein.

ANARK OF WILDENFELS (d. 1539).
†O Herre Gott, dein göttlich Wort.

MATTHÄUS AVENARIUS (1625-92).
O Jesu, meine Lust.

CORNELIUS BECKER (1561-1604).
Der Herr ist mein getreuer Hirt.

MARTIN BEHM (1557-1622).
O Jesu Christ, mein's Lebens Licht.

CASPAR BIENEMANN (1540-91).
Herr, wie du willt, so schick's mit mir.

FRANZ JOACHIM BURMEISTER (1633?-72).
Es ist genug: so nimm, Herr, meinen Geist.

ELISABETHE CRUCIGER (d. 1535).
Herr Christ, der einig' Gott's Sohn.

NICOLAUS DECIUS (d. 1541).
O Lamm Gottes unschuldig.

DAVID DENICKE (1603-80).
†*Ich will zu aller Stunde.
Kommt, lasst euch den Herren lehren.
†Schau', lieber Gott, wie meine Feind'.
†Wenn einer alle Ding verstünd[1].

PAUL EBER (1511-69).
Helft mir Gott's Güte preisen.
Herr Gott, dich loben alle wir.
Herr Jesu Christ, wahr'r Mensch und Gott.

[1] See Cantata 77.

INTRODUCTION

JAKOB EBERT (1549–1614).
  Du Friedefürst, Herr Jesu Christ.
EMILIE JULIANE COUNTESS OF SCHWARZ-
BURG-RUDOLSTADT (1637–1706).
  *Wer weiss, wie nahe mir mein Ende.
PAUL FLEMMING (1609–40).
  In allen meinen Thaten.
JOHANN FRANCK (1618–77).
  Du, O schönes Weltgebäude.
  Ihr Gestirn, ihr hohlen Lüfte.
  Jesu, meine Freude.
  *Schmücke dich, O liebe Seele.
MICHAEL FRANCK (1609–67).
  Ach wie flüchtig.
JOHANN BURCHARD FREYSTEIN (1671–1718).
  Mache dich, mein Geist, bereit.
AHASHUERUS FRITSCH (1629–1701).
  Hast du denn, Jesu, dein Angesicht gäntzlich verborgen.
  Liebster Immanuel, Herzog der Frommen.
CASPAR FUGER (d. c. 1592).
  Wir Christenleut'.
PAUL GERHARDT (1607–76).
  *Barmherzger Vater, höchster Gott.
  Befiehl du deine Wege.
  Fröhlich soll mein Herze springen.
  Gott Vater, sende deinen Geist.
  Ich hab' in Gottes Herz und Sinn.
  Ich steh' an deiner Krippen hier.
  Nun danket all' und bringet Ehr'.
  O Haupt voll Blut und Wunden.
  O Welt, sieh' hier dein Leben.

Schaut! schaut! was ist für Wunder dar[1].
Schwing' dich auf zu deinem Gott.
Wach auf, mein Herz, und singe.
Warum sollt' ich mich denn grämen.
Was alle Weisheit in der Welt.
Weg, mein Herz, mit den Gedanken.
Wie soll ich dich empfangen.
Wir singen dir, Immanuel.
Zeuch ein zu deinen Thoren.

JUSTUS GESENIUS (1601–73).
†O Gott, der du aus Herzensgrund[2].

JOHANNES G. GIGAS (1514–81).
Ach, lieben Christen, seid getrost.

JOHANN GRAUMANN (1487–1541).
Nun lob', mein' Seel', den Herren.

GEORG GRÜENWALD (d. 1530).
Kommt her zu mir, spricht Gottes Sohn.

JOHANN HEERMANN (1585–1647).
Herzliebster Jesu, was hast du verbrochen.
O Gott, du frommer Gott.
So wahr ich lebe, spricht dein Gott.
Treuer Gott, ich muss dir klagen.
Was willst du dich betrüben.
Wo soll ich fliehen hin.
Zion klagt mit Angst und Schmerzen.

LUDWIG HELMBOLD (1532–98).
Nun lasst uns Gott dem Herren.
Von Gott will ich nicht lassen.

VALERIUS HERBERGER (1562–1627).
Valet will ich dir geben.

---

[1] Wagner's version begins, "O seht was ist für Wunder dar."
[2] The Hymn occurs in a Cantata of doubtful authenticity.

INTRODUCTION

NICOLAUS HERMAN (c. 1485–1561).
Erschienen ist der herrlich' Tag.
Lobt Gott, ihr Christen alle gleich [allzugleich].
Wenn mein Stündlein vorhanden ist.

JOHANN HERMANN (fl. ? 1548–63).
Jesu, nun sei gepreiset.

SEBALD HEYDEN (1494–1561).
O Mensch, bewein' dein' Sünde gross.

ERNST CHRISTOPH HOMBURG (1605–81).
Ist Gott mein Schild und Helfersmann.

MARTIN JANUS (c. 1620–82).
Jesu, meiner Seelen Wonne.

JUSTUS JONAS (1493–1555).
Wo Gott der Herr nicht bei uns hält.

CHRISTIAN KEIMANN (1607–62).
Freuet euch, ihr Christen alle.
Meinen Jesum lass' ich nicht.

CHRISTOPH KNOLL (1563–1650).
Herzlich thut mich verlangen.

JOHANN KOLROSS (d. c. 1558).
Ich dank' dir, lieber Herre.

SALOMO LISCOW (1640–89).
Also hat Gott die Welt geliebt.

MARTIN LUTHER (1483–1546).
Ach Gott, vom Himmel sieh' darein.
Aus tiefer Noth schrei ich zu dir.
Christ lag in Todesbanden.
Christ unser Herr zum Jordan kam.
Christum wir sollen loben schon.

Ein' feste Burg ist unser Gott.
Erhalt' uns, Herr, bei deinem Wort.
Es woll' uns Gott genädig sein.
Gelobet seist du, Jesu Christ.
Herr Gott dich loben wir.
Komm, Gott Schöpfer, heiliger Geist[1].
Komm, heiliger Geist, Herre Gott.
Mit Fried' und Freud' ich fahr' dahin.
Nun bitten wir den heiligen Geist.
Nun komm, der Heiden Heiland.
Vater unser im Himmelreich.
Verleih' uns Frieden gnädiglich.
Vom Himmel hoch da komm ich her.
Wär' Gott nicht mit uns diese Zeit.

WOLFGANG MEUSEL (1497–1563).
Der Herr ist mein getreuer Hirt.

MARTIN MOLLER (1547–1606).
†Ach Gott, wie manches Herzeleid.
Nimm von uns, Herr, du treuer Gott.

HEINRICH MÜLLER (1631–75).
Selig ist die Seele.

JOACHIM NEANDER (1650–80).
*Lobe den Herren, den mächtigen König der Ehren.

CASPAR NEUMANN (1648–1715).
*Auf, mein Herz, des Herren Tag.
*Liebster Gott, wann werd' ich sterben?

GEORG NEUMARK (1621–81).
Wer nur den lieben Gott lässt walten.

[1] The Hymn occurs in one of the Cantatas of doubtful authenticity.

PHILIPP NICOLAI (1556–1608).
Wachet auf, ruft uns die Stimme.
Wie schön leuchtet der Morgenstern.

JOHANNES OLEARIUS (1611–84).
Gelobet sei der Herr.
Tröstet, tröstet, meine Lieben.

GEORG MICHAEL PFEFFERKORN (1645–1732).
*Was frag ich nach der Welt[1].

SYMPHORIANUS POLLIO (fl. 1507–33).
Meine Seel' erhebt den Herren.

ADAM REISSNER (1496–c. 1575).
In dich hab' ich gehoffet, Herr.

BARTHOLOMÄUS RINGWALDT (1532–c. 1600).
Herr Jesu Christ, du höchstes Gut.
Herr Jesu Christ, ich weiss gar wohl.

MARTIN RINKART (1586–1649).
Nun danket alle Gott.

JOHANN RIST (1607–67).
Du Lebensfürst, Herr Jesu Christ.
Ermuntre dich, mein schwacher Geist.
Hilf, Herr Jesu, lass gelingen.
Jesu, der du meine Seele.
Jesu, du mein liebstes Leben.
O Ewigkeit, du Donnerwort.
O Gottes Geist, mein Trost und Rath.
Werde munter, mein Gemüthe.

SAMUEL RODIGAST (1649–1708).
Was Gott thut, das ist wohlgethan.

[1] Wagner has a different text.

JOHANN CHRISTOPH RUBE (1665–1746).
  Wohl dem, der sich auf seinen Gott.
CHRISTOPH RUNGE (1619–81).
  Lasst Furcht und Pein.
GOTTFRIED WILHELM SACER (1635–99)
  Gott fähret auf gen Himmel.
HANS SACHS (1494–1576).
  †Warum betrübst du dich, mein Herz.
MARTIN SCHALLING (1532–1608).
  Herzlich lieb hab' ich dich, O Herr.
JOHANN HERMANN SCHEIN (1586–1630).
  Mach's mit mir, Gott, nach deiner Güt'.
CYRIACUS SCHNEEGASS (1546–97).
  —Ach Herr, mich armen Sünder.
  —Das neugebor'ne Kindelein.
JOHANNES SCHNEESING (d. 1567).
  Allein zu dir, Herr Jesu Christ.
BALTHASAR SCHNURR (1572–1644).
  O grosser Gott von Macht.
JOHANN JAKOB SCHÜTZ (1640–90).
  *Sei Lob und Ehr' dem höchsten Gut.
NICOLAUS SELNECKER (1532–92).
  Ach bleib' bei uns, Herr Jesu Christ.
LAZARUS SPENGLER (1479–1534).
  Durch Adams Fall ist ganz verderbt.
PAUL SPERATUS (1484–1551).
  Es ist das Heil uns kommen her.

INTRODUCTION

PAUL STOCKMANN (1602?–36).
    Jesu Leiden, Pein und Tod.

CHRISTOPH TIETZE (1641–1703).
    Ich armer Mensch, ich armer Sünder.

JOSUA WEGELIN (1604–40).
    Auf Christi Himmelfahrt allein.

SIGISMUND WEINGÄRTNER (fl. 1607).
    †Auf meinen lieben Gott.

MICHAEL WEISSE (1480?–1534).
    Christus, der uns selig macht.

GEORG WEISSEL (1590–1635).
    Nun liebe Seel', nun ist es Zeit.

GEORG WERNER (1589–1643).
    *Ihr Christen auserkoren.

CASPAR ZIEGLER (1621–90).
    Ich freue mich in dir.

ANONYMOUS.
    Ach Gott und Herr.
    Christ ist erstanden.
    *Christe, du Lamm Gottes.
    Christus, der ist mein Leben.
    Ein Kind geborn zu Bethlehem.
    Freu' dich sehr, O meine Seele.
    Herr Jesu Christ, ich schrei zu dir.
    Komm, Jesu, komm, mein Leib ist müde.
    Singen wir aus Herzensgrund.

† The authorship of these Hymns is doubtful.
* The eleven Hymns marked with an asterisk are not in Paul Wagner's Hymn book.

The Hymn Tunes used by Bach

During his Cantorship at Leipzig Bach systematically collected, harmonised, and in some cases refashioned, Hymn tunes whose qualities attracted him. At the time of his death he had brought together about two hundred and forty melodies in a manuscript which unfortunately has disappeared. In 1764 it was in the possession of the Leipzig music seller, Bernhard Christoph Breitkopf, into whose hands it passed, presumably, in the lean years that befell Bach's widow after his death in 1750. In Breitkopf's catalogue (1764) the work is described as "Bachs, J. S. Vollständiges Choralbuch mit in Noten aufgesetzten Generalbasse an 240 in Leipzig gewöhnlichen Melodien." Copies of it were offered at the price of ten thalers[1]. But, as none exist, it is doubtful whether the "Choralbuch" in fact was published in that form and year.

It would appear, however, that the greater part of Bach's collection was published in different works before and after his death. In 1736 Georg Christian Schemelli, "Schloss-Cantor" at Naumburg-Zeitz, in Saxony, published a "Musicalisches Gesang-Buch, Darinnen 954 geistreiche, sowohl alte als neue Lieder und Arien, mit wohlgesetzten Melodien, in Discant und Bass, befindlich sind"

---

[1] See Spitta, III. chap. iv.

INTRODUCTION 57

(Breitkopf, Leipzig, 1736). Bach was invited to prepare the collection for the press. Its tunes, the Preface declared, were either "ganz neu" composed by him, or had been supplied by him with a Bass. The 954 Hymns share between them no more than sixty-nine melodies, about a quarter of which are Bach's own compositions[1]. The Preface announced that about two hundred more melodies were ready for a second edition, should one be called for, as unhappily was not the case. It would seem, therefore, that Bach proposed to place his whole collection at Schemelli's service.

Bach continued his collection of Hymn tunes, in spite of the cold reception given to Schemelli's volume. To his own copy of the book he added eighty-eight harmonised Chorals. Among the effects of Philipp Emmanuel Bach in 1790 appears "The Naumburg Hymn book, containing printed Chorals and also eighty-eight Chorals written out in parts." Unhappily, it cannot be traced. Meanwhile in 1764 Breitkopf of Leipzig acquired a MS. containing one hundred and fifty four-part Hymn tunes harmonised by Bach. Simultaneously, the Berlin printer Friedrich Wilhelm Birnstiel resolved

[1] Spitta follows C. F. Becker's edition of the "Kirchengesänge" in supposing that Bach wrote twenty-nine tunes for Schemelli (III. 111 n.). Zahn, however, VI. 316, accounts positively for forty-eight tunes. Twenty-one remain. Not all of them are Bach's. On the whole question of Bach's original Hymn tunes see *infra*, p. 67.

to issue a printed edition of Bach's Chorals. He invited Philipp Emmanuel Bach to edit and preface it with an Introduction. In 1765 the book was issued. It numbered fifty pages containing one hundred Hymn tunes, and bore the title: "Johann Sebastian Bachs vierstimmige Choralgesänge gesammlet von Carl Philipp Emmanuel Bach" (Berlin & Leipzig, 1765). A second Part, with which Philipp Emmanuel was not associated, was published in 1769. It contained one hundred more Hymn tunes, among them, "O Herzensangst, O Bangigkeit," "Gottlob, es geht nunmehr zum Ende," and "Nicht so traurig, nicht so sehr."

Twenty years followed the publication of the first Part of Birnstiel's edition before Breitkopf issued a completer collection of Bach's Chorals in four Parts between the years 1784 and 1787. Philipp Emmanuel edited this collection also. Its first Part, published at Leipzig in 1784, bore the title: "Johann Sebastian Bachs vierstimmige Choralgesänge, Erster Theil. Leipzig bey Johann Gottlob Immanuel Breitkopf." The second, third, and fourth Parts were issued in 1785, 1786, and 1787 respectively, the whole collection containing three hundred and seventy[1] Chorals, including a large number from Bach's extant Church compositions.

[1] A 3rd edition, dated 1831, contains three hundred and seventy-one.

Finally, in 1843, Carl Ferdinand Becker (1804-77), Organist of St Nicholas' Church, Leipzig, issued a collection of two hundred and ten four-part Hymn settings, under the title "Joh. Seb. Bachs vierstimmige Kirchengesänge" (Leipzig: Robert Friese). Two more recent collections of Bach's Chorals are accessible and inexpensive. The earlier, Ludwig Erk's "Johann Sebastian Bach's mehrstimmige Choralgesänge und geistliche Arien," is published by C. F. Peters, Leipzig, in two volumes (Prefaces dated 1850 and 1865) which contain three hundred and nineteen Choral settings. Erk gives some of the longer as well as the simple Hymn settings, besides some tunes drawn from other sources than those which the second of the two collections explores. The latter, "Johann Sebastian Bach's Werke. Für Gesang. Gesammtausgabe für den praktischen Gebrauch. VII. Choralgesänge" (Leipzig, 1898), edited by Bernhard Friedrich Richter, contains three hundred and eighty-nine Chorals, including one hundred and eighty-five edited by Philipp Emmanuel Bach 1784-87 which were not used in Bach's extant Cantatas. They are printed from B. G. xxxix ("Arien und Lieder"), which contains them all. Richter's edition also includes a complete collection of the Simple Chorals used in Bach's Oratorios, "Passions," Cantatas, and Motetts. Reference is made to it throughout the following pages, and to Erk in cases where he prints a setting not found in Richter's "Choralgesänge."

Of this great *corpus* of Choral music Bach introduces into his concerted Church works—the "Passions," Oratorios, Cantatas, Motetts—one hundred and four Hymn tunes, including, however, one which occurs in a Cantata of doubtful authenticity. Besides these one hundred and four melodies, Bach uses twenty-eight in his Organ works that are not found elsewhere in his music. Therefore, excluding his own compositions, it appears that he introduced into the works that have come down to us the following one hundred and thirty-two Hymn tunes:

JOHANN RODOLF AHLE (1625-73).
> Es ist genug; so nimm, Herr, meinen Geist.
> *Liebster Jesu, wir sind hier*[1].

HEINRICH ALBERT (1604-51).
> Gott des Himmels und der Erden.

JOHANN MICHAEL ALTENBURG (1584-1640).
> *Herr Gott, nun schleuss den Himmel auf.*

LOUIS BOURGEOIS (fl. 1541-61).
> Ainsi qu'on oit le cerf bruire[2].
> *Leve le cœur, ouvre l'oreille*[3].

[1] Originally (1664) set to "Ja, er ists, das Heil der Welt." The melodies in italic type occur only in the Organ works.
[2] Also known as "Freu' dich sehr, O meine Seele," and "Wie nach einer Wasserquelle."
[3] In Bach, "Wenn wir in höchsten Nöthen sein."

On a beau son maison bastir[1].
Or sus, serviteurs du Seigneur[2].

SETH CALVISIUS (1556–1615).
In dich hab' ich gehoffet, Herr.

JOHANN CRÜGER (1598–1662).
Du, O schönes Weltgebäude.
Herzliebster Jesu, was hast du verbrochen.
Jesu, meine Freude.
Jesus, meine Zuversicht[3].
Nun danket alle Gott.
O Ewigkeit, du Donnerwort[4].
Schmücke dich, O liebe Seele.

WOLFGANG DACHSTEIN (d. c. 1561).
An Wasserflüssen Babylon[3].

NICOLAUS DECIUS (d. 1541).
Allein Gott in der Höh' sei Ehr'.
O Lamm Gottes unschuldig.

JOHANN GEORG EBELING (1637–76).
Warum sollt' ich mich denn grämen.

WOLFGANG FIGULUS (c. 1520–91).
Helft mir Gott's Güte preisen (second melody).

MELCHIOR FRANCK (d. 1639).
O grosser Gott von Macht[3].

MICHAEL FRANCK (1609–67).
Ach wie flüchtig.

[1] In Bach, "Herr Jesu Christ, wahr'r Mensch und Gott."
[2] In Bach, "Herr Gott, dich loben alle wir."
[3] Authorship doubtful.
[4] A reconstruction of Johann Schop's "Wach auf, mein Geist."

CASPAR FUGER (d. 1617).
Wir Christenleut'.

GIOVANNI GIACOMO GASTOLDI (1556?-1622).
In dir ist Freude.

BARTHOLOMÄUS GESIUS (1555?—1613-4).
Du Friedefürst, Herr Jesu Christ.
Heut' triumphiret Gottes Sohn.

MATTHÄUS GREITTER (d. 1550 or 1552).
Es sind doch selig alle[1].

ANDREAS HAMMERSCHMIDT (1612-75).
Freuet euch, ihr Christen alle[2].
Meinen Jesum lass' ich nicht[2].

HANS LEO HASSLER (1564-1612).
Herzlich thut mich verlangen[3].

BARTHOLOMÄUS HELDER (1585?-1635).
Das Jesulein soll doch mein Trost.

NICOLAUS HERMAN (1485?-1561).
Erschienen ist der herrlich' Tag.
Lobt Gott, ihr Christen alle gleich [allzugleich].
Wenn mein Stündlein vorhanden ist.

HEINRICH ISAAK (b. *c.* 1440).
O Welt, ich muss dich lassen[4].

JOHANN KUGELMANN (d. 1542).
Nun lob', mein' Seel', den Herren[2].

[1] Better known as "O Mensch, bewein' dein' Sünde gross."
[2] Authorship doubtful.
[3] Also known as "O Haupt voll Blut und Wunden," and "Ach Herr, mich armen Sünder."
[4] Also sung to "Nun ruhen alle Wälder."

MARTIN LUTHER (1483–1546).
Aus tiefer Noth schrei ich zu dir[1].
Ein' feste Burg ist unser Gott.
Mit Fried' und Freud' ich fahr' dahin[1].
Vom Himmel hoch da komm ich her[1].

GEORG NEUMARK (1621–81).
Wer nur den lieben Gott lässt walten.

PHILIPP NICOLAI (1556–1608).
Wachet auf, ruft uns die Stimme[1].
Wie schön leuchtet der Morgenstern[1].

JOHANN ROSENMÜLLER (1619–84).
Welt, ade! ich bin dein müde.

JOHANN HERMANN SCHEIN (1586–1630).
Mach's mit mir, Gott, nach deiner Güt'.

JOHANN SCHOP (d. *c.* 1665).
Ermuntre dich, mein schwacher Geist.
Werde munter, mein Gemüthe.

JOHANN STEURLEIN (1546–1613).
Das alte Jahr vergangen ist[2].

CASPAR STIELER (1679).
Wo soll ich fliehen hin[1].

MELCHIOR TESCHNER (1614).
Valet will ich dir geben.

DANIEL VETTER (d. 1721).
Liebster Gott, wann werd' ich sterben?

[1] Authorship doubtful.
[2] Originally set to Herman's "Gott Vater, der du deine Sonn."

GOTTFRIED VOPELIUS (1645–1715).
Also hat Gott die Welt geliebt.
Sei gegrüsset, Jesu gütig[1].

MELCHIOR VULPIUS (1560?–1615).
Christus, der ist mein Leben.
Das neugebor'ne Kindelein.
Jesu Kreuz, Leiden und Pein.

JOHANN WALTHER (1496–1570).
Christ unser Herr zum Jordan kam[1].
Erbarm' dich mein, O Herre Gott[1].
Jesus Christus, unser Heiland, Der den Tod[1].
Jesus Christus, unser Heiland, Der von uns[1].
Wär' Gott nicht mit uns diese Zeit[1].

ANONYMOUS.
Ach Gott und Herr.
Ach Gott, vom Himmel sieh' darein.
Alle Menschen müssen sterben (1715).
Alle Menschen müssen sterben (1687).
Allein zu dir, Herr Jesu Christ.
Auf meinen lieben Gott[2].
Christ, der du bist der helle Tag.
Christ ist erstanden.
Christ lag in Todesbanden.
Christe, du Lamm Gottes.
Christum wir sollen loben schon[3].
Christus, der uns selig macht.
Da Jesus an dem Kreuze stund[4].

[1] Authorship doubtful.
[2] Or "Wo soll ich fliehen hin."
[3] Or "Was fürcht'st du, Feind, Herodes, sehr."
[4] Originally set to "In dich hab' ich gehoffet, Herr."

INTRODUCTION

Danket dem Herrn, heut' und allzeit[1].
Der Tag, der ist so freudenreich.
Dies sind die heil'gen zehn Gebot.'
Durch Adams Fall ist ganz verderbt.
Ein Kind geborn zu Bethlehem (Puer natus in Bethlehem)[2].
Erhalt' uns, Herr, bei deinem Wort.
Erstanden ist der heil'ge Christ.
Es ist das Heil uns kommen her.
Es woll' uns Gott genädig sein.
Gelobet seist du, Jesu Christ.
Gottes Sohn ist kommen[3].
Herr Christ, der einig' Gott's Sohn[4].
Herr Gott dich loben wir.
Herr Jesu Christ, dich zu uns wend'.
Herr Jesu Christ, du höchstes Gut.
Herr Jesu Christ, mein's Lebens Licht[5].
Herr, wie du willt, so schick's mit mir.
Herzlich lieb hab' ich dich, O Herr.
Hilf Gott, dass mir's gelinge.
Ich hab' mein Sach' Gott heimgestellt.
Ich dank' dir, lieber Herre.
Ich freue mich in dir.
Ich ruf' zu dir, Herr Jesu Christ.
In dich hab' ich gehoffet, Herr (1560).
In dulci jubilo.
Ist Gott mein Schild und Helfersmann.
Jesu, der du meine Seele.

---

[1] Also sung to "Ach bleib' bei uns, Herr Jesu Christ."
[2] Also known as "Vom Himmel kam der Engel Schaar."
[3] Originally "Ave ierarchia Celestis et pia." Also known as "Gott, durch deine Güte."
[4] Also sung to Selnecker's "Herr Gott, nun sei gepreiset."
[5] Also known as "Ach Gott, wie manches Herzeleid."

INTRODUCTION

Jesu, nun sei gepreiset.
Komm, Gott Schöpfer, heiliger Geist[1].
Komm, heiliger Geist, Herre Gott.
Kommt her zu mir, spricht Gottes Sohn.
Kyrie, Gott Vater in Ewigkeit[2].
Liebster Immanuel, Herzog der Frommen.
Lob sei dem allmächtigen Gott[3].
Lobe den Herren, den mächtigen König der Ehren[4].
Meine Seele erhebt den Herren.
Nun bitten wir den heiligen Geist.
Nun freut euch, lieben Christen g'mein[5].
Nun komm, der Heiden Heiland.
Nun lasst uns Gott dem Herren.
O Gott, du frommer Gott (1646)[6].
O Gott, du frommer Gott (1679)[7].
O Gott, du frommer Gott (1693).
O Herre Gott, dein göttlich Wort.
Schwing' dich auf zu deinem Gott.
Singen wir aus Herzensgrund[8].
Straf mich nicht in deinem Zorn[9].
Vater unser im Himmelreich.
Verleih' uns Frieden gnädiglich.
Von Gott will ich nicht lassen[10].
Warum betrübst du dich, mein Herz.

[1] The tune occurs in a Cantata of doubtful authenticity.
[2] Included in this title are the second and third stanzas: "Christe, aller Welt Trost," and "Kyrie, Gott heiliger Geist."
[3] Originally "Conditor alme siderum."
[4] Or "Kommst du nun, Jesu, vom Himmel herunter," or "Hast du denn, Jesu, dein Angesicht gäntzlich verborgen."
[5] Also known as "Es ist gewisslich an der Zeit."
[6] Originally "Gross ist, O grosser Gott."
[7] Also known as "Die Wollust dieser Welt."
[8] Also known as "Da Christus geboren war."
[9] Also known as "Mache dich, mein Geist, bereit."
[10] Also known as "Helft mir Gott's Güte preisen."

INTRODUCTION

Was Gott thut, das ist wohlgethan.
Was mein Gott will, das g'scheh' allzeit.
Wo Gott der Herr nicht bei uns hält[1].
Wir danken dir, Herr Jesu Christ[2].
Wir glauben all' an einen Gott, Schöpfer.
Wir glauben all' an einen Gott, Vater.

Bach's Original Hymn Tunes

Though the topic is engrossing, little effort has been made to identify Bach's original Hymn tunes and to sift those which unquestionably are his from others attributed to him wrongly. Carl von Winterfeld, who first gave the subject critical examination, left a heavy legacy of error, which Ludwig Erk did somewhat to lighten. Spitta[3] devotes a few pages to the subject, but they are disfigured by very serious mistakes. Schweitzer carries the investigation no farther and merely records the conjectures of others. It will be useful, therefore, though the enquiry is not directly relative to the Cantatas and Motetts, to explore the subject in the light of information which Spitta did not possess.

[1] Also known as "Ach lieben Christen, seid getrost."
[2] Attributed doubtfully to Johann Eccard (1553–1611). Originally "Herr Jesu Christ, wahr'r Mensch und Gott."
[3] Vol. III. 111–115. Schweitzer, II. 300, gives a list of Hymn tunes "supposed to be by Bach" but does not determine their genuineness. In addition to those discussed below he includes "Ich lass dich nicht," a melody (Zahn, No. 7455) first printed in a Leipzig collection in 1727 and without any indication of Bach's style.

At the outset, it is advisable to clear the ground by eliminating tunes which have been or are asserted to be by Bach and demonstrably are not. Spitta names[1] ten Hymn tunes which are stated to be Bach's by Winterfeld or others. In fact not one of them is by him. They are as follows:

(1) *Alles ist an Gottes Segen* (*Choralgesänge*, No. 19). Zahn, Nos. 3839–3842 b, prints five settings of the Hymn from German Hymn books between 1731 and Bach's death in 1750. Their common source appears to be G. Voigtländer's secular tune (1647), "Fillis sass an einem Böttgen" (Zahn, No. 3838). Bach's is a variation of the original tune. König has two settings closely cognate to Bach's (Zahn, Nos. 3841, 3842 a).

(2) *Auf, auf, mein Herz, und du mein ganzer Sinn* (Erk, No. 162; *Choralgesänge*, No. 24). The melody (Zahn, No. 824) is by Johann Staden (1581–1634).

(3) *Dank sei Gott in der Höhe* (*Choralgesänge*, No. 54). The tune was published by Bartholomäus Gesius in 1605 (Zahn, No. 5391) to the anonymous Hymn, "Jesus Christ, unser Herre," and perhaps is his own composition.

(4) *Das walt' Gott Vater und Gott Sohn* (*Choralgesänge*, No. 58; Erk, No. 182). The tune

---

[1] Vol. III. 115 n.

was published by Daniel Vetter in 1713 (Zahn, No. 673).

(5) *Herr, nun lass' in Friede* (*Choralgesänge*, No. 148; Erk, No. 227). The tune is found in the Hymn book of the Bohemian Brethren in 1694 (Zahn, No. 3302).

(6) *Ist Gott mein Schild und Helfersmann* (*Choralgesänge*, No. 216; Erk, No. 78). The tune is printed in a Dresden collection of 1694 (Zahn, No. 2542. See Cantata 85).

(7) *Meinen Jesum lass' ich nicht.* There are two tunes to this Hymn in Bach's collections. One, which Bach uses in several Cantatas (see Cantata 70), is perhaps by Andreas Hammerschmidt and dates from 1658 (Zahn, No. 3449; *Choralgesänge*, No. 242; Erk, No. 88). The second (*Choralgesänge*, No. 241) dates from 1686 (Zahn, No. 3448 a).

(8) *O Jesu, du mein Bräutigam* (*Choralgesänge*, No. 145). The melody is the old tune "Rex Christe factor omnium," and is found in print in 1527 (Zahn, No. 314 a).

(9) *O Mensch, schau Jesum Christum an* (*Choralgesänge*, No. 287; Erk, No. 282). The melody is as old as 1555, when it appears in association with Triller's Hymn, "Der Herr Gott sei gepreiset" (Zahn, Nos. 3984, 3994 a). It is found also in a collection dated 1603, to which the *Choralgesänge* refers it.

(10) *Schwing dich auf zu deinem Gott* (*Choralgesänge*, No. 305; Erk, No. 114). The tune is as old as 1680 (Zahn, No. 4870). See Cantata 40.

Spitta himself attributes the following melodies to Bach, inaccurately in every case:

(1) *Also hat Gott die Welt geliebt* (it is neither in the *Choralgesänge* nor Erk). The tune is by Gottfried Vopelius and dates from 1682 (Zahn, No. 5920). See Cantata 68.

(2) *Alle Menschen müssen sterben.* There are two tunes to this Hymn in Bach's collections. One (*Choralgesänge*, No. 17; Erk, No. 158) is by Jakob Hintze (1622–1702) (Zahn, No. 6778). It is in *Hymns A. & M.*, No. 127 ("At the Lamb's high feast we sing"). The second melody (*Choralgesänge*, No. 18; Erk, No. 159) demands a more intricate examination. It occurs in Cantata 162 and is discussed there *infra* at length.

(3) *Da der Herr Christ zu Tische sass* (*Choralgesänge*, No. 52; Erk, No. 178). The tune dates from 1611 (Zahn, No. 2503).

(4) *Für Freuden lasst uns springen* (*Choralgesänge*, No. 106). The tune occurs in 1648 (Zahn, No. 2339).

(5) *Herr Jesu Christ, du hast bereit* (*Choralgesänge*, No. 140; Erk, No. 222). The tune is found in a Silesian MS. collection dated 1742 as well as in

Reimann's collection in 1747 (Zahn, No. 4711). Bach's version differs slightly from both.

(6) *Ich freue mich in dir* (*Choralgesänge*, No. 181 ; Erk, No. 64). The melody occurs in Cantata 133 and is there discussed. The balance of probability is against Bach's authorship.

(7) *Meines Lebens letzte Zeit* (*Choralgesänge*, No. 248). The tune is found in a Gotha Psalter of 1726 (Zahn, No. 6380).

(8) *So giebst du nun, mein Jesu, gute Nacht* (*Choralgesänge*, No. 310). The tune dates from 1694 (Zahn, No. 849).

We can pass now to a number of tunes which are found for the first time in one or other of the Bach collections and, for that reason, establish a presumptive right to be regarded as his compositions. They number forty-two.

In the *Notenbüchlein vor Anna Magdalena Bach*, which bears the date 1725 on the cover, there are seven Choral tunes which are not found in print before that date :

1 Dir, dir, Jehovah, will ich singen.
2 Gedenke doch, mein Geist, zurücke.
3 Gieb dich zufrieden und sei stille.
4 Gieb dich zufrieden und sei stille (another tune, in F ma.).
5 Schaffs mit mir, Gott, nach deinem Willen.

6 Warum betrübst du dich Und beugest dich zur Erden.
7 Wie wohl ist mir, O Freund der Seelen.

In Schemelli's Hymn book of 1736 there are twenty-one tunes not found in any earlier collection:

8 Ach, dass nicht die letzte Stunde.
9 Auf, auf, die rechte Zeit ist hier.
10 Beschränkt, ihr Weisen dieser Welt.
11 Dich bet ich an, mein höchster Gott.
12 Eins ist noth; ach Herr, dies eine.
13 Gott, wie gross ist deine Güte.
14 Ich halte treulich still.
15 Ich liebe Jesum alle Stund.
16 Ich steh' an deiner Krippen hier.
17 Jesu, deine Liebeswunden.
18 Jesu, Jesu, du bist mein.
19 Komm, süsser Tod! komm, selge Ruh!
20 Kommt, Seelen, dieser Tag.
21 Kommt wieder aus der finstern Gruft.
22 Liebster Herr Jesu, wo bleibst du.
23 Mein Jesu, was vor Seelenweh.
24 O finstre Nacht, wann wirst du doch vergehen.
25 O liebe Seele, zieh die Sinnen.
26 Selig, wer an Jesum denkt.
27 So wünsch ich mir zu guterletzt.
28 Vergiss mein nicht, mein allerliebster Gott.

In the second Part (1769) of F. W. Birnstiel's *Choralgesänge* there are three new Choral tunes:

29 Gottlob, es geht nunmehr zum Ende.
30 Nicht so traurig, nicht so sehr.
31 O Herzensangst, O Bangigkeit und Zagen.

INTRODUCTION 73

In the third Part of Carl Philipp Emmanuel's *Choralgesänge* (1786) there is one new melody:

    32 Ich bin, ja, Herr, in deiner Macht.

In Becker's collection (1843) there are two Choral tunes attributed to Bach by Zahn:

    33 Singt dem Herren, singet.
    34 Was betrübst du dich, mein Herze.

Spitta prints[1] five Choral tunes which have come down to us through Bach's pupil, Johann Ludwig Krebs:

    35 Das walt' mein Gott, Gott Vater, Sohn.
    36 Gott, mein Herz dir Dank zusendet.
    37 Hier lieg ich nun, O Vater aller Gnaden.
    38 Ich gnüge mich an meinem Stande.
    39 Meine Seele, lass' es gehen.

Finally there are two Choral *Arias* in the "Christmas Oratorio," Nos. 38–40, 42:

    40 Hilf, Herr Jesu, lass' gelingen.
    41 Jesu, du mein liebstes Leben.

And another in the fifth Motett:

    42 Komm, Jesu, komm, mein Leib ist müde.

The last three are the only tunes of his own composition which Bach has wedded to the stanzas of a congregational Hymn in the whole range of his concerted Church music[2].

---

[1] Vol. III. 401–403.
[2] See *Bach's Chorals*, Part I, 53, 54.

74 INTRODUCTION

"Ach, dass nicht die letzte Stunde"
Schemelli 1736 no. 831

Zahn, No. 6721, regards the above melody as "probably," and the Bass as "certainly," by Bach.

INTRODUCTION 75

The melody is not found in any other Hymn book. It has the characteristics of Bach's Hymn tunes, and may be attributed to him.

"AUF, AUF, DIE RECHTE ZEIT IST HIER"
Schemelli 1736 no. 171

Zahn, No. 705, regards this melody as "perhaps" by Bach. It is not found elsewhere. Apart from that circumstance the tune does not suggest Bach's authorship. The repeated concluding phrase is not required by Martin Opitz' Hymn, which is one of four lines. As is so often the case where Bach's Hymn tunes are in question, Johann Balthasar König (1691-1758) has a melody on the Hymn in his *Harmonischer Lieder-Schatz* (1738). As the

Hymn practically had been neglected since Jakob Hintze gave it a melody in 1666, it is curious that Bach and König, the one at Leipzig and the other at Frankfurt a. Main, should have turned their attention to it simultaneously.

"Beschränkt, ihr Weisen dieser Welt"
Schemelli 1736 no. 689

Zahn, No. 7765, attributes the above melody to Bach without qualification. Indeed, it declares his authorship unmistakeably. It is not found in any other Hymn book.

"Das walt' mein Gott, Gott Vater, Sohn"

Krebs MS.

The Hymn's earliest tune is found in the Gotha *Cantional* of 1648. Zahn (No. 4217) conjectures that it was derived from a secular source. It had a wide vogue in Hymn books of the second half of the

INTRODUCTION 79

seventeenth and first half of the eighteenth century. Jakob Hintze in 1690 wrote a minor melody indirectly based upon it, the last phrase of which is identical with Krebs' MS. The latter cannot be regarded as an original tune, and is not at all in Bach's idiom.

"DICH BET ICH AN, MEIN HÖCHSTER GOTT"
Schemelli 1736 no. 396

80 INTRODUCTION

[musical notation]

Zahn, No. 2437, attributes the above melody to Bach without qualification. It is characteristic of his *Aria* form and is certainly his. It is not found elsewhere.

"Dir, dir, Jehovah, will ich singen"
Notenbüchlein 1725 p. 51

[musical notation]

Bach's authorship of the tune is vouched for by Philipp Emmanuel Bach. On p. 50 of the *Notenbüchlein*[1] the tune is also printed in four-part harmony over the same Bass (Erk, No. 19; *Choralgesänge*, No. 67). Zahn, No. 3068, prints the melody only, from Schemelli, No. 397. Erk, No. 20, adds the figured Bass from the latter book. It differs from the *Notenbüchlein*. The tune is not found in other Hymn books.

[1] B. G. xliii (ii).

82   INTRODUCTION

"Eins ist noth; ach Herr, dies eine"
Schemelli 1736 no. 112

INTRODUCTION 83

The groundwork of the customary melody of the above Hymn is Joachim Neander's "Grosser Prophete, mein Herze begehret," published in 1680 (Zahn, No. 3947). A large number of variations of that tune exist, one of which (Zahn, No. 7127) is set to the Hymn "Eins ist noth" in Freylinghausen's Hymn book (1704). That Bach was familiar with the tune appears from the fact that, with an altered first part, it is among the *Choralgesänge* of 1769, set to the same Hymn (Erk, No. 193; *Choralgesänge*, No. 77). The Schemelli tune, though modelled on the Neander-Freylinghausen form, is a new melody. Zahn, No. 7129, attributes it to Bach without qualification, and certainly correctly. It is not found in any other eighteenth century Hymn book.

"GEDENKE DOCH, MEIN GEIST, ZURÜCKE"
Notenbüchlein 1725 p. 52

84 INTRODUCTION

The melody is an *Aria*—it is so called in the MS.—rather than a Hymn tune. It is copied in Anna Magdalena's hand[1] and indubitably is by Bach.

"Gieb dich zufrieden und sei stille"
Notenbüchlein 1725 p. 31

---
[1] Spitta, II. 150.

INTRODUCTION 85

The melody and Bass are by Bach. Spitta[1] draws attention to the "lofty and individual beauty" of the tune. The Bass is unfigured.

On the same page of the *Notenbüchlein* the melody, with a slightly altered Bass, is given in E minor (*Choralgesänge*, No. 111). Erk, Nos. 43 and 208, gives both forms. Zahn, No. 7417a, and Erk, No. 44, give the E mi. version in a somewhat different form.

[1] Vol. III. 113.

"Gieb dich zufrieden und sei stille"
Notenbüchlein 1725 p. 30

Spitta remarks[1] of the melody, that it "leaves us in doubt as to its composer; it is strikingly simple for a composition of Bach's; but at all events it is new." König prints an almost identical melody to the same Hymn in 1738 (Zahn, No. 7419). Probably the parent of the Bach-König melody is Johann Georg Ebeling's setting of the Hymn in a minor key published in 1666 (Zahn, No. 7414). The opening phrases of all three are identical, as are the closing cadence of Ebeling's and König's settings. Had König received the tune as Bach's it is difficult to suppose that he would have altered it. Moreover, he uses it in a much more changed form for another Hymn (Zahn, No. 1815). Bach's authorship therefore is improbable.

"GOTT, MEIN HERZ DIR DANK ZUSENDET" Krebs MS.

---

[1] Vol. III. 113.

88   INTRODUCTION

The melody has the Bach *Aria* character, and may be regarded as by him. Spitta's notes upon the tune[1] are not very intelligible in the translation. It is sufficient to remark that both of the Hymns to which he alludes are by the Countess Emilie Juliane, and that neither possessed a proper melody of its own until Bach wrote "Gott, mein Herz" for one of them.

"Gott, wie gross ist deine Güte"

Schemelli 1736 no. 360

[1] Vol. III. 288.

INTRODUCTION 89

* Schemelli has E flat.

Zahn, No. 7937, attributes the melody and Bass to Bach without qualification. The character of

90 INTRODUCTION

the tune and the fact that the words of the Hymn are by Schemelli establish the conclusion. The tune is not found elsewhere.

"Gottlob, es geht nunmehr zum Ende"
Choralgesänge 1769 no. 198

INTRODUCTION 91

Erk, No. 212, and *Choralgesänge*, No. 118, print the harmonised melody. The former follows Winterfeld in attributing it to Bach without qualification; the latter regards it as "wahrscheinlich" his. There seems to be no ground on which to base either conclusion. The tune is without distinction, and is not in the least possessed of Bach's characteristics. It is included in some nineteenth century Hymn books, and seems to be another form of a tune, to the same Hymn, found in various versions (Zahn, Nos. 2852-2857).

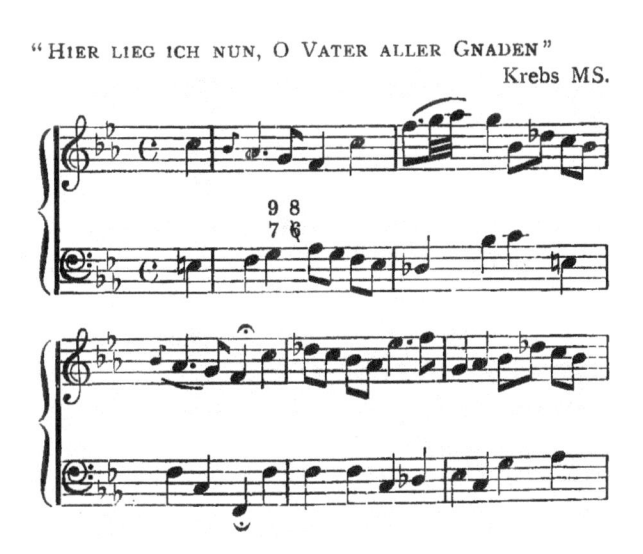

"HIER LIEG ICH NUN, O VATER ALLER GNADEN"
Krebs MS.

The melody is not found elsewhere. It has an unmistakeable Bach curve. Spitta[1] points out that the Hymn "Hier lieg ich nun, O Vater" was not given a tune of its own in Schemelli's Hymn book, nor, in fact, did it possess one. Meanwhile the Hymn, "Hier lieg ich nun, mein Gott, zu deinen Füssen," had been rendered popular by Freylinghausen's Hymn book (1704). Spitta hazards the suggestion that Krebs' melody was written by Bach in anticipation of a demand for a new edition of Schemelli's book. Spitta's guess is supported by an interesting fact. Zahn, Nos. 953–954, prints two forms of the tune "Hier lieg ich nun, mein Gott," dated respectively 1708 and 1719. In the latter

[1] Vol. III. 288.

the opening phrase is identical with Bach's opening phrase, and its general character leaves little doubt that in writing a melody for " Hier lieg ich nun, O Vater," Bach had in his mind that of "Hier lieg ich nun, mein Gott."

"ICH BIN, JA, HERR, IN DEINER MACHT"
Choralgesänge 1786 III. no. 251

94   INTRODUCTION

Zahn, No. 5878 a, remarks, "Mel. bei (von?) J. S. Bach." Erk, No. 236, and *Choralgesänge*, No. 174, suggest, without endorsing, Bach's authorship. Spitta[1] attributes the tune to Bach without qualification. It bears the stamp of Bach's workmanship and is not found in the Hymn books.

"ICH GNÜGE MICH AN MEINEM STANDE"   Krebs MS.

[1] Vol. III. 115 n.

The melody is not found elsewhere. Its form is compatible with Bach's authorship. Spitta[1] points out that in Schemelli's Hymn book (1736) the Hymn "Ich gnüge mich" was sung to the tune "Wer nur den lieben Gott lässt walten." In fact it possessed no melody of its own. As in the case of "Hier lieg ich nun, O Vater," the Krebs melody therefore may have been composed by Bach in preparation for a revised edition of the Schemelli Hymn book. But the compass of the tune is incompatible with congregational use.

"ICH HALTE TREULICH STILL"

Schemelli 1736 no. 657

[1] Vol. III. 288.

Zahn, No. 5082, attributes the melody to Bach without qualification. Its opening phrase is reminiscent of "O Gott, du frommer Gott" (see

INTRODUCTION 97

Cantata 45), but Bach's hand is unmistakeable. The tune is not found in any of the regular Hymn books.

"ICH LIEBE JESUM ALLE STUND"
Schemelli 1736 no. 737

Zahn, No. 4732, remarks, "Mel. und Bass von (?) S. Bach." The Hymn had its own melody (1693). Schemelli's tune improbably is by Bach. It is not found elsewhere.

"Ich steh' an deiner Krippen hier"

Schemelli 1736 no. 195

Zahn, No. 4663, attributes the melody to Bach without qualification. There was in existence already, but not in very general use, a melody to the Hymn by Johann Georg Ebeling (1667). Another, in the Dresden Hymn book, 1694, has an opening phrase, but in a major key, to which Bach's opening line bears a close resemblance (Zahn, Nos. 4659, 4661). It is worth noticing that when Bach used the words in the "Christmas Oratorio," No. 59, he set them to Luther's "Nun freut euch, lieben Christen g'mein." That he should have given the Hymn a distinctive melody of its own two years later is explicable from that circumstance. The tune itself establishes a conviction that Bach composed it. It is not found in the regular Hymn books.

"JESU, DEINE LIEBESWUNDEN" Schemelli 1736 no. 139

Zahn, No. 1302, regards the melody as "probably" by Bach. The probable author of the Hymn, Christoph Wegleiter, died in 1706. Since it had no distinctive melody of its own, its inclusion in Schemelli's collection suggested the provision of one. Whether Bach was the author the tune does not help to decide. It bears a very close resemblance to an anonymous melody (1729) to the Hymn "Sollt es gleich bisweilen scheinen" (Zahn, No. 1356), and is not found elsewhere. König also appears to have drawn upon the 1729 melody in 1738 to set the Hymn "Sollt es gleich" (Zahn, No. 1360).

"JESU, JESU, DU BIST MEIN"   Schemelli 1736 no. 741

Zahn, No. 6446, and *Choralgesänge*, No. 191, concur in regarding the tune as probably by Bach. Spitta[1] expresses himself positively to that effect. The Hymn was wedded to a proper melody of its own since 1687, and Zahn reveals the existence of four others. But none of them had much vogue, and on that ground, perhaps, Bach provided a new

[1] Vol. III. 113.

one for Schemelli's Hymn book. It is not found in any other eighteenth century collection, and its *Aria* character seems to justify a positive ascription of it to Bach. König (1738) has a tune to the same Hymn which, greatly inferior to Bach's, has the appearance of being a melody evolved out of it (Zahn, No. 6447).

"Komm, süsser Tod"   Schemelli 1736 no. 868

Erk, No. 82, and Zahn, No. 4400, attribute the melody to Bach without qualification. It is characteristic of his *Aria* type, and indubitably is his. The anonymous Hymn has no earlier melody, but König (?) set it again in 1738 (Zahn, No. 4401). Bach's tune does not occur in any Hymn book but Schemelli's.

104 INTRODUCTION

"Kommt, Seelen, dieser Tag"

Schemelli 1736 no. 936

INTRODUCTION 105

Zahn, No. 5185, attributes the melody to Bach without qualification. It is in the form of a Gigue and is his unmistakeably. It is not found elsewhere.

"KOMMT WIEDER AUS DER FINSTERN GRUFT"

Schemelli 1736 no. 938

The stamp of Bach's authorship is upon the melody, and Zahn, No. 4709, attributes it to him without qualification. It is not found in other Hymn books than Schemelli's.

"Liebster Herr Jesu, wo bleibst du so lange?"
Schemelli 1736 no. 874

INTRODUCTION 107

108   INTRODUCTION

Zahn, No. 3969, attributes the melody to Bach without qualification. The Hymn had a melody of its own (1676), which König uses, and another more recent (1711). But neither had much vogue in the Hymn books, and Bach's provision of a new melody is intelligible. If the pauses be neglected the *Aria* form of the melody appears, and justifies the ascription of the tune to Bach. It is not found elsewhere.

"MEIN JESU, WAS VOR SEELENWEH"

Schemelli 1736 no. 283

Zahn, No. 8383, attributes the melody and Bass to Bach without qualification. The assumption is confirmed by the fact that the words probably are by Schemelli himself, and that the tune is in Bach's *Aria* form. It is not found elsewhere.

"MEINE SEELE, LASS' ES GEHEN"   Krebs MS.

110 INTRODUCTION

The melody, which is not found elsewhere, reads like Bach. That he should have prepared an original tune for a future edition of Schemelli is explicable in view of the fact that the Hymn had no distinctive melody of its own; the one in moderately general use was a reconstruction (1715) of "Meine Hoffnung stehet feste" (see Cantata 40). König (1738) adapted another well-known tune to the Hymn. In Schemelli, 1736, it was directed to be sung to the tune, "Herr, ich habe missgehandelt" (see Cantata 162).

"NICHT SO TRAURIG, NICHT SO SEHR"

Choralgesänge 1769 no. 153

INTRODUCTION   111

[musical notation]

Zahn, No. 3355, remarks, "Mel. bei (von?) Seb. Bach." Elsewhere he speaks of it as "vermutlich von Bach[1]." Erk, No. 268, queries, and *Choralgesänge*, No. 253, accepts Bach's authorship. Spitta[2] attributes the tune to Bach without qualification. It is not found in any other Hymn book, and Bach's authorship may be admitted. See also B.G. xxxix. No. 53.

"O FINSTRE NACHT"   Schemelli 1736 no. 891

[musical notation with figured bass: 6 4 2 / 6 5 / 6 5 5 / 6]

[1] Vol. VI. 347.   [2] Vol. III. 115 n.

INTRODUCTION

INTRODUCTION 113

The melody is not found in any other Hymn book. The Hymn had been set by Johann Ludwig Steiner in 1723, but his tune was little known. That Bach should have provided one for the Hymn in Schemelli's Hymn book therefore is intelligible. Zahn, No. 6171, regards the melody as "probably" by Bach. It is so distinctive of his style that his authorship may be accepted.

"O HERZENSANGST, O BANGIGKEIT UND ZAGEN"
Choralgesänge 1769 no. 178

114   INTRODUCTION

Zahn, No. 1003, regards the melody as "probably" Bach's. *Choralgesänge*, No. 284, holds it "very probably" his. It differs greatly in character from earlier tunes in the same metre (11. 11. 11. 5), and its *quasi Aria* form perhaps justifies the conclusion that Bach composed it. It is not found in any Hymn book earlier than the nineteenth century.

"O LIEBE SEELE, ZIEH DIE SINNEN"
Schemelli 1736 no. 575

116   INTRODUCTION

Zahn, No. 7787, attributes the melody to Bach without qualification. It is, in fact, unmistakeably his, and is not found in any of the regular Hymn books.

"Schaffs mit mir, Gott, nach deinem Willen"
Notenbüchlein 1725 p. 48

Erk, No. 111, regards the melody, in form a Minuet, as "wahrscheinlich" Bach's. Zahn, No. 2883, expresses no opinion; he quotes the melody, slightly altered, from a later text (1780). Spitta[1] regards it as exhibiting "plainer tokens" of Bach's style. It certainly has Bach's characteristics, and having regard to where it occurs can hardly be other than his composition. It is found in a few modern Hymn books.

[1] Vol. III. 113.

118   INTRODUCTION

"Selig, wer an Jesum denkt"

Schemelli 1736 no. 292

Zahn, No. 4846, attributes the melody to Bach without qualification. Its intrinsic qualities do not justify his confidence. The Bass unquestionably is Bach's. The tune is not found elsewhere.

"SINGT DEM HERREN, SINGET"
Becker 1843 no. 196

Zahn, No. 6267, regards the melody as "probably" by Bach. In fact it was composed by Apelles von Löwenstern, and was published in 1644, to his own Hymn, "Singt dem Herrn ein neues Lied," as the *Choralgesänge*, No. 309, points out.

"SO WÜNSCH ICH MIR ZU GUTER LETZT"
Schemelli 1736 no. 901

The melody is not found elsewhere. Zahn, No. 5892, regards it as "probably," and the Bass as certainly by Bach. The opening phrase of the tune is reminiscent of "Was Gott thut, das ist wohlgethan" (see Cantata 12). That fact, and especially its general atmosphere, rouse a conviction that the melody is of earlier date than 1736 and that Bach was not the author of it.

INTRODUCTION 121

"Vergiss mein nicht, mein allerliebster Gott"
Schemelli 1736 no. 627

The melody is headed: "Aria adag. di S. Bach D. M. Lips.," and is the only one in Schemelli's book thus distinguished. It is unfigured.

122 INTRODUCTION

"Warum betrübst du dich und beugest"
Notenbüchlein 1725 p. 46

The tune, an obvious Bach *Aria*, is unfigured.

INTRODUCTION 123

"WAS BETRÜBST DU DICH, MEIN HERZE"
Becker 1843 no. 187[1]

---

[1] The text has been copied from B.G. xxxix. 267.

INTRODUCTION

Zahn, No. 6830, remarks, " Mel. bei (von ?) Seb. Bach." *Choralgesänge*, No. 334, holds it "wahrscheinlich" his. Spitta[1] attributes the melody to Bach without qualification. The Hymn, by Zacharias Hermann (1643-1716), was published in 1690, without a melody. Possibly Becker's tune is one of those prepared by Bach for Schemelli. The tune occurs in a single, nineteenth century, Hymn book, and may be accepted as Bach's.

"WIE WOHL IST MIR, O FREUND DER SEELEN"
Notenbüchlein 1725 p. 51

[1] Vol. III. 115 n.

Perhaps this unfigured *Aria* may have been designed by Bach for a future edition of Schemelli's Hymn book. The melody obviously is Bach's.

From the foregoing examination the following tunes emerge as being either positively or with practical certainty Bach's original compositions:

    8 Ach, dass nicht die letzte Stunde.
10 Beschränkt, ihr Weisen dieser Welt.
11 Dich bet ich an, mein höchster Gott.

1	Dir, dir, Jehovah, will ich singen.
12	Eins ist noth; ach Herr, dies eine.
2	Gedenke doch, mein Geist zurücke.
3	Gieb dich zufrieden und sei stille.
36	Gott, mein Herz dir Dank zusendet.
13	Gott, wie gross ist deine Güte.
37	Hier lieg ich nun, O Vater aller Gnaden.
32	Ich bin, ja, Herr, in deiner Macht.
38	Ich gnüge mich an meinem Stande.
14	Ich halte treulich still.
16	Ich steh' an deiner Krippen hier.
18	Jesu, Jesu, du bist mein.
19	Komm, süsser Tod! komm, selge Ruh!
20	Kommt, Seelen, dieser Tag.
21	Kommt wieder aus der finstern Gruft.
22	Liebster Herr Jesu, wo bleibst du so lange?
23	Mein Jesu, was vor Seelenweh.
39	Meine Seele, lass es gehen.
30	Nicht so traurig, nicht so sehr.
24	O finstre Nacht, wann wirst du doch vergehen.
31	O Herzensangst, O Bangigkeit und Zagen.
25	O liebe Seele, zieh die Sinnen.
5	Schaffs mit mir, Gott, nach deinem Willen.
28	Vergiss mein nicht, mein allerliebster Gott.
6	Warum betrübst du dich und beugest dich zur Erden.
34	Was betrübst du dich, mein Herze.
7	Wie wohl ist mir, O Freund der Seelen.

As Schweitzer points out[1], Bach's Hymn tunes are sacred *Arias* rather than Chorals. "Their peculiar loveliness comes from the fact that they are the work of an artist brought up on the German

[1] Vol. I. 22.

Choral, writing under the influence of the formally perfect Italian melodic form." They are not appropriate to congregational singing, and in fact have been used very little for that purpose[1]. "Their charm," Spitta remarks[2], "is like that of a pious family circle, musically cultured, and we may delight to fancy that these touching hymns, so delicately worked out in their small limits, were sung, at the master's household devotions, by one or other of the members of his family."

[1] All the Schemelli melodies and those in the *Notenbüchlein*, except the one at page 86 *supra*, are included by Ernst Naumann in a volume of "Lieder und Arien. Für eine Singstimme mit Pianoforte (Orgel oder Harmonium)," Leipzig, 1901. The Schemelli tunes are arranged by Franz Wüllner in another volume, published, like Naumann's, for the New Bach Society. The Editors do not attempt to distinguish Bach's melodies from the others.

[2] Vol. III. 112.

THE CANTATAS

CANTATA I. WIE SCHÖN LEUCHTET DER MORGENSTERN[1]. Feast of the Annunciation of the B.V.M. (*c.* 1740)

Melody: "*Wie schön leuchtet der Morgenstern*"
?Philipp Nicolai 1599

A Choral Cantata, upon Philipp Nicolai's Hymn, "Wie schön leuchtet der Morgenstern," founded on Psalm xlv, first published, with the melody, in Nicolai's *Frewden Spiegel dess ewigen Lebens* (Frankfort a. Main, 1599). The Hymn was written during the plague of 1597. The initial

[1] An English version of the Cantata, "How brightly shines," is published by Novello & Co.

letters of its seven stanzas (W.E.G.U.H.Z.W.) stand for "Wilhelm Ernst Graf und Herr zu Waldeck," Nicolai's former pupil.

Nicolai was born at Mengeringhausen in 1556. He was educated at Erfurt and Wittenberg, and in 1601 became chief pastor of St Katherine's Church, Hamburg. He died there in 1608.

It is improbable that Nicolai composed the melody. Probably he adjusted it to the Hymn. The secular love song, "Wie schön leuchten die Aeugelein," is of later date; therefore the tune cannot be regarded as a secular one transferred to the Hymn. It bears a partial resemblance to that of the fourteenth century Carol, "Resonet in laudibus."

The melody also occurs in Cantatas 36, 37, 49, 61, and 172. There is another harmonisation of it in the *Choralgesänge*, No. 375, where, for the second part of the melody, Bach follows Gottfried Vopelius' reconstruction of the tune, in his *Neu Leipziger Gesangbuch* (Leipzig, 1682 [1681]). Organ Works, Novello, xix. 23.

(*a*)

The words of the opening movement are the first stanza of Nicolai's Hymn:

    Wie schön leuchtet der Morgenstern
    Voll Gnad' und Wahrheit von dem Herrn,
    Die süsse Wurzel Jesse!

CANTATA I

Du Sohn Davids aus Jacobs Stamm,
Mein König und mein Bräutigam,
Hast mir mein Herz besessen;
Lieblich, freundlich,
Schön und herrlich, gross und ehrlich,
Reich von Gaben,
Hoch und sehr prächtig erhaben.

B.G. i. 1.

English translations of the Hymn are noted in the *Dictionary of Hymnology*, pp. 807, 1727.

Form. Choral Fantasia (2 *Corni*, 2 *Oboi da caccia*, Strings, *Continuo*[1]).

(*b*)

The words of the concluding Choral are the seventh stanza of Nicolai's Hymn:

Wie bin ich doch so herzlich froh,
Dass mein Schatz ist das A und O,
Der Anfang und das Ende;
Er wird mich doch zu seinem Preis
Aufnehmen in das Paradeis,
Dess klopf' ich in die Hände.
Amen! Amen!
Komm du schöne Freudenkrone,
Bleib' nicht lange,
Deiner wart' ich mit Verlangen.

B.G. i. 51.

Form. Embellished (2 *Corni*, 2 *Ob. da caccia*, Strings, *Continuo*). *Choralgesänge*, No. 378.

[1] See Spitta, III. 101.

CANTATA II. ACH GOTT, VOM HIMMEL SIEH DAREIN[1]. Second Sunday after Trinity (*c.* 1740)

Melody: "*Ach Gott, vom Himmel sieh' darein*"
Anon. 1524

A Choral Cantata, on Luther's Hymn, "Ach Gott, vom Himmel sieh' darein," a free rendering of Psalm xii, probably written in 1523, and first published in the so-called "Achtliederbuch," *Etlich Christlich lider Lobgesang, und Psalm* (Wittenberg, 1524), where it is set to the melody, "Es ist das Heil uns kommen her" (see No. 9 *infra*). The Hymn was published in the same year in the Erfurt *Enchiridion Oder eyn Handbuchlein*, in association with the melody printed above. The tune, which Bach uses in the first and last movements of the Cantata, has a pre-Reformation origin and, no doubt, owes its present form to Johann Walther, Luther's collaborator. Walther arranged yet a third melody for the Hymn in his *Geystliche gesangk Buchleyn* (Wittenberg, 1524).

[1] An English version of the Cantata, "Ah God, in mercy look from Heaven," is published by Breitkopf & Haertel.

CANTATA II 133

The melody occurs also in Cantatas 77 and 153.

(a)

The words of the opening Chorus are the first stanza of Luther's Hymn:

> Ach Gott, vom Himmel sieh darein
> Und lass dich's doch[1] erbarmen:
> Wie wenig sind der Heil'gen dein,
> Verlassen sind wir Armen:
> Dein Wort man nicht lässt[2] haben wahr,
> Der Glaub' ist auch verloschen gar
> Bei allen Menschenkindern.
> B.G. i. 55.

English translations of the Hymn are noted in the *Dictionary of Hymnology*, p. 9.

Form. Choral Motett (2 *Ob.*, 4 *Trombones, Strings, Continuo*[3]). Erk, No. 149.

(b)

The words of the last movement are the sixth stanza of Luther's Hymn:

> Das wollst du, Gott, bewahren rein
> Für diesem arg'n Geschlechte,
> Und lass uns dir befohlen sein,
> Dass sich's in uns nicht flechte.
> Der gottlos' Hauf' sich umher find't,
> Wo solche[4] lose Leute sind
> In deinem Volk erhaben.
> B.G. i. 72.

Form. Simple (2 *Ob.*, 4 *Trombones, Strings, Continuo*). *Choralgesänge*, No. 7.

[1] 1524 das. [2] 1524 lesst nicht.
[3] On the movement, see Parry, p. 380. [4] 1524 dise.

CANTATA III. ACH GOTT, WIE MANCHES HERZE-LEID[1]. Second Sunday after the Epiphany (*c.* 1740)

Melody: "*O Jesu Christ, mein's Lebens Licht*"
Anon. 1625

Melody: "*Hilf mir, Herr Jesu, weil ich leb'*" MS. 1602

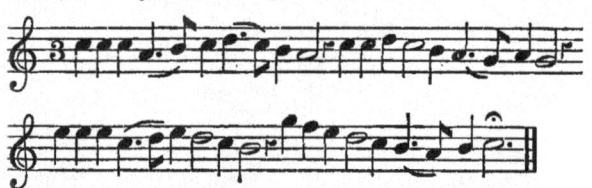

A Choral Cantata, on the Hymn, "Ach Gott, wie manches Herzeleid," first published in Martin Moller's *Meditationes Sanctorum Patrum* (Görlitz, 1587, 2nd ed.). The Hymn is a free paraphrase of Bernard of Clairvaulx' "Jesu dulcis memoria," attributed to Martin Moller.

Moller was born at Kropstädt, near Wittenberg, in 1547, became Cantor at Löwenberg in

[1] An English version of the Cantata, "O God, how many pains of heart," is published by Breitkopf & Haertel.

Silesia and eventually deacon there. In 1600 he became chief pastor at Görlitz, and died there in 1606.

The Hymn is attributed also to Conrad Hojer, Sub-Prior at Möllenbeck, near Rinteln on the Weser.

In the first, second, and last movements of the Cantata Bach uses the melody generally known as "Ach Gott, wie manches Herzeleid." By prescriptive right it should bear the name of Martin Behm's finest Hymn, "O [Herr] Jesu Christ, mein's Lebens Licht," first published in 1610. The earliest version of the tune is set to Behm's Hymn in *As hymnodus sacer* (Leipzig, 1625). It bears, however, so close a resemblance to a Königsberg MS. melody of 1602[1] that it must be considered a derivative of that tune or of some common source. The proper, and quite distinct, melody of "Ach Gott, wie manches Herzeleid" probably was composed by Bartholomäus Gesius and appeared first in his *Ein ander new Opus Geistlicher Deutscher Lieder* (Frankfort a. Oder, 1605).

Bach uses the melody also in Cantatas Nos. 44, 58, 118, and 153. Invariably he prefers the form of lines 1–3 in Joseph Clauder's *Psalmodia nova* (Leipzig, 1630).

---

[1] Zahn, vol. I. No. 532.

CANTATA III

(*a*)

The words of the opening movement are part of the first stanza of the Hymn:

> Ach Gott, wie manches Herzeleid
> Begegnet mir zu dieser Zeit.
> Der schmale Weg ist trübsalvoll,
> Den ich zum Himmel wandern soll.
> B.G. i. 75.

English translations of the Hymn are noted in the *Dictionary of Hymnology*, p. 10.

Form. Choral Fantasia (2 *Ob. d'amore*, Trombone (*col Basso*), *Strings, Continuo*). The *cantus* is with the Basses.

(*b*)

The Choral of the second movement (*Recitativo*) is part of the first and second stanzas of the Hymn:

> Wie schwerlich lässt sich Fleisch und Blut
> Zwingen zu dem ewigen Gut!
> Wo soll ich mich denn wenden hin?
> Zu dir, O[1] Jesu, steht mein Sinn.
> B.G. i. 84.

Form. The Chorus (S.A.T.B.) is intersected by *Recitativo* passages for all the four voices, which take the place of the orchestral *ritornelli* usual in this Extended form (*Continuo*[2]).

---

[1] 1587 Herr.   [2] See p. 44 *supra*.

(c)

The words of the concluding Choral are part of the twelfth stanza of the Hymn:

> Erhalt' mein Herz im Glauben rein,
> So leb' und sterb' ich dir allein.
> Jesu, mein Trost, hör' mein Begier':
> O mein Heiland, wär' ich bei dir!
> B.G. i. 94.

Form. Simple (2 *Ob. d'amore, Corno, Strings, Continuo*). *Choralgesänge*, No. 8.

CANTATA IV. CHRIST LAG IN TODESBANDEN[1].
Easter Day (1724[2])

Melody: "Christ lag in Todesbanden"   Anon. 1524

(1)

---

[1] English versions of the Cantata are published by Novello & Co., "Christ lay in Death's dark prison," and Breitkopf & Haertel, "Christ lay fast bound in Death's harsh chain."

[2] Perhaps founded on an earlier work.

(2)

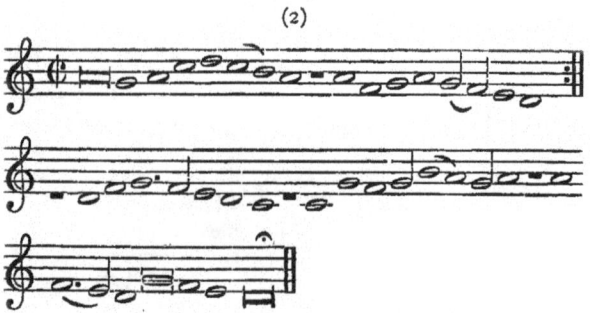

A Choral Cantata, on Luther's Easter Hymn, "Christ lag in Todesbanden[1]," described in 1524 as "'Christ ist erstanden' improved." In fact only slight traces of the latter ancient Hymn are found in Luther's version, stanzas iv and v of which are based on the Sequence "Victimae paschali." The Hymn, with the tune, was published in 1524, in Johann Walther's *Geystliche gesangk Buchleyn* (Wittenberg), and in *Enchiridion Oder eyn Handbuchlein* (Erfurt). The tune, like the words, is based on old material ("Christ ist erstanden": see Cantata 66), and probably owes its reconstruction to Johann Walther, who gives it in the two versions printed above, the second of which excludes the "Hallelujah!" A version of (1) appears in every movement of this Cantata.

Bach uses the melody also in Cantata 158. Other harmonisations of the tune are in the

[1] See Spitta, II. 392.

CANTATA IV 139

Choralgesänge, Nos. 38, 39. Organ Works, N. xv. 79; xviii. 16, 19.

VERSE I.
(*a*)
Christ lag in Todesbanden
Für unser Sünd' gegeben,
Er[1] ist wieder erstanden
Und hat uns bracht das Leben;
Dess wir sollen fröhlich sein,
Gott loben und ihm dankbar[2] sein
Und singen Hallelujah!
Hallelujah!
B.G. i. 98.

English translations of the Hymn are noted in the *Dictionary of Hymnology*, p. 225.

Form. Choral Fantasia (*Cornetto*, 3 *Trombones, Strings, Continuo*).

(*b*)
VERSE II.
Den Tod Niemand zwingen kunnt
Bei allen Menschenkindern;
Das macht alles unser Sünd',
Kein Unschuld war zu finden.
Davon kam der Tod so bald
Und nahm über uns Gewalt,
Hielt uns in seinem Reich gefangen.
Hallelujah!
B.G. i. 110.

Form. Soprano and Alto *Duetto*, the former voice having a somewhat free treatment of the *cantus* (*Cornetto, Trombone I, Continuo*).

[1] 1524 Der.   [2] 1524 und dankbar.

VERSE III.

(c)

Jesus Christus, Gottes Sohn,
An unser Statt ist kommen
Und hat die Sünde weggethan[1],
Damit dem Tod genommen
All' sein Recht und sein' Gewalt,
Da bleibet nichts denn Tod's Gestalt;
Den Stach'l hat er verloren.
    Hallelujah! B.G. i. 112.

Form. Tenor Unison Choral, having the *cantus* in Simple form (*Violino I and II, Continuo*).

(d)

VERSE IV.

Es war ein wunderlicher[2] Krieg,
Da Tod und Leben rungen,
Das Leben das behielt[3] den Sieg
Es hat den Tod verschlungen.
Die Schrift hat verkündiget[4] das,
Wie ein Tod den andern frass,
Ein Spott aus dem Tod ist worden.
    Hallelujah! B.G. i. 114.

Form. Choral Fantasia in Motett form (*Continuo*). The *cantus* is with the Altos.

(e)

VERSE V.

Hier ist das rechte Osterlamm,
Davon Gott hat geboten[5],
Das ist hoch an des[6] Kreuzes Stamm
In heisser Lieb' gebraten,

[1] 1524 abgethon. [2] 1524 wunderlich.
[3] 1524 Das leben behielt. [4] 1524 verkundet.
[5] 1524 gepotten. [6] 1524 Das ist an des.

Das Blut zeichnet unser Thür,
Das hält der Glaub' dem Tode für,
Der Würger kann uns nicht mehr schaden[1].
    Hallelujah!   B.G. i. 118.

Form. Bass Unison Choral; a free treatment of the *cantus* (*Violino I and II, Viola I and II, Continuo*).

VERSE VI.
(*f*)
So feiern wir das hohe Fest
Mit Herzensfreud' und Wonne,
Das uns der Herre scheinen lässt;
Er ist selber die Sonne,
Der durch seiner Gnaden Glanz
Erleuchtet unsre Herzen ganz:
Der Sünden Nacht ist verschwunden[2].
    Hallelujah!   B.G. i. 122.

Form. Soprano and Tenor *Duetto*, treating the *cantus* somewhat freely in canon (*Continuo*).

VERSE VII.
(*g*)
Wir essen und leben wohl
Im rechten Osterfladen;
Der alte Sauerteig nicht soll
Sein bei dem Wort der Gnaden.
Christus will die Koste sein
Und speisen die Seel' allein:
Der Glaub' will keins andern leben.
    Hallelujah!   B.G. i. 124.

Form. Simple (*Cornetto, 3 Trombones, Strings, Continuo*). *Choralgesänge*, No. 41[3].

[1] 1524 uns nicht ruren.   [2] 1524 vergangen.

[3] Spitta (II. 394) points out that this is the only work by Bach which in its text and treatment is a Church Cantata in the sense in which Buxtehude, Pachelbel, and Kuhnau used the term.

Cantata V. Wo soll ich fliehen hin.
Nineteenth Sunday after Trinity (1735)

Melody: "*Venus du und dein Kind*" Anon. 1574

Melody: "*Auf meinen lieben Gott*" Anon. 1609

A Choral Cantata, on Johann Heermann's Lenten Hymn, "Wo soll ich fliehen hin," first published in his *Devoti Musica Cordis* (Leipzig, 1630), to the melody, "Auf meinen lieben Gott."

The melody which Bach uses in the first and last movements was generally sung to Heermann's

Hymn, "Wo soll ich fliehen hin." By prescriptive right it belongs to the Hymn, "Auf meinen lieben Gott," which was published in 1607 (see Cantata No. 188) and received the melody two years later. Heermann's Hymn was not published until 1630 (see *supra*), and received its own proper melody in 1679 (see Cantata 163). B.G. xxxiii. Pref. xxi, follows Spitta in attributing the melody, "Auf meinen lieben Gott," to Johann Pachelbel (1653–1706). The tune, however, has a secular origin and is found in association with the song, "Venus du und dein Kind," in 1574[1]. Bartholomäus Gesius used the tune for the Hymn, "Man spricht: Wen Gott erfreut," in his *Ein ander new Opus Geistlicher Deutscher Lieder* (Frankfort a. Oder, 1605), and Melchior Vulpius associated it with the Hymn, "Auf meinen lieben Gott," in his *Ein schön geistlich Gesangbuch* (Jena, 1609).

The melody also occurs in Cantatas 89, 136, 148, and 188. Bach adopts a reconstruction of the melody published by Johann Hermann Schein in his *Cantional, Oder Gesangbuch Augspurgischer Confession* (Leipzig, 1627[2]). Organ Works, N. xvi. 4; xix. 32.

---

[1] Zahn, vol. II. No. 2160.
[2] The title of the second edition of Schein's work (see Part I, p. 32, of *Bach's Chorals*) varies in details from that of the first.

(*a*)

The words of the opening movement are the first stanza of the Hymn:

> Wo soll ich fliehen hin,
> Weil ich beschweret bin
> Mit viel und grossen Sünden?
> Wo soll[1] ich Rettung finden?
> Wenn alle Welt herkäme,
> Mein' Angst sie nicht wegnähme.
> B.G. i. 127.

An English translation of the Hymn is noted in the *Dictionary of Hymnology*, p. 506.

Form. Choral Fantasia (*Tromba da tirarsi*, 2 *Ob., Strings, Continuo*[2]).

(*b*)

The words of the concluding Choral are the eleventh stanza of the Hymn:

> Führ' auch mein Herz und Sinn
> Durch deinen Geist dahin,
> Dass ich mög' alles meiden,
> Was mich und dich kann scheiden,
> Und ich an deinem Leibe
> Ein Gliedmass ewig bleibe.
> B.G. i. 150.

Form. Simple (*Tromba da tirarsi*, 2 *Ob., Strings, Continuo*). *Choralgesänge*, No. 28.

The melody also appears in the Oboe part in the Alto *Recitativo*, "Mein treuer Heiland" (B.G. i. 142).

[1] 1630 kan.
[2] See Spitta, III. 101, on the form of the movement.

CANTATA VI. BLEIB' BEI UNS, DENN ES WILL ABEND WERDEN[1]. Easter Monday (1736)

Melody: "Danket dem Herrn, heut' und allzeit"

Anon. 1594

[1] English versions of the Cantata are published by Novello & Co., "Bide with us," and Breitkopf & Haertel, "Stay with us, the evening approaches."

(a)

The Alto melody of the above four-part setting, which Bach uses in the third movement ("Choral"), is associated also with the Hymns, "Ach bleib' bei uns, Herr Jesu Christ," "Wir danken dir, O frommer Gott," and "Hinunter ist der Sonnenschein." The Alto melody was in use at Leipzig in 1589, and the above four-part setting is found in Seth Calvisius' *Hymni sacri Latini et germanici* (Erfurt, 1594). No doubt it is by him.

There are other harmonisations of the Alto melody in the *Choralgesänge*, Nos. 1, 313. Organ Works, N. xvi. 10.

The words of the movement are the first and second stanzas of Nicolaus Selnecker's Hymn, "Ach bleib' bei uns, Herr Jesu Christ."

The first stanza, which is a translation of Melanchthon's "Vespera jam venit, nobiscum Christe maneto" (founded on St Luke xxiv. 29), first appeared as a broadsheet in 1579, with Nicolaus Herman's "Danket dem Herrn." The whole Hymn was first published in Selnecker's *Geistliche Psalmen* (Nürnberg, 1611). Only stanzas iii–ix are by him.

Selnecker was born at Hersbruck in 1532. He was a favourite pupil of Melanchthon at Wittenberg, was appointed Court Preacher at Dresden 1557, Professor of Theology at Jena 1565 and, later, at

Leipzig. He was a very prominent figure in ecclesiastical Germany and died at Leipzig in 1592:

*Ach bleib' bei uns, Herr Jesu Christ,
Weil es nun Abend worden ist;
Dein göttlich Wort, das helle Licht,
Lass ja bei uns auslöschen nicht.
*In dieser letzt betrübten Zeit
Verleih' uns, Herr, Beständigkeit,
Dass wir dein Wort und Sacrament
Rein behalt'n bis an unser End'.

B.G. i. 168.

Translations of the Hymn are noted in the *Dictionary of Hymnology*, pp. 1040, 1599.

Form. Soprano Unison Choral (*Violoncello piccolo, Continuo*)[1].

Melody: "Erhalt' uns, Herr, bei deinem Wort"

Anon. 1543

(*b*)

The melody, "Erhalt' uns, Herr, bei deinem Wort," which Bach uses in the concluding Choral of the Cantata, was first published in Joseph

---

* *Unverfälschter Liedersegen* (Berlin, 1878), No. 207, gives the third line of stanza i as "Dein Wort, O Herr, das ewig Licht," and "alln" for "Herr" in the second line of stanza ii.

[1] The movement is No. 5 of the Schübler Chorals (N. xvi. 10).

Klug's *Geistliche Lieder zu Wittemberg* (Wittenberg, 1543). It bears a close resemblance to the melody of Luther's Hymn, "Verleih' uns Frieden gnädiglich" (see Cantata 42), both being derived from the tune of the Antiphon, "Da pacem, Domine," of which Luther's "Verleih' uns Frieden" is a translation. The similarity between the melodies is matched by the intimate association of the two Hymns. In many districts of Germany Luther's stanza was sung immediately after the sermon, either by itself or with the Hymn, "Erhalt' uns, Herr."

Bach uses the melody also in Cantata No. 126. The sharpened fourth note of the tune in this movement is found in an early text (1593).

The words of the concluding Choral are the second stanza of Luther's Hymn, "Erhalt' uns, Herr, bei deinem Wort," written, probably in 1541, for a service at Wittenberg against the Turks. Luther called the Hymn "Ein Kinderlied zu singen wider die zween Ertzfeinde Christi und seiner heiligen Kirchen, den Babst und Türcken." The Hymn was first printed as a broadsheet at Wittenberg in 1542, and, with the tune, in Klug (see *supra*):

>Beweis' dein Macht, Herr Jesu Christ,
>Der du Herr aller Herren bist:
>Beschirm' dein' arme Christenheit,
>Dass sie dich lob' in Ewigkeit.

B.G. i. 176.

English translations of the Hymn are noted in the *Dictionary of Hymnology*, No. 353.
Form. Simple (2 *Ob.*, *Oboe da caccia, Strings, Continuo*). *Choralgesänge*, No. 79.

CANTATA VII. CHRIST UNSER HERR ZUM JORDAN KAM. Feast of St John Baptist (*c.* 1740)

Melody: "*Christ unser Herr zum Jordan kam*"
? Johann Walther 1524

A Choral Cantata, on Luther's Baptismal Hymn, "Christ unser Herr zum Jordan kam." It was written, probably, in 1541 and published as a broadsheet in that year.

The melody, "Christ unser Herr zum Jordan kam," or properly, " Es woll' uns Gott genädig sein," which Bach uses in the first and last movements, was published first in Johann Walther's *Geystliche gesangk Buchleyn* (Wittenberg, 1524), where it is set to Luther's Hymn, "Es woll' uns Gott." It may be attributed with great probability to Walther himself. From 1543 (Joseph Klug) it was attached to "Christ unser Herr."

Bach uses the melody also in Cantata 176. There is another harmonisation of it in *Choralgesänge*, No. 43. Organ Works, N. xvi. 62, 67.

(*a*)

The words of the opening movement are the first stanza of Luther's Hymn:

> Christ unser Herr zum Jordan kam
> Nach seines Vaters Willen,
> Von Sanct Johann's die Taufe nahm,
> Sein Werk und Amt zu erfüllen;
> Da wollt' er stiften uns ein Bad,
> Zu waschen uns von Sünden,
> Ersäufen auch den bittern Tod
> Durch sein selbst Blut und Wunden;
> Es galt ein neues Leben. B.G. i. 179.

English translations are noted in the *Dictionary of Hymnology*, p. 226.

Form. Choral Fantasia (2 *Ob. d'amore, Violino concertante, Strings, Continuo*). The *cantus* is with the Tenor[1].

[1] In this Chorus, Schweitzer remarks (II. 363), Bach paints on a large scale the picture he had already sketched in the Choral

(*b*)

The words of the concluding Choral are the seventh stanza of Luther's Hymn:

> Das Aug' allein das Wasser sieht,
> Wie Menschen Wasser giessen:
> Der Glaub' allein[1] die Kraft versteht
> Des Blutes Jesu Christi;
> Und ist für ihn ein' rothe Fluth
> Von Christi Blut gefärbet,
> Die allen Schaden heilet gut[2]
> Von Adam her geerbet,
> Auch von uns selbst begangen.
> B.G. i. 210.

Form. Simple (2 *Ob. d'amore, Strings, Continuo*). *Choralgesänge,* No. 44.

CANTATA VIII. LIEBSTER GOTT, WANN WERD' ICH STERBEN[3]? Sixteenth Sunday after Trinity (*c.* 1725)

Melody: "*Liebster Gott, wann werd' ich sterben?*"

Daniel Vetter 1713

Preludes upon the melody. The movement assumes the form of a *Concerto grosso*, the *concertino* consisting of a Solo Violin and two oboi d'amore (Spitta, III. 103).

[1] 1543 im Geist.   [2] 1543 heilen thut.

[3] An English version of the Cantata, "When will God recall my spirit?" is published by Novello & Co.

CANTATA VIII

A Choral Cantata[1], on Caspar Neumann's Hymn, "Liebster Gott, wann werd' ich sterben?" published in the ninth edition of the Breslau *Vollständige Kirchen- und Hauss-Music* (Breslau, n.d. *c.* 1700).

Neumann was a native of Breslau, where he was born in 1648. He became pastor of St Elizabeth's Church there, and died in 1715.

The melody of Neumann's Hymn, which Bach uses in the first and last movements of the Cantata, was composed by Daniel Vetter, and was first published in the second Part (first Part 1709) of his *Musicalische Kirch- und Hauss-Ergötzlichkeit* (Leipzig, 1713). Vetter wrote the tune for Neumann's Hymn at the suggestion of Jakob Wilisius, Cantor of St Bernhardin's Church at Breslau, at whose funeral, at his express wish, the Hymn was sung in 1695.

Vetter, a native of Breslau, succeeded his master Werner Fabricius as Organist of the Church of St Nicolas, Leipzig, in 1679. He died in 1721.

Bach has not used the melody elsewhere. But another version of it (melody and figured Bass),

---
[1] See p. 32 *supra*.

from Georg Christian Schemelli's *Musicalisches Gesang-Buch* (Leipzig, 1736), is in B.G. xxxix. "Arien und Lieder," No. 47.

(*a*)

The words of the opening movement are the first stanza of Neumann's Hymn:

* Liebster Gott, wann werd' ich sterben?
Meine Zeit läuft immer hin,
Und des alten Adams Erben,
Unter denen ich auch bin,
Haben dies zum Vatertheil,
Dass sie eine kleine Weil
Arm und elend sein auf Erden.
Und dann selber Erde werden.   B.G. i. 213.

Form. Choral Fantasia (*Corno* (*con Soprano*), *Flauto*, 2 *Ob. d'amore, Strings, Continuo*).

(*b*)

The words of the concluding Choral are the fifth stanza of Neumann's Hymn:

* Herrscher über Tod und Leben,
Mach' einmal mein Ende gut,
Lehre mich den Geist aufgeben
Mit recht wohlgefasstem Muth.
Hilf, dass ich ein ehrlich Grab
Neben frommen Christen hab'
Und auch endlich in der Erde
Nimmermehr zu Schanden werde.
          B.G. i. 241.

Form. Simple (*Corno, Flauto,* 2 *Ob. d'amore, Strings, Continuo*). *Choralgesänge,* No. 227.

CANTATA IX. ES IST DAS HEIL UNS KOMMEN HER. Sixth Sunday after Trinity (? 1731)

Melody: "*Es ist das Heil uns kommen her*" Anon. 1524

A Choral Cantata[1], on Paul Speratus' Hymn, "Es ist das Heil uns kommen her," founded on Romans iii. 28. It was published in the *Etlich Christlich lider Lobgesang, und Psalm* (Wittenberg, 1524) and repeated in the Erfurt *Enchiridion* of the same year.

Speratus (Hoffer or Offer) was born in Suabia in 1484. He was among the earliest and most able supporters of Luther and visited Wittenberg in 1523 to help him in the preparation of the first Lutheran Hymn book, the "Achtliederbuch" (*supra*), to which he contributed three hymns. He drafted the Prussian *Book of Church Order* (1526), became Bishop of Pomerania in 1529, and died in 1551.

[1] See p. 32 *supra*.

CANTATA IX 155

The melody of Speratus' Hymn, which Bach uses in the opening and closing movements of the Cantata, was published, along with the Hymn, in the "Achtliederbuch" of 1524. The tune originally was sung to the Easter Hymn, "Freu' dich du werthe Christenheit," which was in use in 1478. Bach uses the melody in Cantatas 86, 117, 155, 186, and in the "Drei Choräle zu Trauungen" (*Choralgesänge*, No. 89). Organ Works, N. xv. 109. There is traditional usage (1535 and 1586) for Bach's version of lines 5 and 6, and also for the C sharp in line 2.

(*a*)

The words of the first movement are the first stanza of Speratus' Hymn :

> Es ist das Heil uns kommen her
> Von Gnad' und lauter Güte ;
> Die Werk' die helfen nimmermehr,
> Sie mögen nicht behüten ;
> Der Glaub' sieht Jesum Christum an ;
> Der hat g'nug für uns all' gethan,
> Er ist der Mittler worden.
> B.G. i. 245.

English translations of the Hymn are noted in the *Dictionary of Hymnology*, p. 1074.

Form. Choral Fantasia (*Flauto, Oboe d'amore, Strings, Continuo*).

(b)

The words of the concluding Choral are the twelfth stanza of Speratus' Hymn :

> Ob sich's anliess, als wollt' er nicht,
> Lass dich es nicht erschrecken ;
> Denn wo er ist am besten mit,
> Da will er's nicht entdecken.
> Sein Wort lass dir[1] gewisser sein,
> Und ob dein Herz[2] spräch lauter Nein,
> So lass doch dir nicht grauen.   B.G. i. 274.

Form. Simple (*Flauto, Oboe d'amore, Strings, Continuo*). *Choralgesänge*, No. 87.

CANTATA X. MEINE SEEL' ERHEBT DEN HERREN[3]. Feast of the Visitation of the B. V. M. (*c.* 1740)

A Choral Cantata, on the *Magnificat*.

The melody of the first and last movements of the Cantata is Tonus Peregrinus, immemorially associated with Psalm cxiv, " In exitu Israel."

Bach introduces the melody into the Terzetto "Suscepit Israel," in the Latin "Magnificat" (No. 10). Two harmonisations of the melody are in the *Choralgesänge*, Nos. 120, 121.   Organ Works, N. xvi. 8 ; xviii. 75.

---

[1] 1524 das las dir.   [2] 1524 fleisch.
[3] An English version of the Cantata, "My soul doth magnify the Lord," is published by Breitkopf & Haertel.

(a)

The words of the first movement are the first three clauses of the *Magnificat*:

> Meine Seel' erhebt den Herren
> Und mein Geist freuet sich Gottes, meines Heilandes.
> Denn er hat seine elende Magd angesehen. Siehe, von nun an werden mich selig preisen alle Kindes Kind.   B.G. i. 277.

Form. Choral Fantasia (*Tromba*, 2 *Ob.*, *Strings*, *Continuo*). The *cantus* is first with the Sopranos and then with the Altos.

(b)

The words of the concluding Choral are the doxology to the *Magnificat*:

> Lob und Preis sei Gott dem Vater, und dem Sohn und dem heiligen Geiste;
> Wie es war im Anfang, jetzt und immerdar, und von Ewigkeit zu Ewigkeit. Amen.   B.G. i. 303.

Form. Simple(*Tromba*, 2 *Ob.*, *Strings*, *Continuo*). *Choralgesänge*, No. 122.

Bach uses the melody as an *obbligato* (2 Ob. and Tromba in unison) to the Alto-Tenor *Duetto* (fifth movement), "Er denket der Barmherzigkeit und hilft seinem Diener Israel auf" (B.G. i. 299)[1].

---

[1] The movement is No. 4 of the Schübler Chorals (N. xvi. 8).

CANTATA XI. LOBET GOTT IN SEINEN REICHEN[1]
Ascension Day (1735[2])

Melody: "*Ermuntre dich, mein schwacher Geist*"
                                  Johann Schop 1641

(a)

The sixth movement of the Cantata is a Choral upon Johann Schop's melody, "Ermuntre dich, mein schwacher Geist," first published in Part I of Johann Rist's *Himlischer Lieder mit...Melodeien* (Lüneburg, 1641).

Bach uses the melody also in Cantata 43, and in the "Christmas Oratorio," No. 12. There is another treatment of it (melody and figured Bass) in Schemelli's Hymn book (1736), No. 187. Invariably Bach follows Johann Crüger's remodelling of

---

[1] English versions of the Cantata are published by Novello & Co., "Praise our God Who reigns in Heaven," and Breitkopf & Haertel, "Praise Jehovah in His splendour."

[2] The date is approximate. The Cantata is held to have been composed at the same time as the Christmas and Easter Oratorios. The former was first performed in 1734 and the latter in 1736.

the tune in the 1648 edition of the *Praxis Pietatis Melica* (Berlin). The words of the Choral are the fourth stanza of Johann Rist's Ascension Hymn, "Du Lebensfürst, Herr Jesu Christ," first published in Part I of his *Himlischer Lieder* (see *supra*), to its own melody. It is set to Schop's tune in Wagner (1697):

> Nun lieget alles unter dir,
> Dich selbst nur ausgenommen;
> Die Engel müssen für und für
> Dir aufzuwarten kommen.
> Die Fürsten stehn auch auf der Bahn,
> Und sind dir willig unterthan;
> Luft, Wasser, Feu'r und Erden
> Muss dir zu Dienste werden.   B.G. ii. 32.

Form. Simple (2 *Fl.*, 2 *Ob.*, *Strings*, *Continuo*). *Choralgesänge*, No. 82.

Melody: "*Von Gott will ich nicht lassen*"
                                        Anon. 1572 [1571]

* A syllable is wanting in the third period of the melody.

160   CANTATA XI

Melody : " Helft mir Gott's Güte preisen "
Wolfgang Figulus 1575 [1569][1]

(b)

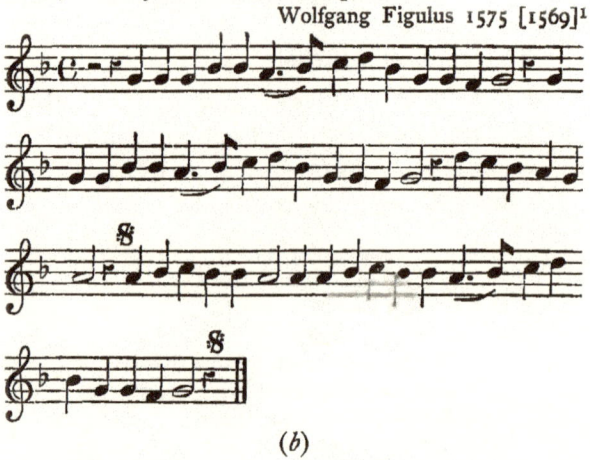

The melody of the concluding movement is known as "Von Gott will ich nicht lassen," from its association with Ludwig Helmbold's Hymn, or "Helft mir Gott's Güte preisen," from its association with Paul Eber's Hymn. Its source is the tune of a secular song, "Ich ging einmal spazieren," which was extant in 1569. As a Hymn tune the melody was first published by Joachim Magdeburg in his *Christliche und Tröstliche Tischgesange* (Erfurt, 1572 [1571]) and by Wolfgang Figulus (two melodies) in his *Weynacht Liedlein* (Frankfort a. Oder, 1575 [1569])[2].

[1] For Figulus' first melody, see *Bach's Chorals*, Part I, p. 63.
[2] See *Bach's Chorals*, Part I, p. 63.

Bach uses the melody "Von Gott" with variations which have earlier sanction. It appears in Cantatas 73, 107. It also occurs in Cantata D 4, "Lobt ihn mit Herz und Munde," attributed to Bach, and there are harmonisations of the tune in the *Choralgesänge*, Nos. 324, 325, 326. Organ Works, N. xvii. 43.

Figulus' second melody (*supra*) belongs exclusively to Eber's Hymn. It appears to originate as a Tenor melody of the first melody, to which its own Tenor bears a clear relation. In spite of its derivation, its individuality permits the tune to be regarded as a separate melody. It occurs in Cantatas 16, 28, 183. Organ Works, N. xv. 39.

The words of the Choral are the seventh stanza of Gottfried Wilhelm Sacer's Ascension Hymn, "Gott fähret auf gen Himmel," published in his *Geistliche, liebliche Lieder* (Gotha, 1714), to the melody, "Von Gott will ich nicht lassen":

> Wann soll es doch geschehen,
> Wann kömmt die liebe Zeit,
> Dass ich ihn werde[1] sehen
> In seiner Herrlichkeit?
> Du Tag, wann wirst du sein,
> Dass wir den Heiland grüssen,
> Dass wir den Heiland küssen?
> Komm, stelle dich doch ein!
>
> B.G. ii. 40.

[1] 1714 wir ihn werden.

English translations of the Hymn are noted in the *Dictionary of Hymnology*, p. 984.

Form. Choral Fantasia (3 *Trombe, Timpani*, 2 *Fl.*, 2 *Ob.*, *Strings, Continuo*).

CANTATA XII. WEINEN, KLAGEN, SORGEN, ZAGEN[1]. Third Sunday after Easter ("Jubilate") (1724 or 1725)

Melody: " *Was Gott thut, das ist wohlgethan*"
Anon. 1690

The concluding Choral is set to the melody, "Was Gott thut, das ist wohlgethan," published in the *Nürnbergisches Gesang-Buch* (Nürnberg, 1690), which contains eight melodies not found in the first (1676) edition of the book. Four of them ("Was Gott thut" being one) are anonymous.

[1] English versions of the Cantata are published by Novello & Co., "Wailing, crying, mourning, sighing," and by Breitkopf & Haertel, "Weeping, wailing, mourning, fearing."

CANTATA XII 163

The authorship of the tune has been attributed to Severus Gastorius of Jena, for whom the Hymn was written. With greater probability it has been assigned to Johann Pachelbel, who was born in 1653 at Nürnberg, and held important positions as organist at Eisenach, Erfurt (1678–90), Stuttgart, Gotha and Nürnberg. He died in 1706. The tune certainly is associated with Pachelbel, who set it in Motett form during his residence at Erfurt, c. 1680.

On the other hand, the first line of the melody is set to the Hymn, "Frisch auf, mein Geist, sei wohlgemuth," in E. C. Homburg's *Geistlicher Lieder, Erster Theil, mit zweystimmigen Melodeyen geziehret von Wernero Fabricio* (Naumburg, 1659 [1658]). Werner Fabricius, born in 1633, was Music Director at St Paul's Church, and Organist of St Nicolas' Church, Leipzig. He died in 1679.

The tune is referred to in the 1693 (Frankfort) edition of the *Praxis Pietatis Melica* as "bekannte Melodie," a statement which disposes of Gastorius', and perhaps of Pachelbel's, claim to it.

Bach uses the melody also in Cantatas 69, 75, 98, 99, 100, 144, and in the " Drei Choräle zu Trauungen" (*Choralgesänge*, No. 339).

The words of the Choral are the sixth stanza of Samuel Rodigast's Hymn, "Was Gott thut, das ist wohlgethan," founded on Deuteronomy xxxii. 4.

Rodigast was born at Gröben near Jena in 1649. He became Co-rector (1680) and Rector (1698) of the Greyfriars Gymnasium at Berlin. He died in 1708. The Hymn is said to have been written in 1675 at Jena for his sick friend, Severus Gastorius, Cantor there. It was published in *Das Hannoverische ordentliche Vollständige Gesangbuch* (Göttingen, 1676):

> Was Gott thut, das ist wohlgethan,
> Dabei will ich verbleiben,
> Es mag mich auf die rauhe Bahn
> Noth, Tod und Elend treiben,
> So wird Gott mich ganz väterlich
> In seinen Armen halten:
> Drum lass' ich ihn nur walten. B.G. ii. 78.

English translations of the Hymn are noted in the *Dictionary of Hymnology*, p. 972.

Form. Embellished ("*Oboe o Tromba*," Fagotto, Strings, Continuo). *Choralgesänge*, No. 340.

CANTATA XIII. MEINE SEUFZER, MEINE THRÄNEN. Second Sunday after the Epiphany (*c.* 1736)

Melody: "*Ainsi qu'on oit le cerf bruire*"

Louis Bourgeois 1542

(a)

The melody of the third movement is known as "Freu' dich sehr, O meine Seele," from its association with that Hymn. The latter, however, has its proper melody, first published, with the Hymn, in Christopher Demantius' *Threnodiae, Das ist: Ausserlesene Trostreiche Begräbnüss Gesänge* (Freiberg, 1620), and probably composed, or adapted, by Demantius himself. Its opening three notes and its seventh line are identical with the opening line of the melody *supra*. The latter tune was first published in Bourgeois' Psalms (1542) and Jean Crespin's *Pseaumes octante trois de David* (Geneva, 1551), set to Beza's version of Psalm xlii. An extract from the Geneva Council archives of July 28, 1552, establishes Louis Bourgeois as the composer of "Ainsi qu'on oit" ("Wie nach einem Wasserquelle"), and the other tunes to Beza's Psalms in the Psalter. In the second edition of Schein's *Cantional* (1645) the tune is set to the anonymous Hymn, "Freu' dich sehr."

166 CANTATA XIII

Bourgeois, born in Paris early in the 16th century, was invited to Geneva in 1541. In 1545 he succeeded Guillaume Franc (d. 1570) as Master of the children and music school there, on Franc's transference to Lausanne Cathedral. In December 1551 Bourgeois was imprisoned for having altered " without leave " the tunes of some of the Psalms, presumably those of the Psalter of 1551. He was released on Calvin's intervention, returned to Paris in 1557, and was living in 1561.

Bach uses the melody also in Cantatas 19, 25, 30, 32, 39, 70, and 194. There appears not to be an earlier example of Bach's treatment of the last phrase of the tune.

The words of the movement are the second stanza of Johann Heermann's " Zion klagt mit Angst und Schmerzen," first published in his *Devoti Musica Cordis* (second edition, Leipzig, 1636), to Bourgeois' tune (*supra*):

>Der Gott, der mir hat versprochen
>Seinen Beistand jederzeit,
>Der lässt sich vergebens suchen
>Itzt in meiner Traurigkeit.
>Ach ! will er denn für und für
>Grausam zürnen über mir?
>Kann und will er sich des[1] Armen
>Itzt nicht wie vorhin erbarmen?
>
>B.G. ii. 87.

[1] 1636 der.

CANTATA XIII

English translations of the Hymn are noted in the *Dictionary of Hymnology*, p. 505.

Form. Alto Unison Choral (*Flauti, Oboe da caccia, Strings, Continuo*).

Melody: "*O Welt, ich muss dich lassen*"
Heinrich Isaak 1539

(*b*)

The melody of the concluding Choral is Heinrich Isaak's "O Welt, ich muss dich lassen," first published in Georg Forster's *Ein ausszug guter alter ūn newer Teutscher liedlein* (Nürnberg, 1539), to the secular song "Innspruck, ich muss dich lassen." It was first associated with Johann Hesse's Hymn, "O Welt, ich muss dich lassen," in 1598[1].

Bach uses the melody in the "St Matthew Passion," Nos. 16 and 44; in the "St John Passion,"

[1] See *Bach's Chorals*, Part I, p. 5.

No. 8; and in Cantatas 44 and 97. There are four other harmonisations of the melody in *Choralgesänge*, Nos. 289–291, 298. By 1598 the tune virtually had assumed the form familiar to Bach's generation. Line 3, however, only began to take modern shape in Schein's *Cantional* of 1627.

The words of the movement are the fifteenth stanza of Paul Flemming's Hymn, "In allen meinen Thaten," first published in his *Teutsche Poemata* (Lübeck, 1642), and set to Isaak's tune (*supra*) in a recension dated 1670.

Flemming was born at Hartenstein in 1609, was laureated as a poet at Leipzig University in 1631, and betook himself to Holstein two years later in order to escape the miseries of the Thirty Years' War. Thence he was sent on an embassy to Russia (1633) and Persia (1635). The Hymn was written in 1633, on the eve of his departure for Russia. In 1640 Flemming graduated M.D. at Leyden and died there in the same year:

    So sei nun, Seele, deine,
    Und traue dem alleine,
    Der dich erschaffen[1] hat.
    Es gehe wie es gehe,
    Dein Vater in der Höhe
    Der weiss zu allen Sachen Rath[2].
                         B.G. ii. 98.

[1] 1642 geschaffen.
[2] 1642 Weiss allen Sachen Raht. Bach's line is a variant reading as old as 1670 (Fischer-Tümpel, 1. 435).

English translations of the Hymn are noted in the *Dictionary of Hymnology*, p. 378.

Form. Simple (*Flauti, Oboe, Strings, Continuo*). *Choralgesänge*, No. 295.

Cantata XIV. Wär' Gott nicht mit uns diese Zeit. Fourth Sunday after the Epiphany (1735)

Melody: "*Wär' Gott nicht mit uns diese Zeit*"
? Johann Walther 1524

A Choral Cantata, on Luther's Hymn, "Wär' Gott nicht mit uns diese Zeit," a version of Psalm cxxiv, first published in the *Geystliche gesangk Buchleyn* (Wittenberg, 1524), with the melody.

The melody may be attributed to Johann Walther, Luther's collaborator, or alternatively, to Luther himself.

Bach has not used the melody elsewhere.

CANTATA XIV

(*a*)

The words of the opening movement are the first stanza of Luther's Hymn:

> Wär' Gott nicht mit uns diese Zeit,
> So soll Israel sagen,
> Wär' Gott nicht mit uns diese Zeit,
> Wir hätten müssen[1] verzagen,
> Die so ein armes Häuflein sind,
> Veracht von so viel Menschenkind,
> Die an uns setzen alle.   B.G. ii. 101.

Translations of the Hymn are noted in the *Dictionary of Hymnology*, p. 1232.

Form. Choral Fantasia, in the Organ Choral form, the vocal themes being used in Counterpoint against the Choral melody in the orchestra (*Corno da caccia*, 2 *Ob.*, *Strings*, *Continuo*)[2].

(*b*)

The words of the concluding Choral are the third stanza of Luther's Hymn:

> Gott Lob und Dank, der nicht zugab,
> Dass ihr Schlund uns mögt fangen.
> Wie ein Vogel des Stricks kömmt ab,
> Ist unsre Seel' entgangen.
> Strick ist entzwei und wir sind frei,
> Des Herren Name steht uns bei,
> Des Gottes Himmels und Erden.
>   B.G. ii. 132.

Form. Simple (2 *Ob.*, *Corno da caccia*, *Strings*, *Continuo*). *Choralgesänge*, No. 330.

---

[1] 1524 must.   [2] See Spitta, III. 66; Parry, p. 420.

CANTATA XV. DENN DU WIRST MEINE SEELE NICHT IN DER HÖLLE LASSEN. Easter Day (1704)

Melody: "*Wenn mein Stündlein vorhanden ist*"
Nicolaus Herman 1569

The melody of the Choral sung in the last thirty bars of the concluding movement is Nicolaus Herman's "Wenn mein Stündlein vorhanden ist," first published, with the Hymn, in Johann Wolff's *Kirche Gesäng, Aus dem Wittenbergischen, und allen andern den besten Gesangbüchern* (Frankfort a. Main, 1569).

Herman was born *circ.* 1485. In 1524 he was acting as Master in the Latin School and Cantor of the church at Joachimsthal in Bohemia. He died there in 1561. He was a great lover of music, a good organist, and is credited with the authorship of the tunes set to his Hymns.

Bach uses the melody also in Cantatas 31 and 95. There are other harmonisations of the tune in the *Choralgesänge*, Nos. 353, 354, 355. The concluding line of Bach's text is a variation of the original melody as old as 1584 (M. Eucharius Zinckeisen's *Kirchen Gesäng*, Frankfort a. Main, 1584). His other variations also are found in earlier texts.

The words of the Choral are the fourth stanza of Nicolaus Herman's Hymn for the Dying, "Wenn mein Stündlein vorhanden ist," first published in his *Die Historien von der Sindfludt*" (Wittenberg, 1562 [1560]):

> Weil' du vom Tod' erstanden bist,
> Werd' ich im Grab' nicht bleiben,
> Mein höchster Trost dein' Auffahrt ist,
> Tod'sfurcht kann sie vertreiben ;
> Denn wo du bist da komm' ich hin,
> Dass ich stets bei dir leb' und bin,
> Drum fahr' ich hin mit Freuden.
>
> B.G. ii. 169.

English translations of the Hymn are noted in the *Dictionary of Hymnology*, p. 1254.

Form. Extended (3 *Clarini, Timpani, Strings, Continuo*).

CANTATA XVI. HERR GOTT DICH LOBEN WIR.
Feast of the Circumcision (New Year's Day)
(? 1724)

Melody: "*Herr Gott dich loben wir*" Anon. 1535

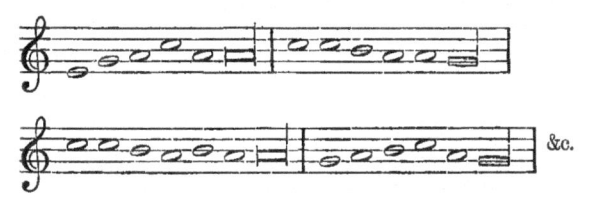

(*a*)

In the opening movement Bach employs the melody, "Herr Gott dich loben wir," a simplified form of the plainsong melody of the Ambrosian "Te Deum laudamus." It was published in Joseph Klug's *Geistliche Lieder* (Wittenberg, 1535), with Luther's version of the "Te Deum," and no doubt had appeared in association with the latter in the first (1529) edition of that book. Only the first four lines of the melody are printed above. See the *Choralgesänge*, No. 133, and Organ Works, N. xviii. 44, for the complete setting.

Bach uses the melody also in Cantatas 119, 120, 190.

The words of the opening movement are the first two clauses of Luther's free version of the

"Te Deum," first published in Joseph Klug's *Geistliche Lieder* (Wittenberg, 1535 [1529]):

> Herr Gott dich loben wir,
> Herr Gott wir danken dir!
> Dich, Gott Vater[1] in Ewigkeit,
> Ehret die Welt weit und breit.
>
> B.G. ii. 175.

English translations of Luther's version are noted in the *Dictionary of Hymnology*, p. 1134.

Form. Choral Fantasia (2 *Ob.*, *Corno da caccia*, *Strings*, *Continuo*).

(*b*)

For the melody of the concluding Choral, "Helft mir Gott's Güte preisen" (second version), see Cantata 11.

The words of the movement are the sixth stanza of Paul Eber's Hymn for the New Year, "Helft mir Gott's Güte preisen," first published in Eichorn's *Geistliche Lieder* (Frankfort a. Oder, *c.* 1580).

Eber was born at Kitzingen, Bavaria, in 1511. He entered the University of Wittenberg in 1532, and eventually held the Chairs of Latin and Hebrew there. He was a friend of Melanchthon and, next to Luther, is the best poet of the Wittenberg School. He died in 1569. The Hymn is an acrostic upon the name "Helena," borne by his

[1] 1535 Dich Vater.

wife and daughter, spelt by the initial letters of the six stanzas:

> All' solch' dein Güt' wir preisen,
> Vater in's Himmels Thron,
> Die du uns thust beweisen
> Durch Jesum[1] deinen Sohn,
> Und bitten ferner[2] dich,
> Gieb uns ein friedlich[3] Jahre,
> Vor alles Leid bewahre
> Und nähr' uns mildiglich. B.G. ii. 198.

An English translation is noted in the *Dictionary of Hymnology*, p. 319.

Form. Simple (2 *Ob.*, *Corno da caccia*, *Strings*, *Continuo*). *Choralgesänge*, No. 125.

CANTATA XVII. WER DANK OPFERT, DER PREISET MICH. Fourteenth Sunday after Trinity (*c.* 1737)

Melody: "*Nun lob', mein' Seel', den Herren*"
? Johann Kugelmann 1540

[1] *c.* 1580 Christum.   [2] *c.* 1580 förder.   [3] *c.* 1580 frölich.

The melody of the concluding Choral, "Nun lob', mein' Seel', den Herren," was first published, with the Hymn, in Johann Kugelmann's *News Gesanng, mit Dreyen stymmen* (Augsburg, 1540), a Hymn book compiled for the use of the Lutheran Church in Prussia and one of the earliest of its kind after Walther's (1524). It contained thirty-nine hymns, for the majority of which (thirty) Kugelmann composed the tunes.

Kugelmann is said to have been born at Augsburg. In 1519 he was in the service of the Emperor Maximilian I at Innspruck as Court Trumpeter. Later he passed into the service of Duke Albert of Prussia in a similar capacity, and eventually became Ducal Capellmeister at Königsberg. He died in 1542.

Bach uses the melody also in Cantatas 28, 29, 51, 167, in Motett 1, " Singet dem Herrn ein neues Lied," and in the so-called Motett, "Sei Lob und Preis mit Ehren." Other harmonisations of the tune are in the *Choralgesänge*, Nos. 269, 270. The variations of the original melody which appear in

CANTATA XVII 177

Bach's versions are found in texts within sixty years of the publication of the tune in 1540.

The words of the Choral are the third stanza of Johann Graumann's (Poliander) "Nun lob', mein' Seel', den Herren," a version of Psalm ciii, first published as a broadsheet at Nürnberg c. 1540, and, with the tune, in Kugelmann's *News Gesanng* (1540).

Graumann was born at Neustadt in the Bavarian Palatinate in 1487. In 1520 he became Rector of the Thomasschule, Leipzig. On Luther's recommendation he was invited to aid the Reformation movement in Prussia, and in 1525 became pastor of the Altstadt Church at Königsberg. He died there in 1541. The Hymn is said to have been written in 1525 at the request of Albert of Hohenzollern, High Master of the Teutonic Order and first Duke of Prussia (d. 1568):

> Wie sich ein Vat'r[1] erbarmet
> Üb'r seine junge Kindlein klein:
> So thut der Herr uns Armen,
> So wir ihn kindlich fürchten rein.
> Er kennt das arm' Gemächte,
> Er[2] weiss, wir sind nur Staub.
> Gleich wie das Gras vom Reche,
> Ein' Blum' und fallend Laub:
> Der Wind nur drüber wehet,
> So ist es nimmer da:
> Also der Mensch vergehet,
> Sein End', das ist ihm nah.   B.G. ii. 225.

[1] 1540 mañ.   [2] 1540 Got.

178   CANTATA XVIII

Translations of the Hymn into English are noted in the *Dictionary of Hymnology*, p. 451.

Form. Simple (2 *Ob.*, *Strings*, *Continuo*). *Choralgesänge*, No. 271.

CANTATA XVIII. GLEICH WIE DER REGEN UND SCHNEE VOM HIMMEL FÄLLT. Sexagesima Sunday (1713 or 1714)

Melody: "*Durch Adams Fall ist ganz verderbt*"
Anon. 1535

The melody of the concluding Choral, "Durch Adams Fall ist ganz verderbt," first appeared in Joseph Klug's *Geistliche Lieder* (Wittenberg, 1535 [1529]), with the Hymn. It is said to be the melody of the song, "Was wöll wir aber heben an," sung at the Battle of Pavia in 1525.

Bach uses the melody also in Cantata 109. Organ Works, N.-xv. 107; xviii. 28.

The words of the Choral are the eighth stanza of Lazarus Spengler's "Durch Adams Fall ist ganz verderbt," first published in Johann Walther's

CANTATA XVIII

Geystliche gesangk Buchleyn (Wittenberg, 1524), with two melodies, probably by Walther himself.

Lazarus Spengler was born at Nürnberg in 1479. He made Luther's acquaintance when the Reformer visited the city in 1518 on his way to Augsburg, and became a leader of the Reformation in Nürnberg, where he was successively Raths Syndikus and Rathsherr. He died in 1534:

> Ich bitt' O Herr, aus Herzens Grund,
> Du wollst nicht von mir nehmen
> Dein heil'ges Wort aus meinem Mund;
> So wird mich nicht beschämen
> Mein' Sünd und Schuld,
> Denn in dein Huld
> Setz' ich all mein Vertrauen.
> Wer sich nur fest
> Darauf verlässt,
> Der wird[1] den Tod nicht schauen.
>
> B.G. ii. 252.

English translations of the Hymn are noted in the *Dictionary of Hymnology*, p. 1072.

Form. Simple (2 *Fl.*, *Fagotto*, 4 *Violas, Continuo*). *Choralgesänge*, No. 73.

Bach introduces the melody into the accompaniment of the Bass *Recitativo*, "Gleich wie der Regen," and the following Chorus, "Mein Gott, hier wird" (B.G. ii. 237).

Four clauses of the Litany are inserted into the second movement (B.G. ii. 238).

[1] 1524 wurd.

CANTATA XIX. ES ERHUB SICH EIN STREIT.
Feast of St Michael the Archangel (1726)
For the melody of the concluding Choral, "Ainsi qu'on oit le cerf," see Cantata 13.

The words of the concluding Choral are the ninth stanza of the anonymous funerary Hymn, "Freu' dich sehr, O meine Seele," first published in Christopher Demantius' *Threnodiae* (Freiberg, 1620), and set to Bourgeois' melody in the second (1645) edition of Schein's *Cantional*:

>Lass' dein' Engel mit mir fahren
>Auf Elias Wagen roth,
>Und mein' Seele wohl bewahren,
>Wie[1] Laz'rum nach seinem Tod.
>Lass' sie ruhn in deinem Schoos,
>Erfüll' sie mit Freud' und Trost,
>Bis der Leib kommt aus der Erde,
>Und mit ihr[2] vereinigt werde. B.G. ii. 288.

Translations of the Hymn into English are noted in the *Dictionary of Hymnology*, p. 395.

Form. Embellished (3 *Trombe, Timpani,* 2 *Ob., Taille*[3], *Strings, Continuo*). *Choralgesänge*, No. 99.

Bach introduces the melody "Herzlich lieb hab' ich dich, O Herr" into the fifth movement, the Tenor *Aria* "Bleibt ihr Engel," as a Tromba *obbligato* (B.G. ii. 279). He had in mind the third stanza of the Hymn. See the Michaelmas Cantata No. 149 for melody and stanza.

[1] 1620 Mit. Bach's version follows Schein.
[2] 1620 Mit Ehr wird.   [3] The Taille was a Tenor Bassoon.

CANTATA XX. O EWIGKEIT, DU DONNERWORT. First Sunday after Trinity (*c.* 1725)

Melody: "*Wach auf, mein Geist*" Johann Schop 1642

Melody: "*O Ewigkeit, du Donnerwort*"
Johann Crüger's reconstruction 1653

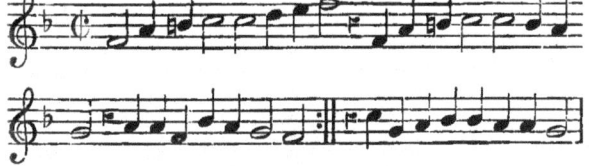

A Choral Cantata[1], on Johann Rist's Hymn, "O Ewigkeit, du Donnerwort," first published in the fourth Part of his *Himlischer Lieder* (Lüneburg, 1642).

The melody which Bach uses in the opening Chorus, and in the concluding Chorals of Parts I

[1] See p. 32 *supra*.

and II, was composed by Johann Schop for Johann Rist's "Wach auf, mein Geist, erhebe dich," and was published, with that Hymn, in Part III (1642) of the *Himlischer Lieder*. Schop also wrote a melody for "O Ewigkeit, du Donnerwort," for Part IV of Rist's collection. Johann Crüger's reconstruction of "Wach auf," which Bach follows almost exactly, was published, with the Hymn "O Ewigkeit, du Donnerwort," in his *Praxis Pietatis Melica* (Berlin, 1653), and also in Christoph Runge's *D. M. Luthers Und anderer vornehmen geistreichen und gelehrten Männer Geistliche Lieder und Psalmen* (Berlin, 1653).

Bach uses the melody in Cantata 60. Other harmonisations of it are in Anna Magdalena Bach's *Notenbüchlein*, and *Choralgesänge*, No. 275.

(*a*)

The words of the opening movement are the first stanza of Rist's Hymn:

> O Ewigkeit, du Donnerwort,
> O Schwert, das durch die Seele bohrt,
> O Anfang sonder Ende!
> O Ewigkeit, Zeit ohne Zeit,
> Ich weiss vor grosser Traurigkeit
> Nicht, wo ich mich hin wende[1];
> Mein ganz erschrocknes Herz erbebt,
> Dass mir die Zung' am Gaumen klebt.
> B.G. ii. 293.

[1] 1642 hin mich wende.

English translations of the Hymn are noted in the *Dictionary of Hymnology*, p. 828.

Form. Choral Fantasia (3 *Ob.*, Tromba da tirarsi, Strings, Continuo).

(*b*)

The words of the concluding Choral of Part I are the eleventh stanza of Rist's Hymn:

> So lang ein Gott im Himmel lebt
> Und über alle Wolken schwebt,
> Wird solche Marter währen:
> Es wird sie plagen Kält' und Hitz',
> Angst, Hunger, Schrecken, Feu'r und Blitz,
> Und sie doch nicht[1] verzehren.
> Denn wird sich enden diese Pein,
> Wenn Gott nicht mehr wird ewig sein.
> B.G. ii. 317.

Form. Simple (*Tromba da tirarsi*, 3 *Ob.*, Strings, Continuo). *Choralgesänge*, No. 276.

(*c*)

The words of the concluding Choral of Part II are the sixteenth stanza of Rist's Hymn:

> O Ewigkeit, du Donnerwort,
> O Schwert, das durch die Seele bohrt,
> O Anfang sonder Ende!
> O Ewigkeit, Zeit ohne Zeit,
> Ich weiss vor grosser Traurigkeit
> Nicht, wo ich mich hin wende.
> Nimm du mich, wenn es dir gefällt,
> Herr Jesu, in dein Freudenzelt. B.G. ii. 327.

Form. Simple (*Tromba da tirarsi*, 3 *Ob.*, Strings, Continuo). *Choralgesänge*, No. 276.

[1] 1642 nie.

CANTATA XXI. ICH HATTE VIEL BEKÜMMERNISS[1]. For General Use[2] (1714)

Melody: "*Wer nur den lieben Gott lässt walten*"
Georg Neumark 1657

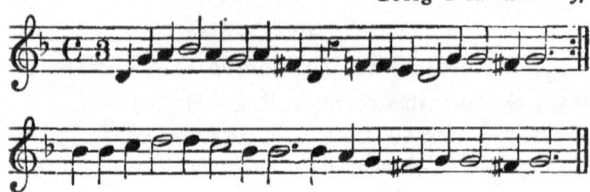

In the ninth movement, the Chorus "Sei nun wieder zufrieden," Bach makes use of the words and melody of Georg Neumark's Hymn, "Wer nur den lieben Gott lässt walten," published together in his *Fortgepflantzter Musikalisch-Poetischer Lustwald* (Jena, 1657).

Georg Neumark was born at Langensalza in Thuringia in 1621. In 1652 (?) the Grand Duke of Saxe-Weimar appointed him Court Poet, Librarian and Registrar of the administration at Weimar. Of the "Fruit-bearing Society," the chief German literary union in the 17th century, he became Secretary in 1656. He died in 1681. The melody was composed by Neumark for the Hymn.

[1] English versions of the Cantata are published by Novello & Co., "My spirit was in heaviness," and Breitkopf & Haertel, "I had great heaviness of heart."
[2] The Score is inscribed, "Per ogni tempo." The Cantata is appropriate particularly to the Third Sunday after Trinity, by whose Epistle it was suggested.

Bach uses the melody also in Cantatas 27, 84, 88, 93, 166, 179, and 197. There is another harmonisation of the tune in the *Choralgesänge*, No. 367. Mendelssohn uses it for the Choral, " To Thee, O Lord, I yield my spirit," in " St Paul," No. 9. Bach's version of the last line of the tune is invariable and is not noted by Zahn as having earlier authority. Organ Works, N. xv. 117; xvi. 6; xix. 21, 22.

The words of the Choral are the second and fifth stanzas of Neumark's Hymn, which was written at Kiel in 1641 :

> Was helfen uns die schweren Sorgen?
> Was hilft uns unser Weh und Ach?
> Was hilft es, dass wir alle Morgen
> Beseufzen unser Ungemach?
> Wir machen unser Kreuz und Leid
> Nur grösser durch die Traurigkeit.
>
> Denk' nicht in deiner Drangsalshitze,
> Dass du von Gott verlassen seist,
> Und dass der Gott[1] im Schoosse sitze,
> Der sich mit stetem Glücke speist.
> Die Folgezeit verändert viel,
> Und setzet Jeglichem sein Ziel.
>
> B.G. v. (i) 36.

Translations of the Hymn into English are noted in the *Dictionary of Hymnology*, p. 796.

Form. Choral Motett (*Oboe, Fagotto,* 4 *Trombones, Strings, Organ, Continuo*). The *cantus* is with the Tenor.

[1] 1657 Gott der.

CANTATA XXII. JESUS NAHM ZU SICH DIE ZWÖLFE. Quinquagesima ("Esto Mihi") Sunday (1723)

Melody: "*Herr Christ, der einig' Gott's Sohn*"
Anon. 1524

Melody: "*Ich hört ein Fräulein klagen*"
Anon. 1549

In the concluding Choral Bach uses the words and melody of the Christmas Hymn, "Herr Christ, der einig' Gott's Sohn," published together in the Erfurt *Enchiridion Oder eyn Handbuchlein* (1524) and in Johann Walther's *Geystliche gesangk Buchleyn* (Wittenberg, 1524). The tune bears a close relation to that of the secular song "Ich hört ein Fräulein klagen," published in 1549. Presumably the secular tune is the earlier, and Walther's influence upon the 1524 version may be assumed. Bach uses the melody also in Cantatas 96, 132, 164. Organ Works, N. xv. 9; xviii. 43.

The words of the Choral are the fifth stanza of Elisabethe Cruciger's Christmas Hymn, "Herr Christ, der einig' Gott's Sohn," first published, with the tune, in the *Enchiridion* and *Buchleyn* of 1524. The authoress was the daughter of a Polish refugee residing at Wittenberg, where she married Caspar Cruciger, a student at the University, in 1524. Cruciger, who was regarded by Luther with great affection and was treated as a son, became one of the Professors of Theology in the University. His wife, a great lover of music, died at Wittenberg in 1535. This is the only Hymn of hers extant or known:

> Ertödt' uns durch dein' Güte,
> Erweck' uns durch dein' Gnad';
> Den alten Menschen kränke,
> Dass der neu' leben mag,
> Wohl hie auf dieser Erden
> Den Sinn und all' Begehrden
> Und G'danken[1] han zu dir.   B.G. v. (i) 89.

Translations of the Hymn into English are noted in the *Dictionary of Hymnology*, p. 271.

Form. Extended (*Oboe, Strings, Continuo*). Erk, No. 48.

[1] 1524 dancken.

CANTATA XXIII. DU WAHRER GOTT UND DAVIDS SOHN[1]. Quinquagesima ("Esto Mihi") Sunday (1724)[2]

Melody: "*Christe, du Lamm Gottes*" Anon. 1557

gieb uns dei-nen Frie-den. A - - - - - men -

In the concluding Choral Bach uses the melody and words of the Antiphon, "Christe, du Lamm Gottes." Words and melody appear together in the Pfalz-Neuburg *Kirchenordnung* (Nürnberg, 1557), and obviously have a pre-Reformation association. The movement originally was the concluding number of the "St John Passion."

Bach introduces the melody into the opening movement of Cantata 127. He has not used it elsewhere in the Cantatas, Oratorios, or Motetts. He made an arrangement of it, however (B.G. xli. 187), in five vocal parts (2 S's.A.T.B.) with *Continuo* accompaniment, for the "Kyrie Eleison." Organ Works, N. xv. 61.

[1] An English version of the Cantata, "Thou very God, and David's Son," is published by Breitkopf & Haertel.
[2] First performed in 1724, the Cantata probably was composed at Cöthen. See Spitta, II. 350.

CANTATA XXIII 189

The words of the Choral are a prose translation of the "Agnus Dei," and are found in Low German in the Brunswick *Kirchenordnung* of 1528, and in High German in the Saxon *Kirchenordnung* of 1540:

> *Christe, du Lamm Gottes,
> Der du trägst die Sünd' der Welt,
> Erbarm' dich unser!
>
> Christe, du Lamm Gottes,
> Der du trägst die Sünd' der Welt,
> Erbarm' dich unser!
>
> Christe, du Lamm Gottes,
> Der du trägst die Sünd' der Welt,
> Gieb uns dein'n Frieden!
>
> B.G. v. (i) 117.

Translations of the Antiphon are noted in the *Dictionary of Hymnology*, p. 31.

Form. Choral Fantasia (*Cornetto*, 3 *Trombones*, 2 *Ob.*, *Strings*, *Continuo*). Neither the *Choralgesänge* nor Erk prints the melody.

Bach introduces the melody into the accompaniment of the Tenor *Recitativo*, "Ach, gehe nicht vorüber," where the Violins and Oboes have it (B.G. v. (i) 104). He employs it in the same manner (Oboes and Horns) in the accompaniment of the "Kyrie" of the Mass in F major (B.G. viii. 3).

Cantata XXIV. Ein ungefärbt Gemüthe.
Fourth Sunday after Trinity (1723)

Melody: "*O Gott, du frommer Gott*" Anon. 1693

In the concluding Choral Bach uses the melody, "O Gott, du frommer Gott," published, in association with Johann Heermann's Hymn, in the *Neuvermehrtes und zu Ubung Christl. Gottseligkeit eingerichtetes Meiningisches Gesangbuch* (Meiningen, 1693). It is among the anonymous melodies in that collection. But the lines which compose it are found among the tunes (the majority of them by Hieronymus Kradenthaller, a Regensburg organist) in *Lust- und Artzneigarten des Königlichen Propheten Davids* (Regensburg, 1675), and may be regarded as a reminiscence of them. The Hymn has other melodies, one of which Bach uses more frequently (see Cantata 45).

CANTATA XXIV

The above melody is also in Cantatas 71 and 164. There is a four-part setting of it in the *Choralgesänge*, No. 282.

Bach's version shows important modifications of the sixth and last lines. Practically identical variations are found in Christian Friedrich Witt's *Psalmodia sacra* (Gotha, 1715).

The set of Variations, or Partite, in N. xix. 44, upon the melody, "O Gott, du frommer Gott," treat another and earlier (1646) tune, originally known as "Gross ist, O grosser Gott."

The words of the Choral are the first stanza of Johann Heermann's "O Gott, du frommer Gott," first published in his *Devoti Musica Cordis* (Leipzig, 1630):

> O Gott, du frommer Gott,
> Du Brunnquell aller[1] Gaben,
> Ohn' den nichts ist, was ist,
> Von dem wir Alles haben :
> Gesunden Leib gieb mir,
> Und dass in solchem Leib'
> Ein' unverletzte Seel'
> Und rein Gewissen bleib'!
>
> B.G. v. (i) 150.

English translations of the Hymn are noted in the *Dictionary of Hymnology*, p. 833.

Form. Extended (*Clarino*, 2 *Ob.*, *Strings*, *Continuo*).

---

[1] 1630 guter.

CANTATA XXV. ES IST NICHTS GESUNDES AN MEINEM LEIBE[1]. Fourteenth Sunday after Trinity (*c.* 1731)
For the melody of the concluding Choral, "Ainsi qu'on oit le cerf," see Cantata 13.

The words of the concluding Choral are the twelfth stanza of Johann Heermann's "Treuer Gott, ich muss dir klagen," first-published in his *Devoti Musica Cordis* (Leipzig, 1630), to the above melody:

> Ich will alle meine Tage
> Rühmen deine starke Hand,
> Dass du meine Plag' und Klage
> Hast so herzlich abgewandt.
> Nicht nur in der Sterblichkeit
> Soll dein Ruhm sein ausgebreit't :
> Ich will's auch hernach erweisen,
> Und dort ewiglich dich preisen.
> B.G. v. (i) 188.

English translations of the Hymn are noted in the *Dictionary of Hymnology*, p. 505.

Form. Simple (*Cornetto*, 3 *Trombones*, 3 *Fl.*, 2 *Ob.*, *Strings*, *Continuo*). *Choralgesänge*, No. 101.

In the opening Chorus of the Cantata (B.G. v. (i) 158) Bach introduces the melody of the penitential hymn, "Ach Herr, mich armen Sünder." The tune is more familiar as "Herzlich thut mich verlangen" (see Cantata 135)[2].

---

[1] English versions of the Cantata are published by Novello & Co., "There is nought of soundness in all my body," and Breitkopf & Haertel, "There is no more soundness in all my body."

[2] See Spitta, II. 466-7, on the movement.

CANTATA XXVI. ACH WIE FLÜCHTIG. Twenty-fourth Sunday after Trinity (*c.* 1740)

Melody: "*Ach wie flüchtig*" Michael Franck 1652

Melody: "*Ach wie flüchtig*"
Johann Crüger's (?) reconstruction 1661

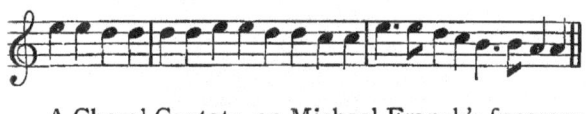

A Choral Cantata, on Michael Franck's funerary Hymn, "Ach wie flüchtig," first published, with the melody, in Franck's *Die Eitelheit, Falschheit und Unbeständigkeit der Welt*" (Coburg, 1652).

Franck was born at Schleusingen in 1609 and in 1628 became a master baker there. In 1640 poverty drove him to Coburg, where he taught in the town school. In 1659 Johann Rist crowned him as a poet and received him into his Order of Elbe Swans. He died in 1667.

CANTATA XXVI

The melody, which Bach uses in the opening and concluding movements of the Cantata, was composed by Franck and published, in four-part harmony, with the Hymn, in 1652. The Hymn was republished in the 1661 (Berlin) edition of Crüger's *Praxis Pietatis Melica* and in the Brunswick *Neuvermehrtes vollständiges Gesangbuch* (Brunswick, 1661), with a reconstruction of Franck's melody which may be attributed to Johann Crüger. The melody does not occur elsewhere in the Cantatas. Organ Works, N. xv. 121.

(a)

The words of the opening movement are the first stanza of Franck's Hymn:

> Ach wie flüchtig,
> Ach wie nichtig
> Ist der Menschen Leben!
> Wie ein Nebel bald entstehet,
> Und auch wieder bald vergehet,
> So ist unser Leben, sehet!
>
> B.G. v. (i) 191.

Translations of the Hymn into English are noted in the *Dictionary of Hymnology*, p. 387.

Form. Choral Fantasia (*Flauto*, 3 *Ob., Corno, Strings, Organ, Continuo*)[1].

---

[1] The movement should be compared with the Prelude upon the melody in the *Orgelbüchlein* (N. xv. 121).

(b)

The words of the concluding Choral are the thirteenth stanza of Franck's Hymn:

> Ach wie flüchtig,
> Ach wie nichtig
> Sind der Menschen Sachen!
> Alles, Alles, was wir sehen,
> Dass muss fallen und vergehen;
> Wer Gott fürcht't, bleibt[1] ewig stehen.

B.G. v. (i) 216.

Form. Simple (*Flauto*, 3 *Ob.*, *Corno*, *Strings*, *Organ*, *Continuo*). *Choralgesänge*, No. 11.

CANTATA XXVII. WER WEISS, WIE NAHE MIR MEIN ENDE[2]. Sixteenth Sunday after Trinity (1731)

(a)

For the melody of the opening Chorus, "Wer nur den lieben Gott lässt walten," see Cantata 21. The Choral words of the opening Chorus are the first stanza of the funerary Hymn, "Wer weiss, wie nahe mir mein Ende," written by Emilie Juliane Countess of Schwarzburg-Rudolstadt.

The authoress was born in 1637, married her cousin, the Count of Schwarzburg-Rudolstadt, and

[1] 1652 wird.
[2] English versions of the Cantata are published by Novello & Co., "O teach me, Lord, my days to number," and Breitkopf & Haertel, "Who knows, how near my latter ending?"

died in 1706. About 600 hymns are attributed to her. The Hymn "Wer weiss" was published, to the above melody, in the Rudolstadt Hymn book of 1682 (Appendix, 1688) and in *M. Joh. Heinrich Häveckers... Kirchen-Echo* (Leipzig, 1695). Its authorship is also claimed by Georg Michael Pfefferkorn (1645-1732):

> Wer weiss, wie nahe mir mein Ende?
> Hingeht die Zeit, herkommt der Tod.
> Ach, wie geschwinde und behende
> Kann kommen meine Todesnoth!
> Mein Gott, ich bitt' durch Christi Blut,
> Mach's nur mit meinem Ende gut.
>
> B.G. v. (i) 219.

Translations of the Hymn into English are noted in the *Dictionary of Hymnology*, p. 330.

Form. Choral Fantasia. The Chorus (S.A.T.B.) is intersected by *Recitativo* passages accompanying the orchestral *ritornelli* (2 Ob., Corno, Strings, Continuo)[1].

Melody: "*Welt, ade! ich bin dein müde*"

Johann Rosenmüller 1682

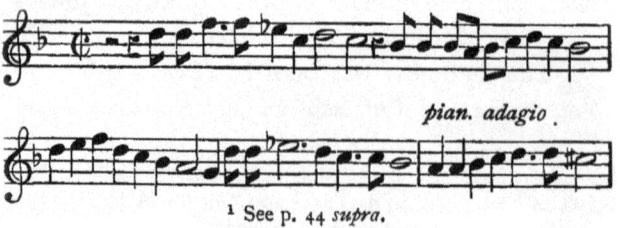

---

[1] See p. 44 *supra.*

forte allegro

(*b*)

The melody of the concluding Choral was composed by Johann Rosenmüller for the Hymn, "Welt, ade! ich bin dein müde" (1649).

Rosenmüller was born at Pelsnitz in Saxony in 1619. In 1642 he was assistant master in St Thomas' School, Leipzig, and a pupil of Tobias Michael, Cantor there. In 1651 he was appointed Organist of St Nicolas' Church, Leipzig. Imprisoned in 1655 for a grave offence, he lived thereafter in Hamburg and Italy. In 1674 he was appointed Kapellmeister at Wolfenbüttel, and died there in 1684.

The five-part setting of the melody which Bach uses here was published by Gottfried Vopelius in his *Neu Leipziger Gesangbuch* (Leipzig, 1682 [1681][1]). Vopelius was born in 1645, at Herwigsdorf, near Löbau, became Cantor of St Nicolas', Leipzig, in 1675, and died in 1715.

Bach uses the melody also in Cantata 158.

[1] The melody and Bass had appeared three years earlier in Johann Quirsfeld's *Geistlicher Harffen-Klang* (Leipzig, 1679).

The words of the concluding Choral are the first stanza of Johann Georg Albinus' funerary Hymn, "Welt, ade! ich bin dein müde." The Hymn was written in 1649 for the funeral of the daughter of Abraham Teller, Archidiaconus of St Nicolas'.

Albinus was born at Unter-Nessa, Saxony, in 1624. He was educated at Leipzig and in 1653 was appointed Rector of the Cathedral School, Naumburg. In 1657 he became pastor of St Othmar's Church there. He died in 1679. The Hymn was published first as a broadsheet in 1649 and later in the Brandenburg *Neu-Vollständigers Gesang-Buch* (Bayreuth, 1668) and *Geistliches Neuvermehrtes Gesang-Buch* (Schleusingen, 1672) :

> Welt, ade! ich bin dein müde,
> Ich will nach dem Himmel zu,
> Da wird sein der rechte Friede
> Und die ew'ge, stolze Ruh.
> Welt, bei dir ist Krieg und Streit,
> Nichts denn lauter Eitelkeit;
> In dem Himmel allezeit
> Friede, Freud' und Seeligkeit.
>
> B.G. v. (i) 244.

Translations of the Hymn into English are noted in the *Dictionary of Hymnology*, p. 37.

Form. Simple (2 *Ob., Corno, Strings, Continuo*). *Choralgesänge*, No. 350. Erk, No. 134, prints Vopelius' 1682 version[1].

[1] See Spitta, II. 452 n.

CANTATA XXVIII. GOTTLOB! NUN GEHT DAS JAHR ZU ENDE[1]. Sunday after Christmas (*c.* 1725[2])

(*a*)

The melody of the second movement is Johann Kugelmann's (?) "Nun lob', mein' Seel', den Herren" (see Cantata 17). The words of the movement are the first stanza of Johann Graumann's Hymn, "Nun lob', mein' Seel', den Herren" (see Cantata 17):

> Nun lob', mein' Seel', den Herren,
> Was[3] in mir ist, den Namen sein!
> Sein Wohlthat thut er mehren,
> Vergiss es nicht, O Herze mein.
> Hat dir dein' Sünd' vergeben,
> Und heilt dein' Schwachheit gross,
> Errett't dein armes Leben,
> Nimmt dich in seinen Schoos;
> Mit reichem Trost beschüttet,
> Verjüngt dem Adler gleich.
> Der Kön'g schafft Recht, behütet
> Die leiden in seinem Reich.   B.G. v. (i) 258.

Form.   Choral Motett (*Cornetto*, 3 *Trombones, 2 Ob., Strings, Continuo*).   Erk, No. 319[4].

[1] English versions of the Cantata are published by Novello & Co., "O praise the Lord for all His mercies," and Breitkopf & Haertel, "Praise God! the year draws to its closing."

[2] Wustmann suggests *c.* 1736.   [3] 1540 Und was.

[4] The third movement ("Sei Lob und Preis mit Ehren") of the otherwise spurious Bach Motett, "Jauchzet dem Herrn alle Welt," is almost identical with the above Chorus, excepting for the substitution of the fifth for the first stanza of Graumann's Hymn. See Spitta, II. 716.

CANTATA XXIX

(*b*)

For the melody of the concluding Choral, "Helft mir Gott's Güte preisen," see Cantata 11.

The words of the concluding Choral are the sixth stanza of Paul Eber's New Year's Hymn, "Helft mir Gott's Güte preisen" (see Cantata 16):

> All' solch' dein' Güt' wir preisen,
> Vater in's Himmelsthron,
> Die du uns thust beweisen,
> Durch Christum, deinen Sohn,
> Und bitten ferner[1] dich:
> Gieb uns ein friedlich's[2] Jahre,
> Für allem Leid bewahre
> Und nähr' uns mildiglich.
> B.G. v. (i) 272.

Form. Simple (*Cornetto*, 3 *Trombones*, 2 *Ob.*, *Taille*[3], *Strings*, *Continuo*). *Choralgesänge*, No. 124.

CANTATA XXIX. WIR DANKEN DIR, GOTT, WIR DANKEN DIR. For the Inauguration of the Town Council, Leipzig (1731)

For the melody of the concluding Choral, Johann Kugelmann's (?) "Nun lob', mein' Seel', den Herren," see Cantata 17.

The words of the concluding Choral are the fifth stanza of Johann Graumann's Hymn, "Nun lob', mein' Seel', den Herren" (see Cantata 17).

[1] *c.* 1580 förder.   [2] *c.* 1580 frölich.
[3] The Taille was a Tenor Bassoon.

The stanza is an addendum to the four published in 1540 and appeared posthumously in a broadsheet reprint of the Hymn at Nürnberg c. 1555:

> * Sei Lob und Preis mit Ehren,
> Gott Vater, Sohn, heiligem Geist!
> Der woll' in uns vermehren,
> Was er uns aus Gnaden verheisst,
> Dass wir ihm fest vertrauen,
> Gänzlich verlass'n auf ihn,
> Von Herzen auf ihn bauen,
> Dass uns'r Herz, Muth und Sinn
> Ihm tröstlich soll'n anhangen;
> Drauf singen wir zur Stund':
> Amen! wir werden's erlangen,
> Glaub'n wir aus Herzens Grund.
> B.G. v. (i) 316.

Form. Embellished (3 *Trombe, Timpani*, 2 *Ob.*, *Strings, Organ, Continuo*). *Choralgesänge*, No. 272.

CANTATA XXX. FREUE DICH, ERLÖSTE SCHAAR[1].
Feast of St John Baptist (1738[2])

For the melody of the concluding Choral of Part I, Louis Bourgeois' "Ainsi qu'on oit le cerf," see Cantata 13.

The words of the concluding Choral of Part I are the third stanza of Johannes Olearius' Hymn

---

[1] An English version of the Cantata, "Come rejoice, ye faithful," is published by Breitkopf & Haertel.
[2] The Cantata is founded upon an earlier secular work. See Spitta, III. 77.

for St John Baptist's Day, "Tröstet, tröstet, meine Lieben," first published in his *Geistliche Singe-Kunst* (Leipzig, 1671), to Bourgeois' melody (*supra*). Olearius was born at Halle in 1611. In 1643 he was appointed Court Preacher and Private Chaplain there to Duke August of Saxe-Weissenfels. After 1680 he held appointments as Kirchenrath and General Superintendent at Weissenfels. He died in 1684. His *Geistliche Singe-Kunst* of 1671 was one of the largest and best German Hymn books of the seventeenth century, and contained 302 hymns by Olearius himself:

> Eine Stimme lässt sich hören
> In der Wüsten, weit und breit,
> Alle Menschen zu bekehren :
> Macht dem Herrn den Weg bereit,
> Machet Gott ein' eb'ne Bahn,
> Alle Welt soll heben an,
> Alle Thäler zu erhöhen,
> Dass die Berge niedrig stehen.
> B.G. v. (i) 360.

English translations of the Hymn are noted in the *Dictionary of Hymnology*, p. 866.

Form. Simple (2 *Fl.*, 2 *Ob.*, Strings, Organ, Continuo). *Choralgesänge*, No. 103.

CANTATA XXXI. DER HIMMEL LACHT, DIE ERDE JUBILIRET. Easter Day (1715[1])

For the words and melody of the concluding Choral, Nicolaus Herman's Hymn, "Wenn mein Stündlein vorhanden ist," see Cantata 15. The words are the fifth stanza of the Hymn, which was posthumously added to its original four stanzas in *Drei schöne geistliche Lieder* (Cöln, 1574)[2]. It is not by Herman:

> So fahr' ich hin[3] zu Jesu Christ,
> Mein' Arm'[4] thu' ich ausstrecken;
> So schlaf' ich ein und ruhe fein,
> Kein Mensch kann mich aufwecken:
> Denn Jesus Christus, Gottes Sohn[5],
> Der wird die Himmelsthür[6] aufthun,
> Mich führ'n zum[7] ew'gen Leben.
>
> B.G. vii. 50.

Form. Embellished (*Tromba*, 3 *Ob.*, *Taille*[8], *Fagotto, Strings, Continuo*). *Choralgesänge*, No. 357.

Bach introduces the melody into the Soprano Aria, "Letzte Stunde, brich herein," as an *obbligato* for the Violins and Viola (B.G. vii. 44).

[1] Schweitzer, II. 141 n., suggests *c.* 1723 as the date of Bach's revision of the 1715 work to the form in which we have it.
[2] Wackernagel, III. 1212, prints from a text of *c.* 1575.
[3] *c.* 1575 Ich fahr dahin. [4] *c.* 1575 hend.
[5] *c.* 1575 war Gottes son.
[6] *c.* 1575 Der wird uns Chor und tempel.
[7] *c.* 1575 Ein lassen zu dem.
[8] The Taille was a Tenor Bassoon.

CANTATA XXXII. LIEBSTER JESU, MEIN VER-
LANGEN[1]. First Sunday after the Epiphany
(c. 1740)

For the melody of the concluding Choral, Louis Bourgeois' "Ainsi qu'on oit," see Cantata 13.

The words of the concluding Choral are the twelfth stanza of Paul Gerhardt's Lenten Hymn, "Weg, mein Herz, mit den Gedanken," first published in Johann Crüger's *Praxis Pietatis Melica* (Berlin, 1647), to another melody ("Zion klagt mit Angst und Schmerzen"):

> Mein Gott, öffne mir die Pforten
> Solcher Gnad' und Gütigkeit,
> Lass mich allzeit aller Orten
> Schmecken deine Süssigkeit!
> Liebe mich, und treib' mich an,
> Dass ich dich, so gut ich kann,
> Wiederum umfang' und liebe,
> Und ja nun nicht mehr betrübe.
> B.G. vii. 80.

Translations of the Hymn into English are noted in the *Dictionary of Hymnology*, p. 412.

Form. Simple (*Oboe, Strings, Continuo*). *Choralgesänge*, No. 102.

---

[1] An English version of the Cantata is published by Breitkopf & Haertel, "Blessed Jesus, priceless treasure."

CANTATA XXXIII. ALLEIN ZU DIR, HERR JESU CHRIST. Thirteenth Sunday after Trinity (*c.* 1740)

Melody: "*Allein zu dir, Herr Jesu Christ*"
Anon. *c.* 1541

* *sic.*

Melody: "*Allein zu dir, Herr Jesu Christ*"   Anon. 1545

A Choral Cantata, on Johannes Schneesing's penitential Hymn, "Allein zu dir, Herr Jesu

Christ," which was published as a Nürnberg broadsheet *c.* 1541 and was included by Luther in Valentin Babst's *Geystliche Lieder* (Leipzig, 1545), with the second version of the melody printed above.

Schneesing, a native of Frankfort a. Main, was pastor of Friemar, near Gotha, where he died in 1567. He is said to have been much interested in teaching children the hymns and tunes which he composed.

The melody of Schneesing's Hymn, which Bach uses in the opening and closing movements of the Cantata in its 1545 form, was first published, with the Hymn, in an undated broadsheet, probably at Wittenberg, *c.* 1541, and thence in Valentin Babst's Hymn book (*supra*). The tune has been attributed to Schneesing.

Bach has not used the melody elsewhere in the Cantatas, Oratorios, or Motetts. There is another harmonisation of it in the *Choralgesänge*, No. 15.

(*a*)

The words of the opening movement are the first stanza of Schneesing's Hymn:

> Allein zu dir, Herr Jesu Christ,
> Mein' Hoffnung steht auf Erden;
> Ich weiss, dass du mein Tröster bist,
> Kein Trost mag mir sonst werden.

Von Anbeginn ist nichts erkor'n,
Auf Erden war[1] kein Mensch gebor'n,
Der mir aus Nöthen helfen kann,
Ich ruf' dich an[2],
Zu dem ich mein[3] Vertrauen hab'.
B.G. vii. 83.

English translations of the Hymn are noted in the *Dictionary of Hymnology*, p. 1015.

Form. Choral Fantasia (2 *Ob.*, *Strings*, *Organ*, *Continuo*).

(*b*)

The words of the concluding Choral are the fourth stanza of Schneesing's Hymn:

> Ehr' sei Gott in dem höchsten Thron,
> Dem Vater aller Güte,
> Und Jesum Christ, sein'm liebsten[4] Sohn,
> Der uns allzeit behüte[5],
> Und[6] Gott, dem heiligen Geiste,
> Der uns sein' Hülf' allzeit leiste,
> Damit wir ihm gefällig sein,
> Hier in dieser Zeit
> Und folgends in der[7] Ewigkeit.
B.G. vii. 114.

Form. Simple (2 *Ob.*, *Strings*, *Organ*, *Continuo*). *Choralgesänge*, No. 16.

[1] *c.* 1541 ist.
[2] *c.* 1541 Dich ruff ich an.
[3] *c.* 1541 all mein.
[4] *c.* 1541 einigen.
[5] *c.* 1541 Der wöll uns all behüten.
[6] *c.* 1541 Auch.
[7] *c.* 1541 im in.

CANTATA XXXVI. SCHWINGT FREUDIG EUCH EMPOR. First Sunday in Advent (c. 1730[1])

Melody: "*Nun komm, der Heiden Heiland*" Anon. 1524

Melody: "*Veni Redemptor gentium*" Anon. 1531[2]

Ve - ni Re-demp-tor gen-ti - um, ost - en-de par-tum vir-gi nis, mi-re-tur om - ne sae-cu - lum, ta - lis de - cet par - tus De - um.

(*a*)

For the second movement of Part I of the Cantata Bach uses the words and melody of Luther's Christmas Hymn, "Nun komm, der Heiden Heiland." The Hymn, a translation of "Veni Redemptor gentium," attributed to St Ambrose, was first published in the Erfurt

---

[1] A revision of an earlier (1726) work. See Spitta, II. 158, 471.

[2] From Michael Weisse's *Ein New Gesengbuchlen* (Jung Bunzlau, 1531), where the melody is set to Weisse's Hymn, "Von Adam her so lange Zeit."

Enchiridion (1524), with the melody, a simplification of that of "Veni Redemptor gentium." Both Hymn and melody are also in Walther's *Geystliche gesangk Buchleyn* (1524), and his assistance in reconstructing the tune may be inferred. Bach uses the melody elsewhere in Cantatas 61 and 62. Organ Works, N. xv. 3; xvii. 46, 49, 52; xviii. 83. The words of the second movement of Part I are the first stanza of Luther's Hymn:

> Nun komm, der Heiden Heiland,
> Der Jungfrauen Kind erkannt,
> Dess sich wundert alle Welt:
> Gott solch' Geburt ihm bestellt. B.G. vii. 236.

Translations of the Hymn into English are noted in the *Dictionary of Hymnology*, p. 1212.

Form. Duetto for Soprano and Alto (2 Ob. d'amore, Organ, Continuo), treating the melody in canon freely.

(*b*)

The words and melody of the concluding Choral of Part I are Philipp Nicolai's "Wie schön leuchtet der Morgenstern" (see Cantata 1). The words are the sixth stanza of the Hymn:

> Zwingt die Saiten in Cythara
> Und lasst die süsse Musica
> Ganz freudenreich erschallen,
> Dass ich möge mit Jesulein,
> Dem wunderschönen Bräut'gam mein,
> In steter Liebe wallen.

Singet, springet,
Jubiliret, triumphiret,
Dankt dem Herren!
Gross ist der König der Ehren. B.G. vii. 243.

Form. Simple (2 *Ob. d'amore, Strings, Organ, Continuo*). *Choralgesänge,* No. 377.

(c)

The words and melody of the second movement of Part II of the Cantata are Luther's "Nun komm, der Heiden Heiland" (see *a supra*). The words are the sixth stanza of the Hymn:

Der du bist dem Vater gleich,
Führ' hinaus den Sieg im Fleisch,
Dass dein ewig Gott's gewalt'
In uns das krank' Fleisch enthalt'.

B.G. vii. 251.

Form. Tenor Unison Choral (2 *Ob. d'amore, Organ, Continuo*).

(d)

The words and melody of the concluding Choral are Luther's "Nun komm, der Heiden Heiland" (see *a supra*). The words are the eighth stanza of the Hymn:

Lob sei Gott dem Vater g'thon[1],
Lob sei Gott sein'm ein'gen Sohn,
Lob sei Gott dem heil'gen Geist,
Immer und in Ewigkeit! B.G. vii. 258.

Form. Simple (2 *Ob. d'amore, Strings, Organ, Continuo*). *Choralgesänge,* No. 264.

[1] 1524 thon.

Cantata XXXVII. Wer da glaubet und getauft wird. Ascension Day (*c.* 1727)

(*a*)

The melody and Hymn of the third movement are Philipp Nicolai's " Wie schön leuchtet der Morgenstern " (see Cantata 1). The words are the fifth stanza of the Hymn:

> Herr Gott Vater, mein starker Held!
> Du hast mich ewig vor der Welt
> In deinem Sohn geliebet.
> Dein Sohn hat mich sich[1] selbst vertraut,
> Er ist mein Schatz, ich bin sein' Braut,
> Sehr hoch in ihm erfreuet.
> Eya, eya!
> Himmlisch Leben wird ergeben
> Mir dort oben;
> Ewig soll mein Herz ihn loben.
>   B.G. vii. 272.

Form. Soprano and Alto *Duetto* (*Continuo*) in canon on the melody.

Melody: "*Lob' Gott getrost mit Singen*"   Anon. 1544

---

[1] 1599 ihm.

Melody: "*Ich dank' dir, lieber Herre*"   Reconstruction 1662

(b)

The words and melody of the concluding Choral are Johann Kolross' (Rhodanthracius) Morning Hymn, "Ich dank' dir, lieber Herre," first published as a broadsheet at Nürnberg, c. 1535, and included in Valentin S. Schumann's *Geistliche lieder auffs new gebessert und gemehrt* (Leipzig, 1539).

The author is said to have been a pastor at Basel and to have died there in 1558.

The melody "Ich dank' dir, lieber Herre" has a secular origin. It was associated in 1532 with the song, "Entlaubt ist uns der Walde." In 1544 Johann Roh or Horn attached it to his Hymn, "Lob' Gott getrost mit Singen," in his *Ein Gesangbuch der Brüder inn Behemen und Merherrn*" (Nürnberg, 1544). In a simplified form the tune was attached to Kolross' Hymn in the 1662 (Frankfort) *Praxis Pietatis Melica*.

The melody does not occur elsewhere in the Cantatas or Oratorios. *Choralgesänge*, Nos. 176, 177.

The words of the concluding Choral are the fourth stanza of the Hymn:

> Den Glauben mir verleihe
> An dein'n Sohn, Jesum Christ,
> Mein' Sünd' mir auch verzeihe
> Allhier zu dieser Frist.
> Du wirst mir's nicht versagen,
> Was[1] du verheissen hast,
> Dass er mein' Sünd' thu' tragen
> Und lös' mich von der Last. B.G. vii. 282.

Translations are noted in the *Dictionary of Hymnology*, p. 631.

Form. Simple (2 *Ob. d'amore, Strings, Continuo*). *Choralgesänge*, No. 178.

CANTATA XXXVIII. AUS TIEFER NOTH SCHREI ICH ZU DIR[2]. Twenty-first Sunday after Trinity (*c.* 1740)

Melody: "*Aus tiefer Noth schrei ich zu dir*"
?Martin Luther 1524

---

[1] *c.* 1535 Wie.
[2] An English version of the Cantata, "From depths of woe I call on Thee," is published by Novello & Co.

A Choral Cantata, on Martin Luther's free translation of Psalm cxxx, written in 1523 and published in 1524, with the melody, in Walther's *Geystliche gesangk Buchleyn* (Wittenberg). An earlier version of the Hymn (with the melody) is in *Eyn Enchiridion oder Handbuchlein* (Erfurt, 1524), and (to another tune) in *Etlich Christlich lider* (Wittenberg, 1524). The tune is known as "Luther's 130th," and may be regarded with some probability as his composition.

The melody does not occur elsewhere in the Cantatas or Oratorios. Organ Works, N. xvi. 68, 72.

(*a*)

The words of the opening movement are the first stanza of Luther's Hymn:

> Aus tiefer Noth schrei ich zu dir,
> Herr Gott, erhör' mein Rufen!
> Dein' gnädig' Ohr' neig her zu mir[1],
> Und meiner Bitt' sie öffne.
> Denn so du willt das sehen an,
> Was Sünd' und Unrecht ist gethan;
> Wer kann, Herr, vor dir bleiben?
> B.G. vii. 285.

Translations of the Hymn into English are noted in the *Dictionary of Hymnology*, pp. 96, 1607.

Form. Choral Motett (2 *Ob.*, 4 *Trombones, Strings, Continuo*). Erk, No. 150.

---

[1] 1524 Deyn gnedig oren ker zu myr.

CANTATA XXXIX 215

(b)

The words of the concluding Choral are the fifth stanza of Luther's Hymn :

> Ob bei uns ist der Sünden viel,
> Bei Gott ist viel mehr Gnade,
> Sein' Hand zu helfen hat kein Ziel,
> Wie gross auch sei der Schade.
> Er ist allein der gute Hirt,
> Der Israel erlösen wird
> Aus seinen Sünden allen.   B.G. vii. 300.

Form. Simple (4 *Trombones*, 2 *Ob.*, *Strings*, *Continuo*). *Choralgesänge*, No. 31.

Bach introduces the melody (*basso marcato*) into the accompaniment of the Soprano *Recitativo a battuta*, "Ach! dass mein Glaube" (B.G vii. 295).

CANTATA XXXIX. BRICH DEM HUNGRIGEN DEIN BROD[1]. First Sunday after Trinity (*c.* 1740)

The melody of the concluding Choral is Louis Bourgeois' "Ainsi qu'on oit" (see Cantata 13).

The words of the concluding Choral are the sixth stanza of David Denicke's paraphrase of the Beatitudes, "Kommt, lasst euch den Herren lehren." The Hymn was first published, to Bourgeois' melody, in the *New Ordentlich Gesangbuch* (Brunswick, 1648), of which Denicke and Justus Gesenius (1601-73) were the editors.

[1] An English version of the Cantata, "Give the hungry man thy bread," is published by Novello & Co.

Denicke was born at Zittau in 1603. In 1629 he became tutor to the sons of Duke Georg of Brunswick-Lüneburg. He held various important public offices in Hanover and died in 1680:

> Selig sind, die aus Erbarmen
> Sich annehmen fremder Noth,
> Sind mitleidig mit den Armen,
> Bitten treulich für sie Gott.
> Die behülflich sind mit Rath,
> Auch, so möglich, mit der That,
> Werden wieder Hülf' empfangen
> Und Barmherzigkeit erlangen.
>
> B.G. vii. 348.

Translations of the Hymn into English are noted in the *Dictionary of Hymnology*, p. 287.

Form. Simple (2 *Fl.*, 2 *Ob.*, *Strings*, *Continuo*). *Choralgesänge*, No. 104.

CANTATA XL. DAZU IST ERSCHIENEN DER SOHN GOTTES[1]. Feast of St Stephen (Christmas) (*c.* 1723)

Melody: " *Wir Christenleut'* "

Caspar Fuger the younger 1593

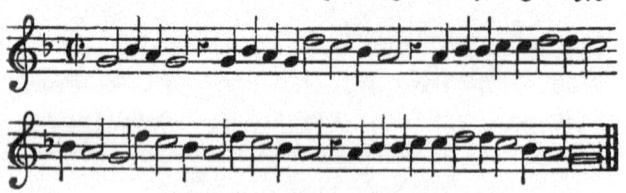

---

[1] An English version of the Cantata, "To this end appeared the Son of God," is published by Breitkopf & Haertel.

CANTATA XL 217

(a)

The words and melody of the third movement are from Caspar Fuger's Christmas Hymn, "Wir Christenleut'." The melody, which is found in MS. 1589 associated with the Hymn, may be attributed to Caspar Fuger, the younger[1], and was first published in Martin Fritzsch's *Gesangbuch. Darinnen Christliche Psalmen unnd Kirchen Lieder* (Dresden, 1593). Bach uses the melody also in Cantatas 110 and 142, and in the "Christmas Oratorio," No. 35. Organ Works, N. xv. 36; xix. 28.

The Hymn, attributed to the elder Caspar Fuger, was probably written about 1552, and was published first in *Drey schöne Newe Geistliche Gesenge* (1592). The words are the third stanza of the Hymn:

> Die Sünd' macht Leid;
> Christus bringt Freud',
> Weil er zu Trost[2] in diese Welt gekommen[3].
> Mit uns ist Gott
> Nun in der[4] Noth:
> Wer ist, der uns als[5] Christen kann verdammen?
> B.G. vii. 377.

Translations of the Hymn into English are noted in the *Dictionary of Hymnology*, p. 401.

Form. Simple (2 *Ob., Corno, Strings, Continuo*). *Choralgesänge*, No. 379.

---

[1] See *Bach's Chorals*, Part I, p. 51. [2] 1592 uns.
[3] 1592 ist kommen. [4] 1592 dieser. [5] 1592 jetzt uns.

218   CANTATA XL

Melody: "Meine Hoffnung stehet feste"   Anon. 1680

Melody: "Bleiches Antlitz, sei gegrüsset"
    Friedrich Funcke 1686

Melody: "Einen guten Kampf hab' ich"   Anon. 1713

(b)

The words and melody of the sixth movement are from Paul Gerhardt's "Schwing' dich auf zu deinem Gott." The Hymn was first published, to another tune, in Johann Crüger's 1653 (Berlin) edition of his *Praxis Pietatis Melica*.

The melody which Bach uses in this movement is found, in identical form, as No. 144 of the second Part of *Johann Sebastian Bachs vierstimmige Choralgesänge gesammlet von Carl Philipp Emmanuel Bach* (Berlin and Leipzig, 1769). According to the *Choralgesänge*, No. 305, the tune is a slight reconstruction ("etwas umgebildet") of a melody (Zahn, iv. No. 6295a) published in the second Part of Daniel Vetter's *Musicalische Kirch- und Hauss-Ergötzlichkeit* (Leipzig, 1713) in association with Heinrich Albert's (1604–51) "Einen guten Kampf hab' ich." Bach's and Vetter's forms clearly are related. But Bach's text is still closer to a melody which occurs in Joachim Neander's (1650–80) *Glaub- und Liebesübung* (Bremen, 1680), set to his own "Meine Hoffnung stehet feste." Described by Neander as a "bekannte Melodie," the apparent original of it is found in the *Lüneburgisches Gesangbuch* (Lüneburg, 1686), set to Johann Rist's "Bleiches Antlitz, sei gegrüsset." The tune there bears the initials "F. F.," i.e. Friedrich Funcke, who was born in 1642, was Cantor of St John's Church, Lüneburg, 1664–94, and died 1699. Bach's melody therefore must either accept Funcke as its author, or the two tunes must be held derivatives of an original now lost. In any case the ascription of the tune to Bach is inaccurate.

The melody does not occur elsewhere in Bach's works.

The words of the sixth movement of the Cantata are the second stanza of Paul Gerhardt's Hymn:

> Schüttle[1] deinen Kopf und sprich:
> Fleuch, du alte Schlange!
> Was erneurst du deinen Stich,
> Machst mir angst und bange?
> Ist dir doch der Kopf zerknickt,
> Und ich bin durch's Leiden
> Meines Heilands dir entrückt[2]
> In den Saal der Freuden. B.G. vii. 387.

Form. Simple (*Corno*, 2 *Ob.*, *Strings, Continuo*). *Choralgesänge*, No. 305.

Melody: "*Freuet euch, ihr Christen alle*"
? Andreas Hammerschmidt 1646

[1] 1653 Schütte. [2] 1653 entzückt.

(c)

The words of the concluding Choral are from Christian Keimann's Christmas Hymn, "Freuet euch, ihr Christen alle," published, with the tune, in Part IV of Andreas Hammerschmidt's *Musicalischer Andachten Geistlicher Moteten undt Concerten* (Freiberg, 1646).

Andreas Hammerschmidt, the composer (?) of the melody, was born at Brüx in Bohemia in 1612. He received his musical education from Stephen Otto, Cantor at Schandau, and in 1635 became Organist of St Peter's Church, Freiberg (Saxony). From thence he went (1639) to Zittau as Organist of St John's Church, and died there in 1675.

Bach has not used the melody elsewhere.

The words of the concluding Choral are the fourth stanza of Keimann's Hymn. Keimann was born in 1607 at Pankratz in Bohemia. In 1634 he was appointed Co-rector, and in 1638 Rector, of the Gymnasium at Zittau. He died in 1662. The Hymn is said to have been written at Christmas 1645. The fourth stanza may refer to the opening of the Peace Congresses at Münster and Osnabrück which concluded the Thirty Years' War:

> Jesu, nimm dich deiner Glieder
> Ferner in Genaden an;
> Schenke, was man bitten kann,
> Zu erquicken deine Brüder;

222   CANTATA XLI

  Gieb der ganzen Christenschaar
  Frieden und ein sel'ges Jahr!
  Freude, Freude über Freude!
  Christus wehret allem Leide.
  Wonne, Wonne über Wonne:
  Er ist die Genadensonne. B.G. vii. 394.
 An English translation of the Hymn is noted in
the *Dictionary of Hymnology*, p. 614.
  Form. Simple (*Corno*, 2 *Ob.*, *Strings, Continuo*).
Choralgesänge, No. 105.

CANTATA XLI. JESU, NUN SEI GEPREISET[1].
 Feast of the Circumcision (New Year's Day)
(*c.* 1740)

Melody: "*Jesu, nun sei gepreiset*"   Anon. 1591

---

[1] An English version of the Cantata, "Jesus, now will we praise Thee," is published by Novello & Co.

A Choral Cantata, on Johann Hermann's New Year's Hymn, "Jesu, nun sei gepreiset." Words and melody were published together in the Wittenberg collection of Christmas Hymns, *Cantilenae latinae et germanicae...Lateinische und Deutsche Weinacht Lieder* (Wittenberg, 1591). Of the author nothing positive is known. It is conjectured that he was a Lutheran theologian resident at Wittenberg 1548–63.

The melody, which Bach uses in the first and last movements, occurs also in Cantatas 171 and 190. In all three cases he introduces an important modification of the original tune by concluding with the opening phrases of the Hymn. There is another version of the melody in the *Choralgesänge*, No. 203, which is closer to the 1591 text.

(*a*)

The words of the opening movement are the first stanza of Hermann's Hymn:

> Jesu, nun sei gepreiset
> Zu diesem neuen Jahr',
> Für dein' Güt', uns beweiset
> In aller Noth und Gefahr,
> Dass wir haben erlebet
> Die neu', fröhliche Zeit,
> Die voller Gnade schwebet
> Und ew'ger Seeligkeit;
> Dass wir in guter Stille
> Das alt' Jahr hab'n erfüllet.

> Wir woll'n uns dir ergeben
> Jetzund und immerdar,
> Behüt' Leib, Seel'[1] und Leben
> Hinfort durch's[2] ganze Jahr ![3]   B.G. x. 3.

Form. Choral Fantasia (3 *Trombe, Timpani,* 3 *Ob., Strings, Organ, Continuo*)[4].

(*b*)

The words of the concluding Choral are the third stanza of Hermann's Hymn:

> Dein ist allein die Ehre,
> Dein ist allein der Ruhm;
> Geduld im Kreuz uns lehre,
> Regier' all' unser Thun,
> Bis wir fröhlich[5] abscheiden
> In's ewig' Himmelreich[6],
> Zu wahrem Fried' und Freude,
> Den Heil'gen Gottes gleich.
> Indess mach's mit uns Allen
> Nach deinem Wohlgefallen:
> Solch's singet heut ohn' Scherzen
> Die christgläubige Schaar,
> Und wünscht mit Mund und Herzen
> Ein selig's neues Jahr.   B.G. x. 58.

Form. Extended (3 *Trombe, Timpani,* 3 *Ob., Strings, Organ, Continuo*). *Choralgesänge,* No. 204.

---

[1] 1593 Behüt uns Leib.   [2] 1593 das.
[3] Wackernagel, v. 195, prints from a text of 1593.
[4] See Spitta, III. 101, on the hybrid form of the movement.
[5] 1593 getrost.   [6] 1593 Vaters Reich.

CANTATA XLII. AM ABEND ABER DESSELBIGEN
SABBATHS. First Sunday after Easter ("Quasimodo geniti") (*c.* 1731[1])

(*a*)

The words of the fourth movement are the first stanza of Johann Michael Altenburg's "Verzage nicht, du Häuflein klein," first published (to no specified tune) as a broadsheet *c.* 1632 (Leipzig), and later in *Andächtige Hertz- und Seelen-Musica* (Nordhausen, *c.* 1635). The Hymn is also attributed, on doubtful evidence, to Gustavus Adolphus of Sweden.

Altenburg was born at Alach, near Erfurt, in 1584. In 1608 he was appointed pastor of Ilversgehofen, near Erfurt, and later to other charges near the city. Forced by the war to seek refuge in Erfurt in 1631, he composed the Hymn "Verzage nicht" there. The rest of his life was passed in Erfurt, where he died in 1640. He was a good musician and in early life was Cantor of St Andrew's Church, Erfurt. A number of hymn melodies by him are known:

> Verzage nicht, O[2] Haüflein klein,
> Obgleich[3] die Feinde willens sein,
> Dich gänzlich zu verstören,
> Und suchen deinen Untergang,
> Davon dir wird rechst[4] angst und bang:
> Es wird nicht lange[5] währen. B.G. x. 82.

[1] See Wustmann, p. 281.   [2] *c.* 1632 du.
[3] *c.* 1632 Ob schon.   [4] *c.* 1632 gantz.   [5] *c.* 1632 lang mehr.

226   CANTATA XLII

Translations of the Hymn into English are noted in the *Dictionary of Hymnology*, pp. 55, 1721.

Form. A Soprano and Tenor *Duetto* (*Fagotto, Violoncello, Organ, Continuo*). Though marked "Choral," Bach does not use the Hymn melody.

Melody: "*Verleih' uns Frieden gnädiglich*"   Anon. 1535

(1) 1531.

Melody: "*Gieb unsern Fürsten*"   Anon. 1566

Gieb un-sern Für-sten und al-ler O-ber-keit Fried und gut

Re-gi-ment, das wir un-ter ih-nen ein ge-ruh-lich und stil-les

Le-ben füh-ren mö-gen in al-ler Gott-se-lig-keit und

Ehr- -bar-keit,

(b)

The melody of the last movement is that of Luther's "Verleih' uns Frieden gnädiglich," published, with the Hymn, in *Kirchē gesenge, mit vil schönen Psalmen unnd Melodey* (Nürnberg, 1531), and in Joseph Klug's *Geistliche Lieder* (Wittenberg, 1535 [1529]). The musical texts are nearly identical, Bach's version conforming rather to the latter. The tune bears relationship to that of Luther's "Erhalt' uns, Herr" (see Cantata 6): both derive from the melody of the Antiphon, "Da pacem, Domine." The melody occurs also in Cantata 126. There is late sixteenth century authority for the F sharp at the fourth note (*supra*), which Bach adopts. But his variation of the second line is not indicated by Zahn as occurring earlier.

The melody of the additional stanza, "Gieb unsern Fürsten," was first published, with the Hymn, in *Das christlich Kinderlied D. Martini Lutheri* (Wittenberg, 1566). The melody occurs also in Cantata 126. The "Amen" which Bach uses is found in association with the melody in 1573.

The words of the concluding Choral are the first stanza of Luther's "Verleih' uns Frieden gnädiglich," a translation of the Antiphon, "Da pacem, Domine." It appeared first in prose in 1527 and in metrical form in Klug's *Geistliche Lieder* (*supra*). The additional stanza, "Gieb

unsern Fürsten," founded on 1 Timothy ii. 1, 2,
was attached to the Hymn in 1566 (*supra*):

> Verleih' uns Frieden gnädiglich,
> Herr Gott, zu unsern Zeiten,
> Es ist ja doch[1] kein Andrer nicht,
> Der für uns könnte streiten,
> Den du uns'r Gott alleine.
>
> Gieb unsern Fürsten und der[2] Obrigkeit
> Fried' und gut Regiment,
> Dass wir unter ihnen
> Ein geruhig[3] und stilles Leben führen mögen
> In aller Gottseligkeit und Ehrbarkeit, Amen!
> B.G. x. 91.

Translations of the Hymn into English are noted in the *Dictionary of Hymnology*, p. 276.

Form. Simple (2 *Ob.*, *Fagotto*, *Strings*, *Organ*, *Continuo*). *Choralgesänge*, No. 322.

CANTATA XLIII. GOTT FÄHRET AUF MIT JAUCHZEN[4]. Ascension Day (1735)

For the melody of the concluding Choral, Johann Schop's "Ermuntre dich, mein schwacher Geist," see Cantata 11.

The words are the first and thirteenth stanzas of Johann Rist's Ascension Hymn, "Du Lebensfürst, Herr Jesu Christ" (see Cantata 11):

---

[1] 1535 denn.   [2] 1566 aller.   [3] 1566 geruhlich.
[4] An English version of the Cantata, "God goeth up with shouting," is published by Novello & Co.

Du Lebensfürst, Herr Jesu Christ,
Der du bist aufgenommen
Gen Himmel, da dein Vater ist
Und die Gemein' der Frommen:
Wie soll ich deinen grossen Sieg,
Den du durch einen[1] schweren Krieg
Erworben hast, recht preisen,
Und dir g'nug Ehr' erweisen?

Zieh' uns dir nach, so laufen wir,
Gieb uns des Glaubens Flügel!
Hilf, dass wir fliehen weit von hier
Auf Israelis Hügel.
Mein Gott! wann fahr' ich doch dahin,
Woselbst ich ewig[2] fröhlich bin?
Wann werd' ich vor dir stehen,
Dein Angesicht zu sehen?
B.G. x. 126.

Form. Simple (3 *Trombe*, 2 *Ob.*, *Strings*, *Continuo*). *Choralgesänge*, No. 81.

CANTATA XLIV. SIE WERDEN EUCH IN DEN BANN THUN[3]. Sixth Sunday after Easter ("Exaudi")[4] (*c.* 1725)

(*a*)

For the melody of the fourth movement, "Ach Gott, wie manches Herzeleid," see Cantata 3.

[1] 1641 Den du uns durch den.
[2] 1641 Wo ich ohn' Ende.
[3] An English version of the Cantata, "You will they put under ban," is published by Breitkopf & Haertel.
[4] The Sunday is the First after Ascension Day.

The words are part of the first stanza of Martin Moller's(?) "Ach Gott, wie manches Herzeleid" (see Cantata 3):

> Ach Gott, wie manches Herzeleid
> Begegnet mir zu dieser Zeit!
> Der schmale Weg ist trübsalvoll,
> Den ich zum Himmel wandern soll.
>
> B.G. x. 143.

Form. Tenor Unison Choral (*Fagotto, Continuo*).

(*b*)

For the melody of the concluding Choral, Heinrich Isaak's "O Welt, ich muss dich lassen," see Cantata 13. The words are the fifteenth stanza of Paul Flemming's "In allen meinen Thaten" (see Cantata 13):

> So sei nun, Seele, deine,
> Und traue dem alleine,
> Der dich erschaffen[1] hat.
> Es gehe, wie es gehe:
> Dein Vater in der Höhe
> Der weiss zu allen Sachen Rath[2].
>
> B.G. x. 150.

Form. Simple (2 *Ob., Fagotto, Strings, Continuo*). *Choralgesänge,* No. 296.

---

[1] 1642 geschaffen.
[2] 1642 Weiss allen Sachen Raht. Bach's last line appears in a recension of the Hymn dated 1670.

CANTATA XLV. ES IST DIR GESAGT, MENSCH, WAS GUT IST. Eighth Sunday after Trinity (c. 1740)

Melody: "Die Wollust dieser Welt"   Anon. 1679

* sic.

The melody of the concluding Choral is generally associated with Johann Heermann's "O Gott, du frommer Gott," but is not to be confused with the melody of 1693 (see Cantata 24). The tune, whose source is not known, appears first in Ahashuerus Fritsch's *Himmels-Lust und Welt-Unlust* (Jena, 1679), in association with Johann Jakob Schütz' (1640–90) "Die Wollust dieser Welt" (published in 1675). A reconstruction of the melody is found in the Darmstadt *Geistreiches Gesang-Buch* (Darmstadt, 1698), which Bach follows more closely.

The melody is used also in Cantatas 64, 94, 128, 129, and in the unfinished Cantata U 1, "Ehre sei Gott in der Höhe." The Choralvariationen or Partite (N. xix. 44) upon the melody, "O Gott, du frommer Gott," treat another tune, originally "Gross ist, O grosser Gott," published in the Hanover *New Ordentlich Gesang-Buch* (Hanover, 1646). Bach's version of "Die Wollust" is founded upon a reconstruction of the tune in 1698. His modifications of lines 4–6 appear to be original.

The words of the concluding Choral are the second stanza of Heermann's "O Gott, du frommer Gott" (see Cantata 24):

> Gieb, dass ich thu' mit Fleiss,
> Was mir zu thun gebühret,
> Wozu mich dein Befehl
> In meinem Stande führet.
> Gieb, dass ich's thue bald,
> Zu der Zeit, da ich soll;
> Und wenn ich's thu', so gieb,
> Dass es gerathe wohl.
>
> B.G. x. 186.

Form. Simple (2 *Fl.*, 2 *Ob.*, *Strings, Continuo*). *Choralgesänge*, No. 278.

CANTATA XLVI. SCHAUET DOCH UND SEHET.
Tenth Sunday after Trinity (*c.* 1725)
Melody: "*O grosser Gott von Macht*"
? Melchior Franck 1632

The melody and words of the concluding Choral are from Balthasar Schnurr's (1572-1644) "O grosser Gott von Macht," published together as a broadsheet, entitled *Ein Andächtiges Buss-Lied, Aus der Vorbitt Abrahams für die Sodomiter* (Leipzig, 1632). The *Cantionale sacrum* (Gotha, Part II, 1648) contains a harmonisation of the melody by Melchior Franck. As that work includes thirty tunes harmonised by him, it may be conjectured that he was the composer of the melody, "O grosser Gott."

Melchior Franck was born at Zittau, *c.* 1573-80. In 1601 he was Town "Musiker" at Nürnberg, and two or three years later became Capellmeister at Coburg. He died there in 1639.

The melody, which Bach does not use elsewhere, is not in the *Choralgesänge*. There does not appear to be earlier sanction for Bach's treatment of the fourth and sixth lines of the tune. The words of the concluding Choral are the ninth stanza of the Hymn, an addendum to the original broadsheet of 1632, first published in Jeremias Weber's *Gesangbuch* (Leipzig, 1638). Its authorship is attributed by Erk[1] and Spitta[2] to Johann Matthäus Meyfart (1590-1642). In Weber's Hymn book, however, it bears the unidentified initials, "M. J. W.":

> O grosser Gott der[3] Treu',
> Weil vor dir Niemand gilt
> Als dein Sohn Jesus Christ,
> Der deinen Zorn gestillt :
> So sieh' doch an die Wunden sein,
> Sein' Marter; Angst und schwere Pein.
> Um seinet-willen schone,
> Und nicht nach Sünden lohne.
>   B.G. x. 236.

Form. Extended (*Tromba or Corno da Tirarsi*[4], 2 *Fl.* (*a due*), *Strings, Continuo*). Erk, No. 280.

---

[1] Vol. II. p. 125, No. 280.
[2] Vol. II. p. 428.   [3] 1638 von.
[4] Both instruments are said to have been a combination of Tromba and Trombone.

CANTATA XLVII. WER SICH SELBST ERHÖHET, DER SOLL ERNIEDRIGET WERDEN. Seventeenth Sunday after Trinity (*c.* 1720)

Melody: "*Warum betrübst du dich, mein Herz*"
Anon. 1565

The words and melody of the concluding Choral are those of the Hymn "Warum betrübst du dich, mein Herz." The melody is found in association with the Hymn in a MS. (1565) of Bartholomäus Monoetius of Crailsheim, among the "cantiones quae pro ratione temporis tum in schola tum etiam in ecclesia Creilsheimensi solent cantari." In B.G. xxxiii. p. 28 it is conjectured that the tune descends from the old Meistersinger.

The melody occurs also in Cantata 138 and in Johann Christian Bach's Motett, "Ich lasse dich nicht." There are other harmonisations of the tune in the *Choralgesänge*, Nos. 331, 332. Bach's modification of the concluding phrase is found in 1588.

The words of the concluding Choral are the eleventh stanza of the Hymn, whose authorship has been attributed, apparently without foundation, to Hans Sachs (1494-1576)[1]. It occurs in *Zwey schöne newe geistliche Lieder* (Nürnberg, c. 1560) and is said to be found in a Polish Hymn book edited by Pastor Seklucyan at Königsberg in 1559:

> Der zeitlichen Ehr' will ich gern entbehr'n,
> Du woll'st mir[2] nur das Ew'ge gewähr'n,
> Das du erworben hast
> Durch deinen herben, bittern Tod.
> Das bitt' ich dich, mein Herr und Gott!
> B.G. x. 274.

Translations of the Hymn into English are noted in the *Dictionary of Hymnology*, pp. 1234, 1724.

Form. Simple (2 *Ob., Strings, Continuo*). *Choralgesänge*, No. 333.

---

[1] Wackernagel, IV. 128, prints the text under Georg Aemilius Oemler.
[2] *c.* 1560 mich.

CANTATA XLVIII. ICH ELENDER MENSCH, WER WIRD MICH ERLÖSEN. Nineteenth Sunday after Trinity (c. 1740)

Melody: "*Ach Gott und Herr*" Anon. 1625

Reconstruction 1655

(a)

The words and melody of the third movement are those of the Lenten Hymn, "Ach Gott und Herr, Wie gross und schwer," first published together in *As hymnodus sacer* (Leipzig, 1625). A reconstruction of the melody, in a major key[1], which Bach follows, first appeared in Christoph Peter's ("Sangmeister" at Guben) *Andachts Zymbeln Oder andächtige und geistreiche...Lieder* (Freiberg, 1655).

[1] Closely follows Crüger's version of the minor.

There is another harmonisation of the tune in *Choralgesänge*, No. 3. Organ Works, N. xviii. 1, 2, 3. The words of the concluding Choral are the fourth stanza of the Hymn. The stanza was first published at Jena (broadsheet) in a sermon by Dr Johann Major (or Gross) in 1613. In a second edition of the broadsheet, printed at Erfurt in the same year, six stanzas of the Hymn were included. Its authorship is attributed to Johann Major (1564–1654), a Professor at Jena University, 1611–54, and to Martin Rutilius (1550–1618), deacon and arch-deacon at Weimar, 1586–1618. It is placed by Fischer-Tümpel[1] among the "Lieder von unbekannten Verfassern"[2]:

> Soll's ja so sein,
> Dass Straf' und Pein
> Auf Sünden folgen müssen:
> So fahr' hier fort
> Und schone dort,
> Und lass mich hier[3] wohl büssen.
> B.G. x. 288.

Translations of the Hymn into English are noted in the *Dictionary of Hymnology*, p. 983.

Form. Simple (*Tromba*, 2 *Ob.*, *Strings*, *Continuo*). *Choralgesänge*, No. 4.

---

[1] Vol. i. No. 52.
[2] See the *Dictionary of Hymnology*, p. 982.
[3] 1613 ja.

CANTATA XLVIII

Melody: "*Herr Jesu Christ, du höchstes Gut*"

Anon. 1593

(*b*)

The words and melody of the concluding Choral are those of the "Kreuz- und Trostlied," "Herr Jesu Christ, ich schrei zu dir," though the melody is more familiar in association with Bartholomäus Ringwaldt's Lenten Hymn, "Herr Jesu Christ, du höchstes Gut." It was published, to another Hymn, in the Dresden *Gesangbuch* of 1593. In Christopher Demantius' *Threnodiae* (Freiberg, 1620) it occurs in association with "Herr Jesu Christ, ich schrei zu dir." The melody is the Tenor (slightly altered) of a four-part setting of "Wenn mein Stündlein vorhanden ist." Its derivation from the latter is patent (see Cantata 15).

The melody occurs also in Cantatas 113, 131, 166, 168. There is another harmonisation of it in the *Choralgesänge*, No. 141.

The words of the concluding Choral are the twelfth stanza of the Hymn "Herr Jesu Christ, ich schrei zu dir," whose author is not identified. Hymn and melody appear together in Demantius' *Threnodiae* (*supra*):

> Herr Jesu Christ, einiger Trost,
> Zu dir will ich mich wenden;
> Mein Herzleid ist dir wohl bewusst,
> Du kannst und wirst es enden.
> In deinen Willen sei's gestellt,
> Mach's, lieber[1] Gott, wie dir's gefällt:
> Dein bin und will ich bleiben. B.G. x. 298.

Form. Simple (*Tromba*, 2 *Ob.*, Strings, Continuo). *Choralgesänge*, No. 144.

In the opening movement Bach introduces the melody in canon in the accompaniment (*Tromba, Oboi*).

CANTATA XLIX. ICH GEH' UND SUCHE MIT VERLANGEN. Twentieth Sunday after Trinity (*c.* 1731)

The melody and words of the concluding Choral are from Philipp Nicolai's "Wie schön leuchtet der Morgenstern" (see Cantata 1).

The words are the seventh stanza of the Hymn:

> Wie bin ich doch so herzlich froh,
> Dass mein Schatz ist das A und O,
> Der Anfang und das Ende.
> Er wird mich doch zu seinem Preis
> Aufnehmen in das Paradeis;

[1] 1620 liebster.

Dess klopf' ich in die Hände!
Amen, Amen!
Komm, du schöne Freudenkrone,
Bleib' nicht lange!
Deiner wart' ich mit Verlangen.
B.G. x. 330.

Form. *Dialogus* for Soprano and Bass, the Soprano having the *cantus* (*Oboe d'amore, Strings, Organ, Continuo*)[1]. It is marked " Duetto."

CANTATA LI. JAUCHZET GOTT IN ALLEN LANDEN. Fifteenth Sunday after Trinity[2] (1731 or 1732)

The words and melody of the fourth movement are from Johann Graumann's "Nun lob', mein' Seel', den Herren " (see Cantata 17).

The words are the fifth stanza of the Hymn:

> * Sei Lob und Preis mit Ehren
> Gott Vater, Sohn, heiligem Geist!
> Der woll' in uns vermehren,
> Was er uns aus Gnaden verheisst,
> Dass wir ihm fest vertrauen,
> Gänzlich verlass'n auf ihn,
> Von Herzen auf ihn bauen,
> Dass uns'r Herz, Muth und Sinn

[1] Into this Cantata Bach incorporates the last movement of the Clavier Concerto in E major. See also Nos. 110, 146, 169, 174, 188.

[2] Also for general use. Spitta, 11. 473, suggests a later revision of the text by Bach with a view to using the Cantata for Michaelmas Day 1737, when that Festival and the Fifteenth Sunday after Trinity coincided.

Ihm festiglich anhangen ;
Drauf singen wir zur Stund' :
Amen ! wir werd'ns erlangen,
Glaub'n wir aus Herzens Grund.

B.G. xii. (ii) 14.

Form. Soprano Unison Choral (*Violino I and II Soli, Continuo*).

CANTATA LII. FALSCHE WELT, DIR TRAU ICH NICHT. Twenty-third Sunday after Trinity (*c.* 1730)

Melody: "*In dich hab' ich gehoffet, Herr*"
Seth Calvisius 1581

The melody, "In dich hab' ich gehoffet, Herr," which Bach uses in the concluding Choral of the Cantata, was composed by Seth Calvisius or Kallwitz (1556–1615), a predecessor of Bach as Cantor of St Thomas' Church, Leipzig. It was published, along with the Hymn, in Gregorius Sunderreitter's *Himlische Harpffe Davids* (Nürnberg, 1581).

The melody occurs elsewhere in Cantata 106, in the "St Matthew Passion," No. 38, and in the "Christmas Oratorio," No. 46. Organ Works, N. xviii. 59. In Johann Hermann Schein's *Cantional* (Leipzig, 1627) it appears in a form very similar to that in which Bach employs it. In the *Orgelbüchlein* (N. xv. 113) the melody called "In dich hab' ich gehoffet" is not by Calvisius, but is an Easter Hymn tune dating at least from the fifteenth century.

The words of the concluding Choral are the first stanza of Adam Reissner's, or Reusner's, Hymn (based on Psalm xxxi), "In dich hab' ich gehoffet, Herr," first published in *Form und Ordnung Gaystlicher Gesang und Psalmen* (Augsburg, 1533):

In dich hab' ich gehoffet, Herr,
Hilf, dass ich nicht zu Schanden werd',
Noch ewiglich zu Spotte.
Dass bitt' ich dich,
Erhalte mich
In deiner Treu', Herr Gotte[1].

B.G. xii. (ii) 50.

Translations of the Hymn into English are noted in the *Dictionary of Hymnology*, p. 955.

Form. Embellished (2 *Cor.*, 3 *Ob.*, *Fagotto*, Strings, Organ, Continuo). *Choralgesänge*, No. 212[2].

[1] 1533 mein Gotte.
[2] The Introduction to the Cantata is the opening movement of the first Brandenburg Concerto.

CANTATA LV. ICH ARMER MENSCH, ICH SÜN-
DENKNECHT. Twenty-second Sunday after
Trinity (1731 or 1732)

Melody: "*Werde munter, mein Gemüthe*"
Johann Schop 1642

The melody of the concluding Choral is Johann Schop's "Werde munter, mein Gemüthe," first published, with the Hymn, in Part III of Johann Rist's *Himlischer Lieder mit Melodeien* (Lüneburg, 1642).

The melody occurs also in Cantatas 146, 147, 154, and in the "St Matthew Passion," No. 48. There are two harmonisations of it in the *Choralgesänge*, Nos. 363, 364. Bach's seventh line is found in Vopelius (1682).

The words of the concluding Choral are the sixth stanza of Johann Rist's Evening Hymn, "Werde munter, mein Gemüthe," first published, with the melody, in Part III of his *Himlischer Lieder* (*supra*):

> Bin ich gleich von dir gewichen,
> Stell' ich mich doch wieder ein;
> Hat uns doch dein Sohn verglichen
> Durch sein' Angst und Todespein.
> Ich verleugne nicht die Schuld,
> Aber deine Gnad' und Huld
> Ist viel grösser als die Sünde,
> Die ich stets in mir befinde.
> B.G. xii. (ii) 86.

English translations of the Hymn are noted in the *Dictionary of Hymnology*, p. 1254.

Form. Simple (*Flauto, Oboe, Strings, Continuo*). *Choralgesänge*, No. 362.

CANTATA LVI. ICH WILL DEN KREUZSTAB GERNE TRAGEN[1] Nineteenth Sunday after Trinity (1731 or 1732)

Melody: "*Du, O schönes Weltgebäude*"
Johann Crüger 1649

---

[1] An English version of the Cantata, "I with my cross-staff gladly wander," is published by Breitkopf & Haertel.

The melody and words of the concluding Choral are from Johann Franck's Hymn, "Du, O schönes Weltgebäude." The melody was first published, with the first stanza only of Franck's Hymn (but with the first line as, "Du geballtes Weltgebäude"), in Johann Crüger's *Geistliche Kirchen-Melodien* (Leipzig, 1649).

The melody does not appear elsewhere in the Cantatas or Oratorios. Another harmonisation of it is in the *Choralgesänge*, No. 71.

The words of the concluding Choral are the sixth stanza of Franck's Hymn. The complete text of it was first published, along with the melody, in Christoph Runge's edition of Crüger's *Praxis Pietatis Melica* (Berlin, 1653):

> Komm, O Tod, du Schlafes Bruder,
> Komm, und führe mich nur fort;
> Löse meines Schiffleins Ruder,
> Bringe mich an[1] sichern Port.
> Es mag, wer da will, dich scheuen,
> Du kannst mich vielmehr erfreuen;
> Denn durch dich komm' ich hinein[2]
> Zu dem schönsten Jesulein.
>
> B.G. xij. (ii) 104.

Translations of the Hymn into English are noted in the *Dictionary of Hymnology*, p. 387.

Form. Simple (2 *Ob.*, *Taille*[3], *Strings*, *Continuo*). *Choralgesänge*, No. 72.

---

[1] 1653 in.   [2] 1653 herein.
[3] The Taille was a Tenor Bassoon.

CANTATA LVII. SELIG IST DER MANN. Feast of St Stephen (Christmas) (*c.* 1740)

Melody: "*Hast du denn, Liebster, dein Angesicht*"
Anon. 1665

The melody of the concluding Choral is generally associated with Joachim Neander's Thanksgiving Hymn, "Lobe den Herren, den mächtigen König der Ehren," and was appropriated for it by him in his *Glaub- und Liebesübung* (Bremen, 1680). The tune originally appeared in Part II of the Stralsund *Ernewertes Gesangbuch, Darinnen 408 Geistreiche Psalmen und Lieder* (Stralsund, 1665), set to "Hast du denn, Liebster, dein Angesicht gäntzlich verborgen," upon which Ahashuerus Fritsch modelled his Hymn (*infra*). Zahn suggests a secular origin for the tune.

There is early eighteenth century authority for Bach's treatment of the second part of the tune.

The melody occurs also in Cantata 137 and in the unfinished Cantata U 3, "Herr Gott, Beherrscher aller Dinge." Organ Works, N. xvi. 14 ("Kommst du nun, Jesu, vom Himmel herunter"). Bach's treatment of bars 1 and 2 after the middle double-bar is not uniform. In the two following bars (3 and 4) his melody is invariable and is found in 1708.

The words of the concluding Choral are the sixth stanza of Ahashuerus Fritsch's Hymn-dialogue between Christ and the Soul, "Hast du denn, Jesu, dein Angesicht gäntzlich verborgen." The Hymn, based upon an earlier model (*supra*), was first published (without the melody) in Fritsch's *Zwey und Siebenzig neue Himmel-süsse Jesus-Lieder* (Jena, 1668).

Fritsch was born at Mücheln, near Merseburg, in 1629. He became Chancellor and President of the Consistory at Rudolstadt, and died there in 1701:

> Richte dich, Liebste, nach meinem Gefallen und gläube,
> Dass ich dein Seelenfreund immer und ewig verbleibe,
> Der dich ergötzt
> Und in den Himmel versetzt
> Aus dem gemarterten Leibe.   B.G. xii. (ii) 132.

Form. Simple (2 *Ob.*, *Taille*[1], *Strings*, *Organ*, *Continuo*). *Choralgesänge*, No. 231.

[1] The Taille was a Tenor Bassoon.

CANTATA LVIII. ACH GOTT, WIE MANCHES HERZELEID. Sunday after the Circumcision (1733)

(a)

The melody of the opening movement is that of Martin Moller's (?) Hymn, "Ach Gott, wie manches Herzeleid" (see Cantata 3). The words of the Choral are part of the first stanza of the Hymn:

> Ach Gott, wie manches Herzeleid
> Begegnet mir zu dieser Zeit!
> Der schmale Weg ist trübsalsvoll,
> Den ich zum Himmel wandern soll.
>
> B.G. xii. (ii) 135.

Form. A *Dialogus* between Soprano and Bass, the Soprano having the melody (2 *Ob.*, *Taille*, *Strings*, *Continuo*).

(b)

For the melody of the fifth movement, "Ach Gott, wie manches Herzeleid," or "Herr Jesu Christ, mein's Lebens Licht," see Cantata 3.

The words of the Choral are the second stanza of Martin Behm's funerary Hymn, "O [Herr] Jesu Christ, mein's Lebens Licht," first published in a collection entitled *Christliche Gebet* (1610), and thence in his *Zehen Sterbegebet Reimweise zugerichtet* (Wittenberg, 1611).

Behm was born at Lauban, in Silesia, in 1557. He was assistant in the Town school, deacon, and eventually chief pastor there. He died in 1622. He was one of the best and most prolific hymn writers of his period:

> Ich hab' vor mir ein' schwere Reis'
> Zu dir in's Himmels Paradeis;
> Da ist mein rechtes Vaterland,
> Daran[1] du dein Blut hast[2] gewandt.
>
> B.G. xii. (ii) 146.

Translations of the Hymn into English are noted in the *Dictionary of Hymnology*, p. 127.

Form. A *Dialogus* between Soprano and Bass, the Soprano having the melody (2 *Ob.*, *Taille*, *Strings*, *Continuo*).

CANTATA LIX. WER MICH LIEBET, DER WIRD MEIN WORT HALTEN. Whit Sunday (1716)

Melody: "*Komm, heiliger Geist, Herre Gott*"

Anon. 1535

---

[1] 1611 Darauff.   [2] 1611 hast dein Blut.

The melody and words of the penultimate movement are from Luther's Whitsuntide Hymn, "Komm, heiliger Geist, Herre Gott," an expansion of the Latin Antiphon, "Veni Sancte Spiritus." The Hymn was first published, with the melody, in Walther's *Geystliche gesangk Buchleyn* (Wittenberg, 1524), and in both editions of the Erfurt *Enchiridion* (1524). An earlier form of the melody (*supra*) appears, with the Hymn, in Klug's *Geistliche Lieder* (Wittenberg, 1535 [1529]).

The melody is found also in Cantata 175 and, in a free form, in Cantata 172. It occurs also in Motett 2, "Der Geist hilft unsrer Schwachheit auf." Organ Works, N. xvii. 1, 10.

The words of the Choral are the first stanza of Luther's Hymn:

> Komm, heiliger Geist, Herre Gott,
> Erfüll' mit deiner Gnaden Gut
> Deiner Gläubigen Herz, Muth und Sinn!
> Dein' brünstig' Lieb' entzünd' in ihn'n!
> O Herr, durch deines Lichtes Glanz[1]
> Zu dem Glauben versammelt hast
> Das Volk aus aller Welt Zungen;
> Das sie dir, Herr, zu Lob' gesungen.
> Alleluja! Alleluja!
> B.G. xii. (ii) 164.

English translations of the Hymn are noted in the *Dictionary of Hymnology*, p. 631.

Form. Embellished (*Strings, Continuo*). *Choralgesänge*, No. 220.

CANTATA LX. O EWIGKEIT, DU DONNERWORT.

Twenty-fourth Sunday after Trinity (1732)

(*a*)

The melody of the opening movement is Johann Schop's "Wach auf, mein Geist," reconstructed by Johann Crüger for Rist's Hymn, "O Ewigkeit, du Donnerwort" (see Cantata 20).

[1] 1524 glast.

The words of the Choral are the first stanza of Rist's Hymn:

> O Ewigkeit, du Donnerwort,
> O Schwert, das durch die Seele bohrt,
> O Anfang sonder Ende!
> O Ewigkeit, Zeit ohne Zeit,
> Ich weiss vor grosser Traurigkeit
> Nicht, wo ich mich hinwende[1];
> Mein ganz erschrock'nes Herze bebt[2],
> Dass mir die Zung' am Gaumen klebt.
> B.G. xii.(ii) 171.

Form. A *Dialogus* between Alto and Tenor, the Alto having the melody (*Corno*, 2 *Ob. d'amore, Strings, Continuo*).

Melody: "*Es ist genug*"   Johann Rodolph Ahle 1662

(*b*)

The melody of the concluding Choral is Johann Rodolph Ahle's setting of Burmeister's "Es ist genug; so nimm, Herr, meinen Geist." The tune was first published, with the Hymn, in Part III (1662) of Ahle's *Neuer Geistlicher Arien, So mit* 1, 2, 3, *oder* 4, *Stimmen* (Mühlhausen, 1660–64).

[1] 1642 hin mich wende.   [2] 1642 Hertz erhebt.

Ahle, born at Mühlhausen in 1625, was Organist of the Blasiuskirche and Burgomaster there. He died in 1673. He was a very prolific composer of "geistliche Arien," and collaborated especially with Burmeister.

The melody does not occur elsewhere in the Cantatas or Oratorios.

The words of the concluding Choral are the fifth stanza of Franz Joachim Burmeister's "Es ist genug," which was published, with the melody, in 1662 (*supra*).

Burmeister was born, probably in 1633, at Lüneburg. He was appointed Deacon of St Michael's Church there in 1670 and held the post until his death in 1672. He was a friend of Johann Rist, who admitted him to his Order of Elbe Swans in 1660:

> Es ist genug : Herr, wenn es dir gefällt,
> So spanne mich doch aus.
> Mein Jesus kommt : nun gute Nacht, O Welt!
> Ich fahr' in's Himmelshaus ;
> Ich fahre sicher hin mit[1] Frieden,
> Mein grosser[2] Jammer bleibt darnieden.
> Es ist genug.
>
> B.G. xii. (ii) 190.

Form. Simple (*Corno*, 2 *Ob. d'amore, Strings, Continuo*). *Choralgesänge*, No. 91.

[1] 1662 inn.   [2] 1662 feuchter.

CANTATA LXI. NUN KOMM, DER HEIDEN HEILAND[1]. First Sunday in Advent (1714)

(a)

The melody of the opening movement is that of Luther's Christmas Hymn, "Nun komm, der Heiden Heiland" (see Cantata 36). The words are the first stanza of the Hymn:

> Nun komm, der Heiden Heiland,
> Der Jungfrauen Kind erkannt,
> Dess sich wundert alle Welt :
> Gott solch' Geburt ihm bestellt.
>
> B.G. xvi. 3.

Form. A Choral Fantasia in the form of a French "Ouverture," into whose opening and closing *Grave* sections the Choral melody is introduced, all of the four vocal parts in turn or together singing the *cantus* (*Fagotto, Strings, Organ, Continuo*[2]).

(b)

The words and melody of the concluding movement are Philipp Nicolai's " Wie schön leuchtet der

---

[1] English versions of the Cantata, "Come, Thou blessed Saviour, come," are published by Breitkopf & Haertel, and by Novello & Co., "Come, Redeemer of our race."

[2] See Spitta, III. 101.

Morgenstern" (see Cantata 1). The words are part of the seventh stanza of the Hymn:

> Amen, Amen!
> Komm du schöne Freudenkrone,
> Bleib' nicht lange.
> Deiner wart' ich mit Verlangen.
> B.G. xvi. 17.

Form. Choral Fantasia (fourteen bars) (*Fagotto, Strings, Organ, Continuo*).

CANTATA LXII. NUN KOMM, DER HEIDEN HEILAND. First Sunday in Advent (after 1734[1])

A Choral Cantata, on Luther's Christmas Hymn, "Nun komm, der Heiden Heiland" (see Cantata 36).

(*a*)

The words of the opening movement are the first stanza of the Hymn:

> Nun komm, der Heiden Heiland,
> Der Jungfrauen Kind erkannt,
> Dess sich wundert alle Welt:
> Gott solch' Geburt ihm bestellt.
> B.G. xvi. 21.

Form. Choral Fantasia (*Corno,* 2 *Ob., Strings, Continuo*).

---

[1] Schweitzer includes the Cantata in the 1728–34 period (II. 242 n.). Wustmann dates it *c.* 1740.

CANTATA LXIV

(*b*)

The words of the concluding Choral are the eighth stanza of the Hymn:

    Lob sei Gott, dem Vater, g'than[1],
    Lob sei Gott, sein'm ein'gen Sohn,
    Lob sei Gott, dem heil'gen Geist,
    Immer und in Ewigkeit.   B.G. xvi. 50.

Form. Simple (*Corno*, 2 *Ob.*, *Strings*, *Continuo*). *Choralgesänge*, No. 265.

CANTATA LXIV. SEHET, WELCH' EINE LIEBE HAT UNS DER VATER ERZEIGET. Feast of St John the Evangelist (Christmas) (? 1723)

Melody: "*Grates nunc omnes reddamus*"   Anon. 1524

Melody: "*Gelobet seist du, Jesu Christ*"   Anon. 1524

---

[1] 1524 thon.

(a)

The melody of the second movement, "Gelobet seist du, Jesu Christ," was first published, with Luther's Hymn, in Johann Walther's *Geystliche gesangk Buchleyn* (Wittenberg, 1524). The tune is a simplification, doubtless by Walther, of the melody of the Latin Sequence, "Grates nunc omnes reddamus," the version of which printed above is found in Thomas Muntzer's *Deutsch Euangelisch Messze* (Altstadt, 1524).

The melody occurs also in Cantata 91 and in the "Christmas Oratorio," Nos. 7 and 28. A treatment of the melody, Simple in form and unaccompanied, is in B.G. xvi. 371 and another will be found there at p. xv. Another harmonisation of the tune is in the *Choralgesänge*, No. 107. An arrangement of it by Bach for accompanying the congregation is in N. xviii. 37. Organ Works, N. xv. 15; xviii. 38, 39.

The words of the second movement are the seventh stanza of Luther's Christmas Hymn, an expansion of the Latin Sequence, "Grates nunc omnes reddamus," first published as a broadsheet at Wittenberg in 1524, and, with the melody, in Walther's Hymn book (*supra*):

> Das hat er Alles uns gethan,
> Sein' gross' Lieb' zu zeigen an.
> Dess freu' sich alle Christenheit
> Und dank' ihm dess in Ewigkeit.
>   Kyrieleis!   B.G. xvi. 118,

CANTATA LXIV

English translations of the Hymn are noted in the *Dictionary of Hymnology*, p. 408.

Form. Simple (*Cornetto*, 3 *Trombones, Strings, Organ, Continuo*). *Choralgesänge*, No. 108.

(*b*)

The melody of the fourth movement is the 1679 tune, "O Gott, du frommer Gott," or "Die Wollust dieser Welt" (see Cantata 45). Another treatment of the melody, to the same words, is printed in B.G. xvi. 372 as an Appendix. It is No. 281 of the *Choralgesänge*.

The words of the fourth movement are the first stanza of Georg Michael Pfefferkorn's Hymn, "Was frag ich nach der Welt," first published as a broadsheet at Altenburg in 1667. It has a distinctive melody of its own, by Jakob Hintze (1679).

Pfefferkorn was born at Ifta, near Creuzburg, in 1645. He became a private tutor and master in the Gymnasium at Altenburg, and, later, tutor to the children of Duke Ernst of Gotha. He was appointed in 1682 Superintendent at Gräfen-Tonna, near Gotha, and died there in 1732.

* Was frag ich nach der Welt
  Und allen ihren Schätzen,
  Wenn ich mich nur an dir,
  Mein Jesu, kann ergötzen?
  Dich hab' ich einzig mir
  Zur Wollust vorgestellt :
  Du, du bist mein Lust ;
  Was frag ich nach der Welt! B.G. xvi. 120.

260   CANTATA LXIV

An English translation of the Hymn is noted in the *Dictionary of Hymnology*, p. 893.

Form. Embellished (*Cornetto*, 3 *Trombones, Strings, Organ, Continuo*). *Choralgesänge*, No. 280.

Melody: "*Jesu, meine Freude*"   Johann Crüger 1653

(c)

The melody of the concluding Choral is Johann Crüger's "Jesu, meine Freude," which first appeared, set to Johann Franck's Hymn, in the 1653 (Berlin) edition of the *Praxis Pietatis Melica*.

The melody also occurs in Cantatas 81 and 87, and in Motett 3, "Jesu, meine Freude." There is another harmonisation of it in the *Choralgesänge*, No. 195. Bach's treatment of the second line varies. Only in Cantatas 64 and 87 and the Organ Preludes does he follow Crüger's text (the C sharp at the fourth note dates from 1674). In the other Cantata and the Motett his version of that line, and also of the penultimate line, appears to be his own and to have been copied into later Hymn books. Organ Works, N, xv. 31; xviii. 64; P. v. 112.

The words of the concluding Choral are the fifth stanza of Johann Franck's "Jesu, meine Freude," first published, with the melody, in 1653 (*supra*). The Hymn was modelled upon a secular song, which had appeared in 1641, "Flora meine Freude; Meiner Seelenweide":

> Gute Nacht, O Wesen,
> Das die Welt erlesen!
> Mir gefällst du nicht.
> Gute Nacht, ihr Sünden,
> Bleibet weit dahinten,
> Kommt nicht mehr an's Licht!
> Gute Nacht,
> Du Stolz und Pracht!
> Dir sei ganz, O[1] Lasterleben,
> Gute Nacht gegeben! B.G. xvi. 132.

Translations of the Hymn into English are noted in the *Dictionary of Hymnology*, pp. 591, 1657.

Form. Simple (*Cornetto*, 3 *Trombones, Strings, Organ, Continuo*). *Choralgesänge*, No. 200.

CANTATA LXV. SIE WERDEN AUS SABA ALLE KOMMEN[2]. Feast of the Epiphany (1724)

Melody: "*Puer natus in Bethlehem*" Anon. 1543

[1] 1653 du.
[2] An English version of the Cantata, "The sages of Sheba," is published by Novello & Co.

CANTATA LXV

Melody: "*Ein Kind geborn zu Bethlehem*"   1553

(a)

The words and melody of the second movement are those of the Christmas Hymn, "Ein Kind geborn zu Bethlehem," a translation of the Latin Hymn, "Puer natus in Bethlehem," which is as old as the fourteenth century. The earlier melody occurs in Joseph Klug's *Geistliche Lieder zu Wittemberg, Anno* 1543 (Wittenberg, 1543), where it is set to both the Latin and German words. Another melody is found in Lucas Lossius' *Psalmodia, hoc est, Cantica sacra veteris ecclesiae selecta* (Nürnberg, 1553 [1550]). Bach uses the later melody here. With alterations the 1543 tune is that of Luther's "Vom Himmel kam der Engel Schaar." The 1553 melody is the descant to the 1543 *canto fermo*, the latter becoming the Tenor in early settings.

Neither melody occurs elsewhere in the Cantatas or Oratorios. Organ Works, N. xv. 13, 22 ("Vom Himmel kam der Engel Schaar").

The words of the second movement are the fourth stanza of the Christmas Hymn, "Ein Kind geborn zu Bethlehem," published, with the melody, by Joseph Klug in 1543 (*supra*):

>Die Kön'ge aus Saba kamen dar,
>Gold, Weihrauch, Myrrhen brachten sie dar,
>Alleluja, Alleluja!
>
>B.G. xvi. 152.

Translations of the Hymn into English are noted in the *Dictionary of Hymnology*, p. 941.

Form. Embellished (2 *Fl.*, 2 *Ob. da caccia*, *Continuo*). *Choralgesänge*, No. 302.

Melody: "*Was mein Gott will*" Anon. 1572 [1571]

(*b*)

The melody of the concluding Choral, "Was mein Gott will, das g'scheh' allzeit," is of French origin, and appears first in Pierre Attaignant's *Trente et quatre chansons musicales* (Paris, [1529]) as the melody of a secular song, "Il me souffit de

264   CANTATA LXV

tous mes maulx[1]." It was attached to the Hymn, "Was mein Gott will," in Joachim Magdeburg's *Christliche und Tröstliche Tischgesenge, mit Vier Stimmen* (Erfurt, 1572 [1571]). The melody occurs also in Cantatas 72, 92, 103, 111, 144, and in the "St Matthew Passion," No. 31. Bach follows the Dresden (1597) form.

The words of the concluding Choral are the tenth stanza of Paul Gerhardt's "Ich hab' in Gottes Herz und Sinn," first published, to the melody "Was mein Gott," in the 1647 (Berlin) edition of Crüger's *Praxis Pietatis Melica*:

> Ei nun, mein Gott, so fall' ich dir
> Getrost in deine Hände.
> Nimm mich, und mach' es so[2] mit mir
> Bis an mein letztes Ende,
> Wie du wohl weisst,
> Dass meinem Geist
> Dadurch sein Weg[3] entstehe,
> Und deine Ehr'
> Je mehr und mehr
> Sich in mir[4] selbst erhöhe.   B.G. xvi. 166.

Translations of the Hymn into English are noted in the *Dictionary of Hymnology*, p. 412.

Form. Simple (*Continuo*). *Choralgesänge*, No. 346.

---

[1] See *Bach's Chorals*, Part I, p. 11.
[2] 1647 du.   [3] 1647 and Bach's MS. Nutz.   [4] 1647 ihr.

CANTATA LXVI. ERFREUT EUCH, IHR HERZEN.
Easter Monday (*c.* 1731)

Melody: "Christ ist erstanden"   Anon. 1535

Stanza .i.

Stanza iii[1].

The words and melody of the concluding Choral are those of the medieval Easter Hymn, "Christ ist erstanden." They are found together in Joseph Klug's *Geistliche Lieder zu Wittemberg* (Wittenberg, 1535 [1529]). The melody occurs in a fifteenth century MS. and its earliest printed form dates from 1513. The words are as old as the thirteenth century.

The melody does not occur elsewhere in the Cantatas and Oratorios. There is a harmonisation of the complete Hymn in the *Choralgesänge*, No. 36. Organ Works, N. xv. 83.

[1] The melody of stanza ii is identical with that of stanza i.

The words of the Choral are the third stanza of the Hymn:

> Alleluja, Alleluja, Alleluja!
> Dess soll'n wir Alle froh sein:
> Christus will[1] unser Trost sein,
> Kyrieleis!
> B.G. xvi. 214.

Translations of the Hymn into English are noted in the *Dictionary of Hymnology*, p. 225.
Form. Simple (*Continuo*). *Choralgesänge*, No. 37.

CANTATA LXVII. HALT' IM GEDÄCHTNISS JESUM CHRIST[2]. First Sunday after Easter ("Quasimodo geniti") (*c.* 1725)

Melody: "*Erschienen ist der herrlich' Tag*"
Nicolaus Herman 1560

---

[1] Orig. scholl.
[2] An English version of the Cantata, "Hold in remembrance Jesus Christ," is published by Breitkopf & Haertel.

Melody: "*Erstanden ist der heil'ge Christ*"   Anon. 1555[1]

(a)

The melody and words of the fourth movement are those of the Easter Hymn, "Erschienen ist der herrlich' Tag," of which Nicolaus Herman was both author and composer. The Hymn and melody were first published in his *Die Sontags Euangelia uber das gantze Jar* (Wittenberg, 1560). Both are reminiscent of the Easter Hymn, "Erstanden ist der heil'ge Christ."

The melody occurs also in Cantata 145. Bach's third line is found in an early seventeenth century (1605) text. Organ Works, N. xv. 91.

The words of the Choral are the first stanza of the Hymn:

> Erschienen ist der herrlich' Tag,
> D'ran sich Niemand g'nug freuen mag:
> Christ, unser Herr, heut' triumphirt,
> All' sein' Feind' er gefangen führt.
>   Alleluja!   B.G. xvi. 233.

Translations of the Hymn into English are noted in the *Dictionary of Hymnology*, p. 514.

[1] *Ein Schlesich singebüchlein aus Göttlicher schrifft* (Breslau, 1555).

CANTATA LXVII

Form. Simple (*Corno da tirarsi, Flauto*, 2 *Ob. d'amore, Strings, Organ, Continuo*). *Choralgesänge*, No. 83.

Melody: "*Du Friedefürst, Herr Jesu Christ*"
Bartholomäus Gesius 1601

(*b*)

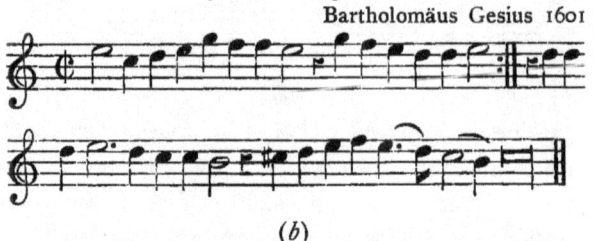

The words of the concluding Choral are from Jakob Ebert's Hymn for Peace, "Du Friedefürst, Herr Jesu Christ."
Ebert was born at Sprottau, in Silesia, in 1549. He was successively Professor of Hebrew, Ethics, and Theology in the University of Frankfort a. Oder, and died there in 1614. The Hymn, with the melody, was first published in Bartholomäus Gesius' *Geistliche deutsche Lieder* (Frankfort a. Oder, 1601).
The melody is by Bartholomäus Gesius. He was born *c.* 1555 at Müncheberg, near Frankfort, and from 1593 onwards was Cantor at Frankfort. He died there in 1613 or 1614.
The melody is used also in Cantatas 116 and 143. The last line of Bach's version of the melody is a variant upon Crüger's text (1649) of the tune.

The words of the Choral are the first stanza of the Hymn:

> Du Friedefürst, Herr Jesu Christ,
> Wahr'r Mensch und wahrer Gott,
> Ein starker Nothhelfer du bist
> Im Leben und im Tod:
> Drum wir allein
> Im Namen dein
> Zu deinem Vater schreien.
>
> B.G. xvi. 246.

Translations of the Hymn into English are noted in the *Dictionary of Hymnology*, p. 319.

Form. Simple (*Corno da tirarsi, Flauto,* 2 *Ob. d'amore, Strings, Organ, Continuo*). *Choralgesänge,* No. 68.

CANTATA LXVIII. ALSO HAT GOTT DIE WELT GELIEBT[1]. Whit Monday (? 1735[2])

Melody: "*Also hat Gott die Welt geliebt*"
                                    Gottfried Vopelius 1682

[1] An English version of the Cantata, "God so loved the world," is published by Novello & Co.

[2] Schweitzer, II. 263, gives the date as 1731. The Cantata in part is constructed out of a secular work composed in 1716. See Spitta, I. 567.

The words and melody of the opening movement are those of the Hymn, "Also hat Gott die Welt geliebt."

Its author, Salomo Liscow or Liscovius, was born at Niemitsch, near Guben, in 1640. After graduating at Wittenberg, where he was crowned a poet, he was ordained pastor at Otterwisch in 1664, and in 1685 was appointed to a similar position at Wurzen. He died there in 1689. The Hymn was first published in his *Christlichen Frauen-Zimmers geistliche Tugend-Spiegel* (Leipzig, 1675).

The melody was composed by Gottfried Vopelius and was attached to the Hymn in his *Neu Leipziger Gesangbuch* (Leipzig, 1682 [1681]).

Bach has not used the melody elsewhere. It is given neither by Erk nor the *Choralgesänge*[1].

The words of the opening movement are the first stanza of the Hymn:

> Also hat Gott die Welt geliebt,
> Dass er uns seinen Sohn gegeben.
> Wer sich im Glauben ihm ergiebt,
> Der soll dort ewig bei[2] ihm leben.

[1] Spitta, III. 114, wrongly regards it as an original melody by Bach.
[2] 1675 mit.

CANTATA LXIX 271

Wer glaubt, dass Jesus ihm geboren,
Der bleibet ewig unverloren,
Und ist kein Leid, das den betrübt,
Den Gott und auch sein Jesus liebt.
B.G. xvi. 249.

Form. Choral Fantasia (*Corno*, 2 *Ob.*, *Taille*[1], *Strings, Continuo*). The treatment of the *cantus* is very free.

CANTATA LXIX. LOBE DEN HERRN, MEINE SEELE. Twelfth Sunday after Trinity[2] (? 1724)

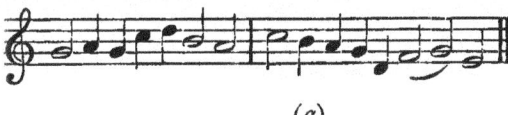

Melody: "*Es woll' uns Gott genädig sein*"   Anon. 1525

(*a*)

The words and melody of the concluding Choral are those of Luther's version of Psalm lxvii, "Es woll' uns Gott genädig sein," published originally in Luther's *Ein weise christlich Mess zuhaltē*

[1] The Taille was a Tenor Bassoon.
[2] Also adapted *c.* 1730 for use as a Rathswahl Cantata. Hence its festival character.

CANTATA LXIX

(Wittenberg, 1524). It is also in Walther's *Geystliche gesangk Buchleyn* of that year, but is set there to the melody better known as "Christ unser Herr zum Jordan kam" (see Cantata 7). Along with the melody printed above—which Erk, No. 201, tentatively attributes to Matthäus Greitter (d. *c.* 1550) —the Hymn was published in the Strassburg *Ordnung des Herren Nachtmal* (1525) and in the Strassburg *Kirchēampt mit lobgsengen* (1525).

The melody occurs also in Cantata 76, and there are other harmonisations of it in the *Choralgesänge*, Nos. 95, 96.

The words of the Choral are the third stanza of the Hymn:

> Es danke, Gott, und lobe dich
> Das Volk in guten Thaten.
> Das Land bringt Frucht und bessert sich;
> Dein Wort ist wohl gerathen.
> Uns segne Vater und der Sohn,
> Uns segne Gott, der heil'ge Geist;
> Dem alle Welt die Ehre thu',
> Vor ihm sich fürchte allermeist,
> Und[1] sprecht von Herzen: Amen!
>
> B.G. xvi. 325.

Translations of the Hymn into English are noted in the *Dictionary of Hymnology*, p. 355.

Form. Embellished (3 *Trombe, Timpani,* 3 *Ob., Fagotto, Strings, Continuo*). *Choralgesänge,* No. 97.

---

[1] 1524 Nu.

CANTATA LXX

(b)

Spitta points out[1] that about 1730 Bach remodelled the Cantata for use at a Rathswahl service. The Appendix to the Bach-Gesellschaft volume contains the following additional number. It is not in the vocal score. The words are the sixth stanza of Samuel Rodigast's "Was Gott thut, das ist wohlgethan" and the melody is that of the Hymn (see Cantata 12):

> Was Gott thut, das ist wohlgethan,
> Dabei will ich verbleihen.
> Es mag mich auf die rauhe Bahn
> Noth, Tod und Elend treiben :
> So wird Gott mich ganz väterlich
> In seinen Armen halten;
> Drum lass' ich ihn nur walten. B.G. xvi. 379.

Form. Embellished (*Tromba*, 3 *Ob.*, *Fagotto*, *Strings*, *Continuo*). Erk, No. 301.

CANTATA LXX. WACHET, BETET, BETET, WACHET[2]. Twenty-sixth Sunday after Trinity[3] (1716)

(a)

For the melody of the closing Choral, Part I,

[1] II. 692.
[2] An English version of the Cantata, "Watch ye, pray ye," is published by Novello & Co.
[3] Originally, for the Second Sunday in Advent (Spitta, I. 570). In its present form the Cantata's date probably is 1723. The *Recitativi* represent Leipzig additions to the original Franck text (Wustmann, p. 293).

Louis Bourgeois' "Ainsi qu'on oit le cerf," see Cantata 13.

The words of the Choral are the tenth stanza of the Hymn, "Freu' dich sehr, O meine Seele" (see Cantata 19):

>Freu' dich sehr, O meine Seele,
>Und vergiss all' Noth und Qual,
>Weil dich nun Christus, dein Herre,
>Ruft aus diesem Jammerthal.
>Seine Freud' und Herrlichkeit
>Sollst du sehn in Ewigkeit,
>Mit den Engeln jubiliren,
>In Ewigkeit triumphiren.
>
>B.G. xvi. 354.

Form. Simple (*Tromba, Oboe, Fagotto, Strings, Continuo*). *Choralgesänge,* No. 98.

Melody: "*Meinen Jesum lass' ich nicht*"
? Andreas Hammerschmidt 1659

CANTATA LXX

(sheet music: phrases (7), (8), (9), (10), (11))

(b)

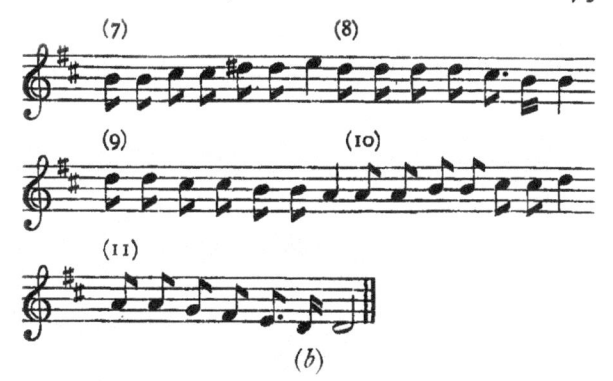

The melody of the concluding Choral of Part II, "Meinen Jesum lass' ich nicht," was first published, with Christian Keimann's Hymn, in Part IV of Andreas Hammerschmidt's *Fest- Bus- und Danck-Lieder, Mit 5 Vocal Stimmen* (Zittau, 1659 [1658]). The melody appears there in an elongated form (eleven phrases) owing to the repetition of lines 3, 4, 5, 6, of the stanza, followed by another repetition of line 6. For use as a Hymn tune the melody has several forms.

The melody occurs also in Cantatas 124, 154, 157, 163. Bach used it also for the discarded closing Choral of Part I of the "St Matthew Passion" (*Choralgesänge*, No. 247), and there is another harmonisation of it in the *Choralgesänge*, No. 242.

Bach's version, which has not earlier sanction, is built up of phrases 1-4, 9, 11, of the original

(1658) text. In Cantata 124 and in two other harmonisations of the tune in the *Choralgesänge*, Nos. 242, 247, he substitutes phrase 10 for phrase 9. There is another melody in the *Choralgesänge*, No. 241, to the same Hymn. It is by Peter Sohren (1676). The words of the Choral are the fifth stanza of Christian Keimann's Hymn, an acrostic upon the words of the dying Elector Johann Georg of Saxony (d. 1656): "Meinen Jesum lass' ich nicht." The first words of stanzas i–v supply these five words, while their last lines repeat the sentence in full. The initial letters of the first five lines of stanza vi stand for: J[ohann] G[eorg] C[hurfürst] Z[u] S[achsen], i.e. Johann Georg Elector of Saxony:

> Nicht nach Welt, nach Himmel nicht
> Meine Seele wünscht und sehnet[1];
> Jesum wünsch' ich[2] und sein Licht;
> Der mich hat mit Gott versöhnet,
> Der mich frei macht[3] vom Gericht,
> Meinen Jesum lass' ich nicht.
>
> B.G. xvi. 368.

English translations of the Hymn are noted in the *Dictionary of Hymnology*, p. 614.

Form. Embellished (*Tromba, Oboe, Fagotto, Strings, Continuo*). *Choralgesänge*, No. 243.

[1] 1658 stöhnet.   [2] 1658 wünscht sie.   [3] 1658 freyet.

(c)

Melody: "Nun freut euch, lieben Christen g'mein"
Anon. 1535

[musical notation]

In the second movement of Part II of the Cantata (B.G. xvi. 360), the Bass *Recitativo*, "Ach, soll nicht dieser grosse Tag," the Tromba has the melody of Luther's Advent Hymn, "Nun freut euch, lieben Christen g'mein," generally known as "Luther's Hymn," and also, through its association with Bartholomäus Ringwaldt's Advent Hymn, as "Es ist gewisslich an der Zeit[1]."

The melody, "Nun freut euch, lieben Christen g'mein," was first published, with Luther's Hymn, in Klug's *Geistliche Lieder* (Wittenberg, 1535 [1529]). It also occurs in the "Christmas Oratorio," No. 59. There is another harmonisation of it in the *Choralgesänge*, No. 262. Organ Works, N. xviii. 80. Bach's text is invariable and is found in sixteenth century Hymn books.

[1] See *Bach's Chorals*, Part I, 58.

CANTATA LXXI. GOTT IST MEIN KÖNIG. For the Inauguration of the Town Council, Mühlhausen (1708)

The Choral melody of the second movement is the 1693 tune, "O Gott, du frommer Gott" (see Cantata 24). The words of the Choral are the sixth stanza of Johann Heermann's "O Gott, du frommer Gott" (see Cantata 24):

> Soll ich auf dieser Welt
> Mein Leben höher bringen,
> Durch manchen sauren Tritt
> Hindurch in's Alter dringen:
> So gieb Geduld; vor Sünd'
> Und Schanden mich bewahr',
> Auf dass ich tragen mag
> Mit Ehren graues Haar[1]. B.G. xviii. 12.

Form. A Tenor "Aria con Corale in Canto" sung by a Soprano, i.e. a *Duetto* (*Organ*)[2].

[1] 1630   Das ich mit Ehren trag
               All meine grawe Haar.
Bach's last two lines are taken from the 1636 edition of the *Devoti Musica Cordis*.

[2] See Spitta, I. 346–348, on Bach's combination of Bible verses with suitable stanzas of Chorals. Strictly, the movement is a *Trio* for Soprano (having the Choral melody), Tenor (having an independent *Aria*), and an accompanying *Continuo*.

CANTATA LXXII. ALLES NUR NACH GOTTES WILLEN. Third Sunday after the Epiphany (c. 1725[1])

For the melody of the concluding Choral, "Was mein Gott will, das g'scheh' allzeit," see Cantata 65. The words of the Choral are the first stanza of Albrecht Margrave of Brandenburg-Culmbach's only Hymn, "Was mein Gott will, das g'scheh' allzeit," first published as a broadsheet at Nürnberg c. 1554, and in *Fünff Schöne Geistliche Lieder* (Dresden, 1556):

> Was mein Gott will, das g'scheh' allzeit',
> Sein Will' der ist der beste[2];
> Zu helfen den'n er ist bereit,
> Die an ihn glauben feste.
> Er hilft aus Noth,
> Der fromme Gott,
> Und züchtiget[3] mit Massen:
> Wer Gott vertraut,
> Fest auf ihn baut,
> Den will er nicht verlassen.   B.G. xviii. 84.

English translations of the Hymn are noted in the *Dictionary of Hymnology*, p. 37.

Form. Simple (2 Ob., Strings, Continuo). *Choralgesänge*, No. 344.

[1] Wustmann (p. 277) suggests a date before 1723.
[2] c. 1554 aller beste.   [3] c. 1554 Er tröst die Welt.

CANTATA LXXIII. HERR, WIE DU WILLT, SO SCHICK'S MIT MIR. Third Sunday after the Epiphany (*c.* 1725)

Melody: "Wo Gott der Herr nicht bei uns hält" Anon. 1535

(*a*)

The Choral melody of the opening movement, "Wo Gott der Herr nicht bei uns hält," was first published, with Justus Jonas' (1493-1555) Hymn bearing that title, in Joseph Klug's *Geistliche Lieder* (Wittenberg, 1535 [1529]). The Hymn was most usually sung to the tune "Ach lieben Christen, seid getrost," but Bach follows Crüger (1709) in associating it with "Wo Gott der Herr."

The melody also occurs in Cantatas 114 and 178, and in Cantata D 3 attributed to Bach, "Siehe, es hat überwunden der Löwe." There are three other harmonisations of the tune in the *Choralgesänge*, Nos. 383, 385, 388.

The words of the Choral are the first stanza of Caspar Bienemann's (Melissander), "Herr, wie du willt, so schick's mit mir," first published in his *Betbüchlein* (Leipzig, 1582).

Bienemann was born at Nürnberg in 1540. He accompanied an Imperial embassy to Greece as interpreter, and there assumed the name Melissander. In 1578 he became pastor and General Superintendent at Altenburg. He died there in 1591. The Hymn was written in 1574, when he was private tutor to the children of Duke Johann Wilhelm of Saxe-Weimar, and was taught as a prayer to the Duchess Maria, then aged three. The initial letters of the three stanzas form an acrostic on her title, "Herzogin zu Sachsen":

> Herr, wie du willt, so schick's mit mir
> In Leben und im Sterben!
> Allein zu dir steht mein Begier,
> Herr, lass mich[1] nicht verderben!
> Erhalt' mich nur in deiner Huld,
> Sonst, wie du willt, gieb mir Geduld;
> Denn dein Will' ist der beste.   B.G. xviii. 87.

Translations of the Hymn into English are noted in the *Dictionary of Hymnology*, p. 142.

Form. Choral Fantasia. The Choral Chorus (S.A.T.B.), Extended in design, is intersected by *Recitativo* passages for S.T.B. which elaborate the ideas suggested by the Hymn. The *Recitativo* passages are sung to orchestral *ritornelli*, always the same, but differing in key (*Corno*, 2 *Ob.*, *Strings*, *Organ obbligato*, *Continuo*)[2].

[1] 1582 Lass mich, Herr.
[2] See Spitta, II. 414, and p. 44 *supra*.

CANTATA LXXIII

(b)

For the melody of the concluding Choral, "Von Gott will ich nicht lassen," see Cantata 11.

The words of the Choral are the ninth stanza of Ludwig Helmbold's "Von Gott will ich nicht lassen," founded on Psalm lxxiii. 23. The Hymn, written during a pestilence at Erfurt in 1563, was first published as a broadsheet in 1563-64 and later in *Hundert Christenliche Haussgesang* (Nürnberg, 1569).

Helmbold was born at Mühlhausen in 1532, was educated at Leipzig and Erfurt, became Dean of the Philosophical Faculty in the latter University, and was crowned a poet by Maximilian II in 1566. He became pastor of St Blasius' Church, Mühlhausen, in 1586, and Superintendent there. He died in 1598:

> Das ist des Vaters Wille,
> Der uns erschaffen[1] hat;
> Sein Sohn hat Gut's die Fülle
> Erworben uns aus Gnad'[2];
> Auch Gott[3], der heil'ge Geist,
> Im Glauben uns regieret,
> Zum Reich des Himmels führet:
> Ihm sei Lob, Ehr' und Preis. B.G. xviii. 104.

English translations of the Hymn are noted in the *Dictionary of Hymnology*, p. 508.

Form. Simple (*Corno*, 2 *Ob.*, *Strings*, *Continuo*). *Choralgesänge*, No. 328.

[1] 1569 geschaffen. [2] 1569 Erworben und Genad. [3] 1569 Gott.

CANTATA LXXIV. WER MICH LIEBET, DER WIRD MEIN WORT HALTEN. Whit Sunday (1735[1])

Melody: "*Kommt her zu mir, spricht Gottes Sohn*"
Anon. 1530

The melody of the concluding Choral is an anonymous tune published as a broadsheet, "Ain schöns newes Christlichs lyed," in 1530, with Georg Grüenwald's (d. 1530) Hymn, "Kommt her zu mir, spricht [sagt] Gottes Sohn."

The melody also occurs in Cantatas 86 and 108. There is earlier authority for Bach's variation of the opening (1534) and closing (1598) phrases of the melody.

The words of the Choral are the second stanza of Paul Gerhardt's "Gott Vater, sende deinen Geist," first published in the 1653 (Berlin) edition of Crüger's *Praxis Pietatis Melica*, to a melody by Johann Crüger, "Den Herren meine Seel' erhebt."

[1] The Cantata is an elaboration of No. 59. See Spitta, I. 511.

CANTATA LXXV

Bach follows general use in associating the Hymn with the tune "Kommt her zu mir" (*supra*) :

> Kein Menschenkind hier auf der Erd'
> Ist dieser edlen Gabe werth,
> Bei uns ist kein Verdienen ;
> Hier gilt gar nichts als Lieb' und Gnad',
> Die Christus uns verdienet hat
> Mit Büssen und Versühnen. B.G. xviii. 146.

Form. Simple (*Tromba, Ob. da caccia,* 2 *Ob., Strings, Continuo*). *Choralgesänge,* No. 223.

CANTATA LXXV. DIE ELENDEN SOLLEN ESSEN.

First Sunday after Trinity[1] (1723)

(*a*)

The melody of the concluding Choral of Part I is that of Samuel Rodigast's Hymn, "Was Gott thut, das ist wohlgethan" (see Cantata 12).

The words of the Choral are the fifth stanza of that Hymn :

> Was Gott thut, das ist wohlgethan !
> Muss ich den Kelch gleich schmecken,
> Der bitter ist nach meinem Wahn:
> Lass ich mich doch nicht[2] schrecken :
> Weil doch zuletzt ich werd' ergötzt
> Mit süssem Trost im Herzen ;
> Da weichen alle Schmerzen. B.G. xviii. 171.

Form. Extended (2 *Ob., Strings, Continuo*).

[1] Spitta, II. 357 n., points out that the Cantata, in an abridged and altered form, beginning with the first *Recitativo,* was known under the title, "Was hilft des Purpurs Majestät."

[2] 1676 nichts.

(b)

The Second Part of the Cantata opens with an Orchestral *Sinfonia*, or Orchestral Choral Fantasia (*Tromba, Strings, Continuo*), on the melody "Was Gott thut." Schweitzer[1] observes that this is the only occasion on which Bach has given a Choral purely orchestral treatment. The Tromba has the *cantus*.

(c)

The words, melody, and form of the Choral concluding the Second Part are identical with those of (a) *supra*.

CANTATA LXXVI. DIE HIMMEL ERZÄHLEN DIE EHRE GOTTES. Second Sunday after Trinity[2] (1723)

(a)

The words and melody of the concluding Choral of Part I are Luther's "Es woll' uns Gott genädig sein" (see Cantata 69). The words are the first stanza of the Hymn:

> Es woll' uns Gott genädig sein
> Und seinen Segen geben;
> Sein Antlitz uns mit hellem Schein
> Erleucht' zum ew'gen Leben:

[1] Vol. II. 150. See also Spitta, II. 355.

[2] Beginning with the opening of the Second Part, and under the title, "Gott segne noch die treue Schaar," the Cantata was used for a Reformation Festival. See Spitta, II. 357 n.

CANTATA LXXVI

> Dass wir erkennen seine Werk'
> Und was ihm lieb auf Erden,
> Und Jesus Christus Heil und Stärk'
> Bekannt den Heiden werden,
> Und sie zu Gott bekehren!
>
> B.G. xviii. 218.

Form. Extended (*Tromba, Strings, Continuo*). Erk, No. 201.

(*b*)

The concluding Choral of Part II is a repetition of (*a*) *supra*, the words being the third stanza of Luther's Hymn:

> Es danke, Gott, und lobe dich
> Das Volk in guten Thaten;
> Das Land bringt Frucht und bessert sich:
> Dein Wort ist wohl gerathen.
> Uns seg'ne Vater und der Sohn,
> Uns seg'ne Gott, der heil'ge Geist;
> Dem alle Welt die Ehre thu',
> Vor ihm sich fürchte allermeist,
> Und[1] sprech von Herzen: Amen!
>
> B.G. xviii. 230.

Form. Extended (*Tromba, Strings, Continuo*). Erk, No. 201.

[1] 1524 Nu.

CANTATA LXXVII. DU SOLLST GOTT, DEINEN HERREN, LIEBEN. Thirteenth Sunday after Trinity (*c.* 1725)

Melody: "*Dies sind die heil'gen zehn Gebot'*" Anon. 1524

Ky - rie - leis

Melody: "*In Gottes Namen fahren wir*" Anon. 1536

(a)

The opening Chorus of the Cantata introduces a Choral melody that does not appear elsewhere in the Cantatas, Oratorios, or Motetts. The movement is a Chorus upon the words, " Du sollst Gott, deinen Herren, lieben von ganzem Herzen, von ganzer Seele, von allen Kraften, von ganzem Gemüthe, und deinen Nächsten als dich selbst" ("Thou shalt love the Lord thy God with all thy heart, and with all thy soul, and with all thy strength, and with all thy mind, and thy neighbour as thyself," St Luke x. 27). As Spitta comments[1], Bach called to mind the continuation of the Scripture text: "On these two commandments hang all the law and the prophets." He therefore enforces the text by the melody of Luther's Hymn, " Dies sind die heil'gen zehn Gebot'" ("These are the sacred ten commandments"). While the Chorus is worked out in quavers from the first line of the melody, the lesser commandment is stated by the Tromba da tirarsi, which announces the tune in crotchets, while the greater commandment is emphasised by the Organ, treating the melody in minims as a *cantus firmus*.

The melody is an adaptation of the tune of the song, "In Gottes Namen fahren wir." Reconstructed for Luther's Hymn, the tune was published both in

[1] Vol. II. 430.

the Erfurt *Enchiridion* of 1524 and in Johann Walther's *Geystliche gesangk Buchleyn* at Wittenberg in the same year. The reconstruction of the tune may be attributed to Walther.

There is a harmonisation of the tune in the *Choralgesänge*, No. 66. Organ Works, N. xv. 103; xvi. 42, 47.

Form. Choral Fantasia (*Tromba da tirarsi, Strings, Continuo*)[1].

(*b*)

For the melody of the concluding Choral, "Ach Gott, vom Himmel sieh' darein," see Cantata 2.

Bach's MS. lacks a text here[2] and the words of the Choral were selected as appropriate by Carl Friedrich Zelter (1758-1833). They are the eighth stanza of the Hymn, "Wenn einer alle Ding verstünd," published in *Das Hannoverische ordentliche, vollständige Gesangbuch* (Lüneburg, 1657), attributed to David Denicke:

> Du stellst, mein Jesu, selber dich[3]
> Zum Vorbild wahrer Liebe:
> Gieb mir auch Gnad' und Kraft, dass ich[4]
> Gott und den Nächsten liebe[5];

[1] See Spitta, II. 430, on the relation of the movement to the Organ Chorals. He regards it as a development between the earlier *Orgelbüchlein* (N. xv. 103) and the later *Clavierübung* (N. xvi. 42) Preludes.

[2] Spitta, II. 429, remarks that the MS. indicates haste and lack of leisure.

[3] 1657 Herr Jesu, du stellst selber dich.

[4] 1657 Verleih, das dem zu folge ich.

[5] 1657 Die lieb am nechsten übe.

Dass ich bei[1] Allem, wo ich kann,
Stets lieb'[2] und helfe Jedermann
Nach deinem Wort und Weise[3].
             B.G. xviii. 254.

Form. Simple[4]. *Choralgesänge,* No. 6.

CANTATA LXXVIII. JESU, DER DU MEINE SEELE.
Fourteenth Sunday after Trinity (after 1734)

Melody: "*Wachet, doch, erwacht, ihr Schläfer*" Anon. 1662

A Choral Cantata, on Johann Rist's Lenten Hymn, "Jesu, der du meine Seele," first published in Part I of his *Himlischer Lieder* (Lüneburg, 1641).

The melody of the opening and concluding movements has, from 1663, been known by its association with Rist's Hymn. In its earliest form it belonged to the secular song, "Daphnis ging für wenig Tagen," and is found in association with it in Theobald Grummer's *Des Daphnis aus Cimbrien*

---
[1] 1657 in.   [2] 1657 Lieb, trew.
[3] 1657 Wie ich mirs wünsch, erweise.
[4] The Score does not indicate the instrumentation.

CANTATA LXXVIII 291

Galathee (Hamburg, 1642). In 1643 it was used for the song, "Ferdinand, du grosser Kaiser." In the 1662 (Frankfort) edition of Johann Crüger's *Praxis Pietatis Melica* the tune is attached to Georg Philipp Harsdörffer's (1607-58) "Wachet doch, erwacht, ihr Schläfer," and in Nicolaus Stenger's *Christlich- neuvermehrt und gebessertes Gesangbuch* (Erfurt, 1663) it was set to Rist's Hymn. With that Hymn it has been particularly associated ever since. The melody occurs also in Cantata 105. There are other harmonisations of the tune in the *Choralgesänge*, Nos. 185, 186, 187. For the first half of the tune (lines 1-4) Bach's text is invariable and follows the Rothenburg Cantor Georg Falck's *Andacht-erweckende Seelen-Cymbeln* (1672). For lines 7 and 8 he uses more than one form. In Cantata 78 he follows the Leipzig organist Daniel Vetter's *Musicalische Kirch- und Hauss-Ergötzlichkeit* (Part II, Leipzig, 1713). Elsewhere his eighth line follows Telemann (1730).

(*a*)

The words of the opening movement are the first stanza of Johann Rist's Hymn:

    Jesu, der du meine Seele
    Hast durch deinen bittern Tod
    Aus des Teufels finstrer Höhle
    Und der schweren Seelennoth[1]
        [1] 1641 Sünden Noth.

Kräftiglich heraus gerissen,
Und mich Solches lassen wissen
Durch dein angenehmes Wort:
Sei doch jetzt, O Gott, mein Hort!
B.G. xviii. 257.

Translations of the Hymn into English are noted in the *Dictionary of Hymnology*, p. 966.
Form. Choral Fantasia[1] (*Corno, Flauto,* 2 *Ob., Strings, Continuo*).

(*b*)

The words of the concluding Choral are the twelfth stanza of Rist's Hymn:

Herr! ich glaube, hilf mir Schwachen,
Lass mich ja verzagen nicht[2]:
Du, du kannst mich stärker machen,
Wenn mich Sünd' und Tod anficht.
Deiner Güte will ich trauen,
Bis ich fröhlich werde schauen
Dich, Herr Jesu, nach dem Streit
In der süssen Ewigkeit.
B.G. xviii. 286.

Form. Simple (*Corno, Flauto,* 2 *Ob., Strings, Continuo*). *Choralgesänge,* No. 188[3]

[1] The movement is built upon the same ground Bass as the *Crucifixus* of the B Minor Mass.
[2] 1641 Lass uns ja verderben nicht.
[3] The last four lines of the second *Recitativo* are from the tenth stanza of the Hymn.

CANTATA LXXIX. GOTT, DER HERR, IST SONN' UND SCHILD[1]. For the Reformation Festival (? 1735)

Melody: "*Nun danket alle Gott*"   Johann Crüger 1648

(*a*)

The melody of the third movement is Johann Crüger's "Nun danket alle Gott," first published, with Martin Rinkart's Hymn, in the 1648 (Berlin) edition of the *Praxis Pietatis Melica*. The tune appears there anonymously; but in the 1653 Crüger-Runge *Geistliche Lieder und Psalmen* Crüger's initials are attached to it. It has been conjectured to be an adaptation by Crüger of a melody either by Rinkart, who was a good musician, or Luca Marenzio, a choirmaster at Rome, who died in 1598.

[1] An English version of the Cantata, "The Lord is a Sun and Shield," is published by Novello & Co.

The melody occurs also in Cantata 192 and in the third of the "Drei Choräle zu Trauungen" (*Choralgesänge*, No. 258). There is another harmonisation of the tune in the *Choralgesänge*, No. 257. Organ Works, N. xvii. 40. Bach's text is invariable. The words of the movement are the first stanza of Martin Rinkart's Hymn, first published in 1648 (*supra*).

Rinkart was born at Eilenburg in 1586. He became a chorister of St Thomas' Church, Leipzig, was briefly Cantor at Eisleben, and in 1617 was appointed Archidiaconus at Eilenburg. He died in 1649. His Hymn of Thanksgiving ("Lob- und Danklied") is founded on Ecclesiasticus l. 22-24:

> Nun danket Alle Gott
> Mit Herzen, Mund und Händen,
> Der grosse Dinge thut
> An uns und allen Enden,
> Der uns von Mutterleib'
> Und Kindesbeinen an
> Unzählig viel zu gut,
> Und noch jetzo gethan!
>
> B.G. xviii. 308.

Translations of the Hymn into English are noted in the *Dictionary of Hymnology*, pp. 963, 1679.

Form. Extended (2 *Cor.*, Timpani, 2 *Fl.*, 2 *Ob.*, Strings, Continuo). *Choralgesänge*, No. 259.

CANTATA LXXIX   295

Melody: "*Nun lasst uns Gott dem Herren*"   Anon. 1575

Melody: "*Nun lasst uns Gott dem Herren*"   Anon. 1587

(*b*)

The melody of the concluding Choral is that of Ludwig Helmbold's Grace after Meat, "Nun lasst uns Gott dem Herren," which was published first in Helmbold's *Geistliche Lieder, den Gottseligen*

Christen zugericht (Mühlhausen, 1575), and repeated in Nicolaus Selnecker's *Christliche Psalmen, Lieder, und Kirchengesenge* (Leipzig, 1587). The monotonous melody, which Bach uses (with some modifications introduced by Crüger [1649]), is founded on the one that accompanies the Hymn in Selnecker's volume. It is clear, however, that Selnecker's is a variation of the descant melody of the four-part setting of the Hymn in Helmbold's *Geistliche Lieder*. The monotony of the tune suggests that the Tenor is the true melody there. Versions of the former, equally monotonous and derived from the 1575 text, are set to the Hymn in other collections between 1575 and 1598.

The melody occurs also in Cantatas 165 and 194. It is sometimes quoted as "Wach auf, mein Herz, und singe," from its association with Paul Gerhardt's Morning Hymn.

The words of the concluding Choral are the eighth stanza of Helmbold's Hymn:

> Erhalt' uns in der Wahrheit,
> Gieb ewigliche Freiheit,
> Zu preisen deinen Namen
> Durch Jesum Christum, Amen!
> B.G. xviii. 316.

English translations of the Hymn are noted in the *Dictionary of Hymnology*, p. 508.

Form. Embellished (2 *Cor.*, *Timpani*, 2 *Fl.* 2 *Ob.*, *Strings*, *Continuo*). *Choralgesänge*, No. 267

CANTATA LXXX. EIN' FESTE BURG IST UNSER
GOTT[1]. For the Reformation Festival (1730[2])

Melody: "*Ein' feste Burg*"   Martin Luther 1535

A Choral Cantata[3], on Luther's Hymn, "Ein' feste Burg," a free version of Psalm xlvi, probably written for the Diet of Speyer in 1529, though an earlier origin has been suggested. It was first published by Klug in 1535 [1529] (*infra*).

The melody, which dominates the Cantata and forms the subject of four of its movements, is quoted above from Joseph Klug's *Geistliche Lieder zu Wittemberg* (Wittenberg, 1535), where it appears in

[1] English versions of the Cantata are published by Novello & Co., "A stronghold sure," and Breitkopf & Haertel, "A stronghold sure is God our Lord."

[2] The work is the enlargement of an early (1716) Cantata, "Alles was von Gott geboren" (Spitta, I. 563), written for the Third Sunday in Lent.

[3] See p. 33 *supra*.

298   CANTATA LXXX

association with Luther's Hymn. Both tune and words, however, are found in Jobst Gutknecht's *Kirchē gesenge, mit vil schönen Psalmen unnd Melodey* (Nürnberg, 1531), and in Klug's collection of Luther's Hymns. That the melody in its present form is by Luther is generally agreed; but the extent to which he was indebted to Gregorian material is in dispute.

The melody does not occur elsewhere in the Cantatas, Oratorios, or Motetts There are two harmonisations of it in the *Choralgesänge*, Nos. 74, 75. Organ Works, N. xviii. 30.

(*a*).

The words of the opening movement are the first stanza of Luther's Hymn:

> Ein' feste Burg ist unser Gott,
> Ein' gute Wehr und Waffen;
> Er hilft uns frei aus aller Noth,
> Die uns jetzt hat betroffen.
> Der alte Böse Feind,
> Mit Ernst er's jetzt meint;
> Gross' Macht und viel' List
> Sein' grausam Rüstung ist,
> Auf Erd' ist nicht sein's Gleichen.
>   B.G. xviii. 319.

Translations of the Hymn into English are noted in the *Dictionary of Hymnology*, pp. 324-325, 1561, 1631, 1729.

Form. Choral Fantasia. The *cantus* is treated freely and fugally (3 *Trombe, Timpani*, 2 *Ob., Strings, Organ*[1]).

(*b*)

The words of the second movement are the second stanza of Luther's Hymn:

> Mit unsrer Macht ist nichts gethan,
> Wir sind gar bald verloren.
> Es streit't für uns der rechte Mann,
> Den Gott selbst hat[2] erkoren.
> Fragst du, wer der ist?
> Er heisst Jesus[3] Christ,
> Der Herre Zebaoth,
> Und ist kein ander Gott;
> Das Feld muss er behalten.
>
> B.G. xviii. 351.

Form. Marked "Aria," the movement is a *Duetto* for Bass and Soprano, the latter singing a

---

[1] The vocal parts of this movement are printed in the Appendix to B.G. xviii. 381 to a Latin version of the first stanza of the Hymn:

> Gaudete omnes populi,
> Habemus Deum fortem!
> Est Sabaoth, qui nullibi
> Vult peccatoris mortem.
> Ecclesiam suam
> Servat securam,
> Et firmissimum
> Eius est fulcrum.
> A malo hoste
> Tuetur optime;
> Vim Satanae ligavit.

[2] 1535 hat selbs.   [3] 1535 Jhesu.

florid and free version of the Choral melody (*Oboe, Strings, Continuo*).

(*c*)

The words of the fifth movement are the third stanza of Luther's Hymn :

> Und wenn die Welt voll Teufel wär',
> Und wollten uns[1] verschlingen,
> So fürchten wir uns nicht so sehr,
> Es soll uns doch gelingen.
> Der Fürst dieser Welt,
> Wie sau'r er sich stellt,
> Thut er uns doch nichts[2];
> Das macht, er ist gericht't ;
> Ein Wörtlein kann ihn fällen.
>
> B.G. xviii. 360.

Form. A Choral Fantasia, in form an Unison Chorus (3 *Trombe, Timpani*, 2 *Ob. d'amore, Strings, Continuo*)[3].

---

[1] 1535 wolt uns gar.   [2] 1535 nicht.
[3] In the Appendix to B.G. xviii. 389, the melody is printed to a Latin version of the fourth stanza of the Hymn :

> Manebit verbum Domini,
> Quid tela hostis dira,
> Nam Spiritus paracleti
> Adest tutela mira.
> Sumat corpora,
> Sumat spolium
> Cara omnia,
> Nil nobis perditum,
> Nam manet regnum Dei.

(d)

The words of the concluding movement are the fourth stanza of Luther's Hymn :

> Das Wort sie sollen lassen stahn
> Und kein'n Dank dazu haben.
> Er ist bei uns wohl auf dem Plan
> Mit seinem Geist und Gaben.
> Nehmen sie uns den Leib[1],
> Gut, Ehr', Kind und Weib;
> Lass fahren dahin,
> Sie haben's kein'n Gewinn ;
> Das Reich muss uns doch bleiben.
> B.G. xviii. 378.

Form. Simple (*Continuo*)[2]. *Choralgesänge*, No. 76.

CANTATA LXXXI. JESUS SCHLÄFT, WAS SOLL ICH HOFFEN[3]? Fourth Sunday after the Epiphany (1724)

The melody of the concluding Choral is Johann Crüger's "Jesu, meine Freude" (see Cantata 64).

[1] 1535 Nemen sie den Leib.
[2] Erk, 1. 114 (No. 24), gives the instrumentation of the movement as: 3 *Trombe, Flauto, Oboe da caccia*, 2 *Ob.*, *Strings, Organ, Continuo.*
[3] English versions of the Cantata are published by Novello & Co., "Jesus sleeps, what hope remaineth ? " and Breitkopf & Haertel, "Jesus sleeps, vain all my hoping."

CANTATA LXXXIII

The words are the second stanza of Johann Franck's "Jesu, meine Freude" (see Cantata 64):

> Unter deinen Schirmen
> Bin ich vor den Stürmen
> Aller Feinde frei.
> Lass den Satan wittern,
> Lass den Feind erbittern,
> Mir steht Jesus bei.
> Ob es jetzt
> Gleich kracht und blitzt,
> Obgleich Sünd' und Hölle schrecken :
> Jesus will mich decken.   B.G. xx. (i) 24.

Form.   Simple (2 *Ob. d'amore, Strings, Continuo*).
Choralgesänge, No. 197.

CANTATA LXXXIII.   ERFREUTE ZEIT IM NEUEN BUNDE.   Purification of the B.V.M. (? 1724)

Melody: "*Mit Fried' und Freud' ich fahr' dahin*"
? Martin Luther 1524

* In later texts a ♭ here.

CANTATA LXXXIII

The melody and words of the concluding Choral are Luther's "Mit Fried' und Freud' ich fahr' dahin," a free rendering of the "Nunc Dimittis," first published, with the melody, in Johann Walther's *Geystliche gesangk Buchleyn* (Wittenberg, 1524). With considerable probability the tune may be attributed to Luther.

The melody occurs also in Cantatas 95, 106, and 125. There is a harmonisation of it in the *Choralgesänge*, No. 249. Organ Works, N. xv. 50.

The words of the Choral are the fourth stanza of Luther's Hymn, being the appointed Hymn for the Festival:

> Er ist das Heil und selig Licht
> Für die Heiden,
> Zur erleuchten[1], die dich kennen nicht,
> Und zu weiden.
> Er ist dein's Volks Israel
> Der Preis, Ehr', Freud' und Wonne.
>
> B.G. xx. (i) 76.

Translations of the Hymn into English are noted in the *Dictionary of Hymnology*, p. 760.

Form. Simple (*Corno*, 2 *Ob.*, *Strings*, *Continuo*). *Choralgesänge*, No. 250.

In the second movement (B.G. xx. (i) 64), marked "Intonazione (Nunc Dimittis) e Recitativo,"

---

[1] 1524 leuchten.

the Bass declaims the words, "Herr, nun lässest du deinen Diener in Friede fahren, wie du gesaget hast," to the old Intonation of the "Nunc Dimittis."

CANTATA LXXXIV. ICH BIN VERGNÜGT MIT MEINEM GLÜCKE. Septuagesima Sunday (1731 or 1732[1])

The melody of the concluding Choral is Georg Neumark's "Wer nur den lieben Gott lässt walten" (see Cantata 21).

The words of the Choral are the twelfth stanza of Emilie Juliane Countess of Schwarzburg-Rudolstadt's funerary Hymn, "Wer weiss, wie nahe mir mein Ende" (see Cantata 27):

> Ich leb' indess in dir vergnüget,
> Und sterb' ohn' alle Kümmerniss.
> Mir g'nüget, wie es mein Gott[2] füget,
> Ich glaub' und bin es ganz gewiss:
> Durch deine Gnad' und Christi Blut
> Machst[3] du's mit meinem Ende gut'.
>
> B.G. xx. (i) 98.

Form. Simple (*Oboe, Strings, Continuo*). *Choralgesänge*, No. 373.

---

[1] The B.G. title page bears the date 1729.
[2] 1695 mein Gott es.   [3] 1695 Mach.

Cantata LXXXV. Ich bin ein guter Hirt[1].
Second Sunday after Easter ("Misericordias Domini") (1735)

Melody: "*Allein Gott in der Höh' sei Ehr'*"
Nicolaus Decius 1539

Melody: "*Gloria in excelsis Deo*" 1545[2]

[1] A Score of this Cantata is also in the *Neue Bachgesellschaft*, ix. (i) 1908.
[2] Johann Spangenberg's *Kirchengesenge Deudtsch* (Magdeburg).

(*a*)

The melody of the third movement is Nicolaus Decius' (or Hovesch) "Allein Gott in der Höh' sei Ehr'," first published, with Decius' rendering of the "Gloria in excelsis," in Valentin Schumann's *Geistliche Lieder auffs new gebessert und gemehrt* (Leipzig, 1539). The melody was formed by putting together phrases 3–4, 7–8, 11 of the "Gloria paschalis." Its association with Becker's Hymn (*infra*) is very general.

The melody occurs also in Cantatas 104, 112, and 128. There is a harmonisation of it in the *Choralgesänge*, No. 12. Bach's version shows slight variations of the original. For the second and third notes following the middle double bar there is early (1545) authority. For his version of the final phrase of the tune in the concluding Choral of Cantata 112 there appears to be none. Organ Works, N. xvi. 39, 40*, 41; xvii. 56, 60, 66; xviii. 4, 5, 7, 11.

The words of the third movement are the first stanza of Cornelius Becker's "Der Herr ist mein getreuer Hirt," a translation of Psalm xxiii, which appeared first in Seth Calvisius' *Harmonia Cantionum ecclesiasticarum* (Leipzig, 1598), and thence in Becker's *Der Psalter Dauids Gesangweis* (Leipzig, 1602).

CANTATA LXXXV

Becker was born at Leipzig in 1561 and became one of the masters in St Thomas' School there. In 1594 he was appointed pastor of St Nicolas' Church, Leipzig, and subsequently Professor of Theology in the University. He died in 1604:

>Der Herr ist mein getreuer Hirt,
>Dem ich mich ganz vertraue :
>Zur Weid' er mich, sein Schäfflein, führt,
>Auf schöner, grüner Aue.
>Zum frischen Wasser leit't er mich,
>Mein' Seel' zu laben kräftiglich
>Durch's sel'ge Wort der Gnaden.
>   B.G. xx. (i) 110.

A translation of the Hymn is noted in the *Dictionary of Hymnology*, p. 121.

Form. Soprano Unison Choral, in the form of a Choral Prelude upon the melody (2 *Ob., Continuo*).

Melody: "*Ist Gott mein Schild und Helfersmann*"
Anon. 1694

(b)

The melody of the concluding Choral, "Ist Gott mein Schild und Helfersmann," was published, with Homburg's Hymn (*infra*), in *Hundert ahnmuthig- und sonderbahr geistlicher Arien* (Dresden, 1694), a collection from which few melodies have passed into common use. The melody has been attributed incorrectly to Bach. He has not used it elsewhere and material is not available to enable the originality of his variations of the tune to be tested.

The words of the concluding Choral are the fourth stanza of Ernst Christoph Homburg's "Ist Gott mein Schild und Helfersmann," or "Gott ist mein Schild und Helfersmann," first published, with a different melody, in Part I of Homburg's *Geistlicher Lieder* (Naumburg, 1659 [1658]).

Homburg was born near Eisenach in 1605. He practised as a lawyer at Naumburg, in Saxony, was regarded by his contemporaries as a poet of high rank, and was admitted a member of Rist's Order of Elbe Swans. He died at Naumburg in 1681:

>Ist Gott mein Schutz und treuer Hirt,
>Kein Unglück mich berühren wird;
>Weicht, alle meine Feinde,
>Die ihr mir stiftet Angst und Pein,
>Es wird zu eurem Schaden sein;
>Ich habe Gott zum Freunde. B.G. xx. (i) 118.

Form. Simple (2 *Ob., Strings, Continuo*). *Choralgesänge*, No. 216.

CANTATA LXXXVI. WAHRLICH, WAHRLICH,
ICH SAGE EUCH. Fifth Sunday after Easter
("Rogate") (*c.* 1725)

(*a*)

The melody of the third movement of the Cantata is Georg Grüenwald's "Kommt her zu mir, spricht Gottes Sohn" (see Cantata 74). The words of the movement are the sixteenth stanza of Grüenwald's Hymn, first published, with the tune, as a broadsheet, entitled "Ain schöns newes Christlichs lyed" (1530).

Grüenwald, an Anabaptist shoemaker, was burnt at the stake as a heretic at Kufstein, in Tyrol, in 1530:

> Und was der ewig güt'ge[1] Gott
> In seinem Wort[2] versprochen hat,
> Geschwor'n bei seinem Namen,
> Das hält und giebt er g'wiss fürwahr[3].
> Er[4] helf' uns zu[5] der Engel[6] Schaar
> Durch Jesum Christum, Amen!
>
> B.G. xx. (i) 127.

English translations of the Hymn are noted in the *Dictionary of Hymnology*, p. 472.

Form. Soprano Unison Choral (2 *Ob.*, *Continuo*)[7].

[1] 1530 gwaltig.   [2] 1530 Geyst.
[3] 1530 unnd war.   [4] 1530 Der.
[5] 1530 in.   [6] 1530 heylig.
[7] In the B.G. Score the voice is not stated.

(*b*)

The concluding Choral is set to the words and melody of Paul Speratus' "Es ist das Heil uns kommen her" (see Cantata 9).

The words are the eleventh stanza of the Hymn:

> Die Hoffnung wart't der rechten Zeit,
> Was Gottes Wort zusaget:
> Wenn das geschehen soll zur Freud',
> Setzt Gott kein' g'wisse Tage.
> Er weiss wohl, wenn's am besten ist,
> Und braucht an uns kein' arge List;
> Dess soll'n wir ihm vertrauen.   B.G. xx. (i) 134.

Form. Simple (*Continuo*). *Choralgesänge*, No. 86.

CANTATA LXXXVII. BISHER HABT IHR NICHTS GEBETEN IN MEINEM NAMEN. Fifth Sunday after Easter ("Rogate") (*c.* 1735)

The melody of the concluding Choral is Johann Crüger's "Jesu, meine Freude" (see Cantata 64).

The words of the Choral are the ninth stanza of Heinrich Müller's "Selig ist die Seele." The Hymn was first published, to a melody of its own, but with the superscription, "Mel.: Jesu, meine Freude," in Müller's *Geistliche Seelen Musik* (Rostock, 1659).

Müller was born at Lübeck in 1631, and from 1653 held various positions at Rostock, as Archdeacon, Professor in the University, pastor of two churches, and Superintendent. He died in 1675:

> Muss ich sein betrübet?
> So mich Jesus liebet,
> Ist mir aller Schmerz
> Über Honig süsse:
> Tausend Zuckerküsse
> Drücket er an's Herz.
> Wenn die Pein
> Sich stellet ein,
> Seine Liebe macht zur Freuden
> Auch das bitt're Leiden. B.G. xx. (i) 152.

Form. Simple (*Oboe*, 2 *Ob. da caccia, Strings, Continuo*). *Choralgesänge,* No. 201.

CANTATA LXXXVIII. SIEHE, ICH WILL VIEL FISCHER AUSSENDEN[1]. Fifth Sunday after Trinity (1732)

The melody and words of the concluding Choral are Georg Neumark's "Wer nur den lieben Gott lässt walten" (see Cantata 21).

The words are the seventh stanza of the Hymn:

> Sing', bet' und geh' auf Gottes Wegen,
> Verricht' das Deine nur getreu,
> Und trau' des Himmels reichem Segen,
> So wird er bei dir werden neu:
> Denn welcher seine Zuversicht
> Auf Gott setzt, den verlässt er nicht.
> B.G. xx. (i) 178.

Form. Simple (2 *Ob. d'amore, Taille*[2], *Strings, Continuo*). *Choralgesänge,* No. 368.

[1] A Score of this Cantata is published by the *Neue Bachgesellschaft,* vii. (i) 1907.
[2] The Taille was a Tenor Bassoon.

CANTATA LXXXIX. WAS SOLL ICH AUS DIR MACHEN, EPHRAIM? Twenty-second Sunday after Trinity (*c.* 1730)

The concluding Choral is set to the melody, " Auf meinen lieben Gott " (see Cantata 5).

The words of the Choral are the seventh stanza of Johann Heermann's Lenten Hymn, " Wo soll ich fliehen hin ? " (see Cantata 5):

>Mir mangelt zwar sehr viel:
>Doch, was ich haben will,
>Ist Alles mir zu gute
>Erlangt mit deinem Blute;
>Damit ich überwinde
>Tod, Teufel, Höll' und Sünde. B.G. xx. (i) 194.

Form. Simple (*Corno,* 2 *Ob., Strings, Continuo*). *Choralgesänge,* No. 26.

CANTATA XC. ES REIFET EUCH EIN SCHRECKLICH ENDE. Twenty-fifth Sunday after Trinity (*c.* 1740)

Melody : " *Vater unser im Himmelreich* " Anon. 1539

CANTATA XC 313

The melody, "Vater unser im Himmelreich," to which the concluding Choral is set, appears first, in association with Luther's versification of the Lord's Prayer, in Valentin Schumann's *Geistliche lieder auffs new gebessert* (Leipzig, 1539). The melody is associated with Moller's Hymn (*infra*) in general use.

The melody also occurs in Cantatas 101 and 102, and in the "St John Passion," No. 5. There is a harmonisation of the tune in the *Choralgesänge*, No. 316, which Bach used for the earlier performances of the "St John Passion." It is noticeable that in that work he keeps to the 1539 text of the melody, whereas in the three Cantatas he substitutes a B natural for G sharp at the thirteenth note of the second line (*supra*) of the 1539 text. Organ Works, N. xv. 105; xvi. 53, 61; xix. 12.

The words of the concluding Choral are the seventh stanza of Martin Moller's "Nimm von uns, Herr, du treuer Gott," a free translation of the Latin "Aufer immensam, Deus, aufer iram," first published (to no specified tune) in Moller's *Meditationes Sanctorum Patrum* (Görlitz, 1584):

> Leit' uns mit deiner rechten Hand,
> Und segne unser' Stadt und Land:
> Gieb uns allzeit dein heil'ges Wort,
> Behüt' vor Teufel's List und Mord;
> Verleih' ein sel'ges Stündelein,
> Auf dass wir ewig bei dir sein! B.G. xx. (i) 214.

English translations of the Hymn are noted in the *Dictionary of Hymnology*, p. 92.

Form. Simple (*Continuo*). *Choralgesänge*, No. 319.

CANTATA XCI. GELOBET SEIST DU, JESU CHRIST.
Christmas Day (*c.* 1740)

A Choral Cantata, on Luther's Christmas Hymn, "Gelobet seist du, Jesu Christ" (see Cantata 64). The melody of the three Choral movements of the Cantata is that of the Hymn (see Cantata 64).

(*a*)

The words of the opening movement are the first stanza of the Hymn:

> Gelobet seist du, Jesu Christ!
> Dass du Mensch geboren bist
> Von einer Jungfrau, das ist wahr,
> Dess freuet sich der Engel Schaar.
> Kyrie eleis!
> B.G. xxii. 3.

Form. Choral Fantasia (2 *Cor.*, *Timpani*, 3 *Ob.*, *Strings*, *Continuo*).

(*b*)

The words of the Choral in the second movement are the second stanza of Luther's Hymn:

> Des ew'gen Vaters einig's Kind
> Jetzt man in der Krippe find't.

In unser armes Fleisch und Blut
Verkleidet sich das ew'ge Gut.
B.G. xxii. 21.

Form. "Recitativ und Choral" for Soprano (*Continuo*)[1].

(c)

The words of the concluding Choral are the seventh stanza of Luther's Hymn:

Das hat er Alles uns gethan,
Sein' gross' Lieb' zu zeigen an;
Dess freu' sich alle Christenheit,
Und dank' ihm dess in Ewigkeit.
Kyrieleis!
B.G. xxii. 32.

Form. Embellished (2 *Cor.*, *Timpani*, 3 *Ob.*, *Strings*, *Continuo*). *Choralgesänge*, No. 109.

CANTATA XCII. ICH HAB' IN GOTTES HERZ UND SINN. Septuagesima Sunday (*c.* 1740)

A Choral Cantata, on Paul Gerhardt's Hymn, "Ich hab' in Gottes Herz und Sinn" (see Cantata 65).

The melody of the five Choral movements is the anonymous "Was mein Gott will, das g'scheh' allzeit," or "Il me souffit de tous mes maulx" (see Cantata 65). Gerhardt's Hymn was published to the tune in 1647.

[1] See p. 44 *supra*.

(a)

The words of the opening movement are the first stanza of Gerhardt's Hymn:

> Ich hab' in Gottes Herz und Sinn
> Mein Herz und Sinn ergeben.
> Was böse scheint, ist mein[1] Gewinn,
> Der Tod selbst ist mein Leben.
> Ich bin ein Sohn
> Dess', der den Thron
> Des Himmels aufgezogen;
> Ob er gleich schlägt
> Und Kreuz auflegt,
> Bleibt doch sein Herz gewogen. B.G. xxii. 35.

Translations of the Hymn are noted in the *Dictionary of Hymnology*, p. 412.

Form. Choral Fantasia (2 *Ob. d'amore, Strings, Continuo*).

(b)

The Choral words in the second movement are the second stanza of Gerhardt's Hymn:

> Es[2] kann mir fehlen nimmermehr!
> Mein Vater muss mich lieben.
> Wenn er mich auch gleich wirft in's Meer,
> So will er mich nur üben
> Und mein Gemüth
> In seiner Güt'
> Gewöhnen fest zu stehen.
> Halt' ich dann Stand,
> Weiss seine Hand
> Mich wieder zu erhöhen. B.G. xxii. 47.

[1] 1647 mir.   [2] 1647 Das.

Form. "Recitativ und Choral" for Bass (*Continuo*)[1].

(c)

The words of the fourth movement are the fifth stanza of Gerhardt's Hymn:

> Zu dem ist Weisheit und Verstand
> Bei ihm ohn' alle Massen;
> Zeit, Ort und Stund' ist ihm bekannt
> Zu thun und auch zu lassen.
> Er weiss, wenn Freud',
> Er weiss, wenn Leid,
> Uns, seinen Kindern, diene,
> Und was er thut,
> Ist alles gut,
> Ob's noch so traurig schiene.   B.G. xxii. 54.

Form. An Alto Unison Choral (2 *Ob. d'amore, Continuo*).

(d)

The Choral words of the seventh movement are the tenth stanza of Gerhardt's Hymn:

> Ei nun, mein Gott, so fall' ich dir
> Getrost in deine Hände;
> Nimm mich, und mache es mit mir[2]
> Bis an mein letztes Ende,
> Wie du wohl weisst,
> Dass meinem Geist
> Dadurch sein Nutz entstehe,
> Und deine Ehr'
> Je mehr und mehr
> Sich in ihr selbst erhöhe.   B.G. xxii. 61.

[1] See p. 44 *supra*.   [2] 1647 mach es du mit mir.

Form. "Choral und Recitativ" (S.A.T.B.). The movement, intersected by *Recitativo* passages for all the vocal parts, is of the Extended *Dialogus* type (*Continuo*).

(*e*)

The words of the concluding Choral are the twelfth stanza of Gerhardt's Hymn:

> Soll ich denn auch des Todes Weg
> Und finst're Strasse reisen;
> Wohlan! ich tret' auf[1] Bahn und Steg,
> Den mir dein' Augen weisen.
> Du bist mein Hirt,
> Der Alles wird
> Zu solchem Ende kehren,
> Dass ich einmal
> In deinem Saal
> Dich ewig möge ehren! B.G. xxii. 68.

Form. Simple (2 *Ob. d'amore, Strings, Continuo*). *Choralgesänge*, No. 347.

CANTATA XCIII. WER NUR DEN LIEBEN GOTT LÄSST WALTEN[2]. Fifth Sunday after Trinity (? 1728)

A Choral Cantata[3], on Georg Neumark's consolatory Hymn, "Wer nur den lieben Gott" (see Cantata 21). All its stanzas (seven) are introduced,

---
[1] 1647 so trät ich.
[2] English versions of the Cantata are published by Novello & Co., "If thou but sufferest God to guide thee," and Breitkopf & Haertel, "He who relies on God's compassion."
[3] See p. 32 *supra*.

but in some cases are subjected to considerable alteration.

As in Cantata 4, "Christ lag in Todesbanden," a single Choral melody, Georg Neumark's "Wer nur den lieben Gott" (see Cantata 21), dominates the present work. But its use is not restricted, as in Cantata 4, to the regular Church Choral forms. Certain numbers, for instance, the fourth and seventh, present the melody clearly. Elsewhere it serves merely as the "motive and incentive," without being the positive *cantus firmus*[1].

(a)

The words of the opening movement are the first stanza of Neumark's Hymn:

> Wer nur den lieben Gott lässt walten
> Und hoffet auf ihn allezeit,
> Den[2] wird er[3] wunderlich erhalten
> In allem Kreuz[4] und Traurigkeit.
> Wer Gott, dem Allerhöchsten, traut,
> Der hat auf keinen Sand gebaut.
> B.G. xxii. 71.

Form. Choral Fantasia (2 *Ob.*, *Strings*, *Continuo*)[5].

[1] Spitta, II. 439.
[2] 1657 Der.
[3] 1657 Ihn.
[4] 1657 aller Noht.
[5] See Spitta, II. 439, on the form of this Chorus.

(*b*)

In the second movement the second stanza of Neumark's Hymn, with important modifications of two of its lines, is involved in the "madrigal" text of the *Recitativo*:

> Was helfen uns die schweren Sorgen?
> Was hilft uns unser Weh und Ach?
> Was hilft es, dass wir alle Morgen
> Es bringt nur bitt'res Ungemach[1].
> Wir machen unser Kreuz und Leid
> Mit christlicher Gelassenheit[2].
>
> B.G. xxii. 83.

Form. "Recitativ und Choral" for Bass[3] (*Continuo*)[4].

(*c*)

The text of the third stanza of Neumark's Hymn is dealt with very freely in the third movement. The Bach-Picander stanza reads:

> Man halte nur ein wenig stille,
> Wenn sich die Kreuzes-Stunde naht,
> Denn unsres Gottes Gnaden-Wille
> Verlässt uns nie mit Rath und That.
> Gott, der die Auserwählten kennt,
> Gott, der sich uns ein Vater nennt,
> Wird endlich allen Kummer wenden,
> Und seinen Kindern Hülfe senden.
>
> B.G. xxii. 84.

[1] 1657 Beseuftzen unser Ungemach.
[2] 1657 Nur grösser durch die Traurigkeit.
[3] See p. 44 *supra*.
[4] See Spitta, II. 438, on the form of this movement.

CANTATA XCIII

The actual text of Neumark's third stanza is as follows:

> Man halte nur ein wenig stille
> Und sey doch in sich selbst vergnügt,
> Wie unsres Gottes Gnadenwille,
> Wie sein' Allwissenheit es fügt.
> Gott der uns Ihm hat auserwehlt,
> Der weis auch sehr wohl, was uns fehlt.

Form. A Tenor *Aria*, suggested by the Choral melody (*Strings, Continuo*).

(d)

The words of the fourth movement are the fourth stanza of Neumark's Hymn:

> Er kennt die rechten Freudenstunden,
> Er weiss wohl, wenn es nützlich sei.
> Wenn er uns nur hat treu erfunden
> Und merket keine Heuchelei:
> So kommt Gott, eh' wir's uns versehn,
> Und lässet uns viel Gut's geschehn.
>
> B.G. xxii. 87.

Form. "Arie (Duett) und Choral" for Soprano and Alto. The Violins and Violas in unison have the melody (*Strings, Continuo*)[1]

(e)

The Choral words of the fifth movement are the fifth stanza of Neumark's Hymn:

> Denk' nicht in deiner Drangsals-Hitze,
> Dass du von Gott verlassen seist,

---

[1] The movement is No. 3 of the Schübler Chorals (N. xvi. 6).

CANTATA XCIII

Dass dieser Gott[1] im Schoosse sitze,
Der sich mit stetem Glücke speist.
Die Folgezeit verändert viel!
Und setzet Jeglichem sein Ziel.
B.G. xxii. 90.

Form. " Recitativ und Choral " for Tenor (*Continuo*)[2].

(*f*)

The text of the sixth movement deals very freely with the sixth stanza of Neumark's Hymn. Similarly, only fragments of the tune appear, the fifth and sixth lines of the melody. The Bach-Picander text is as follows :

Ich will auf den Herren schau'n,
Und stets meinem Gott vertrau'n.
Er ist der rechte Wundersmann,
Der die Reichen arm und bloss,
Und die Armen reich und gross
Nach seinem Willen machen kann.
B.G. xxii. 91.

The actual text of Neumark's sixth stanza reads:

Es sind ja Gott sehr schlechte Sachen
Und ist dem Höchsten alles gleich,
Den Reichen klein und arm zu machen
Den Armen aber gross und reich.
Gott ist der rechte Wundermann,
Der bald erhöhn, bald stürzen kan.

Form. Soprano *Aria*, with fragments of the melody (*Oboe, Continuo*).

[1] 1657 Und dass Gott der.   [2] See p. 44 *supra*.

CANTATA XCIV 323

(g)

The words of the concluding Choral are the seventh stanza of Neumark's Hymn:

> Sing', bet' und geh' auf Gottes Wegen,
> Verricht' das Deine nur getreu,
> Und trau' des Himmels reichem Segen,
> So wird er bei dir werden neu;
> Denn welcher seine Zuversicht
> Auf Gott setzt, den verlässt er nicht.
> B.G. xxii. 94.

Form. Simple (2 *Ob.*, *Strings, Continuo*). *Choralgesänge*, No. 369.

CANTATA XCIV. WAS FRAG ICH NACH DER WELT. Ninth Sunday after Trinity (? 1735)

A Choral Cantata, on Georg Michael Pfefferkorn's Hymn, "Was frag ich nach der Welt" (see Cantata 64).

The melody of the Choral movements is "Die Wollust dieser Welt," or "O Gott, du frommer Gott" (1679) (see Cantata 45).

(a)

The words of the opening movement are the first stanza of Pfefferkorn's Hymn:

> * Was frag ich nach der Welt
> Und allen ihren Schätzen,
> Wenn ich mich nur an dir,
> Mein Jesu, kann ergötzen!
> Dich hab' ich einzig mir

> Zur Wollust vorgestellt,
> Denn du bist meine Ruh':
> Was frag ich nach der Welt!
>
> B.G. xxii. 97.

Form. Choral Fantasia (*Flauto, Strings, Organ, Continuo*)[1].

(*b*)

The Choral words of the third movement are the third stanza of Pfefferkorn's Hymn:

> * Die Welt sucht Ehr' und Ruhm
> Bei hoch erhab'nen Leuten.
> Und denkt nicht einmal dran,
> Wie bald doch diese gleiten!
> Das aber, was mein Herz
> Vor Anderm rühmlich hält,
> Ist Jesus nur allein:
> Was frag ich nach der Welt!
>
> B.G. xxii. 107.

Form. "Recitativ und Choral" for Tenor (2 *Ob., Organ, Continuo*)[2].

(*c*)

The Choral words of the fifth movement are the fifth stanza of Pfefferkorn's Hymn:

> * Die Welt bekümmert sich,
> Im Fall sie wird verachtet,
> Als wenn man ihr mit List
> Nach ihren Ehren trachtet.

---

[1] See Spitta, III. 101, on the form of the movement.
[2] See p. 44 *supra*.

Ich trage Christi Schmach,
So lang es ihm gefällt.
Wenn mich mein Jesus ehrt :
Was frag ich nach der Welt !
                    B.G. xxii. 115.

Form. "Recitativ und Choral" for Bass (*Organ and Continuo*)[1].

(*d*)

The words of the concluding Choral are the seventh and eighth stanzas of Pfefferkorn's Hymn:

* Was frag ich nach der Welt!
Im Hui muss sie verschwinden,
Ihr Ansehn kann durchaus
Den blassen Tod nicht binden.
Die Güter müssen fort,
Und alle Lust verfällt ;
Bleibt Jesus nur bei mir:
Was frag ich nach der Welt !

* Was frag ich nach der Welt!
Mein Jesus ist mein Leben,
Mein Schatz, mein Eigenthum,
Dem ich mich ganz ergeben,
Mein ganzes Himmelreich,
Und was mir sonst gefällt.
Drum sag ich noch einmal :
Was frag ich nach der Welt!
                    B.G. xxii. 127.

Form. Simple (*Flauto*, 2 *Ob.*, *Strings*, *Organ, Continuo*). *Choralgesänge*, No. 281.

---

[1] See p. 44 *supra*.

CANTATA XCV. ·CHRISTUS, DER IST MEIN LEBEN. Sixteenth Sunday after Trinity (? 1732)

Melody: "*Christus, der ist mein Leben*"
Melchior Vulpius 1609

(*a*)

The first of the two Chorals in the opening movement is the anonymous funerary Hymn, "Christus, der ist mein Leben," the oldest accessible form of which is in Melchior Vulpius' *Ein schön geistlich Gesangbuch* (Jena, 1609), where it is set to Vulpius' tune. It has been attributed both to Simon Graf and Anna Countess of Stolberg.

The melody is not found elsewhere in the Cantatas or Motetts or Oratorios. There are harmonisations of it in the *Choralgesänge*, Nos. 46, 47. Bach's treatment of the third line of the tune follows the 1662 (Frankfort) edition of the *Praxis Pietatis Melica*. His treatment of the last line varies: sometimes he uses the 1609 form, and sometimes (*Choralgesänge*, No. 46) the 1662 form.

The words are the first stanza of the Hymn:

> Christus, der ist mein Leben,
> Sterben ist mein Gewinn;
> Dem thu' ich mich ergeben,
> Mit Freud'[1] fahr' ich dahin.
>
> B.G. xxii. 131.

Translations of the Hymn are noted in the *Dictionary of Hymnology*, p. 233.

The words of the second Choral in the first movement are the first stanza of Luther's Hymn, "Mit Fried' und Freud' ich fahr' dahin." The melody also is that of the Hymn (see Cantata 83 for Hymn and melody):

> Mit Fried' und Freud' ich fahr' dahin
> Nach[2] Gottes Willen;
> Getrost ist mir mein Herz und Sinn,
> Sanft und stille.
> Wie Gott mir verheissen hat:
> Der Tod ist mein Schlaf worden.
>
> B.G. xxii. 138.

Form. The two Choral (S.A.T.B.) sections, Extended in form, are separated by *ritornelli*, partly orchestral, partly vocal (Tenor *Recitativo*) (*Corno, 2 Ob. d'amore, 2 Ob., Strings, Continuo*)[3].

---

[1] 1609 Fried.   [2] 1524 Ynn.

[3] See Spitta, II. 462, and Schweitzer, II. 248, on the structure of this funerary Cantata. The first movement may be placed also in the *Dialogus* group.

328   CANTATA XCV

Melody: "*Valet will ich dir geben*"
Melchior Teschner 1614

(b)

The Choral in the second movement is Valerius Herberger's funerary Hymn, "Valet will ich dir geben," first published, words and melody, as a broadsheet at Leipzig in 1614[1]. The melody was composed by Melchior Teschner and bears a close resemblance to the tune "Sellenger's Round." There is another harmonisation of it in the *Choralgesänge*, No. 314. Early (1648) authority exists for Bach's change of the third note before the first double bar, and also (1668) for the changed sixth note from the end of the tune. "St John Passion," No. 28. Organ Works, N. xix. 2, 7.

The words of the Choral are the first stanza of the Hymn:

> Valet will ich dir geben,
> Du arge, falsche Welt,
> Dein sündlich böses Leben
> Durchaus mir nicht[2] gefällt.

[1] See *Bach's Chorals*, Part I, pp. 34–35.   [2] 1614 nichts.

CANTATA XCV

Im Himmel ist gut wohnen,
Hinauf steht mein' Begier,
Da wird Gott ewig[1] lohnen
Dem der[2] ihm dient allhier.

B.G. xxii. 142.

Translations of the Hymn into English are noted in the *Dictionary of Hymnology*, p. 511. *Form*. "Recitativ und Choral" for Soprano. The Unison Choral follows a short *Recitativo* of twelve bars (2 *Ob. d'amore* (*unis.*), *Continuo*).

(c)

The melody and words of the concluding Choral are those of Nicolaus Herman's funerary Hymn, "Wenn mein Stündlein vorhanden ist" (see Cantata 15). The words are the fourth stanza of the Hymn:

Weil du vom Tod erstanden bist,
Werd' ich im Grab nicht bleiben;
Dein letztes Wort mein'[3] Auffahrt ist,
Tod'sfurcht kannst du[4] vertreiben:
Denn wo du bist, da komm' ich hin,
Dass ich stets bei dir leb' und bin.
Drum fahr' ich hin mit Freuden!

B.G. xxii. 153.

Form. Embellished (*Corno*, 2 *Ob. d'amore*, *Strings*, *Continuo*). *Choralgesänge*, No. 356.

[1] 1614 ehrlich. [2] 1614 wer.
[3] 1562 Mein höchster trost dein. [4] 1562 sie.

CANTATA XCVI. HERR CHRIST, DER EIN'GE GOTTES-SOHN. Eighteenth Sunday after Trinity (c. 1740)

A Choral Cantata, on Elisabethe Cruciger's Christmas Hymn, "Herr Christ, der einig' Gott's Sohn" (see Cantata 22). The melody of the opening and concluding movements is that of the Hymn (see Cantata 22).

(a)

The words of the opening movement are the first stanza of the Hymn:

> Herr Christ, der ein'ge Gottes Sohn,
> Vaters in Ewigkeit,
> Aus seinem Herzen entsprossen,
> Gleich wie geschrieben steht.
> Er ist der Morgensterne,
> Sein'n Glanz streckt er so ferne
> Vor andern Sternen klar.   B.G. xxii. 157.

Form. Choral Fantasia (*Corno, Trombone, Flauto piccolo,* 2 *Ob., Strings, Continuo*). The *cantus firmus* is with the Altos.

(b)

The words of the concluding Choral are the fifth stanza of the Hymn:

> Ertödt' uns durch dein' Güte,
> Erweck' uns durch dein' Gnad';
> Den alten Menschen kränke,
> Dass der neu' leben mag,

Wohl hier auf dieser Erden
Den Sinn und all' Begehrden
Und G'danken[1] hab'n zu dir.   B.G. xxii. 184.

Form. Simple (*Corno*, 2 *Ob.*, *Strings, Continuo*). *Choralgesänge*, No. 128.

CANTATA XCVII. IN ALLEN MEINEN THATEN (1734[2])

A Choral Cantata, on Paul Flemming's Hymn, "In allen meinen Thaten" (see Cantata 13).

The melody of the two Choral movements of the Cantata is Heinrich Isaak's "O Welt, ich muss dich lassen" (see Cantata 13), styled in the B.G. Score "Nun ruhen alle Walder." The latter (Paul Gerhardt's) Hymn was first published in 1647, with the direction: "Nach der Melod. O Welt, ich muss dich lassen." Isaak's melody has been attached to Johann Hesse's "O Welt" since 1598[3]. From 1670, at least, the tune is associated with Paul Flemming's "In allen meinen Thaten."

(*a*)

The words of the opening movement are the first stanza of Paul Flemming's Hymn:

[1] 1524 dancken.

[2] Every movement of the Cantata is a stanza of the Hymn. The Score does not indicate the occasion for which the Cantata was written. Schweitzer, II. 242 n., conjectures that it was used for a wedding.

[3] See *Bach's Chorals*, Part I, 5.

CANTATA XCVIII

> In allen meinen Thaten
> Lass' ich den Höchsten rathen,
> Der Alles kann und hat;
> Er muss zu allen Dingen,
> Soll's anders wohl gelingen,
> Selbst geben Rath und That.
> B.G. xxii. 187.

Form. Choral Fantasia (2 *Ob.*, *Fagotti*, *Strings* (*including Violone*), *Organ*).

(*b*)

The words of the concluding Choral are the fifteenth stanza of Flemming's Hymn:

> So sei nun, Seele, deine,
> Und traue dem alleine,
> Der dich erschaffen[1] hat.
> Es gehe, wie es gehe:
> Mein[2] Vater in der Höhe
> Weiss allen Sachen Rath.
> B.G. xxii. 230.

Form. Embellished (2 *Ob.*, *Strings*, *Organ*, *Continuo*). *Choralgesänge*, No. 297.

CANTATA XCVIII. WAS GOTT THUT, DAS IST WOHLGETHAN. Twenty-first Sunday after Trinity (*c.* 1732)

The words and melody of the opening movement are from Samuel Rodigast's Hymn, "Was

---

[1] 1642 geschaffen.   [2] 1642 Dein.

Gott thut, das ist wohlgethan" (see Cantata 12). The words are the first stanza of the Hymn:

> Was Gott thut, das ist wohlgethan,
> Es bleibt gerecht sein Wille;
> Wie er fängt meine[1] Sachen an
> Will ich ihm halten stille.
> Er ist mein Gott, der in der Noth
> Mich wohl weiss zu erhalten:
> Drum lass' ich ihn nur walten. B.G. xxii. 233.

Form. Choral Fantasia (2 *Ob.*, *Taille*[2], Strings, Continuo).

CANTATA XCIX. WAS GOTT THUT, DAS IST WOHLGETHAN. Fifteenth Sunday after Trinity (*c.* 1733)

A Choral Cantata[3], on Samuel Rodigast's Hymn, "Was Gott thut, das ist wohlgethan." The melody of the first and last movements is that of the Hymn (see Cantata 12).

(*a*)

The words of the first movement are the first stanza of the Hymn:

> Was Gott thut, das ist wohlgethan,
> Es bleibt gerecht sein Wille;
> Wie er fängt meine[1] Sachen an
> Will ich ihm halten stille.
> Er ist mein Gott, der in der Noth
> Mich wohl weiss zu erhalten:
> Drum lass' ich ihn nur walten. B.G. xxii. 253.

[1] 1676 seine.   [2] The Taille was a Tenor Bassoon.
[3] See p. 32 *supra*.

334 CANTATA C

Form. Choral Fantasia (*Corno, Flauto, Oboe d'amore, Strings, Continuo*).

(*b*)

The words of the concluding Choral are the sixth stanza of the Hymn:

> Was Gott thut, das ist wohlgethan,
> Dabei will ich verbleiben;
> Es mag mich auf die rauhe Bahn
> Noth, Tod und Elend treiben:
> So wird Gott mich ganz väterlich
> In seinen Armen halten:
> Drum lass' ich ihn nur walten.
>
> B.G. xxii. 276.

Form. Simple (*Corno, Flauto, Oboe d'amore, Strings, Continuo*). *Choralgesänge*, No. 341.

CANTATA C. WAS GOTT THUT, DAS IST WOHLGETHAN (*c.* 1735)[1]

A Choral Cantata, on Samuel Rodigast's Hymn, "Was Gott thut, das ist wohlgethan." The melody of the first and last movements is that of the Hymn (see Cantata 12).

---

[1] The Score does not indicate the occasion for which the Cantata was composed. Wustmann, p. 177, assigns it to the Fifteenth Sunday after Trinity (cf. No. 99). Schweitzer, II. 242 n., conjectures that Bach used it as a Wedding Cantata, and dates it in the early thirties. Spitta, II. 460, puts it *c.* 1735 or 1736. Wustmann marks it "um 1735." Every movement of the Cantata is a stanza of the Hymn.

(*a*)

The words of the first movement are the first stanza of the Hymn:

> Was Gott thut, das ist wohlgethan,
> Es bleibt gerecht sein Wille;
> Wie er fängt meine[1] Sachen an
> Will ich ihm halten stille.
> Er ist mein Gott, der in der Noth
> Mich wohl weiss zu erhalten:
> Drum lass' ich ihn nur walten.
>
> B.G. xxii. 279.

Form. Choral Fantasia (2 *Cor.*, *Timpani*, *Flauto*, *Oboe d'amore*, *Strings*, *Organ*, *Continuo*).

(*b*)

The words of the concluding Choral are the sixth stanza of the Hymn:

> Was Gott thut, das ist wohlgethan,
> Dabei will ich verbleiben;
> Es mag mich auf die rauhe Bahn
> Noth, Tod und Elend treiben:
> So wird Gott mich ganz väterlich
> In seinen Armen halten:
> Drum lass' ich ihn nur walten.
>
> B.G. xxii. 323.

Form. Extended (2 *Cor.*, *Timpani*, *Flauto*, *Ob. d'amore*, *Strings*, *Organ*, *Continuo*).

---

[1] 1676 seine.

CANTATA CI. NIMM VON UNS, HERR, DU TREUER GOTT. Tenth Sunday after Trinity (*c.* 1740)

A Choral Cantata, on Georg Moller's Hymn, "Nimm von uns, Herr, du treuer Gott" (see Cantata 90).

As in Cantatas 4 and 93, where Bach employs a single Hymn as his text, this also is dominated by one melody throughout its Choral movements, the anonymous "Vater unser im Himmelreich" (see Cantata 90).

(*a*)

The words of the opening movement are the first stanza of Moller's Hymn:

> Nimm von uns, Herr, du treuer Gott,
> Die schwere Straf' und grosse Noth[1],
> Die wir mit Sünden ohne Zahl
> Verdienet haben allzumal.
> Behüt' vor Krieg und theurer Zeit,
> Vor Seuchen, Feu'r und grossem Leid.
>
> B.G. xxiii. 3.

Form. Choral Fantasia (*Cornetto*, 3 *Trombones, Flauto*, 2 *Ob., Taille*[2], *Strings, Continuo*[3]).

[1] 1584 Ruth.
[2] The Taille was a Tenor Bassoon.
[3] A suggestion of the melody will be noticed in bars 18–21 of the accompaniment in the second movement.

CANTATA CI

(b)

The Choral words of the third movement are the third stanza of the Hymn:

> Ach! Herr Gott, durch die Treue dein
> Mit Trost und Rettung uns erschein!
> Beweis' an uns deine grosse Gnad',
> Und straf' uns nicht auf frischer That.
> Wohn' uns mit deiner Güte bei,
> Dein Zorn und Grimm fern von uns sei.
>
> B.G. xxiii. 19.

Form. "Recitativ und Choral" for Soprano (*Continuo*)[1].

(c)

The words of the fourth movement are a paraphrase of the fourth stanza of Moller's Hymn:

> Warum willst du so zornig sein?
> Es schlagen deines Eifers Flammen
> Schon über unserm Haupt zusammen.
> Ach, stelle doch die Strafen ein,
> Und trag' aus väterlicher Huld
> Mit unserm schwachen Fleisch Geduld.
>
> B.G. xxiii. 21.

The actual text of Moller's fourth stanza is as follows:

> Warumb wiltu doch zornig sein
> Uber uns arme Würmelein?
> Weistu doch wol, du grosser Gott,
> Das wir nichts sind denn Erd uñ kot.
> Es ist ja für deim Angesicht
> Unser schwacheit verborgen nicht.

[1] See p. 44 *supra*.

Form. A Bass *Aria,* with snatches of the melody (2 *Ob., Taille, Continuo)*[1].

(*d*)

The Choral words of the fifth movement are the fifth stanza of Moller's Hymn :

> Die Sünd' hat uns verderbet sehr;
> Der Teufel plagt uns noch viel mehr.
> Die Welt, auch[2] unser Fleisch und Blut
> Uns allezeit verführen thut.
> Solch' Elend kennst du, Herr, allein :
> Ach, lass' uns dir befohlen sein![3]
>
> B.G. xxiii. 25.

Form. " Recitativ und Choral " for Tenor (*Continuo*)[4].

(*e*)

The words of the sixth movement are a paraphrase of the sixth stanza of Moller's Hymn :

> Gedenk' an Jesu bittern Tod,
> Nimm, Vater, deines Sohnes Schmerzen
> Und seiner Wunden Pein zu Herzen :
> Sie[5] sind ja für die ganze Welt
> Die Zahlung und das Lösegeld ;
> Erzeig' auch mir zu aller Zeit,
> Barmherz'ger Gott, Barmherzigkeit.
> Ich seufze stets in meiner Noth.
> Gedenk' an Jesu bittern Tod.
>
> B.G. xxiii. 27.

---

[1] See Spitta, III. 97–98, upon the Arie-Choral movement.
[2] 1584 und.
[3] 1584 Ach lass es dir zu Hertzen gehn !
[4] See p. 44 *supra*.   [5] Bach's MS. Die.

The actual text of Moller's sixth stanza is as follows:

> Gedenck an deins Sohns bittern Todt,
> Sih an sein heilig Wunden roth:
> Die sind ja für die gantze Welt
> Die Zalung und das Lösegeldt:
> Des trösten wir uns allezeit
> Und hoffen auff Barmherzigkeit.

Form. "Arie (Duett)" for Soprano and Alto, "mit Benutzung der Choral-Melodie" (*Flauto, Ob. da caccia, Continuo*).

(*f*)

The words of the concluding Choral are the seventh stanza of Moller's Hymn:

> Leit' uns mit deiner rechten Hand
> Und segne unsre Stadt und Land;
> Gieb uns allzeit dein heil'ges Wort,
> Behüt' vor's Teufels List und Mord.
> Verleih' ein sel'ges Stündelein,
> Auf dass wir ewig bei dir sein!

B.G. xxiii. 32.

Form. Embellished (*Cornetto*, 3 *Trombones, Flauto*, 2 *Ob., Taille, Strings, Continuo*). *Choralgesänge*, No. 318.

CANTATA CII. HERR, DEINE AUGEN SEHEN NACH DEM GLAUBEN. Tenth Sunday after Trinity (? 1731)

The melody of the concluding Choral is the anonymous "Vater unser im Himmelreich" (see Cantata 90).

The words of the Choral are the sixth and seventh stanzas of Johann Heermann's Lenten Hymn, "So wahr ich lebe, spricht dein Gott," first published in his *Devoti Musica Cordis* (Leipzig, 1630), to the melody "Vater unser" (*supra*):

> Heut' lebst du, heut' bekehre dich!
> Eh' morgen kommt, kann's ändern sich:
> Wer heut' ist frisch, gesund und roth,
> Ist morgen krank, ja wohl gar todt.
> So du nun stirbest ohne Buss',
> Dein Leib und Seel'[1] dort brennen muss.
>
> Hilf, O Herr Jesu, hilf du mir,
> Dass ich noch heute komm' zu dir
> Und Busse thu' den Augenblick,
> Eh' mich der schnelle Tod hinrück':
> Auf dass ich heut' und jederzeit
> Zu meiner Heimfahrt sei bereit. B.G. xxiii. 66.

Translations of the Hymn are noted in the *Dictionary of Hymnology*, p. 1065.

Form. Simple (*Flauto*, 2 *Ob.*, *Strings*, *Continuo*). *Choralgesänge*, No. 320.

CANTATA CIII. IHR WERDET WEINEN UND HEULEN. Third Sunday after Easter ("Jubilate") (? 1735)

The melody of the concluding Choral is the anonymous "Was mein Gott will, das g'scheh' allzeit" (see Cantata 65).

---
[1] 1630 Seel und Leib,

CANTATA CIV 341

The words of the concluding Choral are the ninth stanza of Paul Gerhardt's Hymn, "Barmherzger Vater, höchster Gott," first published in the Berlin (1653) edition of Johann Crüger's *Praxis Pietatis Melica*, to the melody "Durch Adams Fall ist ganz verderbt," to which it is generally set in the Hymn books:

> Ich hab' dich einen Augenblick,
> O liebes Kind, verlassen;
> Sieh' aber, sieh' mit grossem Glück
> Und Trost ohn' alle Maassen
> Will ich dir schon
> Die Freuden-Kron'
> Aufsetzen und verehren.
> Dein kurzes Leid
> Soll sich in Freud'
> Und ewig Wohl[1] verkehren.
>   B.G. xxiii. 94.

Form. Simple (*Tromba, Flauto,* 2 *Ob. d'amore, Strings, Continuo*). *Choralgesänge,* No. 348.

CANTATA CIV. DU HIRTE ISRAEL, HÖRE[2].
    Second Sunday after Easter ("Misericordias Domini") (*c.* 1725)

The melody of the concluding Choral is Nicolaus Decius' "Allein Gott in der Höh' sei Ehr'" (see Cantata 85).

[1] 1653 ewges heyl.
[2] An English version of the Cantata, "Thou Guide of Israel," is published by Novello & Co.

The words of the Choral are the first stanza of Cornelius Becker's Hymn, "Der Herr ist mein getreuer Hirt" (see Cantata 85):

> Der Herr ist mein getreuer Hirt,
> Dem ich mich ganz vertraue;
> Zur Weid' er mich, sein Schäflein, führt,
> Auf schöner, grüner Aue:
> Zum frischen Wasser leit't er mich,
> Mein' Seel' zu laben kräftiglich
> Durch's sel'ge Wort der Gnaden. B.G. xxiii. 116.

Form. Embellished (2 *Ob.*, *Taille*[1], *Strings, Continuo*). *Choralgesänge*, No. 13.

CANTATA CV. HERR, GEHE NICHT IN'S GERICHT.

Ninth Sunday after Trinity (*c.* 1725)

The melody of the concluding Choral is the anonymous "Wachet, doch, erwacht, ihr Schläfer" (see Cantata 78).

The words of the Choral are the eleventh stanza of Johann Rist's Lenten Hymn, "Jesu, der du meine Seele" (see Cantata 78):

> Nun, ich weiss, du wirst mir stillen
> Mein Gewissen, das mich plagt.
> Es wird deine Treu' erfüllen,
> Was du selber hast gesagt:
> Dass auf dieser weiten Erden
> Keiner soll[2] verloren werden,
> Sondern ewig leben soll,
> Wenn er nur ist glaubensvoll. B.G. xxiii. 144.

Form. Extended (2 *Corni*, 2 *Ob.*, *Viola*[3], *Continuo*).

---

[1] The Taille was a Tenor Bassoon.
[2] 1641 je.   [3] See Spitta, II. 426.

CANTATA CVI 343

CANTATA CVI. GOTTES ZEIT IST DIE ALLER-
BESTE ZEIT[1]. "Actus Tragicus[2]" (1711)

Melody: "Ich weiss mir ein Röslein hübsch und fein"
Anon. 1589

---

[1] English versions of the Cantata are published by Novello & Co., "God's time is the best," and Breitkopf & Haertel, "God's time is best."

[2] Spitta, I. 456, suggests that the Cantata was written for the funeral of Philipp Grossgebauer, Rector of the school at Weimar, in 1711. Schweitzer, II. 125, conjectures that the libretto was written by Bach himself.

Melody: "*Ich hab' mein Sach' Gott heimgestellt*"
Anon. 1609

(a)

Into the opening movement Bach introduces a melody which he has not employed elsewhere in the Cantatas, Motetts, or Oratorios. It is found in Johann Rhau's *Gesangbuch* (Frankfort a. Main, 1589) as the Tenor in a four-part setting of the secular song, "Ich weiss mir ein Röslein hübsch und fein," and becomes the melody of the Hymn "Ich hab' mein Sach' Gott heimgestellt" in Melchior Vulpius' *Ein schön geistlich Gesangbuch* (Jena, 1609). Bach uses it in the orchestral accompaniment of this movement. The first line of the melody is identical with the 1565 tune, "Warum betrübst du" (see Cantata 47). The 1589 descant melody was appropriated to the same Hymn in 1598 and is used by Bach in *Choralgesänge*, No. 182; Organ Works, N. xviii. 54, 58.

(*b*)

The words and melody of the Choral in the third movement are from Luther's version of the "Nunc Dimittis," "Mit Fried' und Freud' ich fahr' dahin" (see Cantata 83). The words are the first stanza of the Hymn:

> Mit Fried' und Freud' ich fahr' dahin
> In Gottes Willen;
> Getrost ist mir mein Herz und Sinn,
> Sanft und stille.
> Wie Gott mir verheissen hat;
> Der Tod ist mein Schlaf worden. B.G. xxiii. 166.

Form. A *Dialogus* for Alto and Bass, the Alto having the melody (2 *Viole da gamba, Continuo*).

(*c*)

The melody of the concluding Choral is Seth Calvisius' "In dich hab' ich gehoffet, Herr" (see Cantata 52).

The words are the seventh stanza of Adam Reissner's Hymn, "In dich hab' ich gehoffet, Herr" (see Cantata 52):

> Glorie, Lob, Ehr' und Herrlichkeit
> Sei dir, Gott Vater[1] und Sohn bereit,
> Dem heil'gen Geist mit Namen!
> Die göttlich' Kraft
> Mach' uns sieghaft
> Durch Jesum Christum. Amen. B.G. xxiii. 173.

Form. Choral Fantasia (2 *Fl.*, 2 *Viole da gamba, Continuo*)[2].

[1] 1533 Sei Gott vatern.
[2] See Spitta, I. 463, on the movement.

CANTATA CVII. WAS WILLST DU DICH BE-
TRÜBEN. Seventh Sunday after Trinity (1735)

Melody: "*Was willst du dich betrüben*"   Anon. 1704

A Choral Cantata, on Johann Heermann's Hymn, "Was willst du dich betrüben," first published, to the melody, "Von Gott will ich nicht lassen," in his *Devoti Musica Cordis* (Leipzig, 1630). In Freylinghausen's *Gesangbuch* (1704 [1703]) the Hymn is set to a tune obviously derived from that melody. Bach uses the latter in the first and last movements of the Cantata (see Cantata 11).

(a)

The words of the opening movement are the first stanza of Heermann's Hymn:

> Was willst du dich betrüben,
> O meine liebe Seel'?
> Ergieb dich den zu lieben[1],
> Der heisst Immanuel;

[1] 1630 Thu den nur hertzlich lieben.

CANTATA CVII

Vertraue¹ ihm allein:
Er wird gut Alles machen
Und fördern² deine Sachen,
Wie dir's wird selig sein.   B.G. xxiii. 181.

Form. Choral Fantasia (*Corno da caccia*, 2 *Fl.*, 2 *Ob. d'amore*, *Strings*, *Organ*, *Continuo*).

(*b*)

The words of the closing Choral are the fourteenth stanza of David Denicke's (?) Hymn, "Ich will zu aller Stunde," first published in the *New Ordentlich Gesang-Buch* (Hanover, 1646), and set there, as here, to the tune " Von Gott will ich nicht lassen" (see Cantata 11)³:

Herr, gieb das ich dein' Ehre
Ja all' mein Leben lang
Von Herzengrund vermehre,
Dir sage Lob und Dank.
O Vater, Sohn und Geist!
Der du aus lauter Gnaden
Abwendest Noth und Schaden,
Sei immerdar gepreist.
   B.G. xxiii. 200.

Form. Extended (*Corno da caccia*, 2 *Fl.*, 2 *Ob. d'amore*, *Strings*, *Organ*, *Continuo*).

[1] 1630 Vertraw dich.   [2] 1630 födern.
[3] The preceding movements are set to the six stanzas of Heermann's Hymn. The addition of an alien stanza is irregular.

CANTATA CVIII. ES IST EUCH GUT, DASS ICH
HINGEHE. Fourth Sunday after Easter ("Cantate") (? 1735)

The melody of the concluding Choral is the anonymous "Kommt her zu mir, spricht Gottes Sohn" (see Cantata 74).

The words of the Choral are the tenth stanza of Paul Gerhardt's Hymn, "Gott Vater, sende deinen Geist" (see Cantata 74). The stanza appeared first in a new version of the Hymn in Gerhardt's *Geistliche Andachten* (Berlin, 1667):

> Dein Geist, den Gott vom Himmel giebt,
> Der leitet Alles, was ihn liebt,
> Auf wohlgebahnten Wegen.
> Er setzt und richtet unsern Fuss,
> Dass er nicht anders treten muss,
> Als wo man find't den Segen.
>
> B.G. xxiii. 230.

Form. Simple (2 *Ob. d'amore*, Strings, Continuo). *Choralgesänge*, No. 224.

CANTATA CIX. ICH GLAUBE, LIEBER HERR, HILF MEINEM UNGLAUBEN. Twenty-first Sunday after Trinity (*c.* 1731)

The melody and words of the concluding Choral are Lazarus Spengler's "Durch Adams Fall ist ganz verderbt" (see Cantata 18).

CANTATA CX

The words are the seventh stanza of Spengler's Hymn:

> Wer hofft in Gott und dem vertraut,
> Der wird nimmer[1] zu Schanden:
> Denn wer auf diesen Felsen baut,
> Ob ihm gleich geht zu Handen
> Viel Unfalls hie:
> Hab' ich doch nie
> Den Menschen sehen fallen,
> Der sich verlässt
> Auf Gottes Trost;
> Er hilft sein'n Gläub'gen allen. B.G. xxiii. 255.

Form. Choral Fantasia (*Corno da caccia*, 2 *Ob.*, Strings, *Continuo*).

CANTATA CX. UNSER MUND SEI VOLL LACHENS. Christmas Day[2] (*c.* or after 1734)

The words and melody of the concluding Choral are from Caspar Fuger's Christmas Hymn, "Wir Christenleut'" (see Cantata 40).

The words are the fifth stanza of Fuger's Hymn:

> Alleluja!
> Gelobt sei Gott[3]!
> Singen wir All' aus unsers Herzens Grunde;
> Denn Gott hat heut'
> Gemacht solch' Freud',
> Der wir vergessen soll'n zu keiner Stunde.
>   B.G. xxiii. 324.

[1] 1524 wurdet nicht.

[2] See Spitta (III. 78) on this Cantata. It is partly constructed out of the Overture of an Orchestral Suite (D major). See Cantatas 49, 146, 169, 174, 188 for other instances of the same process.

[3] 1592 Alleluia. Bach's line follows Martin Fritzsch's Dresden *Gesangbuch* of 1593.

Form. Simple (*Tromba,* 2 *Fl.,* 2 *Ob., Oboe da caccia, Strings, Organ, Continuo*). *Choralgesänge,* No. 380.

CANTATA CXI. WAS MEIN GOTT WILL, DAS G'SCHEH' ALLZEIT. Third Sunday after the Epiphany (*c.* 1740)

A Choral Cantata, on Albrecht Margrave of Brandenburg-Culmbach's Hymn, "Was mein Gott will, das g'scheh' allzeit" (see Cantata 72). The melody of the opening and concluding movements is that of the Margrave's Hymn (see Cantata 65).

(*a*)

The words of the opening movement are the first stanza of the Hymn:

    Was mein Gott will, das g'scheh' allzeit,
    Sein Will' der ist der beste[1];
    Zu helfen den'n er ist bereit,
    Die an ihn glauben feste.
    Er hilft aus Noth,
    Der fromme Gott,
    Und züchtiget[2] mit Maassen:
    Wer Gott vertraut,
    Fest auf ihn baut,
    Den will er nicht verlassen.   B.G. xxiv. 3.

Form. Choral Fantasia[3] (2 *Ob., Strings, Continuo*).

[1] *c.* 1554 aller beste.   [2] *c.* 1554 Er tröst die Welt.
[3] Bach here combines the Choral Fantasia and instrumental Concerto forms. See Spitta, III. 103.

(b)

The words of the concluding Choral are the fourth stanza of the Hymn:

> Noch eins, Herr, will ich bitten dich,
> Du wirst mir's nicht versagen :
> Wann mich der böse Geist anficht,
> Lass' mich doch[1] nicht verzagen!
> Hilf, steur' und wehr'[2],
> Ach Gott, mein Herr,
> Zu Ehren deinem Namen.
> Wer das begehrt,
> Dem wird's gewährt ;
> Drauf sprech' ich fröhlich : Amen!
>
> B.G. xxiv. 28.

Form. Simple (2 *Ob.*, *Strings*, *Continuo*). *Choralgesänge*, No. 345.

CANTATA CXII. DER HERR IST MEIN GE-TREUER HIRT[3]. Second Sunday after Easter ("Misericordias Domini") (*c.* 1731)

A Choral Cantata, on Wolfgang Meusel's (Musculus) version of Psalm xxiii, "Der Herr ist mein getreuer Hirt," first published in the Augsburg *Gesangbuch* of 1530 or 1531, and again in the edition of 1533.

Meusel was born at Dieuze, in Lorraine, in 1497. In 1512 he entered the Benedictine monastery at

---

[1] *c.* 1554 Herr. [2] *c.* 1554 Hillf unnd auch wehr.

[3] An English version of the Cantata, "The Lord is my Shepherd," is published by Novello & Co. Every movement of the Cantata is a stanza of the Hymn.

Lixheim, near Saarburg. He embraced Lutheranism, and in 1537 became chief pastor of the Cathedral Church of Augsburg. In 1549 he settled at Bern as Professor of Theology, and died there in 1563.

The melody of the opening and concluding movements is Nicolaus Decius' "Allein Gott in der Höh' sei Ehr'" (see Cantata 85), to which Meusel's Hymn generally was sung.

(a)

The words of the opening movement are the first stanza of Meusel's Hymn:

> Der Herr ist mein getreuer[1] Hirt,
> Hält mich in seiner Hute,
> Darin mir gar nichts mangeln wird
> Irgend an einem Gute.
> Er weidet mich ohn' Unterlass,
> Darauf wächst das wohlschmeckend' Gras
> Seines heilsamen Wortes.   B.G. xxiv. 31.

Translations of the Hymn into English are noted in the *Dictionary of Hymnology*, p. 732.

Form. Choral Fantasia (2 *Cor.*, 2 *Ob. d'amore*, *Strings, Continuo*).

(b)

The words of the concluding Choral are the fifth stanza of Meusel's Hymn:

[1] 1533 Der Herre ist mein trewer.

Gutes und die Barmherzigkeit
Folgen[1] mir nach im Leben,
Und ich werd' bleiben allezeit
Im Haus des Herren eben:
Auf Erd' in christlicher[2] Gemein'
Und nach dem Tod da[3] werd' ich sein
Bei Christo, meinem Herren.

B.G. xxiv. 48.

Form. Embellished (2 *Cor.*, 2 *Ob. d'amore, Strings, Continuo*). *Choralgesänge*, No. 14.

CANTATA CXIII. HERR JESU CHRIST, DU HÖCHSTES GUT. Eleventh Sunday after Trinity (*c.* 1740)

A Choral Cantata, on Bartholomäus Ringwaldt's Lenten Hymn, "Herr Jesu Christ, du höchstes Gut," published in his *Christliche Warnung des Trewen Eckarts* (Frankfort a. Oder, 1588).

Ringwaldt was born at Frankfort a. Oder in 1532. In 1566 he became pastor at Langfeld, or Langenfeld, near Sonnenburg, in Brandenburg, and died there *c.* 1600. He was one of the most prolific Hymn writers of the sixteenth century.

The melody, which Bach uses directly or by suggestion throughout the Cantata, is that usually associated with Ringwaldt's Hymn (see Cantata 48).

[1] 1533 lauffen.   [2] 1533 der Christlichen.   [3] 1533 Tode.

(*a*)

The words of the first movement are the first stanza of Ringwaldt's Hymn:

> Herr Jesu Christ, du höchstes Gut,
> Du Brunnquell aller Gnaden[1],
> Sieh' doch, wie ich in meinem Muth
> Mit Schmerzen bin beladen,
> Und in mir hab' der Pfeile viel,
> Die im Gewissen ohne Ziel
> Mich armen Sünder drücken.   B.G. xxiv. 51.

English translations of the Hymn are noted in the *Dictionary of Hymnology*, p. 962.

Form. Choral Fantasia (2 *Ob.*, *Strings*, *Continuo*). The melody is treated freely[2].

(*b*)

The words of the second movement are the second stanza of the Hymn:

> Erbarm' dich mein in solcher Last,
> Nimm sie aus meinem Herzen,
> Dieweil du sie gebüsset hast
> Am Holz mit[3] Todesschmerzen:
> Auf dass ich nicht für grossem Weh'
> In meinen Sünden untergeh',
> Noch[4] ewiglich verzage[5].   B.G. xxiv. 59.

Form. An Alto Unison Choral ("*Violini all' unisono*," *Continuo*).

[1] 1588 der Genaden.
[2] Bach here combines the Choral Fantasia and instrumental Concerto forms. See Spitta, III. 103.
[3] 1588 im.   [4] 1588 Und.   [5] 1588 vorzage.

(c)

The Choral words of the fourth movement are the fourth stanza of the Hymn:

> Jedoch[1] dein heilsam Wort, das macht
> Mit seinem süssen Singen,
> Dass mir das Herze wieder lacht,
> Als wenn's[2] begünnt' zu springen.
> Dieweil Gott[3] alle Gnad' verheisst,
> Wenn wir nur[4] mit zerknirschtem Geist
> Zu unserm Jesu[5] kommen.   B.G. xxiv. 67.

Form. "Recitativ" and Choral for Bass[6] (*Continuo*[7]).

(d)

The words of the seventh movement are a paraphrase of the seventh stanza of the Hymn:

> Ach Herr, mein Geist, vergieb mir's doch,
> Womit ich deinen Zorn erreget,
> Zerbrich das schwere Sündenjoch,
> Das mir der Satan auferleget,
> Dass sich mein Herz zufrieden gebe
> Und dir zum Preis und Ruhm hinfort
> Nach deinem Wort in kindlichem Gehorsam lebe.
>   B.G. xxiv. 76.

[1] 1588 Aber.   [2] 1588 Und was.   [3] 1588 es.
[4] 1588 Denen die.   [5] 1588 Zu dir, O Jesu.
[6] See p. 44 *supra*.
[7] In the fifth movement (B.G. xxiv. 69) the Tenor *Aria*, "Jesus nimmt die Sünder an," the last line of the melody is brought forward prominently each time to the words, "dein' Sünd' ist dir vergeben." This seems to be the only instance of Bach's setting a Choral melody to new words. See Spitta, III. 96.

The actual text of the seventh stanza is as follows:

> O Herr, vergib, vergib mir's doch
> Umb deines Namens willen,
> Und thu in mir das schwere joch
> Der ubertrettung stillen,
> Das sich mein Hertz zu frieden geb
> Und dir hinfort zu Ehren leb
> Mit Kindtlichem gehorsam.

Form. An "Arie (Duett)" for Soprano and Alto, built upon the first and last lines of the melody (*Continuo*).

(e)

The words of the concluding Choral are the eighth stanza of Ringwaldt's Hymn:

> Stärk' mich mit deinem Freudengeist,
> Heil' mich mit deinen Wunden;
> Wasch' mich mit deinem Todesschweiss
> In meiner letzten Stunden;
> Und nimm mich einst, wann dir's gefällt,
> Im wahren[1] Glauben von der Welt
> Zu deinen Auserwählten.

B.G. xxiv. 80.

Form. Simple[2]. *Choralgesänge*, No. 142.

[1] 1588 rechten.
[2] The orchestration is not indicated, and there is no *Continuo* part.

CANTATA CXIV. ACH, LIEBEN CHRISTEN, SEID
GETROST. Seventeenth Sunday after Trinity
(c. 1740)

A Choral Cantata, on Johannes Gigas', or Heune's, Hymn, "Ach, lieben Christen, seid getrost," first published in a collection of *Geistliche Lieder* (Frankfort a. Oder, 1561). Johannes G. Gigas was born at Nordhausen in 1514. In 1543 he was appointed first Rector of the Fürstlichen Land-Schule at Pforta, and later served as pastor at Freystadt and Schweidnitz. He died at the latter place in 1581.

The melody which Bach uses throughout the Choral movements is the anonymous "Wo Gott der Herr nicht bei uns hält" (see Cantata 73), to which the Hymn was set in 1561.

(a)

The words of the first movement are the first stanza of Gigas' Hymn:

> Ach, lieben Christen, seid getrost;
> Wie thut ihr so verzagen
> Weil uns der Herr heimsuchen thut?
> Lasst uns von Herzen sagen:
> Die Straf' wir wohl verdienet ha'n,
> Solch's muss bekennen[1] Jedermann,
> Niemand darf sich ausschliessen.
> B.G. xxiv. 83.

Form. Choral Fantasia (*Corno, 2 Ob., Strings, Continuo*).

[1] 1561 Solches bekenn ein.

(*b*)

The words of the fourth movement are the third stanza of Gigas' Hymn:

> Kein' Frucht das Weizen-Körnlein bringt,
> Es fall' denn in die Erden;
> So muss auch unser ird'scher Leib
> Zu Staub und Aschen werden,
> Eh' er kommt zu der Herrlichkeit,
> Die du, Herr Christ, uns hast bereit't
> Durch deinen Gang zum Vater.
>
> B.G. xxiv. 101.

Form. A Soprano Unison Choral (*Continuo*).

(*c*)

The words of the concluding Choral are the sixth stanza of Gigas' Hymn:

> Wir wachen[1] oder schlafen ein,
> So sind wir doch[2] des Herren;
> Auf Christum wir getaufet sein,
> Der kann dem Satan wehren.
> Durch Adam auf uns kömmt der Tod,
> Christus hilft uns aus aller Noth.
> Drum loben wir den Herren.
>
> B.G. xxiv. 108.

Form. Simple (*Corno*, 2 *Ob.*, *Strings*, *Continuo*). *Choralgesänge*, No. 386.

[1] 1561 Wie warten hie.   [2] 1561 Sind wir doch ja.

CANTATA CXV. MACHE DICH, MEIN GEIST, BEREIT[1]. Twenty-second Sunday after Trinity (*c.* 1740)

Melody: "*Straf mich nicht in deinem Zorn*"
Anon. 1694

A Choral Cantata, on Johann Burchard Freystein's Hymn, "Mache dich, mein Geist, bereit," first published in the Halle *Geistreiches Gesang-Buch* (1698).

Freystein was born at Weissenfels in 1671. He was educated at Leipzig and Jena Universities, practised at Dresden as a lawyer, and died there in 1718.

The melody of the opening and concluding movements was first published in the *Hundert ahnmuthig- und sonderbahr geistlicher Arien* (Dresden, 1694). It is set there to Johann Georg Albinus' Hymn, "Straf mich nicht in deinem Zorn." From 1712 it was also associated with Freystein's Hymn in the Hymn books.

[1] An English version of the Cantata, "Christian stand with sword in hand," is published by Breitkopf & Haertel.

Bach has not used the melody elsewhere. He had recent (1715) authority for the variations he introduces into bars 3 and 4 of the original tune.

(*a*)

The words of the opening movement of the Cantata are the first stanza of Freystein's Hymn:

> * Mache dich, mein Geist, bereit,
> Wache, fleh' und bete,
> Dass dich nicht die böse Zeit
> Unverhofft betrete;
> Denn es ist
> Satans List
> Über viele Frommen
> Zur Versuchung kommen.   B.G. xxiv. 111.

Translations of the Hymn into English are noted in the *Dictionary of Hymnology*, p. 397.

Form. Choral Fantasia (*Corno, Flauto, Oboe d'amore, Strings, Continuo*).

(*b*)

The words of the concluding Choral are the tenth stanza of Freystein's Hymn:

> * Drum so lasst uns immerdar
> Wachen, fliehen, beten,
> Weil dir Angst, Noth und Gefahr
> Immer näher treten;
> Denn die Zeit
> Ist nicht weit,
> Da uns Gott wird richten
> Und die Welt vernichten.   B.G. xxiv. 132.

Form. Simple (*Corno, Flauto, Oboe d'amore, Strings, Continuo*). *Choralgesänge*, No. 312.

CANTATA CXVI. DU FRIEDEFÜRST, HERR JESU CHRIST[1]. Twenty-fifth Sunday after Trinity (1744)

A Choral Cantata, on Jakob Ebert's Hymn, "Du Friedefürst, Herr Jesu Christ" (see Cantata 67). For Bartholomäus Gesius' melody, see Cantata 67.

(a)

The words of the opening movement are the first stanza of Ebert's Hymn:

> Du Friedefürst, Herr Jesu Christ,
> Wahr'r Mensch und wahrer Gott,
> Ein starker Nothhelfer du bist
> Im Leben und im Tod.
> Drum wir allein
> Im Namen dein
> Zu deinem Vater schreien. B.G. xxiv. 135.

Form. Choral Fantasia (*Corno*, 2 *Ob. d'amore*, Strings, Continuo).

(b)

The words of the concluding Choral are the seventh stanza of Ebert's Hymn:

> Erleucht' auch[2] unsern Sinn und Herz
> Durch den Geist deiner Gnad',
> Dass wir nicht treiben draus ein'n Scherz,
> Der unsrer Seele schad't.

[1] An English version of the Cantata, "O Jesu Christ, Thou Prince of Peace," is published by Novello & Co.
[2] 1601 doch.

O Jesu Christ,
Allein du bist,
Der Solch's wohl kann ausrichten.
B.G. xxiv. 158.

Form. Simple (*Corno*, 2 *Ob. d'amore, Strings, Continuo*). *Choralgesänge,* No. 69.

CANTATA CXVII. SEI LOB UND EHR' DEM HÖCHSTEN GUT (*c.* 1733)[1]

A Choral Cantata, on Johann Jakob Schütz' Hymn of Thanksgiving, "Sei Lob und Ehr' dem höchsten Gut," first published in his *Christliches Gedenckbüchlein, zu Beförderung eines anfangenden neuen Lebens* (Frankfort a. Main, 1675).

Schütz was born at Frankfort a. Main in 1640, practised as an advocate, and died there in 1690.

The melody "Es ist das Heil uns kommen her" (see Cantata 9), which Bach uses for the Hymn, is generally associated with it in the Hymn books.

(*a*)

The words of the opening movement are the first stanza of Schütz' Hymn :

* Sei Lob und Ehr' dem höchsten Gut,
  Dem Vater aller Güte,

[1] The Score does not indicate the occasion for which the Cantata was designed. Every movement of the Cantata is a stanza of the Hymn.

Dem Gott, der alle Wunder thut,
Dem Gott, der mein Gemüthe
Mit seinem reichen Trost erfüllt,
Dem Gott, der allen Jammer stillt.
Gebt unserm Gott die Ehre!
 B.G. xxiv. 161.

Translations of the Hymn into English are noted in the *Dictionary of Hymnology*, p. 1018.

Form. Choral Fantasia (2 *Fl.*, 2 *Ob.*, Strings, Continuo).

(*b*)

The words of the fourth movement are the fourth stanza of Schütz' Hymn:

* Ich rief dem Herrn in meiner Noth:
Ach Gott, vernimm mein Schreien!
Da half mein Helfer mir vom Tod
Und liess mir Trost gedeihen.
Drum dank', ach Gott, drum dank' ich dir;
Ach danket, danket Gott mit mir!
Gebt unserm Gott die Ehre! B.G. xxiv. 172.

Form. Simple (*Continuo*). *Choralgesänge*, No. 90.

(*c*)

The words of the concluding Choral are the ninth stanza of Schütz' Hymn:

* So kommet vor sein Angesicht
Mit jauchzenvollem Springen;
Bezahlet die gelobte Pflicht,
Und lasst uns fröhlich singen:

CANTATA CXVIII

> Gott hat es Alles wohl bedacht
> Und Alles, Alles wohl gemacht!
> Gebt unserm Gott die Ehre!
> B.G. xxiv. 172.

Form. Simple (*Continuo*). *Choralgesänge,* No. 90.

CANTATA CXVIII. O JESU CHRIST, MEIN'S LEBENS LICHT (*c.* 1737)[1]

The melody of the single movement which forms the Cantata is the anonymous "Ach Gott, wie manches Herzeleid" (see Cantata 3).

The words of the movement are the first stanza of Martin Behm's funerary Hymn, "O [Herr] Jesu Christ, mein's Lebens Licht" (see Cantata 58):

> O Jesu Christ, mein's Lebens Licht,
> Mein Hort, mein Trost, mein' Zuversicht,
> Auf Erden bin ich nur ein Gast,
> Und drückt mich sehr der Sünden Last.
> B.G. xxiv. 185.

Form. Choral Motett (*Lituus* 1 *and* 2, *Cornetto,* 3 *Trombones*)[2].

---

[1] The Score does not indicate the occasion for which the Cantata was written. Schweitzer, II. 371, supposes that it was composed for and performed originally at a funeral in the open air. The fact would explain the orchestration of the Cantata. Another Score of it exists, in which Strings (and perhaps Wood Wind) replace the brass instruments.

[2] The *Lituus* probably was a member of the Cornet family.

CANTATA CXIX. PREISE, JERUSALEM, DEN HERRN[1］ For the Inauguration of the Town Council, Leipzig (1723)

Melody: "Herr Gott dich loben wir" Anon. 1535

The words and melody of the concluding Choral of the Cantata are from Luther's translation of the "Te Deum," "Herr Gott dich loben wir" (see Cantata 16). The melody printed above is that portion of the Plainsong to which the clauses Bach uses here were sung. Bach's version of the "Amen" is not found in the 1535 text.

The words of the Choral are the twenty-second and twenty-third clauses of the "Te Deum":

> Hilf deinem Volk, Herr Jesu Christ,
> Und segne das dein Erbtheil ist,
> Wart' und pfleg' ihr'r zu aller Zeit,
> Und heb' sie hoch in Ewigkeit.
>
> B.G. xxiv. 246.

Form. Simple. *Choralgesänge,* No. 134[2].

[1] An English version of the Cantata, "Praise thou the Lord, Jerusalem," is published by Novello & Co.
[2] The orchestration is not stated in the Score. The work was the first of Bach's Rathswahl Cantatas at Leipzig.

CANTATA CXX. GOTT, MAN LOBET DICH IN DER
STILLE. For the Inauguration of the Town
Council, Leipzig (c. 1730[1])

Melody: "*Herr Gott dich loben wir*"　　　Anon. 1535

The words and melody of the concluding Choral of the Cantata are from Luther's translation of the "Te Deum" (see Cantata 16). The melody printed above is that portion of the Plainsong to which the clauses Bach uses here were sung.

[1] The Cantata probably had served for the celebration of the Augsburg Confession in Leipzig, June 26, 1730 (Spitta, II. 469).

The words of the Choral are clauses xx–xxiii of the "Te Deum":

> Nun hilf uns, Herr, den Dienern dein,
> Die mit dein'm Blut[1] erlöset sein.
> Lass' uns im Himmel haben Theil
> Mit den Heil'gen im ew'gen Heil.
> Hilf deinem Volk, Herr Jesu Christ,
> Und segne, was[2] dein Erbtheil ist,
> Wart' und pfleg' ihr'r zu aller Zeit,
> Und heb' sie hoch in Ewigkeit.

B.G. xxiv. 284.

Form. Simple (*Continuo*). *Choralgesänge*, No. 135.

CANTATA CXXI. CHRISTUM WIR SOLLEN LOBEN SCHON. Feast of St Stephen (Christmas) (*c.* 1740)

Melody: "*A solis ortus cardine*"   Anon. 1537

[1] 1535 tewrn Blut.   [2] 1535 das.

Melody: "*Christum wir sollen loben schon*"   Anon. 1524

A Choral Cantata, on Luther's Christmas Hymn, "Christum wir sollen loben schon," a full and close translation of Coelius Sedulius' Christmas Hymn, "A solis ortus cardine," first published, with the melody, in Johann Walther's *Geystliche gesangk Buchleyn* (Wittenberg, 1524) and the *Enchiridion Oder eyn Handbuchlein* (Erfurt, 1524).

The melody is an adjustment of that of the Latin Hymn, and in its simplified form may be attributed to Walther. The original Plainsong is printed above from *Psalmen und geystliche Lieder, die man zu Strassburg, und auch die man inn anderen Kirchen pflegt zu singen* (Strassburg, 1537).

Bach has not used the tune elsewhere in the Cantatas, Oratorios, or Motetts. Organ Works, N. xv. 33; xviii. 23.

(*a*)

The words of the opening movement are the first stanza of Luther's Hymn:

>Christum wir sollen loben schon,
>Der reinen Magd Marien Sohn,
>So weit die liebe Sonne leucht't
>Und an aller Welt Ende reicht.   B.G. xxvi. 3.

Translations of the Hymn into English are noted in the *Dictionary of Hymnology*, p. 4.

Form. Choral Motett (*Cornetto, 3 Trombones, Oboe d'amore, Strings, Continuo*).

(*b*)

The words of the concluding Choral are the eighth stanza of Luther's Hymn:

> Lob, Ehr' und Dank sei dir gesagt,
> Christ, gebor'n von der reinen Magd,
> Sammt[1] Vater und dem heil'gen Geist,
> Von nun an bis in Ewigkeit.
>
> B.G. xxvi. 20.

Form. Simple (*Cornetto, 3 Trombones, Oboe d'amore, Strings, Continuo*). *Choralgesänge*, No. 42.

CANTATA CXXII. DAS NEUGEBOR'NE KINDELEIN. Sunday after Christmas (*c.* 1742)

Melody: "*Das neugebor'ne Kindelein*"

Melchior Vulpius 1609

[1] 1524 Mit.

370   CANTATA CXXII

A Choral Cantata[1], on Cyriacus Schneegass' Christmas Hymn, "Das neugebor'ne Kindelein," probably first published in his *Weihenacht und New Jahrs-Gesäng* (Erfurt, 1595), and thence in his *Geistliche Lieder und Psalmen* (Erfurt, 1597).

Schneegass was born at Buffleben, near Gotha, in 1546. In 1573 he was appointed pastor of St Blasius' Church at Freidrichoda, near Gotha, and died there in 1597.

The melody was first published, with the Hymn, in Melchior Vulpius' *Ein schön geistlich Gesangbuch* (Jena, 1609). It may be attributed confidently to Vulpius himself.

The melody does not occur elsewhere in the Cantatas, Oratorios, or Motetts.

(*a*)

The words of the opening movement are the first stanza of Schneegass' Hymn:

> Das neugebor'ne Kindelein,
> Das herzeliebe Jesulein,
> Bringt abermal ein neues Jahr
> Der auserwählten Christenschaar.
>
> B.G. xxvi. 23.

Translations of the Hymn into English are noted in the *Dictionary of Hymnology*, p. 1014.

Form. Choral Fantasia (2 *Ob.*, *Taille*[2], *Strings*, *Continuo*).

[1] See p. 33 *supra*.   [2] The Taille was a Tenor Bassoon.

CANTATA CXXII

In the third movement, the Soprano *Recitativo*, "Die Engel, welche sich," the Choral melody is in the accompaniment (3 *Flutes and Continuo*).

(*b*)

The Choral words of the fourth movement are the third stanza of the Hymn:

> Ist Gott versöhnt und unser Freund,
> Was kann[1] uns thun der arge Feind?
> Trotz Teufel und der[2] Höllen Pfort'!
> Das Jesulein ist unser Hort.
> B.G. xxvi. 35.

Form. An "Arie" (*Terzetto*) for Soprano, Alto, and Tenor, the Alto (with *Violino I* and *II* and *Viola* in unison) having the melody (*Continuo*).

(*c*)

The words of the concluding Choral are the fourth stanza of the Hymn:

> Es bringt das rechte Jubeljahr;
> Was trauern wir denn immerdar?
> Frisch auf! itzt ist es[3] Singenszeit,
> Das Jesulein wend't alles Leid.
> B.G. xxvi. 40.

Form. Simple (2 *Ob.*, *Taille*, *Strings*, *Continuo*). *Choralgesänge*, No. 57.

[1] 1597 mag.   [2] 1597 Trotz Türcken, Bapst und.
[3] 1597 es ist itzt.

CANTATA CXXIII. LIEBSTER IMMANUEL, HERZOG DER FROMMEN. Feast of the Epiphany (c. 1740)

Melody: "*Liebster Immanuel*"   Anon. 1679

Melody: "*Schönster Immanuel*"   Anon. 1698

* *sic.*

A Choral Cantata, on Ahashuerus Fritsch's "Liebster [Schönster] Immanuel, Herzog der Frommen," first published in his *Himmels-Lust und Welt-Unlust* (Jena, 1679), with the melody.

CANTATA CXXIII

The melody appears either to be derived from, or to be the original of, a "Courant," which is found in a MS. collection of dance tunes dated 1681. The former alternative is the more probable.

The melody does not occur elsewhere in the Cantatas, Oratorios, or Motetts. Erk, No. 113, who attributes the tune tentatively to Johann Rodolph Ahle, prints the melody, with figured Bass, from Schemelli's *Gesang-Buch* (1736). The tune is very freely treated in the Hymn books. Bach's version follows a reconstruction of it in the Darmstadt *Geistreiches Gesang-Buch* (Darmstadt, 1698). His substitution of an F sharp for A natural as the third note of the third bar of the reconstructed melody (*supra*) is found in a version of the tune in 1715. For his treatment of bars 5 and 6 also there is (1731) authority. His closing cadence, based on the 1679 text, is repeated in Schemelli's *Gesang-Buch* (1736).

(*a*)

The words of the opening movement are the first stanza of Fritsch's Hymn:

> Liebster Immanuel, Herzog der Frommen,
> Du meiner Seelen Heil[1], komm, komm nur[2] bald!
> Du hast mir, höchster Schatz, mein[3] Herz genommen,
> So ganz vor Liebe brennt und nach dir wallt.

[1] 1679 Trost.   [2] 1679 doch.
[3] 1679 Denn du hast mir, mein Schatz, das.

Nichts kann auf Erden
Mir Lieb'res werden,
Als wenn ich meinen Jesum stets behalt'[1].

B.G. xxvi. 43.

A translation of the Hymn into English is noted in the *Dictionary of Hymnology*, p. 675.

Form. Choral Fantasia (2 *Fl.*, 2 *Ob. d'amore*, Strings, Continuo)[2].

(*b*)

The words of the concluding Choral are the fifth stanza of Fritsch's Hymn:

> Drum fahrt nur immerhin[3], ihr Eitelkeiten!
> Du, Jesu, du bist mein, und ich bin dein;
> Ich will mich von der Welt zu dir bereiten;
> Du sollt in meinem Herz und Munde sein[4]!
> Mein ganzes Leben
> Sei dir ergeben,
> Bis man mich einstens legt in's[5] Grab hinein.

B.G. xxvi. 60.

Form. Simple (2 *Fl.*, 2 *Ob. d'amore*, Strings, Continuo). *Choralgesänge*, No. 229.

---

[1] 1679 Wenn ich, mein Jesu, dich nur stets behalt.

[2] Spitta, III. 102, draws attention to Bach's evident desire to conceal the secular character of the melody, which is a sarabande in form.

[3] 1679 Drumb fahret immerhin.

[4] 1679 Mund und Herze sein.

[5] 1679 Bis man mich leget in das.

CANTATA CXXIV. MEINEN JESUM LASS' ICH
NICHT. First Sunday after the Epiphany
(c. 1740)

A Choral Cantata, on Christian Keimann's Hymn, "Meinen Jesum lass' ich nicht" (see Cantata 70). For Andreas Hammerschmidt's (?) melody, see Cantata 70.

(a)

The words of the opening movement are the first stanza of Keimann's Hymn:

> Meinen Jesum lass' ich nicht,
> Weil er sich für mich gegeben,
> So erfordert meine Pflicht,
> Klettenweis' an ihm zu kleben.
> Er ist meines Lebens Licht:
> Meinen Jesum lass' ich nicht. B.G. xxvi. 63.

Form. Choral Fantasia (*Corno, Oboe d'amore, Strings, Continuo*).

(b)

The words of the concluding Choral are the sixth stanza of Keimann's Hymn[1]:

> Jesum lass' ich nicht von mir,
> Geh' ihm ewig an der Seiten;
> Christus lässt mich für und für
> Zu den Lebens-Bächlein leiten.
> Selig, der[2] mit mir so spricht:
> Meinen Jesum lass' ich nicht. B.G. xxvi. 82.

Form. Simple (*Corno, Oboe d'amore concertante, Strings, Continuo*). *Choralgesänge*, No. 246.

[1] See Cantata 70 for the acrostic of this stanza. [2] 1659 wer.

CANTATA CXXV. MIT FRIED' UND FREUD' ICH FAHR' DAHIN. Purification of the B.V.M. (c. 1740)

A Choral Cantata, on Luther's version of the "Nunc Dimittis" (see Cantata 83, for the Hymn and the melody).

(a)

The words of the opening movement are the first stanza of Luther's Hymn:

> Mit Fried' und Freud' ich fahr' dahin
> In Gottes Willen;
> Getrost ist mir mein Herz und Sinn,
> Sanft und stille;
> Wie Gott mir verheissen hat,
> Der Tod ist mein Schlaf worden.
> B.G. xxvi. 85.

Form. Choral Fantasia (*Corno, Flauto, Oboe, Strings, Continuo*).

(b)

The Choral words of the third movement are the second stanza of Luther's Hymn:

> Das macht Christus, wahr'r Gottes Sohn,
> Der treue Heiland,
> Den du mich, Herr, hast sehen lahn,
> Und machst bekannt,
> Dass Er sei das Leben und Heil,
> Im Tod und auch im Sterben[1]. B.G. xxvi. 101.

Form. "Recitativ" and Choral for Bass (*Strings, Continuo*[2]).

[1] 1524 Ynn nott und sterben. [2] See p. 44 *supra*.

(c) The words of the concluding Choral are the fourth stanza of Luther's Hymn:

> Er ist das Heil und sel'ge Licht
> Für die Heiden:
> Zu erleuchten[1], die dich kennen nicht,
> Und zu weiden.
> Er ist dein's Volks Israel
> Der Preis, Ehr', Freud' und Wonne.
> B.G. xxvi. 110.

Form. Simple (*Corno, Flauto, Oboe, Strings, Continuo*). *Choralgesänge*, No. 251.

CANTATA CXXVI. ERHALT' UNS, HERR, BEI DEINEM WORT. Sexagesima Sunday (*c.* 1740)

A Choral Cantata, on Luther's Hymn, "Erhalt' uns, Herr" (see Cantata 6). Bach's association (in the concluding Choral of the Cantata) of Luther's "Verleih' uns Frieden" with the Hymn, "Erhalt' uns, Herr," was in accordance with customary use. In many parts of Germany the stanza was sung immediately after the sermon, either by itself, or in association with Luther's "Erhalt' uns." For the melody of the latter Hymn, which Bach uses in the first and third movements of the Cantata, see Cantata 6.

[1] 1524 leuchten.

(a)

The words of the opening movement are the first stanza of Luther's "Erhalt' uns, Herr":

> Erhalt' uns, Herr, bei deinem Wort,
> Und steur' des Papsts und Türken Mord,
> Die Jesum Christum, deinen Sohn,
> Stürzen wollen von seinem Thron[1].
>
> B.G. xxvi. 113.

Form. Choral Fantasia (*Tromba*, 2 *Ob., Strings, Continuo*)[2].

(b)

The Choral words of the third movement are the third stanza of Luther's "Erhalt' uns, Herr":

> Gott heil'ger Geist, du Tröster werth,
> Gieb dein'm Volk einerlei Sinn auf Erd'.
> Steh' bei uns in der letzten Noth,
> Gleit' uns in's Leben aus dem Tod.
>
> B.G. xxvi. 126.

Form. "Recitativ," or *Dialogus*, for Tenor and Alto (*Continuo*), the Choral melody and *Recitativo* passages being shared by both voices.

(c)

The words and melody of the concluding Choral are those of Luther's Hymn, "Verleih' uns Frieden gnädiglich," with its additional stanza, "Gieb unserm Fürst'n" (see Cantata 42):

---

[1] 1543 Wolten stürtzen von deinem thron.
[2] See Spitta, III. 101, on the form of the movement.

Verleih' uns Frieden gnädiglich,
Herr Gott, zu unsern Zeiten;
Es ist ja doch[1] kein And'rer nicht,
Der für uns könnte streiten,
Denn du, unser Gott, alleine.

Gieb unsern Fürst'n und aller Obrigkeit
Fried' und gut Regiment,
Dass wir unter ihnen
Ein geruh'g[2] und stilles Leben führen mögen
In aller Gottseligkeit und Ehrbarkeit. Amen.
B.G. xxvi. 131.

Form. Simple (*Tromba*, 2 *Ob.*, *Strings*, *Continuo*). *Choralgesänge*, No. 321.

CANTATA CXXVII. HERR JESU CHRIST, WAHR'R MENSCH UND GOTT. Quinquagesima ("Esto Mihi") Sunday (*c.* 1740)

Melody: "*On a beau son maison bastir*".

Louis Bourgeois 1551

A Choral Cantata, on Paul Eber's funerary Hymn, "Herr Jesu Christ, wahr'r Mensch und

[1] 1535 denn.   [2] 1566 geruhlich.

Gott," written in 1557, and first published in the Hamburg *Enchiridion Geistliker Leder und Psalmen D. Mar. Luth.* (Hamburg, 1565). The melody appears first in the Geneva Psalter, *Pseaumes octante trois de David, mis en rime Francoise* (Geneva, 1551), where it is set to Psalm cxxvii. In Lutheran Hymn books it is generally associated with Eber's Hymn. Psalm cxxvii, included in the Geneva Psalter of 1551, was one of the thirty-four recently translated by Theodore Beza. The melody must therefore be assigned to Louis Bourgeois (see Cantata 13).

The melody does not occur elsewhere in the Cantatas, Oratorios, or Motetts. For the first note of the first line and last note of the second in Bach's version there is late sixteenth century authority (Calvisius' *Hymni sacri Latini et germanici*, Erfurt, 1594).

(*a*)

The words of the opening movement of the Cantata are the first stanza of Eber's Hymn:

> Herr Jesu Christ, wahr'r Mensch und Gott,
> Der du litt'st Marter, Angst und Spott,
> Für mich am Kreuz auch endlich starbst,
> Und mir dein's Vaters Huld erwarbst,
> Ich bitt' durch's bittre Leiden dein;
> Du woll'st mir Sünder gnädig sein!
>   B.G. xxvi. 135.

Translations of the Hymn into English are noted in the *Dictionary of Hymnology*, p. 319.

Form. Choral Fantasia (2 *Fl.*, 2 *Ob.*, *Strings*, *Continuo*).

As Quinquagesima heralds the season of the Passion, Bach introduces into the orchestral accompaniment of the movement the melody, "Christe, du Lamm Gottes" (see Cantata 23), the Strings and Wind instruments playing alternate lines of it[1].

(*b*)

The words of the concluding Choral are the eighth stanza of Eber's Hymn:

> Ach Herr, vergieb all' unsre Schuld,
> Hilf, dass wir warten mit Geduld,
> Bis unser Stündlein kömmt herbei,
> Auch unser Glaub' stets wacker sei,
> Dein'm Wort zu trauen festiglich,
> Bis wir einschlafen seliglich. B.G. xxvi. 160.

Form. Simple (2 *Fl.*, 2 *Ob.*, *Strings*, *Continuo*). *Choralgesänge*, No. 147.

CANTATA CXXVIII. AUF CHRISTI HIMMEL-FAHRT ALLEIN. Ascension Day (? 1735)

(*a*)

For the melody of the opening movement, Nicolaus Decius' "Allein Gott in der Höh' sei Ehr'," see Cantata 85.

[1] See Spitta, III. 101, on the form of the movement.

The words of the opening movement are the first stanza of Josua Wegelin's, or Wegelein's, Ascension Hymn, "Auf Christi Himmelfahrt allein," first published in Wegelin's *Andächtige Versöhnung mit Gott* (Nürnberg, 1636), with a first stanza beginning, "Allein auf Christi Himmelfahrt," and to the tune "Allein Gott" (*supra*). The Hymn was reconstructed and published as "Auf Christi Himmelfahrt allein" in the Lüneburg *Vollständiges Gesang-Buch* (Lüneburg, 1661).

Wegelin was born at Augsburg in 1604, and was successively Deacon, Archdeacon, and pastor there. In 1635 he was appointed pastor at Pressburg. He died in 1640:

> Auf Christi Himmelfahrt allein
> Ich meine Nachfahrt gründe,
> Und allen Zweifel, Angst und Pein
> Hiermit stets überwinde;
> Denn weil das Haupt im Himmel ist,
> Wird seine Glieder Jesus Christ
> Zu rechter Zeit nachholen. B.G. xxvi. 163.

English translations of the Hymn are noted in the *Dictionary of Hymnology*, p. 1246.

Form. Choral Fantasia (2 *Cor.*, 2 *Ob.*, Oboe da caccia, Strings, Continuo).

(*b*)

For the melody of the concluding Choral, the anonymous (1679) "O Gott, du frommer Gott," see Cantata 45.

The words of the concluding Choral are the fourth stanza of Matthäus Avenarius' Hymn, "O Jesu, meine Lust," first published (to no specified melody) in Heinrich Ammersbach's *Vermehrtes Gesang-Büchlein* (Halberstadt, 1673). Its proper melody dates from 1677 and appears to have been little used. Avenarius' Hymn is set to "O Gott, du frommer Gott," in Wagner (1697).

Avenarius was born at Eisenach in 1625, became Cantor at Schmalkalden in 1650, pastor at Steinbach-Hallenberg in 1662, and died in 1692:

> Alsdann so wirst du mich
> Zu deiner Rechten stellen,
> Und mir, als deinem Kind,
> Ein gnädig Urtheil fällen,
> Mich bringen zu der Lust,
> Wo deine Herrlichkeit
> Ich werde schauen an
> In alle Ewigkeit.   B.G. xxvi. 184.

Form. Embellished (2 *Cor*, 2 *Ob.*, Oboe da caccia, Strings, Continuo). *Choralgesänge*, No. 279.

CANTATA CXXIX. GELOBET SEI DER HERR.
Trinity Sunday (1732)

A Choral Cantata, on Johannes Olearius' Hymn for Trinity Sunday, "Gelobet sei der Herr," founded on the Gospel for the Day. The Hymn was first published in Olearius' *Christliche Bet-Schule* (Leipzig, 1665), to the tune, "Nun danket alle Gott[1]." Bach sets it here to the anonymous (1679) "O Gott, du frommer Gott" (see Cantata 45). In Wagner (1697) the Hymn is set to "Nun danket alle Gott."

(a)

The words of the first movement are the first stanza of Olearius' Hymn:

> Gelobet sei der Herr,
> Mein Gott, mein Licht, mein Leben,
> Mein Schöpfer, der mir hat
> Mein'n Leib und Seel' gegeben;
> Mein Vater, der mich schützt
> Von Mutterleibe an,
> Der alle Augenblick'
> Viel Gut's an mir gethan. B.G. xxvi. 187.

Translations of the Hymn into English are noted in the *Dictionary of Hymnology*, p. 866.

Form. Choral Fantasia (3 *Trombe, Timpani*, 2 *Ob., Strings, Continuo*).

(b)

The words of the concluding Choral are the fifth stanza of Olearius' Hymn:

> Dem wir das Heilig itzt
> Mit Freuden lassen klingen,
> Und mit der Engelschaar
> Das Heilig, Heilig singen;
> Den herzlich lobt und preist
> Die ganze Christenheit:
> Gelobet sei mein Gott
> In alle Ewigkeit! B.G. xxvi. 224.

[1] Every movement of the Cantata is a stanza of the Hymn.

CANTATA CXXX 385

Form. Extended (3 *Trombe, Timpani, Flauto,* 2 *Ob., Strings, Continuo*).

CANTATA CXXX. HERR GOTT, DICH LOBEN ALLE WIR. Feast of St Michael the Archangel (*c.* 1740)

Melody: "*Or sus, serviteurs du Seigneur*"
Louis Bourgeois 1551

Melody: "*Il n'y a icy celluy*"   Anon. *c.* 1551[1]

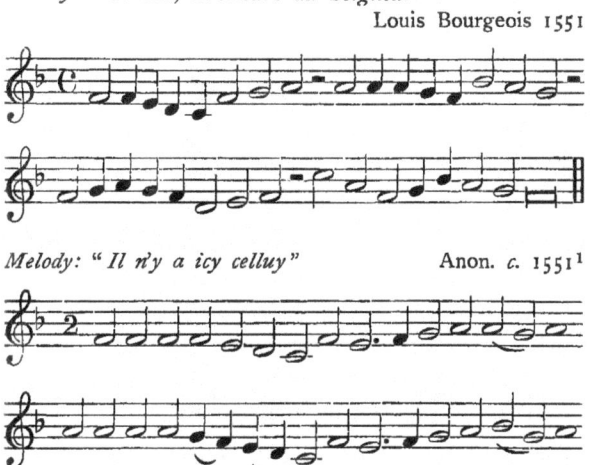

[1] Sung to the words of the French *chanson*:

    Il n'y a icy celluy
    Qui n'ait sa belle amye.
    Je ne le dy pas pour my,
    La myenne n'y est mye.
    Elle est bien a son plaisir,
    Celle qui a son desir,
    Elle est bien a son plaisir,
    Mais je ne l'ouse dire.

A Choral Cantata, on Paul Eber's Hymn, a free translation of Philipp Melanchthon's "Dicimus grates tibi, summe rerum," first published as a broadsheet at Nürnberg c. 1554 as "Ein schön New Geistlich Lobgesang" and thence in Johann Eichorn's *Geistliche Lieder D. Mart. Lut. und anderer frommen Christen* (Frankfort a. Oder, 1561).

The melody, which was associated with Eber's Hymn before Bartholomäus Gesius wrote for the latter its proper melody in 1601[1], was published originally in the Geneva Psalter, *Pseaumes octante trois de David* (Geneva, 1551), where it is set to Psalm cxxxiv, "Or sus, serviteurs du Seigneur," one of the thirty-four Psalms translated by Theodore Beza and included in that book. The tune in its present and familiar form, therefore, must be attributed to Louis Bourgeois (see Cantata 13). But, like the other Psalm tunes in that collection, "Or sus, serviteurs" probably has a secular origin. Its first two lines bear a distinct

[1] Zahn, I. No. 460.

resemblance to the melody of a French *chanson*, "Il n'y a icy celluy¹." The tune was set to Psalm c in John Knox' Anglo-Genevan Psalter of 1561 and also in Sternhold and Hopkins' *The whole Book of Psalmes* (1562). Claude Goudimel harmonised it in 1565. Upon the issue in 1696 of Tate and Brady's *A New Version of the Psalms of David, Fitted to the Tunes Used in Churches*, the word "Old" was added to the titles of the tunes that were retained in use from the older Psalter. Thus Bourgeois' tune, which from 1562 to 1696 was the "Hundredth," was thenceforth known as the "Old Hundredth." The name is peculiar to British use.

The melody does not occur elsewhere in the Cantatas, Oratorios, or Motetts. There are harmonisations of the tune in the *Choralgesänge*, Nos. 129, 130², 132.

(*a*)

The words of the opening movement are the first stanza of Eber's Hymn:

<blockquote>
Herr Gott dich loben alle wir
Und sollen billig danken dir
Für dein' Geschöpf' der Engel schon,
Die um dich schweb'n in deinem Thron.
B.G. xxvi. 233.
</blockquote>

¹ The melody is printed *supra* from Gaston Paris and Auguste Gevaert's *Chansons du XVᵉ siècle, publiées d'après le manuscrit de la Bibliothèque nationale de Paris* (Paris, 1875).

² 'See (*b*) *infra*.

Translations of the Hymn into English are noted in the *Dictionary of Hymnology*, p. 293.

Form. Choral Fantasia (3 *Trombe, Timp.*, 3 *Ob.*, Strings, Continuo).

(*b*)

The words of the concluding Choral are the eleventh and twelfth stanzas of Eber's Hymn:

> Darum wir billig loben dich
> Und danken dir, Gott, ewiglich,
> Wie auch der lieben Engel Schaar
> Dich preisen heut' und immerdar.
>
> Und bitten dich : wollst[1] allezeit
> Dieselben heissen sein bereit,
> Zu schützen deine kleine Heerd',
> So hält dein göttlich's Wort in Werth.
>
> B.G. xxvi. 268.

Form. Embellished (3 *Trombe, Timp.*, 3 *Ob.*, Strings, Continuo). *Choralgesänge*, No. 131[2].

[1] *c.* 1554 du wölst.
[2] Erk, No. 220, and *Choralgesänge*, No. 130, print a setting of the melody in Simple form orchestrated for 2 Clarini, which Erk conjectures to have been intended as a simpler substitute for the closing Choral. He prints the arrangement from an old MS. which he thinks may be in Karl Philipp Emmanuel Bach's hand. Bernhard Friedrich Richter, in the *Choralgesänge*, questions its genuineness.

Cantata CXXXI. Aus der Tiefe rufe ich, Herr, zu dir (1707–8)[1]

The Hymn and Choral melody which Bach uses in the second and fourth movements of the Cantata are Bartholomäus Ringwaldt's Lenten Hymn, "Herr Jesu Christ, du höchstes Gut" (see Cantatas 48 and 113).

(*a*)

The Choral words of the second movement are the second stanza of Ringwaldt's Hymn:

> Erbarm' dich mein in solcher Last,
> Nimm sie aus meinem Herzen,
> Dieweil du sie gebüsset hast
> Am Holz mit[2] Todesschmerzen:
> Auf dass ich nicht mit[3] grossem Weh
> In meinen Sünden untergeh',
> Noch[4] ewiglich verzage[5].
>
> B.G. xxviii. 11.

Form. *Duetto* for Soprano and Bass, the former having the Choral melody, while the Bass independently sings verses iii and iv of Psalm cxxx (*Oboe, Continuo*)[6].

---

[1] The Score does not indicate the occasion for which the Cantata was composed. The B.G. edition bears the statement, "Componirt zu Mühlhausen 1707–1708."

[2] 1588 im.   [3] 1588 für.
[4] 1588 Und.   [5] 1588 vorzage.
[6] See Spitta, I. 451, on the construction of this movement.

(b)

The Choral words of the fourth movement are the fifth stanza of Ringwaldt's Hymn:

> Und weil ich denn in meinem Sinn,
> Wie ich zuvor geklaget,
> Auch ein betrübter Sünder bin,
> Den sein Gewissen naget,
> Und wollte gern[1] im Blute dein
> Von Sünden abgewaschen[2] sein,
> Wie David und Manasse. B.G. xxviii. 20.

Form. *Duetto* for Alto and Tenor, the Alto having the Choral melody while the Tenor sings independently verse vi of Psalm cxxx (*Continuo*)[3].

CANTATA CXXXII. BEREITET DIE WEGE, BEREITET DIE BAHN. Fourth Sunday in Advent (1715)

The words and melody of the concluding Choral are those of Elisabethe Cruciger's Christmas Hymn, "Herr Christ, der einig' Gott's Sohn" (see Cantata 22).

The Choral is a substitution, for use at Leipzig, of the movement originally written for and performed at Weimar[4], necessitated by the fact that at St Thomas' Church figurate music was given only on the first of the Sundays in Advent. Hence

---

[1] 1588 gerne möcht. [2] 1588 absoluiret.
[3] See Spitta, I. 454. [4] See Schweitzer, II. 142.

Bach's earlier Advent Cantatas had to be adapted to another season.

The words of the concluding Choral are the fifth stanza of Elisabethe Cruciger's Hymn:

> Ertödt' uns durch dein' Güte,
> Erweck' uns durch dein' Gnad';
> Den alten Menschen kränke,
> Dass der neu' leben mag,
> Wohl hier auf dieser Erden
> Den Sinn und all' Begehrden
> Und G'danken[1] hab'n zu dir.
>
> B.G. xxviii. 50.

Form. Simple[2].

CANTATA CXXXIII. ICH FREUE MICH IN DIR.
Feast of St John the Evangelist (Christmas) (1735-37)

Melody: "*Ich freue mich in dir*"   Bach's MS. *c.* 1735

* *sic.*

---

[1] 1524 dancken.

[2] The Score simply contains the stanza, the name of the tune, and the direction "Choral semplice stylo."

Melody: "*Ich freue mich in dir*"   Bach's version 1735–37

Melody: "*O stilles Gottes Lamm*"
König's version 1738

A Choral Cantata, on Caspar Ziegler's Christmas Hymn, "Ich freue mich in dir," first published in the Halle *Geistreiches Gesang Buch* (Halle, 1697).

Ziegler was born at Leipzig in 1621, and from 1655 was Professor of Law in the University of Wittenberg. He was distinguished as a lawyer, teacher, scholar, and poet. He died in 1690.

The melody, "Ich freue mich in dir," which Bach uses in the opening and concluding movements of the Cantata, is one of two[1] that occur for the first time in his Church Cantatas. That the tune is by Bach himself has been stated, and the following considerations support the conclusion. The tune is not found in any Hymn book of earlier date than the Cantata, i.e. 1735–37. The earliest sketch of it is in Bach's autograph in the MS. of the fugal subject "pleni sunt coeli" of the *Sanctus* of the B minor Mass[2], upon which he was engaged in the period 1735–37. On the other hand, another version of the melody is found in the *Harmonischer Lieder-Schatz, oder Allgemeines Evangelisches Choral-Buch*, published in 1738 by Johann Balthasar König (1691–1758), "Director Chori Musices in Franckfurt am Mayn." The tune is set there to Gottfried Arnold's (1666–1714) Hymn, "O stilles Gottes Lamm," while the first line of the melody is appropriated to another tune, set to the Hymn, "Ich will des Herren Zorn." It is most improbable that König, actually Bach's contemporary, would take liberties with the tune if it was Bach's own composition. The melody, also, entirely lacks the *Aria* character which

[1] The other melody is "Alle Menschen müssen sterben." See Cantata 162.
[2] B.G. xxviii. p. xxv. It is printed *supra*, p. 391.

distinguishes Bach's Hymn tunes from seventeenth and eighteenth century melodies. It is reminiscent, too, of the many reconstructions of Melchior Franck's (?) "O grosser Gott von Macht" (1632) (see Cantata 46), and of the tune "O Gott, du frommer Gott" (1693) (see Cantata 24), whose composite construction has been noticed. Ziegler's Hymn, "Ich freue mich in dir," actually was published in 1697 to the melody, "O Gott, du frommer Gott," and it was quite contrary to Bach's practice in a Choral Cantata to set the Hymn to a new or unfamiliar tune. The balance of probability, therefore, is against Bach's authorship of the tune.

The melody is not found elsewhere in the Cantatas, Oratorios, or Motetts.

(a)

The words of the opening movement are the first stanza of Ziegler's Hymn:

> Ich freue mich in dir
> Und heisse dich willkommen,
> Mein liebes Jesulein!
> Du hast dir vorgenommen
> Mein Brüderlein zu sein.
> Ach, wie ein süsser Ton!
> Wie freundlich sieht er aus
> Der grosse Gottessohn!
>
> B.G. xxviii. 53.

Form. Choral Fantasia (*Cornetto*, 2 *Ob. d'amore, Strings, Continuo*).

(b)

The words of the concluding Choral are the fourth stanza of the Hymn:

> Wohlan! so will ich mich
> An dich, O Jesu, halten,
> Und sollte gleich die Welt
> In tausend Stücke spalten.
> O Jesu! dir, nur dir,
> Dir leb' ich ganz allein;
> Auf dich, allein auf dich,
> O[1] Jesu, schlaf' ich ein.
> B.G. xxviii. 80.

Form. Simple (*Cornetto*, 2 *Ob. d'amore, Strings, Continuo*). *Choralgesänge*, No. 181.

CANTATA CXXXV. ACH HERR, MICH ARMEN SÜNDER. Third Sunday after Trinity (*c.* 1740)

Melody: "*Herzlich thut mich verlangen*"
Hans Leo Hassler 1601

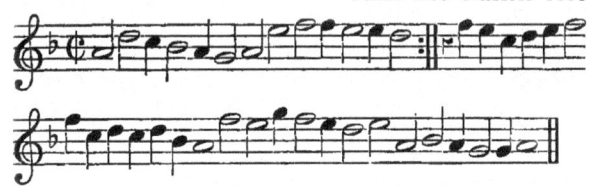

A Choral Cantata, on Cyriacus Schneegass' Hymn on Psalm vi, "Ach Herr, mich armen Sünder," first published in his *Geistliche Lieder und Psalmen* (Erfurt, 1597).

[1] 1697 Mein.

The melody, "Herzlich thut mich verlangen," which Bach uses in the first and last movements of the Cantata, first occurs, as a secular song, in Hans Leo Hassler's *Lustgarten Neuer Teutscher Gesäng* (Nürnberg, 1601). In 1613 it was attached to Christoph Knoll's (1563-1650) "Herzlich thut mich verlangen," and in 1656 to Paul Gerhardt's "O Haupt voll Blut[1]." Christopher Demantius, in his *Threnodiae* (Freiberg, 1620), set it to Schneegass' "Ach Herr, mich armen Sünder," and the Hymn is still generally sung to it.

The melody occurs also in Cantatas 25, 135, 153, 159, 161; in the "St Matthew Passion," Nos. 21, 23, 53, 63, 72; and in the "Christmas Oratorio," Nos. 5, 64. There are other harmonisations of the tune in the *Choralgesänge*, Nos. 157, 158. For the B flat which Bach substitutes for D at the eleventh note in the second part of the tune, and for the C natural in place of G at the penultimate note, there is early authority (1679 and 1694 respectively). Organ Works, N. xviii. 53.

(*a*)

The words of the opening movement are the first stanza of Schneegass' Hymn:

>Ach Herr, mich armen Sünder
>Straf' nicht[2] in deinem Zorn;

---

[1] See *Bach's Chorals*, Part I, p. 8.
[2] 1597 Nicht straff.

Dein'n ernsten Grimm doch linder'[1],
Sonst ist's mit mir verlor'n.
Ach Herr, wollst mir vergeben
Mein' Sünd' und gnädig sein,
Dass ich mag ewig leben,
Entfliehn der Höllenpein.
  B.G. xxviii. 121.

Form. Choral Fantasia (*Trombone,* 2 *Ob.,
Strings, Continuo*). The *cantus* is with the Basses.

(*b*)

The words of the concluding Choral are the sixth stanza of the Hymn[2]:

* Ehr' sei in's Himmels Throne
  Mit hohem Ruhm und Preis,
  Dem Vater und dem Sohne,
  Und auch zu gleicher Weis'
  Dem heil'gen Geist mit Ehren,
  In alle Ewigkeit!
  Der woll' uns All'n bescheren
  Die ew'ge Seligkeit.
   B.G. xxviii. 136.

Form. Simple (*Cornetto,* 2 *Ob., Strings, Continuo*). *Choralgesänge,* No. 156.

[1] 1597 erlinder.
[2] The doxology used here is a later addition to the Hymn, which originally contained only five stanzas. It is found, as stanza vi of Schneegass' Hymn, in the Dresden *Gesangbuch Christlicher Psalmen und Kirchenlieder* (Dresden, 1625).

CANTATA CXXXVI. ERFORSCHE MICH, GOTT, UND ERFAHRE MEIN HERZ. Eighth Sunday after Trinity (c. 1725[1])

The melody which Bach uses in the concluding Choral of the Cantata is known both as "Auf meinen lieben Gott" and "Wo soll ich fliehen hin" (see Cantata 5). The words of the Choral are the ninth stanza of Johann Heermann's Lenten Hymn, "Wo soll ich fliehen hin" (see Cantata 5):

> Dein Blut, der edle Saft,
> Hat solche Stärk' und Kraft,
> Dass auch ein Tröpflein kleine
> Die ganze Welt kann reine,
> Ja, gar aus Teufels Rachen
> Frei, los und ledig[2] machen.
>
> B.G. xxviii. 164.

Form. Embellished (*Corno*, 2 *Ob.*, *Strings*, *Continuo*). *Choralgesänge*, No. 27.

CANTATA CXXXVII. LOBE DEN HERREN, DEN MÄCHTIGEN KÖNIG DER EHREN. Twelfth Sunday after Trinity (? 1732[1])

A Choral Cantata, on Joachim Neander's Hymn of Thanksgiving, "Lobe den Herren," first published in his *Glaub- und Liebesübung* (Bremen, 1680).

[1] Rust suggests the second Leipzig period. [2] 1630 selig.

Neander was born at Bremen in 1650. In 1674 he was appointed Rector of the Latin School at Düsseldorf, and five years later (1679) returned to Bremen as unordained assistant in the Church of St Martin. He died in 1680.

For the melody, "Hast du denn, Liebster," which Bach uses throughout the Cantata, see Cantata 57.

(a)

VERSE I.

* Lobe den Herren, den mächtigen König der Ehren,
Meine geliebte Seele, das ist mein Begehren.
Kommet zu Hauf,
Psalter und Harfen, wacht auf!
Lasset die Musicam hören.   B.G. xxviii. 167.

Translations of the Hymn into English are noted in the *Dictionary of Hymnology*, pp. 683, 1665.

Form. Choral Fantasia (3 *Trombe, Timp.*, 2 *Ob.*, *Strings, Continuo*).

(b)

VERSE II[1].

* Lobe den Herren, der Alles so herrlich regieret,
Der dich auf Adelers Fitigen sicher geführet,
Der dich erhält,
Wie es dir selber gefällt;
Hast du nicht dieses verspüret?   B.G. xxviii. 186.

Form. Unison Choral for Alto. The *cantus* is treated freely (*Violino Solo, Continuo*[2]).

[1] Verse iii in the third movement is not set to the Choral melody.
[2] The movement is No. 6 of the Schübler Chorals (N. xvi. 14).

(c)
VERSE IV.

* Lobe den Herren, der deinen Stand sichtbar gesegnet,
Der aus dem Himmel mit Strömen der Liebe geregnet!
Denke d'ran,
Was der Allmächtige kann,
Der dir mit Liebe begegnet.   B.G. xxviii. 193.

Form. Tenor *Aria*, the *cantus* being in the Tromba *obbligato* (*Tromba, Continuo*).

(d)
VERSE V.

* Lobe den Herren; was in mir ist, lobe den Namen!
Alles was Odem hat, lobe mit Abraham's Samen!
Er ist dein Licht.
Seele, vergiss es ja nicht!
Lobende schliesse mit Amen!   B.G. xxviii. 196.

Form. Embellished (3 *Trombe, Timp.*, 2 *Ob., Strings, Continuo*). *Choralgesänge,* No. 230.

CANTATA CXXXVIII. WARUM BETRÜBST DU DICH, MEIN HERZ. Fifteenth Sunday after Trinity (*c.* 1740[1])

A Choral Cantata, on the Hymn "Warum betrübst du dich, mein Herz" attributed to Hans Sachs (see Cantata 47). The tune which Bach uses in the first, third, and last movements is that of the Hymn (see Cantata 47).

[1] Rust dates it *c.* 1730.

CANTATA CXXXVIII

(*a*)

The Choral in the opening movement is the first stanza of the Hymn:

> Warum betrübst du dich, mein Herz?
> Bekümmerst dich und trägest Schmerz
> Nur um das zeitliche Gut?
> Vertrau' du deinem Herren Gott[1],
> Der alle Ding' erschaffen hat.
>
> B.G. xxviii. 199.

Form. Choral Fantasia, with orchestral and *Recitativo* interludes (2 *Ob. d'amore, Strings, Continuo*)[2].

(*b*)

The Choral in the third movement is the second stanza of the Hymn:

> Er kann und will dich lassen[3] nicht;
> Er weiss gar wohl, was dir gebricht:
> Himmel und Erd' ist sein!
> Dein[4] Vater und dein[4] Herre Gott,
> Der dir[5] beisteht in aller Noth.
>
> B.G. xxviii. 205.

Form. The Choral (S.A.T.B.) is prefaced and its sequence is broken by the interposition of *Recitativo* passages (2 *Ob. d'amore, Strings, Continuo*)[2].

---

[1] *c.* 1560 Herren unnd Gott.
[2] See Spitta, III. 88, on the movement. It has relations with the *Dialogus* type.
[3] *c.* 1560 dich verlassen.   [4] *c.* 1560 Mein.
[5] *c.* 1560 mir.

(c)

The words of the concluding movement are the third stanza of the Hymn :

> Weil du mein Gott und Vater bist,
> Dein Kind wirst du verlassen nicht,
> Du väterliches Herz!
> Ich bin ein armer Erdenkloss,
> Auf Erden weiss ich keinen Trost.
> B.G. xxviii. 217.

Form. Choral Fantasia (2 *Ob. d'amore, Strings, Continuo*).

CANTATA CXXXIX. WOHL DEM, DER SICH AUF SEINEN GOTT. Twenty-third Sunday after Trinity (*c.* 1740)

Melody: "*Mach's mit mir, Gott, nach deiner Güt'*"
 Johann Hermann Schein 1628

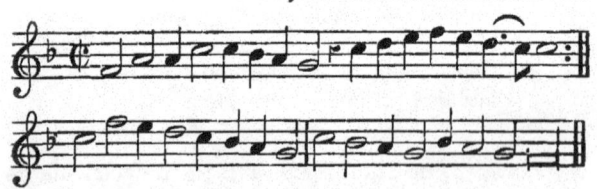

A Choral Cantata, on Johann Christoph Rube's, or Ruben's, Hymn, "Wohl dem, der sich auf seinen Gott," first published in Andreas Luppius' *Andächtig Singender Christen-Mund* (Wesel, 1692), and, to its own melody, in the 1694 edition of the Dresden *Hundert Arien*.

Rube was born in 1665, his father being then pastor near Sondershausen. He was appointed judge (Amtmann) at Burggemünden, near Alsfeld, and from about 1704 held a similar appointment at Battenberg. He died at Battenberg in 1746. The melody to which Bach sets the Hymn in the first and last movements is associated with it in the 1709 edition of Crüger's *Praxis*. It was composed by Johann Hermann Schein for his Hymn, " Mach's mit mir, Gott, nach deiner Güt'," with which it was published in a broadsheet at Leipzig in 1628 as a "Trost-Liedlein" for five voices.

The melody occurs also in Cantata 156 and in the "St John Passion," No. 22. There is another harmonisation of it in the *Choralgesänge*, No. 237. The B flat which Bach substitutes for A natural as the third note of the tune has earlier (1714) authority.

(a)

The words of the opening movement are the first stanza of Rube's Hymn:

* Wohl dem, der sich auf seinen Gott
  Recht kindlich kann verlassen!
  Den mag gleich Sünde, Welt und Tod,
  Und alle Teufel hassen,
  So bleibt er dennoch wohl vergnügt,
  Wenn er nur Gott zum Freunde kriegt.

B.G. xxviii. 225.

Form. Choral Fantasia (2 *Ob. d'amore*, Strings, Organ, Continuo)[1].

(*b*)

The words of the concluding Choral are the fifth stanza of the Hymn:

* Dahero Trotz der Höllen Heer!
Trotz auch des Todes Rachen!
Trotz aller Welt! mich kann nicht mehr
Ihr Pochen traurig machen!
Gott ist mein Schutz, mein Hülf' und Rath:
Wohl dem, der Gott zum Freunde hat.
B.G. xxviii. 248.

Form. Simple (2 *Ob. d'amore*, Strings, Continuo). *Choralgesänge*, No. 238.

CANTATA CXL. WACHET AUF, RUFT UNS DIE STIMME[2]. Twenty-seventh Sunday after Trinity[3] (1731[4])

Melody: "*Wachet auf, ruft uns die Stimme*"
? Philipp Nicolai 1599

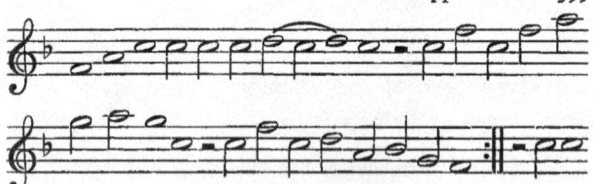

---

[1] See Spitta, III. 101, on the movement.

[2] English versions of the Cantata are published by Novello & Co., "Sleepers, wake! for night is flying," and Breitkopf & Haertel, "Sleepers wake, loud sounds the warning."

[3] The Sunday, only occurring when Easter falls early, becomes the Sunday before Advent.   [4] Rust dates it 1742.

A Choral Cantata[1], on Philipp Nicolai's Hymn, "Wachet auf, ruft uns die Stimme," first published in his *Frewden Spiegel dess ewigen Lebens* (Frankfort a. Main, 1599), with the melody. The Hymn is a reversed acrostic, the initial letters of its three stanzas, W. Z. G., standing for "Graf zu Waldeck," Nicolai's former pupil, who died in 1598, aged fifteen. The Hymn probably was written in 1597, during the pestilence at Unna in Westphalia, where Nicolai then was pastor.

The melody was published with the Hymn in 1599. Whether Nicolai composed it cannot be determined positively. As in the case of his "Wie schön leuchtet der Morgenstern" (see Cantata 1), it is probable that he adapted old material to his purpose. It may be observed that the opening line of "Wachet auf" is identical with the opening line of "O Lamm Gottes[2]," and that the Hymn ends with the words, "in dulci jubilo," a Hymn the beginning of whose melody is practically identical with "Wachet auf," except in metre.

[1] See *supra*, p. 32.   [2] See *infra*, p. 495.

The melody does not occur elsewhere in the Cantatas, Oratorios, or Motetts. Organ Works, N. xvi. 1. Bach's variation of the second line of the tune is not revealed by Zahn as having earlier sanction.

(a)

The words of the opening movement are the first stanza of Nicolai's Hymn:

> Wachet auf! ruft uns die Stimme
> Der Wächter sehr hoch auf der Zinne:
> Wach auf, du Stadt Jerusalem!
> Mitternacht heisst diese Stunde;
> Sie rufen uns mit hellem Munde:
> Wo seid ihr klugen Jungfrauen?
> Wohl auf! der Bräutigam kommt!
> Steht auf! die Lampen nehmt!
> Alleluja!
> Macht euch bereit zu der Hochzeit,
> Ihr müsset ihm entgegen gehn.
>
> B.G. xxviii. 251.

Translations of the Hymn into English are noted in the *Dictionary of Hymnology*, pp. 806, 1613, 1722.

Form. Choral Fantasia (*Corno*, 2 *Ob.*, *Taille*[1], *Strings* (*including Violino piccolo*), *Continuo*).

[1] The Taille was a Tenor Bassoon.

(b)

The words of the fourth movement are the second stanza of Nicolai's Hymn:

> Zion hört die Wächter singen;
> Das Herz thut ihr vor[1] Freuden springen:
> Sie wachet, und steht eilend auf.
> Ihr Freund kommt vom Himmel prächtig,
> Von Gnaden stark, von Wahrheit mächtig:
> Ihr Licht wird hell, ihr Stern geht auf.
> Nun komm, du werthe Kron',
> Herr Jesu, Gottes Sohn!
> Hosianna!
> Wir folgen All' zum Freudensaal,
> Und halten mit das Abendmahl.
>
> B.G. xxviii. 274.

Form. Unison Choral for Tenor (*Vn. I and II and Viola in unison, Continuo*)[2].

(c)

The words of the concluding Choral are the third stanza of Nicolai's Hymn:

> Gloria sei dir gesungen
> Mit Menschen und englischen Zungen,
> Mit Harfen und mit Cymbeln schon.
> Von zwölf Perlen sind die Pforten
> An deiner Stadt; wir sind Consorten
> Der Engel hoch um deinen Thron.

---
[1] 1599 von.
[2] The movement is No. 1 of the Schübler Chorals (N. xvi. 1).

Kein Aug' hat je gespürt,
Kein Ohr hat je[1] gehört
Solche Freude.
Dess sind wir froh, Io! Io!
Ewig in dulci jubilo.
B.G. xxviii. 284.

Form. Simple (*Corno*, 2 *Ob.*, *Taille*, *Strings* (*including Violino piccolo*), *Continuo*). *Choralgesänge*, No. 329.

CANTATA CXLII. UNS IST EIN KIND GEBOREN[2].
Christmas Day (1712 or 1714)

The words and melody of the concluding Choral are those of Caspar Fuger's Christmas Hymn, "Wir Christenleut'" (see Cantata 40).

The words are the fifth stanza of the Hymn:

Alleluja,
Gelobet sei Gott[3]!
Singen wir all' aus unsers Herzens Grunde:
Denn Gott hat heut'
Gemacht solch' Freud',
Der wir vergessen soll'n zu keiner Stunde.
B.G. xxx. 40.

Form. Extended (*Flauti, Oboi, Strings, Continuo*).

[1] 1599 mehr.
[2] Bach's authorship of this Cantata has been challenged (*Bachjahrbuch*, 1912, p. 132).
[3] 1592 Alleluia. Bach's line appears in a text of 1593.

CANTATA CXLIII. LOBE DEN HERRN, MEINE SEELE. Feast of the Circumcision (New Year's Day) (1735)

(a)

The melody of the second movement is Bartholomäus Gesius' setting of Jakob Ebert's Hymn for Peace, "Du Friedefürst, Herr Jesu Christ" (see Cantata 67).

The words are the first stanza of the Hymn[1]:

> Du Friedefürst, Herr Jesu Christ,
> Wahr'r Mensch und wahrer Gott,
> Ein starker Nothhelfer du bist
> Im Leben und im Tod.
> Drum wir allein
> Im Namen dein
> Zu deinem Vater schreien.
>
> B.G. xxx. 53.

Form. Unison Choral for Soprano (*Violini, Continuo*).

In the sixth movement, a Tenor *Aria*, the melody is played by the Violins and Violas in octaves (*Fagotto, Strings, Continuo*). The words are not a stanza of the Hymn.

---

[1] The subject was suggested, no doubt, by the War of the Polish Election, in which Bach's sovereign, Augustus III of Poland-Saxony, was closely interested. The war was brought to a conclusion in his favour in 1735.

(b)

The words of the concluding movement are the third stanza of Ebert's Hymn:

> Gedenk', Herr Jesu[1], an dein Amt,
> Dass du ein Friedfürst bist,
> Und hilf uns gnädig allesammt
> Jetzt und zu dieser Frist;
> Lass uns hinfort
> Dein göttlich Wort
> In Fried' noch länger hören[2].
>
> B.G. xxx. 66.

Form. Choral Fantasia (3 *Cor. da caccia, Timpani, Fagotto, Strings, Continuo*). The *cantus* is in the Soprano part. The other voices accompany on the single word "Halleluja."

CANTATA CXLIV. NIMM, WAS DEIN IST, UND GEHE HIN. Septuagesima Sunday (*c.* 1725)

(a)

The words and melody of the third movement are those of Samuel Rodigast's Hymn, "Was Gott thut, das ist wohlgethan" (see Cantata 12).

The words are the first stanza of the Hymn:

> Was Gott thut, das ist wohlgethan,
> Es bleibt gerecht sein Wille;
> Wie er fängt meine Sachen an,
> Will ich ihm halten stille.

[1] 1601 itzundt. [2] 1601 schallen.

Er ist mein Gott, der in der Noth
Mich wohl weiss zu erhalten:
Drum lass' ich ihn nur walten.
B.G. xxx. 87.

338. *Form.* Simple (*Continuo*). *Choralgesänge*, No.

(*b*)

The words and melody of the concluding Choral are those of Albrecht Margrave of Brandenburg-Culmbach's Hymn, "Was mein Gott will, das g'scheh' allzeit" (see Cantatas 65 and 72). The words are the first stanza of the Hymn:

> Was mein Gott will, das g'scheh' allzeit,
> Sein Wille[1] ist der beste[2];
> Zu helfen den'n er ist bereit,
> Die an ihn glauben feste.
> Er hilft aus Noth,
> Der fromme Gott,
> Und züchtiget[3] mit Maassen.
> Wer Gott vertraut,
> Fest auf ihn baut,
> Den will er nicht verlassen.

B.G. xxx. 92.

343. *Form.* Simple (*Continuo*). *Choralgesänge*, No.

---

[1] Bach's MS. Will der.
[2] *c.* 1554 der ist der aller beste.
[3] *c.* 1554 Er tröst die Welt.

CANTATA CXLV. SO DU MIT DEINEM MUNDE BEKENNEST JESUM. Easter Tuesday[1] (1729 or 1730)

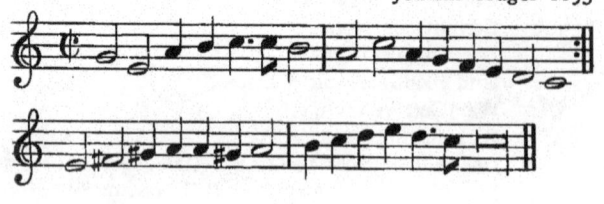

Melody: "Jesus, meine Zuversicht"
? Johann Crüger 1653

Melody: "Jesus, meine Zuversicht"
? Johann Crüger 1653

(a)

The melody of the opening Choral, set to Luise Henriette Electress of Brandenburg's Hymn,

[1] The Cantata is marked merely "Am Osterfeste." Its relation to the Gospel for Easter Tuesday reveals the particular occasion for which it was written. See Spitta, II. 442 n. He quotes the Cantata by the title of the opening Choral, "Auf, mein Herz! des Herren Tag."

CANTATA CXLV 413

"Jesus, meine Zuversicht," was published in 1653 in Christoph Runge's *Geistliche Lieder und Psalmen* (Berlin) and in the Berlin edition of Johann Crüger's *Praxis Pietatis Melica*. The melody is generally attributed to Crüger and was published in 1668, after his death, with his initials attached to it. Perhaps the *Praxis* version (the second *supra*) is a reconstruction of the Runge melody. The melody does not occur elsewhere in the Cantatas, Oratorios, or Motetts. There is another harmonisation of it in the *Choralgesänge*, No. 208, where, as here, Bach uses the tune in its *Praxis* form. His variation of notes 3 and 4 of the second bar of it (*supra*) has earlier (1704) sanction. His treatment of bar 3 varies here and in the *Choralgesänge*. Organ Works, N. xviii. 69.

The words of the Choral are the first stanza of Caspar Neumann's Easter Hymn, "Auf, mein Herz," published in the Breslau *Vollständige Kirchen- und Haus-Music* (Breslau, c. 1700) to the melody, "Jesus, meine Zuversicht" (*supra*):

* Auf, mein Herz! des Herren Tag
  Hat die Nacht der Furcht vertrieben :
  Christus, der im Grabe lag,
  Ist im Tode nicht geblieben.
  Nunmehr bin ich recht getröst't,
  Jesus hat die Welt erlöst.   B.G. xxx. 95.

Form. Simple[1]. *Choralgesänge*, No. 209.

[1] The orchestration is not stated.

(b)

The words and melody of the concluding Choral are those of Nicolaus Herman's Easter Hymn, "Erschienen ist der herrlich' Tag" (see Cantata 67). The words are the fourteenth stanza of the Hymn:

> Drum wir auch billig fröhlich sein,
> Singen das Halleluja fein,
> Und loben dich, Herr Jesu Christ;
> Zu Trost du uns erstanden bist.
> Halleluja! B.G. xxx. 122.

Form. Simple (*Continuo*). *Choralgesänge*, No. 84.

CANTATA CXLVI. WIR MÜSSEN DURCH VIEL TRÜBSAL IN DAS REICH GOTTES EINGEHEN. Third Sunday after Easter ("Jubilate") (*c.* 1740)[1]

The melody of the concluding Choral (B.G. xxx. 190) is Johann Schop's "Werde munter, mein Gemüthe" (see Cantata 55). The words of the Choral are lacking in the MS. and in the B.G. Score.

Form. Simple[2].

---

[1] In the Cantata Bach uses the *Allegro* of the Concerto for two Violins or Clavier (D minor) as a symphony, and the Chorus that follows is its *Adagio* section. Bach uses the same Concerto in Cantata No. 188. See also Nos. 49, 110, 169, 174. Bach's authorship of Cantata 146 has been challenged (*Bachjahrbuch*, 1912).

[2] Only the vocal parts are printed in the Score.

CANTATA CXLVII. HERZ UND MUND UND THAT UND LEBEN. Feast of the Visitation of the B. V. M.[1] (1716)

The melody of the two Choral movements, the sixth and the last, of the Cantata is Johann Schop's "Werde munter, mein Gemüthe" (see Cantata 55). The words of both Choral movements are from Martin Janus', or Jahn's, "Jesu, meiner Seelen Wonne," first published, to Schop's "Werde munter" (*supra*), in the *Frommer Christen Tägliches Bet-Kämmerlein* (Görlitz, 1661). The Hymn is sometimes attributed erroneously to Johann Scheffler (1624–77).

Janus was born *c.* 1620 and probably was a native of Silesia. He was precentor at Sorau and later at Sagan. He died about 1682 at Ohlau, where he is said to have been precentor.

(*a*)

The words of the sixth movement are the sixth stanza of Janus' Hymn:

Wohl mir, das ich Jesum habe,
O wie feste halt' ich ihn,
Dass er mir mein Herze labe,
Wenn ich krank und traurig bin.

---

[1] Spitta, II. 412, states that the Cantata was written originally for the Fourth Sunday in Advent and was adjusted to the Visitation Feast at Leipzig, where there was no opportunity for its use on the Sunday for which it was composed.

Jesum hab' ich, der mich liebet
Und sich mir zu eigen giebet[1].
Ach drum lass' ich Jesum nicht,
Wenn mir gleich mein[2] Herze bricht.
B.G. xxx. 213.

An English translation of the Hymn is noted in the *Dictionary of Hymnology*, p. 579.

Form. Extended (*Tromba, Oboi, Strings, Continuo*).

(*b*)

The words of the concluding Choral are the seventeenth stanza of Janus' Hymn :

Jesus bleibet meine Freude,
Meines Herzens Trost und Saft,
Jesus wehret[3] allem Leide,
Er ist meines Lebens Kraft,
Meiner Augen Lust und Sonne,
Meiner Seele Schatz und Wonne,
Darum lass'[4] ich Jesum nicht
Aus dem Herzen und Gesicht. B.G. xxx. 229.

Form. Extended (*Tromba, Oboi, Strings, Continuo*).

CANTATA CXLVIII. BRINGET DEM HERRN EHRE SEINES NAMENS. Seventeenth Sunday after Trinity (*c.* 1725)

The melody of the concluding Choral is the anonymous "Auf meinen lieben Gott," or "Wo soll ich fliehen hin" (see Cantata 5).

[1] 1661 Und sein Leben für mich giebet.   [2] 1661 das.
[3] 1661 steuret.   [4] 1661 O! drumb lass.

CANTATA CXLIX

The words of the concluding Choral are the eleventh stanza of Johann Heermann's Lenten Hymn, "Wo soll ich fliehen hin" (see Cantata 5)[1]:

    Führ' auch mein Herz und Sinn
    Durch deinen Geist dahin,
    Dass ich mög' alles meiden,
    Was mich und dich kann scheiden,
    Und ich an deinem Leibe
    Ein Gliedmass ewig bleibe. B.G. xxx. 260.

Form. Simple (*Continuo*). *Choralgesänge*, No. 29.

CANTATA CXLIX. MAN SINGET MIT FREUDEN VOM SIEG[2]. Feast of St Michael the Archangel (1731)

Melody: "*Herzlich lieb hab' ich dich, O Herr*" Anon. 1577

[1] The words are lacking in the MS. The introduction of the eleventh stanza of Heermann's Hymn in the B.G. Score is in accordance with Spitta's suggestion (II. 694). Erk, No. 13, proposes stanza vi of Sigismund Weingärtner's (?) "Auf meinen lieben Gott":

    Amen! zu aller Stund'
    Sprech' ich aus Herzensgrund:
    Du wollest selbst uns leiten,
    Herr Christ, zu allen Zeiten,
    Auf dass wir deinen Namen
    Ewiglich preisen. Amen!

[2] An English version of the Cantata, "Let songs of rejoicing be raised," is published by Novello & Co. See Spitta, II. 445, on the source of the Cantata.

The melody, "Herzlich lieb hab' ich dich, O Herr," which Bach uses in the concluding Choral, was first published in Bernhard Schmidt's *Zwey Bücher Einer Neuen Kunstlichen Tabulatur auf Orgel und Instrument* (Strassburg, 1577). The germ of it had appeared six years before in *Newe Symbola etlicher Fürsten* (Nürnberg, 1571), where it is set to the Hymn whose name it bears[1].

The melody occurs also in Cantata 174 and in the "St John Passion," No. 37. There is another harmonisation of it in the *Choralgesänge*, No. 152. Bach's treatment of the tune is not uniform in the four places in which he employs it. There does not appear to be earlier authority for the F sharp which he substitutes for F natural at the fifth and thirteenth notes (*supra*) in this movement, nor does he repeat it elsewhere.

The words of the concluding Choral are the third stanza of Martin Schalling's Hymn for the Dying, "Herzlich lieb hab' ich dich, O Herr," first published in 1571 (*supra*):

---

[1] See *Bach's Chorals*, Part I, p. 39.

Ach Herr, lass dein' lieb' Engelein
Am letzten End' die Seele mein[1]
In Abraham's Schoos tragen;
Den Leib in seim Schlafkämmerlein
Gar sanft, ohn' ein'ge Qual und Pein,
Ruh'n bis am jüngsten Tage!
Alsdann vom Tod erwecke mich,
Dass meine Augen sehen dich
In aller Freud', O Gottes Sohn,
Mein Heiland und mein Gnadenthron!
Herr Jesu Christ, erhöre mich,
Ich will dich preisen ewiglich!

B.G. xxx. 299.

Translations of the Hymn into English are noted in the *Dictionary of Hymnology*, pp. 1004, 1648.

Form. Embellished (3 *Trombe, Timp.*, 3 *Ob.*, *Fagotto, Strings, Continuo*). *Choralgesänge*, No. 155.

CANTATA CLI. SÜSSER TROST, MEIN JESUS KOMMT. Feast of St John the Evangelist (Christmas) (*c.* 1740)

Melody: "*Lobt Gott, ihr Christen alle gleich*"
Nicolaus Herman 1554

---

[1] 1571 An meinem end mein Seelelein.

The words and melody of the concluding Choral are Nicolaus Herman's Christmas Hymn, "Lobt Gott, ihr Christen alle gleich," written c. 1554, and first published in Herman's *Die Sontags Euangelia uber das gantze Jar* (Wittenberg, 1560), where it is set to the melody printed above.

The melody, of which Herman was the composer, appeared first in a broadsheet published in 1554. It is set there to his own words:

> Kommt her, ihr lieben Schwesterlein,
> An diesen Abendtanz;
> Lasst uns ein geistlichs Liedelein
> Singen um einen Kranz.

The melody occurs also in Cantata 195 and there are harmonisations of it in the *Choralgesänge*, Nos. 233, 234. Organ Works, N. xv. 29; xviii. 74. Bach's version of the tune practically was established before the end of the sixteenth century.

The words of the concluding Choral are the eighth stanza of Herman's Hymn:

> Heut' schleusst er wieder auf die Thür
> Zum schönen Paradeis,
> Der Cherub steht nicht mehr dafür;
> Gott sei Lob, Ehr' und Preis!
>   B.G. xxxii. 16.

Translations of the Hymn are noted in the *Dictionary of Hymnology*, p. 514.

Form. Simple (*Flauto, Oboe d'amore, Strings, Continuo*). *Choralgesänge*, No. 235.

CANTATA CLIII. SCHAU', LIEBER GOTT, WIE MEINE FEIND'. Sunday after the Circumcision (1724)

(a)

For the melody of the opening Choral, "Ach Gott, vom Himmel sieh' darein," see Cantata 2. The words of the Choral are the first stanza of David Denicke's (?) Hymn, "Schau', lieber Gott, wie meine Feind'," first published in the *New Ordentlich Gesang-Buch* (Hanover, 1646), to the tune, "Ach Gott, vom Himmel" (*supra*):

> Schau', lieber Gott, wie meine Feind',
> Damit ich stets muss kämpfen,
> So listig und so mächtig seind,
> Dass sie mich leichtlich dämpfen!
> Herr, so mich deine Gnad' nicht hält,
> So kann der Teufel, Fleisch und[1] Welt
> Mich leicht in Unglück stürzen[2].
>
> B.G. xxxii. 43.

Form. Simple (*Strings, Continuo*). *Choralgesänge*, No. 5.

(b)

For the melody of the fifth movement, Hans Leo Hassler's "Herzlich thut mich verlangen," see Cantata 135.

[1] 1646 und die. Bach's text follows the edition of 1652.
[2] 1646 Das Fleisch geschwind verführen. In the 1652 edition the line reads: Mich leicht in sünde stürtzen.

The words of the Choral are the fifth stanza of Paul Gerhardt's Hymn, "Befiehl du deine Wege," first published in the Berlin (1653) edition of the *Praxis Pietatis Melica*. The Hymn is an acrostic on Luther's version of Psalm xxxvii. 5, "Befiehl dem Herren dein Weg und hoff auf ihn, er wirds wol machen," formed by the initial words of the stanzas. It was published to another melody, but was generally sung to Hassler's tune (*supra*):

> Und obgleich alle Teufel
> Dir[1] wollten widerstehn,
> So wird doch ohne Zweifel
> Gott nicht zurücke gehn.
> Was er ihm fürgenommen
> Und was er haben will,
> Das muss doch endlich kommen
> Zu seinem Zweck und Ziel.
> B.G. xxxii. 46.

English translations of the Hymn are noted in the *Dictionary of Hymnology*, pp. 125, 1611.

Form. Simple (*Strings, Continuo*). *Choralgesänge*, No. 160.

(*c*)

For the melody of the concluding Choral, the anonymous "Herr Jesu Christ, mein's Lebens Licht," or "Ach Gott, wie manches Herzeleid," see Cantata 3.

[1] 1653 Hie.

The words of the Choral are the eleventh and twelfth stanzas of Martin Moller's (?) Hymn, "Ach Gott, wie manches Herzeleid" (see Cantata 3), arranged as three verses:

> Drum will ich, weil ich lebe noch,
> Das Kreuz dir fröhlich tragen nach;
> Mein Gott, mach' mich darzu bereit;
> Es dient zum Besten allezeit.
> Hilf mir mein' Sach' recht greifen an,
> Dass ich mein Lauf vollenden kann,
> Hilf mir auch zwingen Fleisch und Blut,
> Für Sünd und Schanden mich behüt'!
> Erhalt' mein Herz im Glauben rein,
> So leb' und sterb' ich dir allein;
> Jesu, mein Trost, hör mein Begier,
> O mein Heiland, wär' ich bei dir!
> B.G. xxxii. 58.

Form. Simple (*Strings, Continuo*). *Choralgesänge*, No. 9.

CANTATA CLIV. MEIN LIEBSTER JESUS IST VERLOREN. First Sunday after the Epiphany (1724)

(*a*)

For the melody of the third movement, Johann Schop's "Werde munter, mein Gemüthe," see Cantata 55.

The words of the Choral are the second stanza of Martin Janus' Hymn, "Jesu, meiner Seelen Wonne" (see Cantata 147):

Jesu, mein Hort und Erretter,
Jesu, meine Zuversicht,
Jesu, starker Schlangentreter,
Jesu, meines Lebens Licht!
Wie verlanget meinem Herzen,
Jesulein, nach dir mit Schmerzen!
Komm', ach komm', ich warte dein,
Komm', O liebstes Jesulein!

B.G. xxxii. 65.

Form. Simple (2 *Ob.*, *Strings*, *Continuo*). *Choralgesänge*, No. 365.

(*b*)

For the melody of the concluding Choral, Andreas Hammerschmidt's (?) "Meinen Jesum lass' ich nicht," see Cantata 70.

The words of the Choral are the sixth stanza of Christian Keimann's Hymn, "Meinen Jesum lass' ich nicht" (see Cantata 70):

Meinen Jesum lass' ich nicht[1],
Geh' ihm ewig an der Seiten;
Christus lässt mich für und für
Zu dem Lebensbächlein leiten.
Selig, der[2] mit mir so spricht:
Meinen Jesum lass' ich nicht!

B.G. xxxii. 82.

Form. Simple (2 *Ob.*, *Strings*, *Continuo*). *Choralgesänge*, No. 244.

[1] 1659 Jesum lass ich nicht von mir.
[2] 1659 wer.

CANTATA CLV. MEIN GOTT, WIE LANG', ACH LANGE. Second Sunday after the Epiphany (1715)

The words and melody of the concluding Choral are those of Paul Speratus' Hymn, "Es ist das Heil uns kommen her" (see Cantata 9).

The words are the twelfth stanza of the Hymn:

> Ob sich's anliess', als wollt' er nicht,
> Lass dich es nicht erschrecken;
> Denn wo er ist am besten mit,
> Da will er's nicht entdecken;
> Sein Wort lass dir[1] gewisser sein,
> Und ob dein Herz[2] spräch' lauter Nein;
> So lass doch dir nicht grauen.
> B.G. xxxii. 96.

Form. Simple (*Strings, Continuo*). *Choralgesänge*, No. 88.

CANTATA CLVI. ICH STEH' MIT EINEM FUSS IM GRABE. Third Sunday after the Epiphany (1729-30)

(*a*)

The melody of the second movement is Johann Hermann Schein's "Mach's mit mir, Gott, nach deiner Güt'" (see Cantata 139).

The words of the Choral are the first stanza of Schein's Hymn. It was written in 1628 for the funeral of Margarita Werner, the wife of a

---

[1] 1524 das las dir.   [2] 1524 fleisch.

Leipzig Town Councillor, and was published in that year as a broadsheet, with the tune. The Hymn is an acrostic; the initial letters of the first and third lines in stanzas i–iv spell the name "Ma-r-g-a-r-i-t-a," and the initial W of stanza v stands for "Werner":

> Mach's mit mir, Gott, nach deiner Güt',
> Hilf mir in meinem Leiden.
> Was ich dich bitt'[1], versag' mir nicht!
> Wenn sich mein' Seel' soll[2] scheiden,
> So nimm sie, Herr, in deine Händ':
> Ist Alles gut, wenn gut das End'.
> B.G. xxxii. 101.

Translations of the Hymn are noted in the *Dictionary of Hymnology*, p. 1008.

Form. "Arie mit Choral" for Soprano and Tenor, i.e. a *Duetto*, the Soprano having the *cantus* and the Tenor an independent subject to other words (*Vn. I and II and Viola in unison, Continuo*)[3].

Melody: "*Herr, wie du willt*"   Anon. 1525

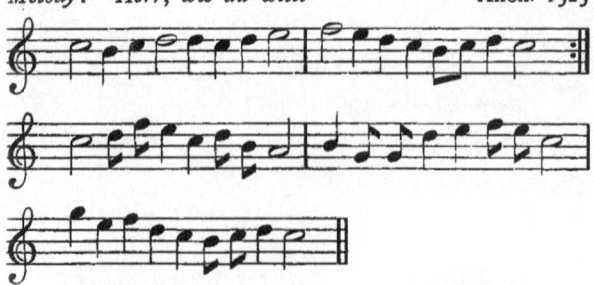

[1] 1628 Ruff ich dich an.   [2] 1628 wil.
[3] See Spitta, II. 441, on the movement.

(*b*)

The melody of the concluding Choral was first published in 1525 in the Strassburg *Ordnung des Herren Nachtmal*, and also, with a slight alteration[1], in the Strassburg *Teutsch Kirchēampt mit lobgsengen, uñ götlichen psalmen* in the same year. It was set in both to Luther's "Aus tiefer Noth," but is generally associated with Bienemann's Hymn (*infra*) in the Hymn books. Bienemann's Hymn has a later (1648) melody of its own, which is less familiar.

The melody does not occur elsewhere in the Cantatas, Oratorios, or Motetts. There is another harmonisation of it in the *Choralgesänge*, No. 151.

The words of the Choral are the first stanza of Caspar Bienemann's Hymn, "Herr, wie du willt, so schick's mit mir" (see Cantata 73):

> Herr, wie du will't, so schick's mit mir
> Im Leben und im Sterben ;
> Allein zu dir steht mein Begehr,
> Herr, lass mich[2] nicht verderben !
> Erhalt' mich nur in deiner Huld:
> Sonst, wie du will't, gieb mir Geduld ;
> Dein Will' der[3] ist der beste.
>   B.G. xxxii. 114.

Form. Simple (*Oboe, Strings, Continuo*). *Choralgesänge*, No. 150.

[1] The penultimate note of the third bar is C instead of B.
[2] 1582 Lass mich, Herr.   [3] 1582 Denn dein Will.

CANTATA CLVII. ICH LASSE DICH NICHT, DU SEGNEST MICH DENN. Purification of the B.V.M.[1] (1727)

The words and melody of the concluding Choral are those of Christian Keimann's Hymn, "Meinen Jesum lass' ich nicht" (see Cantata 70). The words are the sixth stanza of the Hymn:

> Meinen Jesum lass' ich nicht[2],
> Geh' ihm ewig an der Seiten;
> Christus lässt mich für und für
> Zu dem Lebensbächlein leiten;
> Selig, wer mit mir so spricht:
> Meinen Jesum lass' ich nicht!
> B.G. xxxii. 140.

Form. Simple (*Flauto, Oboe, Strings, Continuo*). *Choralgesänge*, No. 245.

CANTATA CLVIII. DER FRIEDE SEI MIT DIR. Purification of the B.V.M. and Easter Tuesday[3] (*c.* 1708–17)

(*a*)

The Choral in the second movement is Johann Georg Albinus' Hymn, "Welt, ade! ich bin dein müde" (Cantata 27). For Johann Rosenmüller's melody, see Cantata 27.

[1] See Spitta, II. 411. Bach performed the Cantata at a funeral four days after using it at the Feast of the Purification.
[2] 1659 Jesum lass ich nicht von mir.
[3] See Spitta, II. 687, on the Cantata.

The words of the Choral are the first stanza of the Hymn:

> Welt, ade! ich bin dein müde,
> Ich will nach dem Himmel zu;
> Da wird sein der rechte Friede
> Und die ew'ge Seelenruh'[1].
> Welt, bei dir ist Krieg und Streit,
> Nichts denn lauter Eitelkeit,
> In dem Himmel allezeit
> Friede, Ruh'[2] und Seeligkeit. B.G. xxxii. 144.

Form. "Arie mit Choral," i.e. *Duetto*, for Soprano and Bass. The Soprano has the *cantus* (*Oboe, Violino solo, Continuo*).

(*b*)

The words and melody of the concluding Choral are Luther's "Christ lag in Todesbanden" (see Cantata 4).

The words are the fifth stanza of the Hymn:

> Hier ist das rechte Osterlamm,
> Davon hat Gott[3] geboten,
> Das ist hoch an[4] des Kreuzes Stamm
> In heisser Lieb' gebraten:
> Dess Blut zeichnet uns're Thür,
> Das hält der Glaub' dem Tode für,
> Der Würger kann uns nicht rühren.
> Halleluja!
> B.G. xxxii. 154.

Form. Simple (*Continuo*). *Choralgesänge*, No. 40.

[1] 1668 stoltze Ruh. Bach follows the 1672 text.
[2] 1668 Freud. Bach follows the 1672 text.
[3] 1524 Gott hat. [4] 1524 Das ist an.

CANTATA CLIX. SEHET, WIR GEH'N HINAUF GEN JERUSALEM. Quinquagesima ("Esto Mihi") Sunday (? 1729)

(a)

For the melody of the second movement, Hassler's "Herzlich thut mich verlangen," see Cantata 135.

The words of the Choral are the sixth stanza of Paul Gerhardt's Passiontide Hymn, "O Haupt voll Blut und Wunden," first published in the 1656 (Frankfort) edition of Crüger's *Praxis Pietatis Melica*:

> Ich will hier bei dir stehen,
> Verachte mich doch nicht!
> Von dir will ich nicht gehen,
> Bis[1] dir dein Herze bricht.
> Wenn dein Haupt[2] wird erblassen
> Im letzten Todesstoss,
> Alsdann will ich dich fassen
> In meinen Arm und Schoos.

B.G. xxxii. 160.

Translations of the Hymn into English are noted in the *Dictionary of Hymnology*, pp. 835, 1681.

Form. "Arie mit Choral" for Soprano and Alto, i.e. a *Duetto*, the Soprano having the Choral melody (*Oboe, Fagotti, Continuo*).

---

[1] 1656 Wann.
[2] 1656 hertz. Bach's line is found in a 1667 text.

CANTATA CLIX 431

Melody: "*Jesu Kreuz, Leiden und Pein*"
Melchior Vulpius 1609: reconstruction 1682

(b)

The melody of the concluding Choral, Melchior Vulpius' "Jesu Kreuz, Leiden und Pein," was first published in 1609, set to Petrus Herbert's Hymn, "Jesu Kreuz, Leiden und Pein[1]. In 1656 it was associated with Paul Stockmann's "Jesu Leiden, Pein und Tod," and a reconstruction of it, set to Stockmann's Hymn, was published by Gottfried Vopelius in his *New Leipziger Gesangbuch, Von den schönsten und besten Liedern verfasset*(Leipzig, 1682).

The melody occurs also in Cantata 182 and in the "St John Passion," Nos. 11, 30, 32. Bach uses it in its reconstructed form. The F sharp which he substitutes for A natural at the seventh note in the second bar (*supra*) has earlier sanction (1714). His variation of the last bar is general to his use of

[1] See the melody in *Bach's Chorals*, Part I, p. 27.

the tune, and is found in an earlier (1714) text. In the "St John Passion" (No. 30) he introduces a C sharp at the sixth note of the first bar (*supra*).

The words of the Choral are the thirty-third stanza of Paul Stockmann's Passiontide Hymn, "Jesu Leiden, Pein und Tod," first published in his *Aller Christen Leib-Stücke* (Leipzig, 1633):

> Jesu, deine Passion
> Ist mir lauter Freude,
> Deine Wunden, Kron' und Hohn
> Meines Herzens Weide;
> Meine Seel' und[1] Rosen geht,
> Wenn ich d'ran gedenke,
> In dem Himmel eine Stätt'
> Mir[2] deswegen schenke!
> B.G. xxxii. 168.

Form. Simple (*Oboe, Strings, Continuo*). *Choralgesänge*, No. 194.

CANTATA CLXI. KOMM, DU SÜSSE TODESSTUNDE. Sixteenth Sunday after Trinity and Feast of the Purification of the B.V.M. (1715)

For the melody of the concluding Choral, Hassler's "Herzlich thut mich verlangen," see Cantata 135.

The words of the Choral are the fourth stanza of Christoph Knoll's funerary Hymn, "Herzlich

---

[1] 1633 auff. [2] 1633 Uns.

thut mich verlangen." The Hymn is said to have been written during a pestilence in 1599. It was first printed at Görlitz in 1605 and also in the Görlitz *Harmoniae sacrae* (1613), where it is set to Hassler's tune.

Christoph Knoll was born at Bunzlau, in Silesia, in 1563. He was successively schoolmaster, Deacon, and Archdeacon at Sprottau, and from 1628 was pastor of the neighbouring village, Wittgendorf. He died there in 1650:

> Der Leib zwar in der Erden
> Von Würmern wird verzehrt:
> Doch auferweckt soll werden[1]
> Durch Christum schön verklärt;
> Wird leuchten als die Sonne
> Und leben ohne Noth[2]
> In himml'scher Freud' und Wonne.
> Was schad't mir dann der Tod[3]?
>
> B.G. xxxiii. 27.

A translation of the Hymn into English is noted in the *Dictionary of Hymnology*, p. 629.

Form. Embellished (2 *Fl.*, *Strings*, *Continuo*). *Choralgesänge*, No. 161.

Bach introduces (Sesquialtera ad Organo) the melody in the opening Alto *Aria*, "Komm, du süsse Todesstunde."

---

[1] 1611 Dort wird erwecket werden.
[2] 1611 ohn alle noth.
[3] 1611 mir der Todt?

CANTATA CLXII. ACH, ICH SEHE, JETZT DA ICH ZUR HOCHZEIT GEHE. Twentieth Sunday after Trinity (1715)

Melody: "Alle Menschen müssen sterben"

Bach's version 1715

Melody: "Jesu, der du meine Seele"

Johann Schop 1641

CANTATA CLXII 435

Melody: "*Herr, ich habe missgehandelt*"
Johann Crüger 1649

Melody: "*Alle Menschen müssen sterben*"
Johann Rosenmüller 1652

The melody of the concluding Choral is one of two which appear for the first time in Bach's Church Cantatas[1]. Erk[2], who prints it, describes it as Johann Schop's "Jesu, der du meine Seele" (1641) "nachgebildet." Spitta[3] declares it to be

---

[1] See Cantata 133.   [2] Vol. II. No. 159.
[3] Vol. III. 115.

"nothing more than a compound produced by the fusion of the melodies, 'Herr, ich habe missgehandelt' (1649) and 'Jesu, der du meine Seele' (1641)." He adds: "I am now thoroughly convinced of Bach being the author of this melody, which occurs nowhere else." Spitta's confidence is inadequately grounded. The Hymn, "Alle Menschen müssen sterben," received in 1652 a five-part setting, by Johann Rosenmüller[1], of which the tune printed *supra* is the descant melody. It is clear that the tune is a derivative, and with great probability may be regarded as the Tenor of an original setting now lost. The German Hymn books between 1652 and 1715, the date of Bach's Cantata, contain a large number of tunes to the Hymn. One of them, dated 1674[2], is, as to the first half of it, certainly constructed upon the Bass of Rosenmüller's setting. Whether Bach's is an original variation or not, Spitta's suggestion that he formed it by dissecting two other tunes by well known composers may be discarded. König prints in 1738 two versions of a tune closely related to Bach's. All three probably are derived from a common source. It was not in accordance with Bach's rule to set a Hymn to a tune not in

[1] Another tune printed by Erk, No. 158, as Rosenmüller's is in fact by Jakob Hintze (1622–1702).
[2] Zahn, IV. No. 6777.

customary use with it. It is therefore improbable that he should have gone out of his way to invent a tune for a Hymn which had its own melody, with one of which, too, he was familiar[1] The circumstances surrounding this case are, in fact, very similar to those attending the doubtful melody in Cantata 133. Of both tunes a large number of variations exist in the Hymn books, evidencing either their composite origin, or their derivation from some common original.

The melody does not occur elsewhere in the Cantatas, Oratorios, or Motetts. In the *Orgelbüchlein*, N. xv. 119, Bach treats a melody found first in the Darmstadt *Das grosse Cantional* (Darmstadt, 1687).

The words of the concluding Choral of the Cantata are the seventh stanza of Johann Georg Albinus' funerary Hymn, "Alle Menschen müssen sterben." It was written and published for the funeral of Paul von Henssberg, a burgher of Leipzig, and was sung to Rosenmüller's setting on that occasion (June 1, 1652). The broadsheet states that both words and music were composed in Henssberg's honour by Johann Rosenmüller. The statement would appear to be conclusive. On the other hand, Rosenmüller is not known as a Hymn writer, and hymnologists unhesitatingly ascribe

---

[1] *Orgelbüchlein*, N. xv. 119.

the Hymn to Albinus, to whose other Hymn for the Dying, "Welt, ade!" Rosenmüller also wrote the music (see Cantata 27):

> Ach, ich habe schon erblicket
> Diese grosse[1] Herrlichkeit!
> Jetzund werd' ich schön geschmücket
> Mit dem weissen Himmelskleid,
> Mit[2] der guld'nen Ehrenkrone;
> Steh' ich da für[3] Gottes Throne,
> Schaue solche Freude an,
> Die kein Ende nehmen kann[4]!
>
> B.G. xxxiii. 46.

Translations of the Hymn into English are noted in the *Dictionary of Hymnology*, p. 36.

Form. Simple (*Corno da tirarsi, Fagotto, Strings, Continuo*). *Choralgesänge*, No. 18.

CANTATA CLXIII. NUR JEDEM DAS SEINE.

Twenty-third Sunday after Trinity (1715)

Melody: "*Wo soll ich fliehen hin*" ? Caspar Stieler 1679

---

[1] 1652 Alle diese.   [2] 1652 Und.   [3] 1652 Stehe da für.
[4] 1652 Die ich nicht beschreiben kan.

The melody of the concluding Choral was first published in Caspar Stieler's *Der Bussfertige Sünder, Oder Geistliches Hand-Büchlein* (Nürnberg, 1679). It is set there to Johann Heermann's Lenten Hymn, "Wo soll ich fliehen hin" (see Cantata 5). Spitta[1] describes the melody as Pachelbel's[2]. Zahn, on the other hand, is of opinion that the anonymous tunes in the *Hand-Büchlein* are by Stieler himself.

Of Stieler, beyond the fact that he calls Ahashuerus Fritsch his "Patron und Gevatter," nothing is known.

The melody occurs also in Cantata 199. The tune, "Wo soll ich fliehen hin," which Bach treats in the Organ Works, is more correctly styled, "Auf meinen lieben Gott" (see Cantata 5).

The MS. of the Cantata and the B.G. Score give no Hymn stanza. Spitta[3] is responsible for the insertion of the eleventh stanza of Johann Heermann's Lenten Hymn, "Wo soll ich fliehen hin" (see Cantata 5), in the vocal Score:

<blockquote>
Führ auch mein Herz und Sinn
Durch deinen Geist dahin,
Dass ich mög' Alles meiden,
Was mich von dir[4] kann scheiden,
Und ich an deinem Leibe
Ein Gliedmass ewig bleibe. [B.G. xxxiii. 64.]
</blockquote>

---

[1] Vol. I. 557.

[2] Spitta incorrectly supposes that the melody is that of Cantata 5 in the major.

[3] Vol. I. 557.   [4] 1630· und dich.

Form. Simple[1]. The melody is neither in Erk nor the *Choralgesänge*.

In the fifth movement of the Cantata (B.G. xxxiii. 61), a *Duetto* ("Arie") for Soprano and Alto, the melody of Andreas Hammerschmidt's (?) "Meinen Jesum lass' ich nicht" (see Cantata 70) accompanies the singers. It is played by the "Violini e Viola all' unisono." The melody is suggested by the words of the movement, which, however, are not a stanza of Christian Keimann's Hymn.

CANTATA CLXIV. IHR, DIE IHR EUCH VON CHRISTO NENNET. Thirteenth Sunday after Trinity (1723 or 1724)

The words and melody of the concluding Choral are from Elisabethe Cruciger's Christmas Hymn, "Herr Christ, der einig' Gott's Sohn" (see Cantata 22).

The words are the fifth stanza of the Hymn:

> Ertödt' uns durch dein' Güte,
> Erweck' uns durch dein' Gnad'!
> Den alten Menschen kränke,
> Dass der neu leben mag,
> Wohl hier auf dieser Erden
> Der Sinn und all Begehrden,
> Nur G'danken[2] hab' zu dir. B.G. xxxiii. 88.

[1] Only the figured Bass, under the title "Choral. In semplice stylo," is given.
[2] 1524 Und dancken.

Form. Simple (2 *Ob.*, *Strings*, *Continuo*). *Choralgesänge*, No. 127.

In the second movement of the Cantata (B.G. xxxiii. 75), the Bass *Recitativo* "Wie hören zwar," Bach gives a brief reference (*Arioso*) to the melody "O Gott, du frommer Gott" (1693) (see Cantata 24). The words are not a stanza of that Hymn.

CANTATA CLXV. O HEIL'GES GEIST- UND WASSERBAD. Trinity Sunday (? 1724)

The words and melody of the concluding Choral are from Ludwig Helmbold's Hymn, "Nun lasst uns Gott dem Herren" (see Cantata 79).

The words are the fifth stanza of the Hymn:

> Sein Wort, sein' Taufe, sein Nachtmahl
> Dient wider allen Unfall:
> Der heil'ge Geist im Glauben
> Lehrt uns darauf vertrauen.
>
> B.G. xxxiii. 104.

Form. Simple (*Fagotto*, *Strings*, *Continuo*). *Choralgesänge*, No. 266.

CANTATA CLXVI. WO GEHEST DU HIN? Fourth Sunday after Easter ("Cantate") (*c.* 1725)

(*a*)

For the melody of the third movement, the anonymous "Herr Jesu Christ, du höchstes Gut," see Cantata 48.

The words of the movement are the third stanza of Bartholomäus Ringwaldt's Hymn, "Herr Jesu Christ, ich weiss gar wohl," first published in *Handbüchlein: Geistliche Lieder und Gebetlin* (Frankfort a. Oder, 1586 [1582], to the tune "Wenn mein Stündlein vorhanden ist." It is associated in Wagner (1697) with the melody, "Herr Jesu Christ" (*supra*):

> Ich bitte[1] dich, Herr Jesu Christ,
> Halt' mich bei den Gedanken
> Und lass mich ja zu keiner Frist
> Von dieser Meinung wanken.
> Sondern dabei verharen fest,
> Bis dass die Seel' aus ihrem Nest
> Wird in den Himmel kommen[2].

B.G. xxxiii. 113.

Form. Soprano Unison Choral ("*Violini e Viola*" *in unison, Continuo*).

(*b*)

The melody of the concluding Choral is Georg Neumark's "Wer nur den lieben Gott lässt walten" (see Cantata 21).

The words are the first stanza of Emilie Juliane Countess of Schwarzburg-Rudolstadt's funerary Hymn, "Wer weiss, wie nahe mir mein Ende" (see Cantata 27):

[1] 1586 So bitt ich.   [2] 1586 fahren.

Wer weiss, wie nahe mir mein Ende,
Hin geht die Zeit, her kommt der Tod.
Ach, wie geschwinde und behende
Kann kommen meine Todesnoth!
Mein Gott, ich bitt' durch Christi Blut,
Mach's nur mit meinem Ende gut!

B.G. xxxiii. 122.

Form. Simple (*Oboe, Strings, Continuo*). *Choralgesänge*, No. 372.

CANTATA CLXVII. IHR MENSCHEN, RÜHMET GOTTES LIEBE[1]. Feast of St John Baptist (*c.* 1725)

The melody of the concluding Choral is Johann Kugelmann's (?) "Nun lob', mein' Seel', den Herren" (see Cantata 17).

The words of the Choral are the fifth stanza of Johann Graumann's Hymn, "Nun lob', mein' Seel', den Herren" (see Cantata 29):

* Sei Lob und Preis mit Ehren
Gott Vater, Sohn, heiliger Geist.
Der woll' in uns vermehren,
Was er uns aus Genad' verheisst.
Dass wir ihm fest vertrauen,
Gänzlich verlassen auf ihn,
Von Herzen auf ihn bauen;
Dass unser Herz, Muth und Sinn

---

[1] An English version of the Cantata "Ye mortals, extol the love of the Father," is published by Breitkopf & Haertel.

CANTATA CLXVIII

Ihm festiglich anhangen:
Darauf singen wir zur Stund'.
Amen, wir werden's erlangen,
Gläub'n wir aus Herzens Grund.
B.G. xxxiii. 140.

Form. Extended (*Clarino, Oboe, Strings, Continuo*).

CANTATA CLXVIII. THUE RECHNUNG! DONNERWORT. Ninth Sunday after Trinity (*c.* 1725)

The words and melody of the concluding Choral are Bartholomäus Ringwaldt's Lenten Hymn, "Herr Jesu Christ, du höchstes Gut" (see Cantatas 48 and 113).

The words are the eighth stanza of the Hymn:

> Stärk' mich mit deinem Freudengeist,
> Heil' mich mit deinen Wunden;
> Wasch' mich mit deinem Todesschweiss
> In meinen letzten Stunden;
> Und nimm mich einst, wenn dir's gefällt,
> In wahrem[1] Glauben von der Welt
> Zu deinen Auserwählten.

B.G. xxxiii. 166.

Form. Simple (2 *Ob. d'amore, Strings, Continuo*). *Choralgesänge,* No. 143.

[1] 1588 rechten.

CANTATA CLXIX. GOTT SOLL ALLEIN MEIN HERZE HABEN. Eighteenth Sunday after Trinity (1731 or 1732)

Melody: "*Nun bitten wir den heiligen Geist*"

Anon. 1524

The words and melody of the concluding Choral are Luther's Whitsuntide Hymn, "Nun bitten wir den heiligen Geist," first published, words and melody, in Johann Walther's *Geystliche gesangk Buchleyn* (Wittenberg, 1524). Undoubtedly the melody is a reconstruction by Walther of the tune, "Nu biten wir den heiligen Geist," one of the few vernacular pre-Reformation Hymns.

The melody also occurs in Cantata 197, and there is another harmonisation of it in the *Choralgesänge*, No. 254.

The words of the Choral are the third stanza of the Hymn, which, with stanzas ii and iv, Luther added to the original "Nu biten wir," which dates certainly from the thirteenth century:

> Du süsse Liebe, schenk' uns deine Gunst,
> Lass uns empfinden der Liebe Brunst,
> Dass wir uns von Herzen einander lieben
> Und in Frieden auf einem Sinn bleiben.
> Kyrie eleison. B.G. xxxiii. 192.

Translations of the Hymn into English are noted in the *Dictionary of Hymnology*, p. 821.

Form. Simple (2 *Ob.*, *Taille*[1], Strings, Continuo). *Choralgesänge*, No. 256[2].

CANTATA CLXXI. GOTT, WIE DEIN NAME, SO IST AUCH DEIN RUHM. Feast of the Circumcision (New Year's Day) (*c.* 1730)

The words and melody of the concluding Choral are Johann Hermann's New Year's Hymn, "Jesu, nun sei gepreiset" (see Cantata 41).

The words are the third stanza of the Hymn:

> Dein ist allein die Ehre,
> Dein ist allein der Ruhm.
> Geduld im Kreuz uns lehre,
> Regier' all' unser Thun,
> Bis wir getrost abscheiden
> In's ew'ge Himmelreich[3]
> Zum wahren Fried' und Freuden,
> Den Heil'gen Gottes gleich.

[1] The Taille was a Tenor Bassoon.
[2] Into this Cantata Bach incorporates the first two movements of the E major clavier Concerto. See also Nos. 49, 110, 146, 174, 188.
[3] 1593 Vaters Reich.

Indess mach's mit uns Allen
Nach deinem Wohlgefallen.
Solch's singet heut' ohn' Scherzen
Die Christgläubige Schaar,
Und wünscht mit Mund und Herzen
Ein sel'ges neues Jahr. B.G. xxxv. 32.

Form. Extended (3 *Trombe, Timp.*, 2 *Ob.*, Strings, Continuo). *Choralgesänge*, No. 204[1].

CANTATA CLXXII. ERSCHALLET, IHR LIEDER.

Whit Sunday (1724 or 1725)

The words and melody of the concluding Choral are Philipp Nicolai's Hymn, "Wie schön leuchtet der Morgenstern" (see Cantata 1).

The words are the fourth stanza of the Hymn:

Von Gott kommt mir ein Freudenschein,
Wenn du mit deinen Äugelein
Mich freundlich thust anblicken.
O Herr Jesu, mein trautes Gut,
Dein Wort, dein Geist, dein Leib und Blut
Mich innerlich erquicken.
Nimm mich freundlich
In dein' Arme, das ich warme
Werd' von Gnaden :
Auf dein Wort komm' ich geladen.
B.G. xxxv. 69.

Form. Embellished (*Fagotto, Strings, Continuo*). *Choralgesänge*, No. 376.

[1] Excepting a difference of key (C major instead of D major) the movement is identical with the concluding Choral of Cantata 41. In the *Choralgesänge* the movement is printed in C major.

In the fifth movement of the Cantata (B.G. xxxv. 62), the Soprano-Alto *Duetto*, "Komm, lass' mich nicht länger warten," the Violin *obbligato* is a very free treatment of the Whitsuntide melody, "Komm, heiliger Geist, Herre Gott" (see Cantata 59), in an abridged form.

CANTATA CLXXIV. ICH LIEBE DEN HÖCHSTEN VON GANZEM GEMÜTHE. Whit Monday (1731 or 1732)

The words and melody of the concluding Choral are Martin Schalling's funerary Hymn, "Herzlich lieb hab' ich dich, O Herr" (see Cantata 149).

The words are the first stanza of the Hymn:

> Herzlich lieb hab' ich dich, O Herr:
> Ich bitt': woll'st sein von mir nicht fern
> Mit deiner Hilf'[1] und Gnaden.
> Die ganze Welt erfreut mich nicht[2],
> Nach Himm'l und Erde frag' ich nicht[3],
> Wenn ich dich nur kann haben.
> Herr[4], wenn mir gleich mein Herz zerbricht,
> So bist du doch[5] mein' Zuversicht,
> Mein Heil[6] und meines Herzens Trost,
> Der mich durch sein Blut hat erlöst.
> Herr Jesu Christ, mein Gott und Herr,
> In Schanden lass mich nimmermehr!
> B.G. xxxv. 157.

[1] 1571 güt.
[2] 1571 nit frewet mich.
[3] 1571 nit frag ich.
[4] 1571 Und.
[5] 1571 doch du.
[6] 1571 theil.

CANTATA CLXXV 449

Form. Embellished (2 *Ob.*, *Taille*[1], *Strings*, *Continuo*). *Choralgesänge*, No. 153[2].

CANTATA CLXXV. ER RUFET SEINEN SCHAFEN MIT NAMEN. Whit Tuesday (? 1735)

For the melody of the concluding Choral, "Komm, heiliger Geist, Herre Gott," see Cantata 59.

The words of the Choral are the ninth stanza of Johann Rist's Hymn for the Sixth Sunday after Easter, "O Gottes Geist, mein Trost und Rath," first published in his *Sabbahtische Seelenlust* (Lüneburg, 1651), to the melody, "Komm, heiliger Geist":

> Nun, werther Geist, ich folg' dir;
> Hilf, dass ich suche für und für
> Nach deinem Wort ein ander Leben,
> Das du mir willt aus Gnaden geben.
> Dein Wort ist ja der Morgenstern,
> Der herrlich leuchtet nah' und fern.
> Drum will ich, die mich anders lehren,
> In Ewigkeit, mein Gott, nicht hören.
>   Alleluja, Alleluja!
>   B.G. xxxv. 177.

Form. Embellished (3 *Fl.*, *Strings*, *Continuo*). *Choralgesänge*, No. 220.

---

[1] The Taille was a Tenor Bassoon.
[2] The Introduction to the Cantata is the first movement of the third Brandenburg Concerto.

Cantata CLXXVI. Es ist ein trotzig und verzagt Ding. Trinity Sunday (? 1735)

For the melody of the concluding Choral, Johann Walther's (?) "Christ unser Herr zum Jordan kam," see Cantata 7. The words of the Choral are the eighth stanza of Paul Gerhardt's Hymn for Trinity Sunday, "Was alle Weisheit in der Welt," first published in the 1653 (Berlin) edition of Crüger's *Praxis Pietatis Melica*, to the melody, "Christ unser Herr":

> Auf dass wir also allzugleich
> Zur Himmelspforte dringen
> Und dermaleinst in deinem Reich
> Ohn' alles Ende singen :
> Dass du alleine König seist,
> Hoch über alle Götter,
> Gott Vater, Sohn und heil'ger Geist,
> Der Frommen Schutz und Retter :
> Ein Wesen, drei Personen.
>
> B.G. xxxv. 198.

Translations of the Hymn into English are noted in the *Dictionary of Hymnology*, p. 411.

Form. Simple (2 *Ob.*, *Oboe da caccia*, *Strings*, *Continuo*). *Choralgesänge*, No. 45.

CANTATA CLXXVII. ICH RUF' ZU DIR, HERR JESU CHRIST[1]. Fourth Sunday after Trinity (1732)

Melody: "*Ich ruf' zu dir, Herr Jesu Christ*"
Anon. 1535

A Choral Cantata, on Johannes Agricola's (Sneider) Hymn, "Ich ruf' zu dir, Herr Jesu Christ," published originally as a broadsheet, and thence in Joseph Klug's *Geistliche Lieder zu Wittemberg* (Wittenberg, 1535 [1529])[2], with the melody.

Agricola was born at Eisleben in 1492. He was educated at Wittenberg, where he was befriended by Luther. He became in 1525 Rector of St Andrew's School and preacher at Eisleben, and later (1540) Court preacher at Berlin. He helped to draw up the "Interim" in 1548 and died in Berlin in 1566. The Hymn is attributed erroneously to Paul Speratus.

[1] Every movement of the Cantata is a stanza of the Hymn.
[2] Wackernagel, III. 54, prints from a 1531 text.

The melody, which was published with the Hymn (*supra*), occurs also in Cantata 185. Organ Works, N. xv. 111.

(*a*)

The words of the opening movement are the first stanza of the Hymn:

> Ich ruf' zu dir, Herr Jesu Christ,
> Ich bitt': erhör' mein Klagen;
> Verleih' mir Gnad' zu dieser Frist,
> Lass mich doch nicht verzagen.
> Den rechten Glauben, Herr, ich mein',
> Den wollest du mir geben,
> Dir zu leben,
> Mein'm Nächsten nutz zu sein[1],
> Dein Wort zu halten eben.
>
> B.G. xxxv. 201.

English translations of the Hymn are noted in the *Dictionary of Hymnology*, pp. 31, 1550.

Form. Choral Fantasia (2 *Ob.*, *Violino concertante*, *Strings*, *Continuo*).

(*b*)

The words of the concluding Choral are the fifth stanza of the Hymn:

> Ich lieg' im Streit und widerstreb':
> Hilf, O Herr Christ, dem Schwachen!
> An deiner Gnad' allein ich kleb';
> Du kannst mich stärker machen.

[1] 1531 nutz sein.

Kömmt nun Anfechtung, Herr, so wehr',
Dass sie mich nicht umstosse.
Du kannst maassen,
Dass mir's nicht bring' Gefahr;
Ich weiss, du wirst's nicht lassen.

B.G. xxxv. 234.

Form. Simple (2 *Ob.*, *Fagotto*, *Strings*, Continuo). *Choralgesänge*, No. 183.

CANTATA CLXXVIII. WO GOTT DER HERR NICHT BEI UNS HÄLT. Eighth Sunday after Trinity (*c.* 1740)

A Choral Cantata, on Justus Jonas' version of Psalm cxxiv, "Wo Gott der Herr nicht bei uns hält," first published in *Eyn Enchiridion oder Handbuchlein* (Erfurt, 1524). It occurs also in *Eyn gesang Buchleyn* (Zwickau, 1525), but to another melody, and in Joseph Klug's *Geistliche Lieder* (Wittenberg, 1535 [1529]), to the tune which Bach uses here (see Cantata 73).

Jonas, the son of Jonas Koch, was born at Nordhausen in 1493. He was educated at Wittenberg and Erfurt and became (1519) Rector of the latter University. As Professor of Church Law at Wittenberg (1521) he was the friend and colleague of Luther and Melanchthon. After Luther's death he became pastor at Eisfeld on the Werra, and died there in 1555.

(*a*)

The words of the first movement are the first stanza of the Hymn:

> Wo Gott der Herr nicht bei uns hält,
> Wenn unsre Feinde toben,
> Und er unsrer Sach' nicht zufällt
> Im Himmel hoch dort oben;
> Wo er Israels Schutz nicht ist
> Und selber bricht der Feinde List:
> So ist's mit uns verloren.
>
> B.G. xxxv. 237.

A translation of the Hymn into English is noted in the *Dictionary of Hymnology*, p. 605.

Form. Choral Fantasia (2 *Ob.*, *Strings*, *Continuo*).

(*b*)

The words of the Choral in the second movement are the second stanza of the Hymn:

> Was Menschen Kraft und Witz ansäht,
> Soll uns billig nicht schrecken;
> Er sitzet an der höchsten Stätt',
> Er[1] wird ihr'n Rath aufdecken,
> Wenn sie's auf's Klügste greifen an,
> So geht doch Gott ein' andre Bahn:
> Es steht in seinen Händen.
>
> B.G. xxxv. 252.

Form. "Recitativ" and Choral for Alto (*Continuo*)[2].

---

[1] 1524 Der.   [2] See p. 44 *supra*.

(*c*)

The words of the fourth movement are the fourth stanza of the Hymn:

> Sie stellen uns wie Ketzern nach,
> Nach[1] unserm Blut sie trachten;
> Noch rühmen sie sich Christen auch[2],
> Die Gott allein gross achten.
> Ach Gott, der theure Name dein
> Muss ihrer Schalkheit Deckel sein!
> Du wirst einmal aufwachen.
> B.G. xxxv. 259.

Form. Tenor Unison Choral (2 *Ob. d'amore, Continuo*).

(*d*)

The words of the Choral in the fifth movement are the fifth stanza of the Hymn:

> Aufsperen sie den Rachen weit
> Und wollen uns verschlingen.
> Lob und Dank sei Gott allezeit:
> Es wird ihn'n nicht gelingen!
> Er wird ihr' Strick' zerreissen gar
> Und stürzen ihre falsche Lahr.
> Sie werden's Gott nicht wehren.
> B.G. xxxv. 262.

Form. "Choral und Recitativ" (S.A.T.B.) in Extended *Dialogus* form (*Continuo*).

[1] 1524 Zu.   [2] 1524 hoch.

(e)

The words of the concluding Choral are the seventh and eighth stanzas of the Hymn:

> Die Feind' sind all' in deiner Hand,
> Dazu all' ihr' Gedanken;
> Ihr' Anschläg' sind[1] dir, Herr[2], bekannt,
> Hilf nur, dass wir nicht wanken.
> Vernunft wider dem Glauben ficht,
> Auf's Künft'ge will sie trauen nicht,
> Da du wirst selber trösten.
>
> Den Himmel und auch die Erden
> Hast du, Herr Gott, gegründet;
> Dein Licht lass uns helle werden,
> Das Herz uns werd' entzündet,
> In rechter Lieb' des Glaubens dein
> Bis an das End' beständig sein;
> Die Welt lass immer murren.
>
> B.G. xxxv. 272.

Form. Simple (2 *Ob.*, *Strings*, *Continuo*). *Choralgesänge*, No. 384.

CANTATA CLXXIX. SIEHE ZU, DASS DEINE GOTTESFURCHT NICHT HEUCHELEI SEI. Eleventh Sunday after Trinity (? 1724)

For the melody of the concluding Choral, Georg Neumark's "Wer nur den lieben Gott lässt walten," see Cantata 21.

The words of the Choral are the first stanza of Christoph Tietze's (Titius) Hymn, "Ich armer

[1] 1524 anschlag ist.   [2] 1524 wol.

Mensch, ich armer Sünder," first published in his *Sünden-Schmertzen, Trost im Hertzen, Todten Kertzen* (Nürnberg, 1663). Tietze was born at Wilkau in 1641, became Deacon and Archdeacon at Hersbruck, near Nürnberg, and died there in 1703. Before the date of this Cantata Tietze's Hymn was usually sung to the tune "Wohl dem, der weit von hohen Dingen," to which it was published. It is set to Neumark's tune in the *Praxis* of 1709 and in the *Unverfälschter Lieder-Segen* of 1878:

> Ich armer Mensch, ich armer Sünder
> Steh' hier vor Gottes Angesicht.
> Ach Gott, ach Gott, verfahr' gelinder
> Und geh' nicht mit mir in's[1] Gericht.
> Erbarme dich, erbarme dich,
> Gott mein Erbarmer, über mich! B.G. xxxv. 292.

Form. Simple (2 *Ob.*, *Strings*, *Continuo*). *Choralgesänge*, No. 371.

CANTATA CLXXX. SCHMÜCKE DICH, O LIEBE SEELE[2]. Twentieth Sunday after Trinity (*c.* 1740)

Melody: "*Schmücke dich, O liebe Seele*"
                                    Johann Crüger 1649

[1] 1663 vor.
[2] An English version of the Cantata, "Soul, array thyself with gladness," is published by Breitkopf & Haertel.

A Choral Cantata, on Johann Franck's Eucharistic Hymn, "Schmücke dich, O liebe Seele," first published, with the melody, in Johann Crüger's *Geistliche Kirchen-Melodien* (Leipzig, 1649), and in the Berlin (1653) edition of Crüger's *Praxis Pietatis Melica*.

The melody does not occur elsewhere in the Cantatas, Oratorios, or Motetts. Organ Works, N. xvii. 22. Zahn does not reveal an earlier instance of Bach's variation of bars 4 and 5 *supra*.

(a)

The words of the opening movement are the first stanza of the Hymn:

> Schmücke dich, O liebe Seele,
> Lass die dunkle Sündenhöhle;
> Komm an's helle Licht gegangen,
> Fange herrlich an zu prangen.
> Denn der Herr voll Heil und Gnaden
> Lässt[1] dich itzt zu Gaste laden.
> Der den Himmel kann verwalten,
> Will selbst[2] Herberg' in dir halten.
> B.G. xxxv. 295.

[1] 1653 Wil.   [2] 1653 jtzt.

Translations of the Hymn into English are noted in the *Dictionary of Hymnology*, pp. 1014, 1699.

Form. Choral Fantasia (2 *Fl.*, 2 *Ob.*, *Oboe da caccia, Strings, Continuo*).

(*b*)

The words of the Choral in the third movement are the fourth stanza of the Hymn :

> Ach, wie hungert mein Gemüthe,
> Menschenfreund, nach deiner Güte !
> Ach, wie pfleg' ich oft mit Thränen
> Mich nach dieser Kost zu sehnen !
> Ach, wie pfleget mich zu dürsten
> Nach dem Trank des Lebensfürsten !
> Wünsche stets, dass mein Gebeine
> Sich[1] durch Gott mit Gott vereine.
>
> B.G. xxxv. 311.

Form. " Recitativ" for Soprano. After seven bars of introductory *Recitativo*, the rest of the movement is a rather free treatment of the melody as a Unison Choral (*Violoncello piccolo, Continuo*).

(*c*)

The words of the concluding Choral are the ninth stanza of the Hymn :

> Jesu, wahres Brod des Lebens,
> Hilf, dass ich doch nicht vergebens
> Oder mir vielleicht zum Schaden
> Sei zu deinem Tisch geladen.

[1] 1653 Mich.

Lass mich durch dies Seelen-Essen
Deine Liebe recht ermessen,
Dass ich auch, wie jetzt auf Erden,
Mög' ein Gast im Himmel werden.

B.G. xxxv. 322.

Form. Simple (*Continuo*). *Choralgesänge*, No. 304.

CANTATA CLXXXII. HIMMELSKÖNIG, SEI WILLKOMMEN. Palm Sunday (1714 or 1715)

For the melody of the penultimate movement, Melchior Vulpius' "Jesu Kreuz, Leiden und Pein," see Cantata 159.

The words of the movement are the thirty-third stanza of Paul Stockmann's Passiontide Hymn, "Jesu Leiden, Pein und Tod" (see Cantata 159):

> Jesu, deine Passion
> Ist mir lauter Freude,
> Deine Wunden, Kron' und Hohn
> Meines Herzens Weide;
> Meine Seel' auf Rosen geht,
> Wenn ich dran gedenke;
> In dem Himmel eine Stätt'
> Uns deswegen schenke.

B.G. xxxvii. 43.

Form. Choral Fantasia in fugal form (*Flauto, Strings, Continuo*).

CANTATA CLXXXIII. SIE WERDEN EUCH IN
DEN BANN THUN. Sixth Sunday after
Easter ("Exaudi")[1] (? 1735)

For the melody of the concluding Choral, the anonymous "Helft mir Gott's Güte preisen," see Cantata 11.

The words of the Choral are the fifth stanza of Paul Gerhardt's Whitsuntide Hymn, "Zeuch ein zu deinen Thoren," first published in the Berlin (1653) edition of Crüger's *Praxis Pietatis Melica*, to its own melody. It is also set in the Hymn books to the tune "Von Gott will ich nicht lassen":

> Du bist ein Geist, der lehret,
> Wie man recht beten soll;
> Dein Beten wird erhöret,
> Dein Singen klinget wohl;
> Es steigt zum Himmel an,
> Es steigt und lässt nicht abe,
> Bis der geholfen habe,
> Der allein[2] helfen kann.
> B.G. xxxvii. 74.

Translations of the Hymn are noted in the *Dictionary of Hymnology*, p. 1300.

Form. Simple (2 *Ob. d'amore*, 2 *Ob. da caccia*, Strings, Continuo). *Choralgesänge*, No. 126.

---

[1] The Sunday is the First after Ascension Day.
[2] 1653 allen.

CANTATA CLXXXIV. ERWÜNSCHTES FREU-
DENLICHT. Whit Tuesday (? 1724)

Melody: "*O Herre Gott, dein göttlich Wort*"
Anon. 1527

The words and melody of the fifth movement are from the Hymn, "O Herre Gott, dein göttlich Wort," attributed to Anark of Wildenfels, published, with the melody, in the 1527 edition of the Erfurt *Enchiridion*.

The author, who died in 1539, was one of the strongest supporters of the Reformation at the Saxon Court and signed the Augsburg Confession.

The melody does not occur elsewhere in the Cantatas, Oratorios, or Motetts. Bach's slight variations from the original, notably the B natural for A natural at the third note *supra*, the C natural for D natural at the fifth note after the first double bar, and the closing cadence, are found in sixteenth century texts.

The words are the eighth stanza of the Hymn:

> Herr, ich hoff' je,
> Du werdest die
> In keiner Noth verlassen,
> Die dein Wort recht
> Als treue Knecht'
> Im Herz'n und Glauben fassen;
> Giebst ihn'n bereit
> Die Seligkeit
> Und läss'st sie nicht verderben.
> O Herr, durch dich
> Bitt' ich, lass mich
> Fröhlich und selig[1] sterben.
>
> B.G. xxxvii. 95.

Translations of the Hymn into English are noted in the *Dictionary of Hymnology*, p. 836.

Form. Simple (2 *Fl.*, *Strings*, *Continuo*). *Choralgesänge*, No. 283[2].

CANTATA CLXXXV. BARMHERZIGES HERZE DER EWIGEN LIEBE. Fourth Sunday after Trinity (1715)

The words and melody of the concluding Choral are from Johannes Agricola's Hymn, "Ich ruf' zu dir, Herr Jesu Christ" (see Cantata 177).

---

[1] 1527 willig.
[2] Spitta, II. 399, supposes that the Choral, which precedes the final Chorus, was inserted when the Cantata was adapted, 1724 (?), to Church use. His inference appears to be incorrect. See Schweitzer, II. 162.

464 CANTATA CLXXXVI

The words are the first stanza of the Hymn :

>Ich ruf' zu dir, Herr Jesu Christ,
>Ich bitt' : erhör' mein Klagen,
>Verleih' mir Gnad' zu dieser Frist,
>Lass mich doch nicht verzagen ;
>Den rechten Weg, O Herr[1], ich mein',
>Den wollest du mir geben,
>Dir zu leben,
>Mein'm Nächsten nütz zu sein[2],
>Dein Wort zu halten eben.
>
>B.G. xxxvii. 118.

Form. Embellished (*Tromba, Oboe, Fagotto, Strings, Continuo*). *Choralgesänge*, No. 184. In the opening movement of the Cantata (B.G. xxvii. 103), the Soprano-Tenor *Duetto* "Barmherziges Herze," the melody of the Choral is introduced upon the Tromba or Oboe. The insertion of the melody transforms the Cantata, whose burden otherwise is a lament over human frailty.

CANTATA CLXXXVI. ÄRGRE DICH, O SEELE, NICHT. Seventh Sunday after Trinity (1723)[3]

The words and melody of the last movement of Part I of the Cantata are Paul Speratus' Hymn, "Es ist das Heil uns kommen her" (see Cantata 9).

---

[1] 1531 glauben, Herr.   [2] 1531 nutz sein.
[3] See Wustmann, p. 287.

The words are the twelfth stanza of the Hymn:

Ob sich's anliess', als wollt' er nicht,
Lass dich es nicht erschrecken;
Denn wo er ist am besten mit,
Da will er's nicht entdecken.
Sein Wort lass dir[1] gewisser sein,
Und ob dein Herz[2] spräch' lauter Nein,
So lass dir doch[3] nicht grauen.

B.G. xxxvii. 136.

Form. Extended (2 *Ob.*, *Strings, Continuo*)[4].

CANTATA CLXXXVII. ES WARTET ALLES AUF DICH. Seventh Sunday after Trinity (1732)

Melody: "*Da Christus geboren war*" Anon. 1544

[1] 1524 das las dir. [2] 1524 fleisch. [3] 1524 doch dir.
[4] On the analogy of Cantatas 75 and 76 Spitta (II. 360) holds that the Choral was repeated at the close of Part II of the Cantata. Schweitzer (II. 152) calls the movement "almost" a Choral Fantasia.

Melody: "*Singen wir aus Herzensgrund*" Anon. 1589

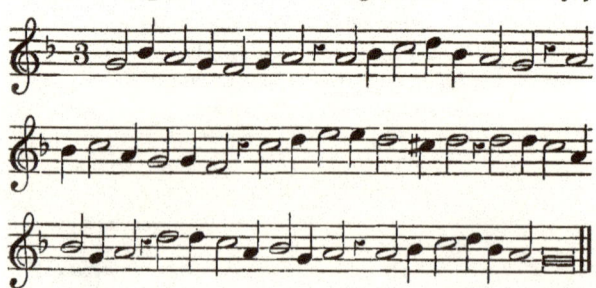

The melody of the concluding Choral is found first in the *Gesangbuch der Brüder inn Behemen und Merherrn* (Nürnberg, 1544), where it is set to Johann Roh's (Horn, Cornu) version of the Latin Christmas Hymn, "In natali Domini." It may be inferred that the melody is adapted from the tune of that Hymn, which probably is of the fourteenth or fifteenth century.

The melody does not occur elsewhere in the Cantatas, Oratorios, or Motetts.

The tune practically had assumed the form in which Bach uses it before the end of the sixteenth century.

The words of the concluding Choral are the fourth and sixth stanzas of the anonymous Hymn, or Grace after Meat, "Singen wir aus Herzensgrund." It appeared first as a broadsheet *c.* 1560 and later in *Hundert Christenliche Haussgesang* (Nürnberg, 1569) and in Johann Eichorn's *Geistliche Lieder*

(Frankfort a. Oder, 1569). In the 1589 edition of the latter Hymn book the Hymn is associated with the tune "Da Christus geboren war":

> Gott hat die Erd' schön zugericht't[1],
> Lässt's an Nahrung mangeln nicht;
> Berg und Thal, die macht er nass,
> Dass dem Vieh auch wächst sein Gras;
> Aus der Erden Wein und Brod
> Schaffet Gott, und giebt's uns satt,
> Dass der Mensch sein Leben hat.
>
> Wir danken sehr und bitten ihn[2],
> Dass er uns geb'[3] des Geistes Sinn,
> Dass wir solches recht versteh'n,
> Stets nach sein'n Geboten geh'n,
> Seinen Namen machen gross
> In Christo ohn' Unterlass:
> So sing'n wir das Gratias.   B.G. xxxvii. 191.

A translation of the Hymn is noted in the *Dictionary of Hymnology*, p. 1060.

Form. Simple (2 *Ob.*, *Strings*, *Continuo*). *Choralgesänge*, No. 308.

CANTATA CLXXXVIII. ICH HABE MEINE ZUVERSICHT[4]. Twenty-first Sunday after Trinity (1730 or 1731)

The melody of the concluding Choral is the anonymous "Auf meinen lieben Gott," or "Wo soll ich fliehen hin" (see Cantata 5).

[1] 1569 Erden zugericht.
[2] 1569 Dancken wir sehr, bitten in.   [3] 1569 Das er geb.
[4] Wustmann, p. 298, contests the authenticity of this Cantata and attributes the greater part of it to Bach's eldest son.

The words of the Choral are the first stanza of the Hymn, "Auf meinen lieben Gott," attributed to Sigismund Weingärtner, first published in *Geistliche Psalmen, Hymnen, Lieder und Gebet* (Nürnberg, 1607). Of Weingärtner nothing certain is known beyond the fact that his name appears as "Sigismund Weingart" in the Index of Authors prefixed to the *Geistliche Psalmen* (*supra*). He seems to have been a preacher in or near Heilbronn *c.* 1600. It is doubtful whether he was the author of the Hymn, whose ascription to him arose from the fact that it stands in the Index immediately under another Hymn to which his initials are attached[1]:

> Auf meinen lieben Gott
> Trau' ich in Angst und Noth.
> Er[2] kann mich allzeit retten
> Aus Trübsal, Angst und Nöthen;
> Mein Unglück kann er wenden:
> Steht all's in seinen Händen.
> B.G. xxxvii. 212.

Translations of the Hymn into English are noted in the *Dictionary of Hymnology*, p. 1247.

Form. Simple (*Continuo*). *Choralgesänge*, No. 25[3].

---

[1] Wackernagel, v. 433, prints two versions of the Hymn, dated 1609 and 1611, under the name of Theodor von Sömeren.
[2] 1609 Der.
[3] In this Cantata, as in No. 146, Bach makes use of Concerto for Clavier or two Violins (D minor). See also Nos. 49, 110, 169, 174.

CANTATA CXC. SINGET DEM HERRN EIN NEUES LIED[1]. Feast of the Circumcision (New Year's Day) (*c.* 1725[2])

(*a*)

The words and melody of the Choral in the second movement are those of Luther's version of the "Te Deum" (see Cantata 16). The words are the first two clauses of the "Te Deum":

> Herr Gott dich loben wir!
> Herr Gott wir danken dir!
> B.G. xxxvii. 244.

Form. Extended; the lines being interrupted by *Recitativo* passages for Bass and Tenor (3 *Trombe, Timp.*, 3 *Ob., Strings, Continuo*).

In two places in the opening Chorus, "Singet dem Herrn," the four voices in unison declaim the first two lines of the Choral (B.G. xxxvii. 236, 240).

(*b*)

The words and melody of the concluding Choral are Johann Hermann's New Year Hymn, "Jesu, nun sei gepreiset" (see Cantata 41).

[1] An English version of the Cantata, "Sing to the Lord a glad new song," is published by Breitkopf & Haertel.
[2] In a revised form Bach used the Cantata for the commemoration of the Augsburg Confession at Leipzig on June 25, 1730 (Spitta, II. 387).

CANTATA CXCII

The words are the second stanza of the Hymn:

Lass' uns das Jahr vollbringen,
Zu Lob dem Namen dein,
Dass wir demselben singen
In der Christengemein ;
Wollst uns das Leben fristen
Durch dein' allmächtig' Hand ;
Erhalt' dein' liebe Christen
Und unser Vaterland.
Dein'n Segen zu uns wende,
Gieb Fried' an allem Ende ;
Gieb unverfälscht im Lande
Dein seligmachend Wort.
Die Heuchler[1] mach' zu Schande
Hier und an allem Ort.
B.G. xxxvii. 257.

Form. Embellished (3 *Trombe, Timp.*, 3 *Ob.*, *Strings, Continuo*). *Choralgesänge*, No. 205.

CANTATA CXCII. NUN DANKET ALLE GOTT
(*c.* 1732[2])

A Choral Cantata, on Martin Rinkart's Hymn, "Nun danket alle Gott" (see Cantata 79). The melody of the opening and concluding movements is Johann Crüger's setting of the Hymn (see Cantata 79).

[1] 1593 Teuffel.
[2] The occasion for which the Cantata was composed is not stated. It is incomplete; the vocal Tenor part is wanting throughout. Every movement is a stanza of the Hymn.

CANTATA CXCII

(a)

The words of the opening movement are the first stanza of Rinkart's Hymn:

> Nun danket alle Gott
> Mit Herzen, Mund und Händen,
> Der grosse Dinge thut
> An uns und allen Enden;
> Der uns von Mutterleib
> Und Kindesbeinen an
> Unzählig viel zu gut
> Und noch jetzund gethan.
> B.G. xli. 67.

Form. Choral Fantasia (2 *Fl.*, 2 *Ob.*, Strings, Continuo).

(b)

The words of the concluding Choral are the third stanza of Rinkart's Hymn:

> Lob, Ehr' und Preis sei Gott,
> Dem Vater und dem Sohne
> Und Dem, der Beiden gleich,
> In hohen[1] Himmelsthrone:
> Dem dreieinigen[2] Gott,
> Als der[3] ursprünglich war,
> Und ist und bleiben wird
> Jetzund und immerdar.   B.G. xli. 88.

Form. Choral Fantasia (2 *Fl.*, 2 *Ob.*, Strings, Continuo).

[1] 1648 höchsten. [2] 1648 dreymahl Einem. [3] 1648 er.

CANTATA CXCIV. HÖCHSTERWÜNSCHTES FREU-
DENFEST[1]. For the Opening of the Organ at
Störmthal (1723)

(a)

For the melody of the concluding movement of
Part I, Louis Bourgeois' "Ainsi qu'on oit le cerf,"
see Cantata 13.

The words of the movement are the sixth and
seventh stanzas of Johann Heermann's Hymn,
"Treuer Gott, ich muss dir klagen" (see Cantata 25):

Heil'ger Geist in's Himmels Throne,
Gleicher Gott von Ewigkeit
Mit dem Vater und dem Sohne,
Der Betrübten Trost und Freud'!
* Allen Glauben den ich find'[2]:
* Hast[3] du in mir angezünd't,
Über mir in[4] Gnaden walte,
Ferner deine Grad'[5] erhalte.

Deine Hülfe zu mir sende,
O du edler Herzensgast!
Und das gute Werk vollende,
* Das[6] du angefangen hast.
* Blas' in mir das Fünklein[7] auf,
Bis dass nach vollbrachten Lauf
Ich den[8] Auserwählten gleiche
Und[9] des Glaubens Ziel erreiche. B.G. xxix. 124.

[1] Bach later adapted the Cantata to Trinity Sunday, 1731.
[2] 1630 So viel ich an Glauben find.   [3] 1630 Der.
[4] 1630 mit.   [5] 1630 Gab.   [6] 1630 Was.
[7] 1630 Blass das kleine Füncklein.   [8] 1630 Allen.
[9] 1630 Ich.

* These lines are found in the 1644 edition of Heermann's
Devoti Musica Cordis.

Form. Simple (3 *Ob.*, *Strings*, *Continuo*). *Choralgesänge*, No. 100.

(*b*)

For the melody of the concluding Choral of the Cantata, the anonymous "Nun lasst uns Gott dem Herren," see Cantata 79. The words of the Choral are the ninth and tenth stanzas of Paul Gerhardt's Morning Hymn, "Wach auf, mein Herz, und singe," first published in the 1647 (Berlin) edition of Crüger's *Praxis Pietatis Melica*, to the above melody:

> Sprich Ja zu meinen Thaten;
> Hilf selbst das Beste rathen;
> Den Anfang, Mitt'l und Ende,
> Ach Herr, zum Besten wende.
>
> Mit[1] Segen mich beschütte[2]:
> Mein Herz sei deine Hütte;
> Dein Wort sei meine Speise,
> Bis ich gen Himmel reise.
>
> B.G. xxix. 138.

Translations of the Hymn are noted in the *Dictionary of Hymnology*, p. 1229.

Form. Embellished (3 *Ob.*, *Strings*, *Continuo*). *Choralgesänge*, No. 268.

---

[1] 1647 Mich. [2] 1647 behüte.

CANTATA CXCV. DEM GERECHTEN MUSS DAS LICHT[1]. For a Wedding (? c. 1726[2])

The melody of the concluding Choral is Nicolaus Herman's "Lobt Gott, ihr Christen alle gleich" (see Cantata 151).

The words of the Choral are the first stanza of Paul Gerhardt's Hymn of Thanksgiving, "Nun danket all' und bringet Ehr'," first published, to Herman's tune (*supra*), in the 1647 (Berlin) edition of Crüger's *Praxis Pietatis Melica*:

> Nun danket all' und bringet Ehr',
> Ihr Menschen in der Welt,
> Dem, dessen Lob der Engel Heer
> Im Himmel stets vermeldt[3].   B.G. xiii. (i) 70.

Form. Embellished (2 *Corni, Timp.*, 2 *Fl.*, 2 *Ob.*, Strings, Continuo). *Choralgesänge*, No. 236.

CANTATA CXCVII. GOTT IST UNS'RE ZUVERSICHT. For a Wedding[4] (c. 1740)

(a)

The words and melody of the concluding movement of Part I (Vor der Trauung) of the Cantata are Luther's "Nun bitten wir den heiligen Geist" (see Cantata 169).

[1] An English version of the Cantata, "For the righteous the light hath awakened," is published by Breitkopf & Haertel.
[2] See Spitta, II. 468.
[3] Only the first line is printed in the Score.
[4] Bach incorporated into this work the Christmas Cantata, "Ehre sei Gott" (No. U 1).

CANTATA CXCVII

The words are the third stanza of the Hymn:

> Du süsse Lieb', schenk' uns deine Gunst,
> Lass uns empfinden der Liebe Brunst,
> Dass wir uns von Herzen einander lieben
> Und in Fried' auf einem Sinne bleiben.
> Kyrie eleis!
> B.G. xiii. (i) 128.

Form. Simple[1]. *Choralgesänge*, No. 255.

(b)

The words and melody of the concluding Choral of the Cantata are Georg Neumark's Hymn, "Wer nur den lieben Gott lässt walten" (see Cantata 21).

The words are the seventh stanza of the Hymn; the first four lines, however, have been rewritten:

> So wandelt froh auf Gottes Wegen,
> Und was ihr thut, das Gott getreu!
> Verdienet eures Gottes Segen,
> Denn der ist alle Morgen neu[2]:
> Denn welcher seine Zuversicht
> Auf Gott setzt, den verlässt er nicht.
> B.G. xiii. (i) 144.

Form. Simple (*Continuo*). *Choralgesänge*, No. 370.

---

[1] The orchestration is not stated in the Score.
[2] 1657 Sing, bet und geh auf Gottes Wegen,
   Verricht das Deine nur getreu
   Und trau des Himmels reichem Segen,
   So wird Er bey dir werden neu.

CANTATA CXCIX. MEIN HERZE SCHWIMMT IM BLUT. Eleventh Sunday after Trinity (*c.* 1714[1])

The melody of the sixth movement is Caspar Stieler's (?) "Wo soll ich fliehen hin" (see Cantata 163). The words of the Choral are the third stanza of Johann Heermann's Hymn, "Wo soll ich fliehen hin" (see Cantata 5):

> Ich Dein betrübtes Kind
> Werf alle meine Sünd,
> So viel ihr in mir stekken
> Und mich so heftig schrecken,
> In Deine tiefen Wunden,
> Da ich stets Heil gefunden.
>
> N.B.G. xiii. (ii) 17.

Form. Soprano Unison Choral (*Viola obbligato, Continuo* [*con Violone*]).

[1] The occasion for which the Cantata was composed is not stated in the Score. Wustmann, p. 156, assigns it to this Sunday because Neumeister wrote a text for the Eleventh Sunday after Trinity bearing the same title.

THE UNFINISHED CANTATAS[1]

I. EHRE SEI GOTT IN DER HÖHE[2]. Christmas Day (? 1728)

The melody of the concluding Choral is the 1679 tune, "O Gott, du frommer Gott," or "Die Wollust dieser Welt" (see Cantata 45). The words of the Choral are the fourth stanza of Caspar Ziegler's Christmas Hymn, "Ich freue mich in dir" (see Cantata 133):

> Wohlan! so will ich mich
> An dich, O Jesu, halten,
> Und sollte gleich die Welt
> In tausend Stücken spalten.
> O Jesu, dir, nur dir,
> Dir leb' ich ganz allein,
> Auf dich, allein auf dich,
> Mein Jesu, schlaf' ich ein. B.G. xli. 114.

Form. Simple[3]. *Choralgesänge,* No. 277.

[1] In B.G. xli there are two sets of unfinished Cantatas: (1) "Nun danket alle Gott" (No. 192), "Ihr Pforten zu Zion" (No. 193), "Ehre sei Gott in der Höhe" (here distinguished as U 1); (2) "O ewiges Feuer, O Ursprung der Liebe" (here distinguished as U 2), "Herr Gott, Beherrscher aller Dinge" (here distinguished as U 3).

[2] The Cantata consists of two *Arias* (one incomplete), a *Recitativo*, and the final Choral. The work is incorporated into the Wedding Cantata, No. 197.

[3] The orchestration is not stated in the Score.

III. HERR GOTT, BEHERRSCHER ALLER DINGE.

For a Wedding[1] (before 1733)

The words and melody of the concluding Choral are Joachim Neander's Hymn of Thanksgiving, "Lobe den Herren, den mächtigen König der Ehren" (see Cantatas 57, 137).

The words are the fourth and fifth stanzas of the Hymn:

> * Lobe den Herren, der deinen Stand sichtbar gesegnet,
> Der aus dem Himmel mit Strömen der Liebe geregnet!
> Denke daran,
> Was der Allmächtige kann,
> Der dir mit Liebe begegnet.
>
> * Lobe den Herren, was in mir ist, lobe den Namen!
> Alles, was Odem hat, lobe mit Abrahams Samen.
> Er ist dein Licht,
> Seele, vergiss es ja nicht;
> Lobende, schliesse mit Amen!
>
> B.G. xli. 174.

Form. Embellished (3 *Trombe, Timpani*, 2 *Ob.*, Strings, Continuo). *Choralgesänge*, No. 230.

---

[1] All instrumental parts except the Viola and Continuo parts are lacking. (See No. 137.) The Cantata is founded, in part, on No. 120 (Spitta, II. 469).

THE CANTATAS OF DOUBTFUL AUTHENTICITY[1]

II. GOTT DER HOFFNUNG ERFÜLLE EUCH[2].
Whit Sunday

Melody: "*Komm, Gott Schöpfer, heiliger Geist*"
Anon. 1524

Melody: "*Komm, Gott Schöpfer, heiliger Geist*"
Anon. 1535

[1] B.G. xli contains four Cantatas of doubtful authenticity. The first of them, "Gedenke, Herr, wie es uns gehet," Spitta, II. 695, does not regard as being by Bach. It appears to have been written for a Public Fast and contains no Chorals.

[2] Spitta, II. 683, holds that the Cantata is not by Bach.

480 CANTATAS OF DOUBTFUL AUTHENTICITY

The words and melody of the concluding Choral are from Luther's Hymn, "Komm, Gott Schöpfer," a translation of the "Veni Creator Spiritus," first published, with the melody, in the Erfurt *Enchiridion Oder eyn Handbuchlein* (Erfurt, 1524) and in Klug's *Geistliche Lieder* (Wittenberg, 1535 [1529]). The melody is that of the Latin Hymn. The melody does not occur elsewhere in the Cantatas, Oratorios, or Motetts. There is another harmonisation of it in the *Choralgesänge*, No. 218. Organ Works, N. xv. 97; xvii. 82.

The words of the Choral are the first stanza of Luther's Hymn:

> Komm, Gott Schöpfer, heiliger Geist,
> Besuch' das Herz der Menschen dein,
> Mit Gnaden sie füll', wie du weisst,
> Das dein' Geschöpf' vorhin sein.
>
> B.G. xli. 238.

Translations of the Hymn into English are noted in the *Dictionary of Hymnology*, p. 1209.

Form. Embellished (2 *Corni, Strings, Continuo*). *Choralgesänge*, No. 219.

III. SIEHE, ES HAT ÜBERWUNDEN DER LÖWE.

Feast of St Michael the Archangel

For the melody of the concluding Choral, the anonymous "Wo Gott der Herr nicht bei uns hält," see Cantata 73.

CANTATAS OF DOUBTFUL AUTHENTICITY

The words of the Choral are the ninth and tenth stanzas of Justus Gesenius' (?) Hymn "für den Schutz der Heil. Engel," "O Gott, der du aus Herzensgrund," first published, to the melody "Wo Gott der Herr" (*supra*), in the *New Ordentlich Gesang-Buch* (Hanover, 1646). Gesenius was born at Esbeck, in Hanover, in 1601. In 1636 he became Court preacher and chaplain at the Cathedral in Hildesheim and in 1642 was appointed chief Court preacher and General Superintendent of Hanover. With David Denicke he edited the Hanoverian Hymn books of 1646–59. He died in 1673:

> Lass' deine Kirch' und unser Land
> Der Engel Schutz empfinden,
> Dass Fried' und Freud'[1] in allem Stand
> Ein Jeder[2] möge finden;
> Lass sie des Teufels Mord und List,
> Und was sein Reich und Anhang ist,
> Durch deine Kraft zerstören.
>
> Zuletzt lass sie an unserm End'
> Den Satan[3] von uns jagen,
> Und unsre Seel' in deine Händ'
> Und Abrahams Schooss tragen,
> Da alles Heer dein Lob erklingt
> Und Heilig! Heilig! Heilig! singt
> Ohn' einiges Aufhören.   B.G. xli. 258.

Form. Embellished (2 *Trombe*). *Choralgesänge*, No. 387.

[1] 1646 Heyl.   [2] 1646 Sich bey uns.   [3] 1646 Bösswicht.

IV. Lobt ihn mit Herz und Munde[1]

The words and melody of the opening Choral are Ludwig Helmbold's Hymn, "Von Gott will ich nicht lassen" (see Cantatas 11 and 73).

The words are the fifth stanza of the Hymn:

> Lobt ihn mit Herz und Munde,
> Welch's er uns beides schenkt.
> Das ist ein' sel'ge Stunde,
> Darin man sein gedenkt;
> Sonst verdirbt alle Zeit,
> Die wir zubring'n auf Erden:
> Wir sollen[2] selig werden
> Und bleib'n in Ewigkeit.
>
> B.G. xli. 259.

Form.   Simple[3].   *Choralgesänge*, No. 327.

---

[1] The occasion for which the Cantata was composed is not stated in the Score.

[2] 1569 Sollen wir.

[3] The orchestration is not stated in the Score.

THE MOTETTS

I. SINGET DEM HERRN EIN NEUES LIED[1]

The middle section of the Double Chorus (*Andante sostenuto*) introduces (Coro II (only the third stanza of Johann Graumann's Hymn, "Nun lob', mein' Seel', den Herren," with Johann Kugelmann's (?) melody (see Cantata 17):

> Wie sich ein Vat'r[2] erbarmet
> Üb'r seine junge Kinderlein[3],
> So thut der Herr uns allen[4],
> So wir ihn kindlich fürchten rein.
> Er kennt das arm' Gemächte,
> Gott weiss, wir sind nur Staub,
> Gleich wie das Gras, vom Rechen,
> Ein' Blum' und fallend Laub!
> Der Wind nur drüber wehet,
> So ist es nicht mehr da[5],
> Also der Mensch vergehet,
> Sein End' das ist ihm nah'.
>
> B.G. xxxix. 18.

[1] English versions of the Motett, "Sing ye to the Lord," are published by Novello & Co. and Breitkopf & Haertel. Spitta (II. 603) suggests that the Motett was composed for New Year's Day
[2] 1540 man.
[3] 1540 kindlein klein.
[4] 1540 armen.
[5] 1540 nymmer da.

Form. Extended. The lines of the Hymn, sung by Coro II, are interrupted by fragments of the first movement (*Allegro moderato*) introduced by Coro I as interludes.

II. DER GEIST HILFT UNSRER SCHWACHHEIT AUF[1] (1729)

The words and melody of the concluding Choral are Luther's Whitsuntide Hymn, " Komm, heiliger Geist, Herre Gott " (see Cantata 59). The words are the third stanza of the Hymn :

> Du heilige Brunst, süsser Trost,
> Nun hilf uns fröhlich und getrost
> In deinem Dienst beständig bleiben,
> Die Trübsal uns nicht abtreiben.
> O Herr, durch dein' Kraft uns bereit'
> Und stärk' des Fleisches Blödigkeit,
> Dass wir hier ritterlich ringen,
> Durch Tod und Leben zu dir dringen.
> Halleluja! Halleluja!   B.G. xxxix. 57.

Form. Simple. *Choralgesänge*, No. 221[2].

III. JESU, MEINE FREUDE[3] (1723)

The melody of the four Choral movements of the Motett is Johann Crüger's setting of Johann Franck's Hymn, " Jesu, meine Freude " (see Cantata 64).

[1] English versions of the Motett, "The Spirit also helpeth us," are published by Novello & Co. and Breitkopf & Haertel.

[2] The Organ and Instrumental accompaniments (2 Ob., "Bassono," Strings, Continuo) of the Motett are in B.G. xxxix. 143.

[3] An English version of the Motett, "Jesu, priceless treasure," is published by Novello & Co.

THE MOTETTS

(a)

The words of the opening Choral are the first stanza of the Hymn:

> Jesu, meine Freude,
> Meines Herzens Weide,
> Jesu, meine Zier:
> Ach, wie lang', ach lange:
> Ist dem Herzen bange
> Und verlangt nach dir!
> Gottes Lamm,
> Mein Bräutigam,
> Ausser dir soll mir auf Erden
> Nichts sonst Liebers werden.
> B.G. xxxix. 61.

Form. Simple. *Choralgesänge,* No. 196.

(b)

The words of the third movement are the second stanza of the Hymn:

> Unter deinen Schirmen
> Bin ich vor den Stürmen
> Aller Feinde frei.
> Lass den Satan wittern,
> Lass den Feind erbittern,
> Mir steht Jesus bei!
> Ob es itzt
> Gleich kracht und blitzt,
> Ob gleich Sünd' und Hölle schrecken:
> Jesus will mich decken.
> B.G. xxxix. 66.

Form. Simple (S.S.A.T.B.). *Choralgesänge,* No. 198.

(c)

The words of the seventh movement are the fourth stanza of the Hymn:

> Weg mit allen Schätzen:
> Du bist mein Ergötzen,
> Jesu, meine Lust!
> Weg, ihr eitlen Ehren,
> Ich mag euch nicht hören;
> Bleibt mir unbewusst!
> Elend, Noth,
> Kreuz, Schmach und Tod
> Soll mich, ob ich viel muss leiden,
> Nicht von Jesu scheiden.
> B.G. xxxix. 75.

Form. Simple. The lower parts, however, exhibit a freedom which is not found in the pure Simple form. *Choralgesänge*, No. 199.

(d)

The words of the concluding Choral are the sixth stanza of the Hymn:

> Weicht, ihr Trauergeister,
> Denn mein Freudenmeister,
> Jesus, tritt herein.
> Denen, die Gott lieben,
> Muss auch ihr Betrüben
> Lauter Zucker sein.
> Duld' ich schon
> Hier Spott und Hohn:
> Dennoch bleibst du auch im Leide,
> Jesu, meine Freude.   B.G. xxxix. 84.

Form. Simple. *Choralgesänge*, No. 196.

IV. FÜRCHTE DICH NICHT, ICH BIN BEI DIR[1]

Melody: "*Warum sollt' ich mich denn grämen*"
Johann Georg Ebeling 1666

[musical notation]

Reconstruction 1713

[musical notation]

The melody of the Choral, upon which the Sopranos of Coro I and II combine in the last section of the Motett, is Johann Georg Ebeling's setting of Paul Gerhardt's Hymn, "Warum sollt' ich mich denn grämen," first published, with the Hymn, in Gerhardt's *Geistliche Andachten Bestehend in hundert und zwanzig Liedern* (Berlin, 1666).

The melody also occurs in the "Christmas Oratorio," No. 33, and there is a harmonisation of

[1] English versions of the Motett, "Be not afraid," are published by Novello & Co. and Breitkopf & Haertel.

it in the *Choralgesänge*, No. 334. In the Oratorio Bach uses only the first half of the tune, and except for the latter half of the second and first part of the third lines of the Hymn, follows Daniel Vetter's reconstruction of the melody in his *Musicalische Kirch- und Hauss-Ergötzlichkeit* (Leipzig, Part II, 1713). There is earlier authority for Bach's innovations, excepting his lines 3 and 6. In the Motett he follows Vetter, excepting the last three bars (*supra*), where his version seems to be his own. The *Choralgesänge* form is identical with the Oratorio movement, but with Vetter's version of the fourth line of the Hymn.

The words of the Choral are the eleventh and twelfth stanzas of Gerhardt's Hymn, first published, to another melody, in the 1653 (Berlin) edition of Crüger's *Praxis Pietatis Melica*:

> Herr, mein Hirt, Brunn aller Freuden!
> Du bist mein, ich bin dein;
> Niemand kann uns scheiden.
> Ich bin dein; weil du dein Leben
> Und dein Blut mir zu gut
> In den Tod gegeben.
> Du bist mein, weil ich dich fasse
> Und dich nicht, O mein Licht,
> Aus dem Herzen lasse!
> Lass mich, lass mich hin gelangen,
> Wo[1] du mich, und ich dich
> Ewig[2] werd' umfangen.   B.G. xxxix. 98.

[1] 1653 Da. [2] 1653 Lieblich.

Form. Choral Fantasia in Motett form, the three lower parts working out a subject *fugato.*

V. KOMM, JESU, KOMM[1]

Melody: "*Komm, Jesu, komm*"   J. S. Bach

The melody of the concluding Choral, in form an *Aria* rather than a Hymn tune (cf. the "Christmas Oratorio," No. 42), is by Bach himself

[1] An English version of the Motett, "Come, Jesu, come," is published by Novello & Co.

and is built upon the subject of the preceding Double Chorus.

The melody does not occur elsewhere.

The words of the Choral are the eleventh stanza of the anonymous Hymn, "Komm, Jesu, komm," published in Paul Wagner's *Andächtiger Seelen geistliches Brand- und Gantz-Opfer. Das ist: vollständiges Gesangbuch* (Leipzig, 1697). In the Jakob-Richter *Allgemeines vierstimmiges Kirchen- und Haus-Choralbuch* (Berlin [1873]) the Hymn is printed to a melody that is said to come from the MS. Hymn book of the Church at Nieder Wiese, 1773. Johann Christoph Schwedler (1672–1730) was assistant there in 1698, after taking his degree at Leipzig in the previous year. Can he be the author of the Hymn, and have communicated it to Wagner at Leipzig? It is not found in any earlier Hymn book:

> * Drauf schliess' ich mich in deine Hände
> Und sage, Welt, zu guter Nacht!
> Eilt gleich mein Lebenslauf zu Ende,
> Ist doch der Geist wohl angebracht.
> Er soll bei seinem Schöpfer schweben,
> Weil Jesus ist und bleibt der wahre Weg zum Leben.
> B.G. xxxix. 125.

Form. Simple[1]. *Choralgesänge*, No. 222.

[1] In the Score the movement is marked "Aria."

APPENDIX I

HYMN MELODIES THAT OCCUR IN THE "PASSIONS" AND ORATORIOS BUT ARE NOT FOUND IN THE CANTATAS AND MOTETTS

(1)

Melody: "*Christus, der uns selig macht*"

"Patris Sapientia" 1531

Melody: "*Christus, der uns selig macht*"

Reconstruction 1598

The melody, "Christus, der uns selig macht," was first published in *Ein New Gesengbuchlen* (Jung Bunzlau, 1531), set to Michael Weisse's free translation of the Hymn, "Patris sapientia, veritas divina." The tune probably is an adaptation of that of the Latin original.

The melody occurs in the "St John Passion," Nos. 12 and 35 (*Choralgesänge*, Nos. 49, 50). There is another harmonisation of it in the *Choralgesänge*, No. 48. The last conforms to the 1531 text of the tune. The two settings in the "St John Passion" follow Seth Calvisius' reconstruction of the melody, published in his *Harmonia Cantionum ecclesiasticarum* (Leipzig, 1598). Organ Works, N. xv. 64 (1531 version).

(2)

Melody: "*Es sind doch selig alle*"   Matthäus Greitter 1525

The melody "Es sind doch selig alle," or "O Mensch, bewein' dein' Sünde gross," most probably

APPENDIX I 493

was composed by Matthäus Greitter, and was published in Part III of the Strassburg *Kirchēampt mit lobgsengen* (Strassburg, 1525). It is set to Greitter's Psalm cxix in the Strassburg *Psalmen* of 1526. Its association with Sebald Heyden's Hymn, "O Mensch, bewein'," dates from *c.* 1584.

The melody occurs in the "St Matthew Passion," No. 35. There is another harmonisation of it in the *Choralgesänge*, No. 286. Organ Works, N. xv. 69.

(3)

Melody: "*Gott des Himmels und der Erden*"
Heinrich Albert 1642

Melody: "*Gott des Himmels und der Erden*"
Reconstruction 1687[1]

[1] Darmstadt *Cantional*.

The melody, "Gott des Himmels und der Erden," was composed by Heinrich Albert and was first published, with the Hymn (of which he was the author), in Part V of his *Arien oder Melodeyen* (Königsberg, 1642).

The melody occurs in the "Christmas Oratorio," No. 53 (*Choralgesänge*, No. 114). In the third bar (*supra*) Bach follows Daniel Vetter's Hymn book (1713). His own closing cadence was prescribed by the fact that his Hymn text contained one syllable more than Albert's original.

(4)

Melody: "Herzliebster Jesu"   Johann Crüger 1640

The melody, "Herzliebster Jesu, was hast du verbrochen," was composed by Johann Crüger for that Hymn (by Johann Heermann), and was first published in his *Newes vollkömliches Gesangbuch* (Berlin, 1640).

The melody occurs in the "St Matthew Passion," Nos. 3, 25, 55; and the "St John Passion," Nos. 4,

APPENDIX I   495

15 (*Choralgesänge*, Nos. 166-169). The F sharp which Bach introduces at the fifth note of the tune dates from 1694.

(5)

Melody: "*O Lamm Gottes unschuldig*"
Nicolaus Decius 1542

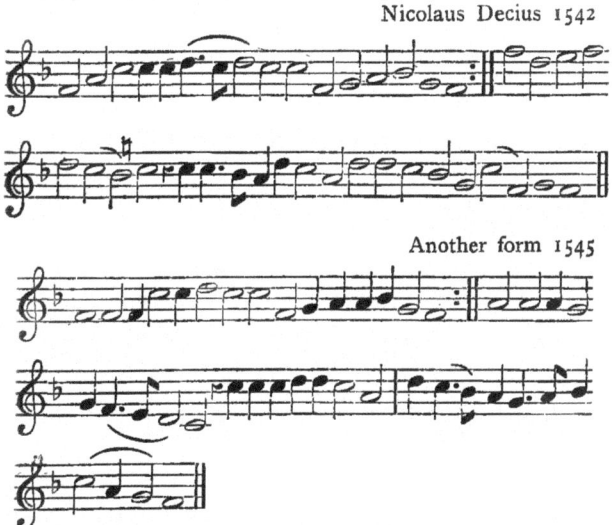

Another form 1545

The melody, "O Lamm Gottes unschuldig," was composed or adapted by Nicolaus Decius for his translation of the "Agnus Dei," and was first published in the *Christliche Kirchen-Ordnung* (Erfurt, 1542).

The melody occurs in the "St Matthew Passion," No. 1. There is a harmonisation of it in the

Choralgesänge, No. 285. Organ Works, N. xv. 58; xvii. 32. Bach generally follows a reconstruction of the melody in Johann Spangenberg's *Kirchengesenge Deudtsch* (Magdeburg, 1545). In the Choral Prelude, N. xvii. 32, he prefers a later (1598) text.

(6)

Melody: "*Vom Himmel hoch*"　　　? Martin Luther 1539

The melody, "Vom Himmel hoch da komm ich her," is with probability attributed to Luther. It was first published, with the Hymn, in Valentin Schumann's *Geistliche lieder auffs new gebessert* (Leipzig, 1539).

The melody occurs in the "Christmas Oratorio," Nos. 9, 17, 23 (*Choralgesänge*, No. 323). Organ Works, N. xv. 21; xix. 14, 16, 19. Bach also wrote a set of five Variations in Canon on the tune (N. xix. 73).

APPENDIX II

TRANSLATIONS

Note. The Roman numerals preceding a stanza indicate its number in the German Hymn. The Arabic numbers in brackets following the first line of a stanza state the Cantata or Motett in which it occurs; plain numerals indicate the Cantatas; M, Motetts; U, Unfinished Cantatas; D, Cantatas of doubtful authenticity. The capital letters at the foot of the translations show the source of the latter, as follows:

 A. Novello & Co.'s Original Octavo Edition.

 B. "The Chorale Book for England; the Hymns from the Lyra Germanica and other sources, translated by Catherine Winkworth; the tunes from the sacred music of the Lutheran, Latin, and other Churches, compiled and edited by William Sterndale Bennett and Otto Goldschmidt." London, 1865.

 C. Breitkopf & Haertel's (J. and W. Chester) English Edition of Bach's Cantatas.

 D. Trans. C. S. T.

 E. "Lyra Germanica: Hymns for the Sundays and Chief Festivals of the Christian Year. Translated from the German." By Catherine Winkworth. New Edition. London, 1864.

APPENDIX II

E (ii). "Lyra Germanica: Second Series: The Christian Life. Translated from the German." By Catherine Winkworth. Fifth Edition. London, 1863.

F. "The Church Hymnary." Edinburgh, 1904.

G. "A Compendious Book of godly and spiritual songs: commonly known as 'The Gude and Godlie Ballatis.' Reprinted from the edition of 1567." Edited by A. F. Mitchell, D.D., LL.D. Scottish Text Society. Edinburgh, 1897.

H. "Songs of Syon. A Collection of Psalms, Hymns, and Spiritual Songs set, for the most part, to their Ancient Proper Tunes, edited by the Rev. G. R. Woodward, M.A., Author of the Cowley Carol-Book." Third Edition, revised and enlarged. London, 1910.

I. "Remains of Myles Coverdale, Bishop of Exeter. Containing...Ghostly Psalms and Spiritual Songs." Edited for the Parker Society, by the Rev. George Pearson. Cambridge, 1846.

K. "Christian Singers of Germany." By Catherine Winkworth. London, 1869.

L. "Psalmodia Germanica: or, A Specimen of Divine Hymns, Translated from the High Dutch." By John Christian Jacobi. London, 1722.

M. "Exotics: A Translation of the Spiritual Songs of Novalis, the Hymn-Book of Luther, and other Poems from the German and Italian." By George Macdonald. London, 1876.

N. "Liturgy and Hymns for the use of the Protestant Church of The Unity of the Brethren or Unitas Fratrum. A New and Revised Edition." London, 1906.

O. "Psalms and Hymns, partly original, partly selected, for the use of the Church of England." By the Rev. Arthur T. Russell. Cambridge, 1851.

P. "The Family Treasury. Containing contributions by well-known writers in all departments of religious literature." London, 1877.

APPENDIX II

1. ACH BLEIB' BEI UNS, HERR JESU CHRIST

    i. O bide with us, Thou Saviour dear, (6)
    Forsake us not when eve is near;
    Thy sacred word, clear guiding light;
    O grant it ne'er be quenched in night.

    ii. In this our last and weakest hour, (6)
    Inspire us, Lord, with steadfast power,
    That undefiled Thy faith we keep,
    Until in death secure we sleep.

    Nicolaus Selnecker (A).

2. ACH GOTT UND HERR

    iv. If pain and woe must follow sin, (48)
    Then be my path still rougher,
    Here spare me not; if heaven I win,
    On earth I gladly suffer.

    Anonymous (B, no. 107).

3. ACH GOTT, VOM HIMMEL SIEH' DAREIN

    i. Ah God, from heaven, look down and view; (2)
    Let it Thy pity waken;
    Behold Thy saints how very few!
    We wretches are forsaken.
    Thy Word they will not grant it right,
    And faith is thus extinguished quite
    Amongst the sons of Adam.

    vi. God will its purity defend (2)
    From this evil generation.
    Let us ourselves to Thee commend,
    Lest we fall from our station;
    The godless rout is all around
    Where these rude wanton ones are found
    Against Thy folk exalted.

    Martin Luther (M, p. 62).

4. Ach Gott, wie manches Herzeleid

 i. O God, how many pains of heart (3, 44, 58)
  Befall me now with cruel smart.
  The narrow way is troublesome,
  By which to heaven I must come.

 ii. How hardly can my flesh and blood (3)
  Aspire to everlasting good?
  Where may I hope to comfort me?
  My mind, O Jesu, turns to Thee.

 xii. O guard my heart, sustain Thine own, (3, 153)
  In life and death, 'tis Thine alone.
  Jesu, my hope, my prayer shall be:
  Dear Saviour, would I were with Thee.
          (C.)

 xi. Then while I live this life of care (153)
  The cross for Thee I'll gladly bear.
  Grant me a patient, willing mood,
  I know that it shall work my good.

xi–xii. Help me to do my task aright, (153)
  That it may stand before Thy sight.
  Let me this flesh and blood control,
  From sin and shame preserve my soul.
     Martin Moller(?) (B, no. 136).

5. Ach Herr, mich armen Sünder

 i. A sinner, Lord, I pray Thee, (135)
  Recall Thy dread decree;
  Thy fearful wrath O spare me,
  From judgment set me free.
  O, dear Lord, grant compassion,
  And toward me turn Thy face,
  That I may dwell beside Thee
  In Heaven's appointed place.

vi. All praise to Thy great merit, (135)
High God on Heaven's throne,
Father and Holy Spirit,
And ever blessed Son.
Our eager voices praise Thee
With joyful ecstasy,
In hope to sing before Thee
For all eternity.
Cyriacus Schneegass (D).

6. ACH, LIEBEN CHRISTEN, SEID GETROST

i. Be of good cheer, good Christians all, (114)
Why stand ye so dejected?
What though our God afflicteth us
Who've His right laws rejected?
How justly falls His chastening hand!
With contrite heart we understand
And bow to His correction.

iii. E'en as the grain to earth doth fall (114)
And rise to harvest from its tomb,
So must our body vile decay
And dust and ashes brief become,
If glorified it hopes to rise
To those far mansions in the skies
Where Christ hath gone before us.

vi. For, though we wake and though we sleep, (114)
The Lord will ever shield us;
Who hath baptized us in His Name
To Satan will not yield us.
Through Adam's sin death on us came.
But Christ the Victim's borne the blame.
Praise God for His great goodness!
Johannes G. Gigas (D).

7. ACH WIE FLÜCHTIG

i. Ah! how fleeting, (26)
Frail and cheating
Are our days' brief measure!
Like a mist that quickly riseth
And the sun's hot ray surpriseth
Is the life that man so prizeth.

xiii. Ah! how cheating, (26)
Hollow, fleeting,
Are our mortal doings.
Nature in deep anguish sigheth;
Where the tree falls, there it lieth.
Who trusts God he never dieth.

Michael Franck (D).

8. ALLE MENSCHEN MÜSSEN STERBEN

vii. Yea, I see what here was told me, (162)
See that wondrous glory shine,
Feel the spotless robes enfold me,
Know a golden crown is mine;
So before the throne I stand,
One amid that glorious band,
Gazing on that joy for aye
That shall never pass away!

Johann Georg Albinus (B, no. 196).

9. ALLEIN ZU DIR, HERR JESU CHRIST

i. Lord Jesu Christ, in Thee alone (33)
My only hope on earth I place,
For other comforter is none,
No help have I but in Thy grace.
There is no man nor creature here,
No angel in the heavenly sphere,
Who at my need can succour me;
I cry to Thee,
For Thou canst end my misery.

iv. Glory to God in highest heaven, (33)
The Father of eternal love;
To His dear Son, for sinners given,
Whose watchful grace we daily prove;
To God the Holy Ghost on high;
Oh ever be His comfort nigh,
And teach us, free from sin and fear,
To please Him here,
And serve Him in the sinless sphere!

     Johannes Schneesing (B, no. 112).

10. ALSO HAT GOTT DIE WELT GELIEBT

i. That God doth love the world we know, (68)
Since He has sent His Son to save us:
To Him be faithful here below,
Then take the endless life He gave us.
To trust in Jesus, our salvation,
Will guard the soul from reprobation:
There is no ill which him can move
Whom God the Lord vouchsafes to love.

     Salomo Liscow (A).

11. AUF CHRISTI HIMMELFAHRT ALLEIN

i. Since Christ is gone to heaven, His home (128)
I too must one day share;
And in this hope I overcome
All anguish, all despair;
For where the Head is, well we know
The members He hath left below
In time He gathers there.

     Josua Wegelin (E (ii), p. 47).

12. AUF, MEIN HERZ! DES HERREN TAG

i. Up, my soul! 'tis Christ's great day, (145)
Death no longer can enthral us.
He who in the dark grave lay
Risen and glorious now doth call us.
Ever will I trust in Him
Who hath bought the world from sin.
                        Caspar Neumann (D).

13. AUF MEINEN LIEBEN GOTT

i. In God, my faithful God, (188)
I trust when dark my road;
Though many woes o'ertake me,
Yet He will not forsake me;
His love it is doth send them,
And when 'tis best will end them.

vi. "So be it," then I say, (148 n.)
With all my heart each day;
Guide us while here we wander,
Till safely landed yonder,
We too, dear Lord, adore Thee,
And sing for joy before Thee.
                (?) Sigismund Weingärtner (B, no. 147).

14. AUS TIEFER NOTH SCHREI ICH ZU DIR

i. From depths of woe I call on Thee, (38)
O God, now hear my crying!
Thy gracious ear incline to me,
To my complaint replying.
If Thou, O Lord, wilt call to mind
The sins and failings of mankind,
  Alas! who may abide it?

v. Yea, though our sin be ne'er so great, (38)
God's grace at last prevaileth;
His arm is ready soon and late,
His mercy never faileth.
Good Shepherd of the flock is He;
His chosen people He shall free
From sin's dark house of bondage.
Martin Luther (A).

15. BARMHERZGER VATER, HÖCHSTER GOTT

ix. Alas! I had forsaken Thee, (103)
O Saviour dear, a moment.
But mark with what deep penitence
I make Thee now atonement.
I bend the knee,
My God, to Thee
In deep humiliation.
The purest joy
Without alloy
Now crowns Thy great Oblation.
Paul Gerhardt (D).

16. BEFIEHL DU DEINE WEGE

v. Through waves and clouds and storms (153)
He gently clears thy way:
Wait thou His time; so shall this night
Soon end in joyous day.
Leave to His sovereign sway
To choose and to command;
So shalt thou, wondering, own His way
How wise, how strong His hand.
Paul Gerhardt (F, no. 277)[1].

[1] This free translation is by John Wesley.

17. CHRIST IST ERSTANDEN

iii. Alleluja, Alleluja, Alleluja! (66)
So let us sing right joyfully;
For Christ our Paschal Lamb is He.
Alleluja!

Anonymous (D).

18. CHRIST LAG IN TODESBANDEN

i. Christ lay in Death's dark prison; (4)
It was our sin that bound Him.
This day hath He arisen,
And sheds new light around Him.
Therefore let us joyful be
And praise our God [right heartily].
Hallelujah!

ii. O'er Death no man can prevail, (4)
If mortal e'er came near him.
Through guilt all our strength would fail,
Our sinful hearts did fear him.
Therefore Death did gain the day,
And lead in triumph us away
Henceforth to dwell with him emprisoned.
Hallelujah!

iii. Now Jesus Christ, the Son of God, (4)
For our defence hath risen,
Our grievous guilt He hath removed,
And Death hath bound in prison.
All his might Death must forego,
For now he's nought but idle show.
His sting is lost for ever.
Hallelujah!

iv. How fierce and dreadful was the strife (4)
    When Life with Death contended;
    For Death was swallowed up by Life
    And all his power was ended.
    God of old, the Scriptures show,
    Did promise that it should be so.
    O Death, where is thy victory?
                    Hallelujah!

v. The Paschal Victim here we see, (4, 158)
    Whereof God's word hath spoken.
    He hangs upon the cruel tree,
    Of saving love the token.
    His blood ransoms us from sin,
    And Death no more can enter in.
    Now Satan cannot harm us.
                    Hallelujah!

vi. So keep we all this holy feast, (4)
    Where every joy invites us;
    Our Sun is rising in the East,
    It is our Lord who lights us.
    Through the glory of His grace
    Our darkness will to-day give place.
    The night of sin is over.
                    Hallelujah!

vii. With grateful hearts we all are met (4)
     To eat the bread of gladness.
     The ancient leaven now forget,
     And every thought of sadness.
     Christ Himself the feast hath spread,
     By Him the hungry soul is fed,
     And He alone can feed us.
                    Hallelujah!
                    Martin Luther (A).

19. CHRIST UNSER HERR ZUM JORDAN KAM

i. Christ bapteist was be Johne in Jordan flude, (7)
For to fulfill for vs all rytcheousnes,
And our Baptisme dotit with sanctitude,
And greit vertew, to wesche our sinfulnes,
To drowne the deide, and hell for to oppres,
Quhen Goddis word with watter Junit[1] be,
Throw Faith, to gif vs lyfe Eternallie.

vii. Our eine seis outward bot the watter cauld, (7)
Bot our pure faith the power spirituall
Of Christis blude, inwart it dois behauld,
Quhilk is ane leuand well Celestiall
Zit for to purge the penitent with all,
Our natiue sin in Adame to expell
And all trespas committit be our sell.

Martin Luther (G, p. 14).

(A reconstruction.)

i. Christ baptized was in Jordan's flood, (7)
(To John the Baptist there He came,)
To wash away our sinfulness
And cleanse us throughly in His name.
For Death is drowned and Hell oppressed
When holy water's on us poured,
And we shall find eternal rest
Through Faith and in the Blood and Breast
Of our all cleansing Lord.

vii. By Faith and power spiritual (7)
Of Christ's own Blood we do behold
Celestial elements, e'en though
Our eyes see nought but water cold.

---

[1] joined.

APPENDIX II

By it the penitent is purged
Of Adam's sin and fear of Hell,
And our low nature's upward urged
To meet the purest God Himself
In raiment fair and spotless. (D.)

20. **CHRISTE, DU LAMM GOTTES**

Lamb of God, O Jesus, (23)
Thou that bearest all men's sins,
Have mercy on us!

Lamb of God, O Jesus,
Thou that bearest all men's sins,
Have mercy on us!

Lamb of God, O Jesus,
Thou that bearest all men's sins,
Grant us Thy peace!

"Agnus Dei" (C).

21. **CHRISTUM WIR SOLLEN LOBEN SCHON**

i. From lands that see the sun arise, (121)
To earth's remotest boundaries,
The Virgin-born to-day we sing,
The Son of Mary, Christ the King.

viii. For that Thine Advent glory be, (121)
O Jesu, Virgin-born, to Thee;
With Father and with Holy Ghost,
From men and from the heavenly host.

Martin Luther, from Coelius Sedulius (H, no. 21).

22. **CHRISTUS, DER IST MEIN LEBEN**

i. My life is hid in Jesus, (95)
And death is gain to me;
Then whensoe'er He pleases,
I meet it willingly.

Anonymous (B, no. 186).

23. DAS NEUGEBOR'NE KINDELEIN
   i. Sing we the birth of God's dear Son, (122)
      From highest heaven to earth come down,
      Bringing to us a glad New Year,
      And to all Christian men good cheer.
   iii. God is our friend and helper true, (122)
      'Gainst Him what can fell Satan do?
      Hell and its iron gates must yield;
      For Jesus is both sword and shield.
   iv. So let us hail this happy year (122)
      And put away all doubt and fear,
      Raise our glad hearts to God's high throne,
      Saved by the grace of Christ His Son.
                    Cyriacus Schneegass (D).

24. DER HERR IST MEIN GETREUER HIRT
   i. The Lord my Guide vouchsafes to be, (85, 104)
      To Him full trust I render;
      And He, my Shepherd, carries me
      To pastures fair and tender:
      He leads me on by waters still,
      My soul with comfort He doth fill,
      My Strength and sure Defender.
                    Cornelius Becker (A).

25. DER HERR IST MEIN GETREUER HIRT
   i. The Lord, He is my shepherd true, (112)
      My steps He safely guideth;
      With all good things in order due
      His bounty me provideth.
      He leadeth me without surcease
      In green and pleasant paths of peace,
      Wherein His grace abideth.

APPENDIX II 511

  v. The Lord is ever at my side, (112)
    His love shall fail me never;
    Therefore my will is to abide
    Within His house for ever.
    On earth His Church doth me sustain,
    And after death I look to reign
    With Christ, my Lord, in glory.
                      Wolfgang Meusel (A).

26. DU FRIEDEFÜRST, HERR JESU CHRIST

  i. O Jesu Christ, Thou Prince of Peace, (67, 116, 143)
    True Man and God in one,
    Our mighty help till life shall cease,
    Our hope when life is run.
    In that dread hour
    We plead Thy power,
    To God our Father crying.

  vii. Now let Thy gracious Spirit shine, (116)
    Our drooping hearts to raise,
    That we in darkness may not pine,
    Nor walk in evil ways.
    O Jesu Christ,
    In Thee we trust,
    For Thou alone canst save us.
                      (A.)

  iii. We thank Thee, Jesu, that indeed (143)
    The Prince of Peace Thou art;
    O help us ever in our need,
    Thy saving grace impart.
    Still year by year
    Grant us to hear
    Thy Word in peace and quiet.
                      Jakob Ebert (D).

27. DU LEBENSFÜRST, HERR JESU CHRIST

   i. O Jesus Christ, Thou dearest Lord, (43)
Thou Prince of life and glory,
Thou with the Father art adored
In heaven, where saints surround Thee.
How best can I the victory sing
Won by Thy might, Thou gracious King?
What strains can I be raising,
Thy love and power praising?

   iv. Now at Thy feet creation lies, (11)
Thy dread commands fulfilling;
Angels must leave the farthest skies
To do Thee service willing.
Princes and Kings shall come to Thee
In reverent love to bow the knee;
Earth, Heaven, Fire and Ocean
Do pay Thee glad devotion.

   xiii. Draw us, to Thee that haste we may, (43)
The wings of Faith aye plying;
Help us to turn from earth away,
The land of bondage flying.
My God, when may I soar to Thee?
When joy and peace my portion be?
When may I stand before Thee?
When reign with Thee in glory?

                             Johann Rist (A).

28. DU, O SCHÖNES WELTGEBÄUDE

   vi. Come, O Death, thou twin of Sleep, (56)
Lead us hence,—I pray Thee come,
Loose my rudder, through the deep
Guide my vessel safely home.

APPENDIX II 513

Thy approach who will may fly,
'Twere a joy to me to die,
Death but opes the gates to Thee,
Jesus, dearest Friend to me!
Johann Franck (E, p. 183).

29. DURCH ADAMS FALL IST GANZ VERDERBT

vii. He that hopeth in God stedfastly (109)
Shall never be confounded:
For doutles God's worde cannot ley,
Though all men shulde resist it.
Great trouble and care
Is every where;
This worlde's sorowe is infinite:
Yet sawe I never
Him perish for ever,
That fast on God's worde trusted.

viii. O Lorde, I praye the hartely (18)
For thy great mercyfull kyndnesse;
Thy wholsome worde take not fro me,
Because of my unthankfulnesse.
My synne is great,
I acknowlege it:
But thy mercy excelleth all thynge.
Therefore will I
Hope styll in the,
To thy blysse that thou mayest me brynge.
Lazarus Spengler (l, p. 557).

30. EIN' FESTE BURG IST UNSER GOTT

i. A stronghold sure our God remains, (80)
A shield and hope unfailing;
In need His help our freedom gains,
O'er all we fear prevailing.

       Our old malignant foe
       Would fain work us woe.
       With craft and great might
       He doth against us fight;
       On earth is not one like him.

ii. Our utmost might is all in vain ; (80)
     We straight had been rejected,
     But for us fights the perfect Man,
     By God Himself elected.
     Ask then, "Who is He?"
     He must Jesus be,
     The God by hosts adored,
     Our great Incarnate Lord,
     Who all His foes shall conquer.

iii. If all the world with fiends were filled, (80)
     A host that would devour us,
     To fear our hearts need never yield,
     For they could not o'erpower us.
     The prince of this world
     From his throne is hurled;
     Why should we then fear,
     Though grim he may appear?
     A single word confounds him.

iv. That word shall still in strength abide, (80)
     Yet they no thanks shall merit;
     For He is ever at our side,
     Both by His gifts and Spirit.
     And should they take our life,
     Wealth, name, child, and wife,
     Tho' these were all gone,
     Yet will they nought have won;
     God's kingdom ours remaineth.

                        Martin Luther (A).

APPENDIX II 515

31. EIN KIND GEBORN ZU BETHLEHEM
   iv. The Princes of Sheba hither came, (65)
      With gold and myrrh and incense they came.
      Hallelujah, Hallelujah!
                            Anon. (C).

32. ERHALT' UNS, HERR, BEI DEINEM WORT
   i. Lord, keep us steadfast in Thy word; (126)
     Curb those who fain by craft or sword
     Would wrest the kingdom from Thy Son,
     And set at nought all He hath done.
   iii. O Comforter, of priceless worth, (126)
      Send peace and unity on earth,
      Support us in our final strife,
      And lead us out of death to life.
                          (B, no. 103.)
   ii. Lord Jesu Christ, Thy power display; (6)
     Thou, Lord, whom other lords obey,
     Thy servants with Thy grace defend,
     That so their thanks may never end.
                        Martin Luther (A).

33. ERSCHIENEN IST DER HERRLICH' TAG
   i. Behold the glorious day of days; (67)
     Let all creation join in praise,
     When Christ our Lord triumphant rose
     And captive led His mighty foes.
                Alleluia!
                  (C.)
   xiv. Then, as is meet, we now will sing (145)
      Glad Hallelujahs to our King:
      To Thee, Lord, doth our praise pertain,
      Who for our joy art risen again.
                  Hallelujah.
            Nicolaus Herman (O, no. 113).

34. ES IST DAS HEIL UNS KOMMEN HER

i. Salvation hath come down to us   (9)
Of freest grace and love.
Works cannot stand before God's law,
A broken reed they prove;
Faith looks to Jesus Christ alone,
He must for all our sins atone,
He is our one Redeemer.
(K, p. 123.)

xi. Hope looketh for the dawning day   (86)
Which God's own Word hath promised.
The tardy hour may e'en delay:
God wills and hath ordained it.
He knoweth what for us is best,
Nor will our strength unduly test.
So therefore let us trust Him.

xii. Should e'er His face seem turned from Thee,
Still be thou not affrighted;   (9, 155, 186)
For when He seems most far from thee
Then art thou least benighted.
So let His Word thy heart restore,
And e'en when doubting, then the more
Know that thou art not slighted.
Paul Speratus (D).

35. ES IST GENUG: SO NIMM, HERR, MEINEN GEIST

v. It is enough! Lord brace me to the test,   (60)
When Death stands at the door.
'Tis Jesus knocks. Vain world, a long farewell!
I wend me hence to God,
Trusting, and most exceeding joyous,
Leaving earth's sorrows far behind me.
It is enough!
Franz Joachim Burmeister (D).

36. ES WOLL' UNS GOTT GENÄDIG SEIN

i. God be mercyfull unto us, (76)
And sende over us his blessynge;
Shewe us his presence glorious,
And be ever to us lovynge;
That men on earth may knowe thy waye,
Thy savynge health and ryghteousnesse;
That they be not led by nyght nor day,
Throwe the pretexte of trewe justice,
To seke salvacyon where none is.

iii. O God, let the people prayse the; (69, 76)
All people, God, mought geve the honoure;
The earth also ryght plenteously
Mought increase ever more and more;
And God, which is oure God over all,
Mought do us good and pleasure.
God blesse us now both great and small,
And all the worlde hym honoure,
Fearynge alwaye his myght and power.

       Martin Luther (I, p. 580).

37. FREU' DICH SEHR, O MEINE SEELE

ix. Let Thine angels close attend me, (19)
As Elias Heaven borne;
May my soul repose upon Thee,
As once Lazarus, poor, forlorn,
In Thy bosom, O receive me,
Fill me full of trust and joy,
Till my risen soul and body
Both unite eternally.   (D.)

x. O my soul, right joyful be thou, (70)
Grief and pain no more to know,
For thy Saviour calleth thee now
From this vale of toil and woe;

Thou shalt see His power and might
Through eternal ages' flight,
With the choir of angels blending
Songs of triumph never ending.
                    Anonymous (A).

38. FREUET EUCH, IHR CHRISTEN ALLE

iv. Jesu, knit in closer union (40)
All Thy members unto Thee,
Pour out all love's energy
To inspire Thy saints' communion.
Grant to all Thy people here
Peace, and blessing through the year,
Joy that earthly joy excelleth,
Christ all power of evil quelleth,
Bliss, that earthly bliss exceedeth.
Christ's our sun, whence grace proceedeth.
                    Christian Keimann (C).

39. GELOBET SEI DER HERR

i. Now praised be the Lord, (129)
My God, my life, my beacon,
Who hath of His great love
My soul and body given ;
Who from my mother's womb
A father's care bestows,
And e'en until the tomb
His goodness ever shows.

v. With praises unto God (129)
Let Heaven's high arches ring.
And let the angel host
Unite with man to sing
The glories of our Prince
With raptured minstrelsy.
Loud praises to His name
Through all Eternity !
                    Johannes Olearius (D).

APPENDIX II 519

40. GELOBET SEIST DU, JESU CHRIST
  i. Now blessed be thou, Christ Jesu; (91)
     Thou art man borne, this is true:
     The aungels made a mery noyse,
     Yet have we more cause to rejoyse.
                   Kirieleyson.
  ii. The blessed Sonne of God onely (91)
     In a crybbe full poore dyd lye:
     With oure poore flesh and oure poore bloude
     Was clothed that everlastynge good.
                   Kirieleyson.
  vii. All this dyd he for us frely, (64, 91)
     For to declare his great mercy:
     All Christendome be mery therfore,
     And geve hym thankes evermore.
                   Kirieleyson.
                   Martin Luther (I, p. 562).

41. GOTT FÄHRET AUF GEN HIMMEL
  vii. When will the night be over? (11)
     When dawns the blissful hour
     That shall to us discover
     The Lord in all His power?
     O day so wondrous dear,
     When first our souls shall meet Him,
     With loving kiss to greet Him!
     Come! quickly now appear!
                   Gottfried Wilhelm Sacer (A).

42. GOTT VATER, SENDE DEINEN GEIST
  ii. There lives no child of man on earth (74)
     Who of Thy grace can boast his worth,
     Not one who is deserving.
     We owe it to Thy love alone,
     To the far merits of Thy Son,
     His death, and His Atonement.

520   APPENDIX II

    x. The Spirit, Whom God sends at need, (108)
       Upon His righteous paths will lead
       And guide our feet aright.
       They shall not wander from those ways,
       Nor be ensnared in evil's maze,
       Who follow His directing.
                    Paul Gerhardt (D).

43. **HAST DU DENN, JESU, DEIN ANGESICHT GÄNTZLICH VERBORGEN**
    vi. Walk in My ways and commandments, beloved
        son. Surely (57)
       Thou may'st on Me rely thy Friend in Heaven
         to be firmly.
       Thou'rt My delight,
       And evermore in My sight
       Shalt thou in glory shine rarely.
                    Ahashuerus Fritsch (D).

44. **HELFT MIR GOTT'S GÜTE PREISEN**
    vi. All people sing Thy praises, (16, 28)
       O Lord on Heaven's high throne,
       For all Thou hast ordained,
       Through Jesus Christ Thy Son.
       O hear Thy children's prayer:
       A year of blessing send us,
       From every ill defend us,
       And keep us in Thy care.   Paul Eber (A).

45. **HERR CHRIST, DER EINIG' GOTT'S SOHN**
    i. Christ is the onlie Sone of God, (96)
      The Father Eternall:
      We haif in Jesse found the rod,
      God and man, naturall.
      He is the Morning Star,
      His bemis send he hes out far,
      Bezond vther sternis all.

v. Awaik vs, Lord, we pray the, (22, 96, 132, 164)
The haly Spreit vs geue,
Quhilk may our auld man mortifie,
That our new man may leue,
Sa will we alway thank the,
That schawis vs sa greit mercy,
And our sinnis dois forgeue.

     Elisabethe Cruciger (G, p. 145).

(Reconstruction.)

i. Christ is the only Son of God, (96)
Father Eternal:
We have in Jesse found the rod,
God and man, natural.
He is the Morning Star,
His beams sends He out far
Other stars beyond all.

v. Awake us, Lord, we pray Thee, (22, 96, 132, 164)
Thy Holy Spirit give,
That our old man may mortify,
That our new man may live.
So will we alway thank Thee,
Who showeth so great mercy
And our sins doth forgive.
         (D.)

46. HERR GOTT, DICH LOBEN ALLE WIR

i. Now praise we all our mighty Lord, (130)
And thank Him and give loud applaud
For those bright beings of the sky
Who circle round His throne on high.

xi. We praise Thee and do Thee adore (130)
And thank Thee, Lord, for evermore,
Whose own dread angels swell the song
That through the ages rolls along.

xii. We pray that God's angelic band (130)
May fulfil ever His command,
And help all people here on earth
God's Word to prize at highest worth.
                              Paul Eber (D).

47. HERR GOTT DICH LOBEN WIR
    i. Thee, Lord our God, we praise, (16, 190)
       To Thee our thanks we raise.
    ii. The whole wide world doth worship Thee, (16)
        Who Father art and e'er shalt be.
    xx. We therefore pray Thee, help us, Lord, (120)
        Whom Thou'st redeemed with Thy Blood;
    xxi. That 'mid the saints we numbered be (120)
         Around Thy throne eternally.   (D.)
    xxii. O Christ, our Lord, Thy people guide, (119, 120)
          For all their wants do Thou provide.
    xxiii. Upon their heads Thy blessings pour, (119, 120)
           Exalt them now and evermore.
                              Martin Luther (A).

48. HERR JESU CHRIST, DU HÖCHSTES GUT
    i. Jesus, Thou source of every good, (113)
       And fountain of salvation,
       Behold me bowed beneath the load
       Of guilt and condemnation:
       My sins indeed are numberless;
       O Lord, regard my deep distress,
       Reject not my petition.
    ii. In pity look upon my need, (113, 131)
        Remove my sore oppression;
        Since Thou hast suffered in my stead,
        And paid for my transgression,
        Let me not yield to dark despair;
        A wounded spirit who can bear?
        O show me Thy salvation.

APPENDIX II

iv. But Thy reviving gospel-word, (113)
    That calls me to repentance,
    Doth joy unspeakable afford,
    Revokes the righteous sentence,
    And tells me Thou wilt not despise
    A broken heart, in sacrifice,
    That turns to Thee, Lord Jesus.

viii. O, for Thy name's sake, let me prove (113, 168)
    Thy mercy, gracious Saviour:
    The yoke which galls me, soon remove,
    Restore me to Thy favour:
    Thy love shed in my heart abroad,
    That I may live to Thee, my God,
    And yield Thee true obedience.

                          (N, no. 278.)

v. Right sore my conscience doth reproach (131)
    The sins that do beset me!
    How can I to God's throne approach,
    Or to my Judge submit me?
    'Tis Jesus' Blood that maketh clean,
    How black soe'er our sin hath been:
    He can and will deliver.

vii. Forgive me, Lord my God, I pray, (113)
    The faults Thy just wrath have incurred,
    And break the heavy load of sin
    Which snares me helpless as a bird.
    So shall my heart find peace and rest,
    To Thy great praise and honour living,
    And Thy dread Word obediently fulfilling[1].

                Bartholomäus Ringwaldt (D).

---

[1] The German text is a paraphrase of Ringwaldt's seventh stanza.

49. HERR JESU CHRIST, ICH SCHREI ZU DIR

xii. O Jesu Christ, man's surest stay, (48)
Who comfort rare dispensest,
My anguish sore is known to Thee,
'Tis Thou alone help sendest.
But as Thou wilt so let it be,
In Thy sure wisdom deal with me;
Thine am I now and ever.
      Anonymous (D).

50. HERR JESU CHRIST, ICH WEISS GAR WOHL

iii. O dear Lord Jesu, watch o'er me (166)
With sheltering care for ever,
Nor let me ever heedless be
Or from my thoughts Thee sever.
O hold me ever in Thy love,
And call my soul to realms above
To part from Jesus never.
     Bartholomäus Ringwaldt (D).

51. HERR JESU CHRIST, WAHR'R MENSCH UND GOTT

i. Lord Jesus Christ, true Man and God, (127)
Who borest anguish, scorn, the rod,
And diedst at last upon the tree,
To bring Thy Father's grace to me;
I pray Thee through that bitter woe,
Let me, a sinner, mercy know.

viii. Dear Lord, forgive us all our guilt, (127)
Help us to wait until Thou wilt
That we depart; and let our faith
Be brave and conquer e'en in death,
Firm resting on Thy sacred Word,
Until we sleep in Thee, our Lord.
      Paul Eber (E, p. 241).

APPENDIX II

52. HERR, WIE DU WILLT, SO SCHICK'S MIT MIR
   i. Lord, as Thou wilt, so deal with me (73, 156)
   Who on Thy will am grounded.
   With Thee alone my soul would be,
   Let me not be confounded.
   O hold me ever in Thy care,
   And give me patience to declare
   "Thy will be ever done, Lord."
   Caspar Bienemann (D).

53. HERZLICH LIEB HAB' ICH DICH, O HERR
   i. Lord, all my heart is fixed on Thee, (174)
   I pray Thee, be not far from me,
   With tender grace uphold me.
   The whole wide world delights me not,
   Of heaven or earth, Lord, ask I not,
   If but Thy love enfold me.
   Yea, though my heart be like to break,
   Thou art my trust that nought can shake,
   My portion and my hidden joy,
   Whose Cross could all my bonds destroy;
   Lord Jesu Christ! My God and Lord!
   Forsake me not who trust Thy word!
   (B, no. 119.)

   iii. My God, when Thou shalt call me home, (149)
   O let my Guardian Angel come
   To bear my soul to Heaven!
   My body in the tranquil tomb
   Shall slumber till the day of doom,
   When graves in twain are riven.
   In that dread hour when I arise,
   O grant to mine unworthy eyes
   With rapture to behold Thy face,
   My Saviour and my throne of grace.

>   O Jesu Christ, hear Thou my cry,
>   That I may dwell with Thee on high.
>   Martin Schalling[1] (A).

54. **HERZLICH THUT MICH VERLANGEN**

>   iv. Though worms destroy my body   (161)
>   Within its earth-bound grave,
>   Yet Christ one day shall call me
>   And from the tomb me save.
>   Then, clothed in radiant glory,
>   Before my God I'll sing
>   Of His great love the story.
>   O Death, where is thy sting!
>   Christoph Knoll (D).

55. **ICH ARMER MENSCH, ICH ARMER SÜNDER**

>   i. Before God's throne I prone do place me,   (179)
>   A sinner frail and mortal wight.
>   Deal with me, Lord, in love I pray Thee,
>   And give me favour in Thy sight.
>   Have mercy on me, Saviour mine,
>   Absolve me, make me wholly Thine.
>   Christoph Tietze (D).

56. **ICH DANK' DIR, LIEBER HERRE**

>   iv. O faith undoubting grant me   (37)
>   In Jesus Christ our Lord;
>   May all my sins forgiven be,
>   And I to grace restored.
>   For sure He'll not deny me
>   But his true word fulfil,
>   Take all my sin upon Him,
>   And free me from its ill.
>   Johann Kolross (D).

---

[1] The melody requires that the second half of the eleventh line of the stanza be repeated.

57. ICH FREUE MICH IN DIR

   i. In Thee will I rejoice (133)
     And ever loving greet Thee;
     For, dearest Saviour mine,
     Thy promise hast Thou given me
     My Brother e'en to stand.
     How sweet the name doth sound!
     And, O! the unmeasured love
     In God's dear Son is found!

  iv. So let what e'er betide, (133, U 1)
     On Jesu will I stay me;
     If earth to atoms break,
     Yet shall it not affray me.
     On Thee, O Jesu mine,
     My heart alone is set,
     Nor, resting on Thy love,
     Can aught on earth me fret.

                             Caspar Ziegler (D).

58. ICH HAB' IN GOTTES HERZ UND SINN

   i. To God's all-gracious heart and mind (92)
     My heart and mind I yield;
     In seeming loss my gain I find,
     In death life stands revealed.
     I am His own,
     Whose glorious throne
     In highest heaven is set;
     Beneath His stroke
     Or sorrow's yoke
     His heart upholds me yet.

  ii. There is but one thing cannot fail, (92)
     That is my Father's love;
     A sea of troubles may assail
     My soul,—'tis but to prove

And train my mind,
By warnings kind,
To love the Good through pain ;
When firm I stand,
Full soon His hand
Can raise me up again.

xii. But must I walk the vale of death (92)
Through sad and sunless ways,
I pass along in quiet faith,
Thy glance my fear allays ;
Through the dark land
My Shepherd's hand
Leads to an end so bright,
That I shall there
With praise declare
That all God's ways are right !

(K, p. 213.)

v. How great the wisdom of our God, (92)
How wise His understanding !
Both time and space obey His nod
And fulfil His commanding !
He sorrow sends
And gladness lends
As best it seemeth to Him ;
His every deed
Supplies our need,
So therefore I will trust Him.

(D.)

x. My God, I give myself to Thee, (65, 92)
On Thy great love relying,
Do Thou in life my helper be,
My light when I am dying.
Incline me still
To do Thy will,

>   Be that my one endeavour,
>   Through all my days
>   To sing Thy praise
>   And worship Thee for ever!
>   Paul Gerhardt (A).

59. ICH RUF' ZU DIR, HERR JESU CHRIST

> i. Lord, hear the voice of my complaint, (177, 185)
>   To Thee I now commend me;
>   Let not my heart and hope grow faint,
>   But deign Thy grace to send me;
>   True faith from Thee, my God, I seek,
>   The faith that loves Thee solely,
>   Keeps me lowly,
>   And prompt to aid the weak,
>   And mark each word that Thou dost speak.
>
> v. Help me, for I am weak; I fight, (177)
>   Yet scarce can battle longer;
>   I cling but to Thy grace and might,
>   'Tis Thou must make me stronger;
>   When sore temptations are my lot,
>   And tempests round me lower,
>   Break their power.
>   So, through deliverance wrought,
>   I know that Thou forsakest me not!
>   Johannes Agricola (B, no. 116).

60. ICH WILL ZU ALLER STUNDE

> xiv. O let me sing God's praises (107)
>   Throughout all my life long!
>   Give me a voice that raises
>   Unfathomed thanks and song.
>   Most Holy Trinity,
>   Whose grace doth e'er abound
>   And care and ill confound,
>   All praise eternally!   ? David Denicke (D).

APPENDIX II

61. IN ALLEN MEINEN THATEN

i. Where'er I go, whate'er my task, (97)
The counsel of my God I ask,
Who all things hath and can ;
Unless He give both thought and deed
The utmost pains can ne'er succeed,
And vain the wisest plan.
(E (ii), p. 108.)

xv. To God, my soul, resign thee, (13, 44, 97)
To faith in Him confine thee,
Who hath thy being given :
Whatever may betide thee,
Through all things He will guide thee,
Thy all-wise Father in heaven.
Paul Flemming (C).

62. IN DICH HAB' ICH GEHOFFET, HERR

i. In Thee, Lord, have I put my trust, (52)
Leave me not helpless in the dust,
Let not my hope be brought to shame,
But still sustain,
Through want and pain,
My faith that Thou art aye the same.
(B, no. 120.)

vii. All glory, praise, and majesty (106)
To Father, Son, and Spirit be,
The holy, blessed Trinity,
Whose power to us
Gives victory,
Through Jesus Christ. Amen, Amen.
Adam Reissner (A).

63. IST GOTT MEIN SCHILD UND HELFERSMANN
　iv.　God is my Shield and Helper true,　(85)
　　　No ills can vex; many or few,
　　　He drives my foes before me.
　　　On their own heads the pains shall fall
　　　'Gainst me designed; for at a call
　　　My God is ever near me.
　　　　　　　　Ernst Christoph Homburg (D).

64. JESU, DER DU MEINE SEELE
　i.　Jesu! Who in sorrow dying　(78)
　　　Didst deliverance bring to me,
　　　Whilst my sins for vengeance crying
　　　Nailed Thee to the shameful tree;
　　　Thou Who Satan's power subduest,
　　　And the sinner's hope renewest,
　　　Biddest all so graciously
　　　That I needs must come to Thee.
　xii.　I believe;—in Thee believing,　(78)
　　　Leave me not, O Lord, to die:
　　　Strength and grace from Thee receiving,
　　　I may sin and death defy.
　　　Now I stay me on Thy blessing,
　　　Till, the sight of Thee possessing,
　　　I shall live from conflict free,
　　　Happy in Eternity.　　　(O, no. 78.)
　xi.　From my guilty soul, I pray Thee,　(105)
　　　Move the heavy load of sin.
　　　Thy sure promise, Lord, O grant me,
　　　Let it ease my heart within;
　　　Through our life's long journey here
　　　Ever may Thy comfort cheer.
　　　Who on Thee in faith believeth
　　　Sure protection e'er receiveth.
　　　　　　　　　　Johann Rist (D).

65. JESU LEIDEN, PEIN UND TOD

xxxiii. Jesu, all Thy bitter pain (159, 182)
Was for my salvation;
Thine the wounds, O Victim slain,
Mine the great Oblation.
Riseth up my soul with joy
Gratefully to thank Thee
For the bliss without alloy
That the Cross hath won me.

Paul Stockmann (D).

66. JESU, MEINE FREUDE

i. Jesu, priceless treasure, (M 3)
Source of purest pleasure,
Truest friend to me;
Ah, how long I've panted,
And my heart hath fainted,
Thirsting, Lord, for Thee!
Thine I am, O spotless Lamb,
I will suffer nought to hide Thee,
Nought I ask beside Thee.

ii. In Thine arm I rest me, (81, M 3)
Foes who would molest me
Cannot reach me here;
Though the earth be shaking,
Every heart be quaking,
Jesus calms my fear;
Fires may flash, and thunders crash,
Yea, and sin and hell assail me;
Jesus will not fail me.

iv. Hence with earthly treasure, (M 3)
Thou art all my pleasure,
Jesu, all my choice.
Hence, thou empty glory,
Nought to me thy story,

APPENDIX II 533

Told with tempting voice;
Pain, or loss, or shame, or cross,
Shall not from my Saviour move me,
Since He deigns to love me.

vi. Hence, all fears and sadness, (M 3)
For the Lord of gladness,
Jesus, enters in ;
They who love the Father,
Though the storms may gather,
Still have peace within ;
Yea, whate'er I here must bear,
Still in Thee lies purest pleasure,
Jesu, priceless treasure. (A.)

v. Fare thee well for ever, (64)
From earth now I sever,
Gone its woe and wail.
Farewell, too, my blackening sin,
All uncleanness foul within,
No more me assail!
Farewell glittering pride and pelf,
Farewell my unworthy self,
Fare thee well for ever!
Johann Franck (D).

67. JESU, MEINER SEELEN WONNE

ii. Jesu, refuge, dearest Saviour, (154)
Jesu, best and strongest stay,
Jesu, Death's all-conquering slayer,
Jesu, brightest guiding ray !
How for Thee my lone heart sigheth,
With what love to Thee it crieth!
Come, O come, I pine for Thee,
Dearest Jesu, come to me!

vi. O how dear is Jesu's loving, (147)
Firmly to Him will I cling.

With sweet care He's e'er removing
From life's troubles smart and sting.
He is mine and me He loveth,
He was dead and for me liveth.
From Him never will I stray,
Nor can Death's dark fears dismay.

xvii. Jesus my dear joy remaineth, (147)
My heart's solace and its stay;
Powers of ill my soul disdaineth,
On Him all my need I lay.
He's my heart's fond hope and pleasure,
My soul's rapture, dearest treasure.
He is with me day and night,
Ever in my heart and sight.

                          Martin Janus (D).

68. JESU, NUN SEI GEPREISET

i. Jesus, now will we praise Thee, (41)
Thus far in safety brought,
And grateful anthems raise Thee,
For all that Thou hast wrought.
Thy gifts are we possessing
In this glad opening year:
How full of grace and blessing
Its advent doth appear.
Through Thee from ill defended
The old year have we ended.
We would to Thee be living
Throughout the coming year,
Ourselves to Thee be giving
Through all our lifetime here.

iii. To Thee alone be glory, (41, 171)
To Thee alone be praise:
Thy Passion's moving story
Shall govern all our ways.

Till, freed from earthly sadness,
We take our heavenward flight,
To dwell with peace and gladness
In God's most holy sight.
To all men shall Thy pleasure
Their good and evil measure:
On Thee then safely staying,
Let Christian people sing,
With hearts and voices praying,
That good this year may bring. (A.)

ii. May this New Year before us (190)
Add praises to God's name.
Good Christians all in chorus
Your loudest carols frame.
Lord by Thy might and power
Grant us long days on earth;
Thy richest blessings shower
On our dear land of birth.
O shield it 'neath thy strong wing,
May this New Year firm peace bring.
Stablish among the nations
Thine own Almighty realm,
And all earth's vain delusions
Right utterly o'erwhelm.

Johann Hermann (D).

69. KOMM, GOTT SCHÖPFER, HEILIGER GEIST

i. Come, Holy Ghost, eternal God, (D 2)
Our hearts and minds inspire
To set on truth and godliness
Our life's one long desire.

Martin Luther[1] (D).

[1] The translation is an adaptation of the version in *Archbishop Parker's Psalter*, 1553-58, quoted in the *Dictionary of Hymnology*, p. 1209.

70. KOMM, HEILIGER GEIST, HERRE GOTT

i. Come, Holy Spirit, God and Lord, (59)
Be all Thy graces now outpoured
On the believer's mind and soul,
And touch our hearts with living coal.
Thy Light this day shone forth so clear,
All tongues and nations gathered near
To learn that faith, for which we bring
Glad praise to Thee, and loudly sing.
Hallelujah! Hallelujah!
(B, no. 72.)

iii. Look down, Holy Dove, Spirit bow; (M 2)
Descend from heaven, and help us now:
Inspire our hearts while humbly kneeling,
To pray with zeal and contrite feeling!
Prepare us, through Thy cleansing power,
For death, at life's expiring hour:
That we may find the grave a portal
To Thee in heaven and life immortal!
Hallelujah! Hallelujah!
Martin Luther (A).

71. KOMM, JESU, KOMM, MEIN LEIB IST MÜDE

xi. When called by Thee I gain Thy portal, (M 5)
Mine will be joys no worlds can give;
There shall I know my pains were mortal,
There will my soul in glory live.
There I around Thy Throne shall hover,
There, my Redeemer, I shall sing Thy praise for ever.
Anonymous (A).

72. KOMMT HER ZU MIR, SPRICHT GOTTES SOHN

xvi. For quhat Eternall God of peace (86)
Hes promeist throw his Spirite of grace,
And syne sworne be his haly name,
That he sall hald baith trew and sune.
God grant that we may sé his Throne,
Throw Faith in Jesus Christ. Amen.
Georg Grüenwald (G, p. 32).

(Reconstruction.)

xvi. For what the eternal God of peace (86)
Has promised of His heavenly grace
And sworn to by His holy name,
That will He truly soon perform.
God grant that we may see His throne,
Through faith in Jesus Christ, His Son.
(D.)

73. KOMMT, LASST EUCH DEN HERREN LEHREN

vi. Blest are they who feel compassion (39)
For another's bitter need,
For the poor make intercession,
And with bread the hungry feed;
They who help with kindly word,
Or to deeds of love are stirred,
Unto them shall help be given,
And a sure reward in heaven.
David Denicke (A).

74. LIEBSTER GOTT, WANN WERD' ICH STERBEN?

i. When will God recall my spirit? (8)
Lives of men run swiftly by;
All who Adam's frame inherit,
One among his heirs am I,

      Know that this befalls the race,
      They but for a little space
      Dwell on earth in want and mourning,
      Soon to earth themselves returning.

v. Thou that life and death ordainest, (8)
    Make it mine in peace to die;
    Let me yield the soul Thou trainest,
    With a courage calm and high.
    Grant that I an honoured grave
    With the holy dead may have,
    Earthly grief and toil forsaking,
    Nevermore to shame awaking.

                    Caspar Neumann (A).

75. LIEBSTER IMMANUEL, HERZOG DER FROMMEN

i. O come, Immanuel, Prince of the lowly, (123)
    Thou, our salvation's hope, quickly appear!
    Thou knowest my heart is Thine, yea, and Thine wholly,
    Burns for Thee, trusts in Thee, knowing no fear.
    Farewell, vain earth,
    Trivial thy worth!
    Comes the Great Day when my God draweth near.

v. How ill content me earth's hollow pleasures! (123)
    Thou, Jesus, art my life, bone of my bone.
    For Thee I sacrifice all this world's treasures;
    Thou shalt direct me e'er, Thou, Thou alone.
    Thou hast my heart,
    Never we'll part,
    Once from the grave I soar to Thy far throne.

                    Ahashuerus Fritsch (D).

76. LOBE DEN HERREN, DEN MÄCHTIGEN KÖNIG
    DER EHREN

i. Praise to the Lord! the Almighty, the King of
    creation! (137)
    O my soul, praise Him, for He is thy health and
    salvation!
    All ye who hear,
    Now to His temple draw near,
    Join me in glad adoration!

ii. Praise to the Lord! who o'er all things so wondrously
    reigneth, (137)
    Shelters thee under His wings, yea so gently sustaineth;
    Hast thou not seen
    How thy desires have been
    Granted in what He ordaineth?

iv. Praise to the Lord! who doth prosper thy work and
    defend thee, (137, U 3)
    Surely His goodness and mercy here daily attend thee;
    Ponder anew
    What the Almighty can do,
    If with His love He befriend thee!

v. Praise to the Lord! Oh let all that is in me adore
    Him! (137, U 3)
    All that hath life and breath, come now with praises
    before Him!
    Let the Amen
    Sound from His people again,
    Gladly for aye we adore Him!

                    Joachim Neander (B, no. 9).

77. LOBT GOTT, IHR CHRISTEN ALLE GLEICH

viii. Wide open stands the once closed door (151)
To Eden's garden ways;
The Angel guardeth it no more.
To God be thanks and praise[1].

                         Nicolaus Herman (D).

78. MACHE DICH, MEIN GEIST, BEREIT

i. Rise, my soul, to watch and pray, (115)
From thy sleep awake thee,
Lest at last the evil day
Suddenly o'ertake thee;
For the foe,
Well we know,
Oft his harvest reapeth
While the Christian sleepeth. (B, no. 125.)

x. Let us then with lowly fear (115)
Watch and pray unceasing;
For the dread hour draweth near,
Judgment fears increasing.
Speeds the day
Unerringly
When the Great Judge cometh
And creation doometh.

                         Johann Burchard Freystein (D).

79. MACH'S MIT MIR, GOTT, NACH DEINER GÜT

i. Deal with me, God, in mercy now, (156)
O help me in my utter woe,
Thine ear to me in pity bow;
When hence my soul must quickly go,
Receive her, as her God and Friend,
For all is right if right the end.

                         Johann Hermann Schein (B, no 191).

---

[1] To fit the tune, the words of the last line must be repeated.

APPENDIX II 541

80. MEINE SEEL' ERHEBT DEN HERREN

My soul doth magnify the Lord, (10)
And my spirit hath rejoiced in God my Saviour.

For He hath regarded the lowliness of His handmaiden.

For behold, from henceforth all generations shall call me blessed.

Glory be to God the Father, and the Son,
And to the Holy Spirit:

As it was in the beginning, and is now,
And shall be world without end. Amen.
(C.)

81. MEINEN JESUM LASS' ICH NICHT

i. Jesus will I never leave, (124)
He's the God of my salvation;
Through His merits I receive
Pardon, life and consolation:
All the powers of my mind
To my Saviour be resigned.

vi. With my Jesus I will stay, (124, 154, 157)
He my soul preserves and feedeth;
He the life, the truth, the way,
Me to living waters leadeth:
Blessed who can say with me,
Christ, I'll never part with Thee.
(N, no. 452.)

v. Not by earth or heaven bright (70)
Is my longing soul beguiled,
But by Jesus and His light
I to God am reconciled.
Saved by Him from judgment sore,
Jesus shall I leave no more.
Christian Keimann (A).

82. Mit Fried' und Freud' ich fahr' dahin

   i. In joy and peace I pass away, (95, 106, 125)
      Whene'er God willeth.
      The fears that vex my anxious soul
      His love stilleth.
      Trusting in His promise sure,
      In death I sleep calm and secure.
                              (A.)

   ii. 'Tis Christ hath wrought this work for me, (125)
      Thy dear and only Son,
      Whom Thou hast suffered me to see,
      And made Him surely known
      As my Help when trouble's rife,
      And even in death itself my Life.

   iv. He is the heathen's saving Light, (83, 125)
      And He will gently lead
      Those who now know Thee not aright,
      And in His pastures feed;
      While His people's joy He is,
      Their Sun, their glory, and their bliss.
               Martin Luther (B, no. 81).

83. Nimm von uns, Herr, du treuer Gott

   i. Remove from us, O faithful God, (101)
      Thy dreadful and avenging Rod,
      The Number of our crying Crimes
      Has well deserved a thousand Times.
      Sad Famine, War, and Pestilence
      Prevent by Thy good Providence.

   iii. To Thee we trust, to Thee we sigh (101)
      And lift our heavy Souls on high.
      Give us an Instance of Thy Grace
      In showing Thy relieving Face;
      By true Repentance bring us Home
      And save us from the Wrath to come.

APPENDIX II   543

iv. Why wilt Thou raise Thy dreadful Storms (101)
    Against so vile and feeble Worms?
    Thou Author of our Being knowst
    That this our Frame is Earth and Dust;
    Our best Endeavours are but frail,
    If Thou dost search we greatly fail.

v. Sin still besets us everywhere,   (101)
    Nor Satan fails to lay his Snare,
    The wicked World with Flesh and Blood
    Conspire to rob us of all Good.
    O Lord, this is not hid from Thee,
    Have mercy on our Misery.

vi. Look on Thy Son's most bitter Death, (101)
    Wounds, Agonies, and parting Breath,
    These dreadful Sufferings of Thy Son
    Atoned for Sins which we had done;
    O! for His Sake our Guilt forgive,
    And let the mourning Sinners live.

vii. O Lord, conduct us by Thy Hand, (90, 101)
     And bless these Realms by Sea and Land;
     Preserve Thy Word amongst us pure,
     Keep us from Satan's Wiles secure;
     Grant us to die in Peace and Love,
     And see Thy glorious Face above.
                    Martin Moller (L, p. 123).

84. NUN BITTEN WIR DEN HEILIGEN GEIST

iii. Thou swete love, graunt us altogether (169, 197)
     To be unfayned in charite;
     That we may all love one another,
     And of one mynde alwaye to be.
            Kirieleyson.
                    Martin Luther (I, p. 543).

(*Reconstruction.*)

iii. O sweetest love, grant to us alway (169, 197)
To be unfeigned in charity;
That we may all love one another,
And of one mind always be.
    Kyrie eleison.   (D.)

85. NUN DANKET ALLE GOTT

i. Now thank we all our God, (79, 192)
With heart and hands and voices,
Who wondrous things hath done,
In whom His world rejoices;
Who from our mother's arms
Hath blessed us on our way
With countless gifts of love,
And still is ours to-day.

iii. All praise and thanks to God (192)
The Father now be given,
The Son, and Him who reigns
With them in highest heaven,
The one eternal God,
Whom earth and heaven adore,
For thus it was, is now,
And shall be evermore!
            Martin Rinkart (B, no. 11).

86. NUN DANKET ALL' UND BRINGET EHR'

i. Now, mortals all, your voices raise, (195)
Acclaim God lustily,
Whom angel hosts throng with their praise
Before His throne on high.
            Paul Gerhardt (D)[1].

[1] The structure of the melody requires that the last line of the stanza be repeated.

APPENDIX II

87. NUN KOMM, DER HEIDEN HEILAND

i. Come, Redeemer of our race, (36, 61, 62)
Virgin born by holy grace,
Hailed by all the wondering earth :
God of old ordained His birth.
(A.)

vi. With the Father equal Thou, (36)
Flesh of our flesh evermore,
Our frail bodies O endow
With grace from Thy plenteous store.

viii. Praise to God the Father be, (36, 62)
Praise and glory to the Son,
Glory, Holy Ghost, to Thee,
While eternal ages run.
Martin Luther (D)[1].

88. NUN LASST UNS GOTT DEM HERREN

v. Thy Word and blessed Blood, (165)
The Font's sin-cleansing flood,
On these Thy Spirit guide us
To stand, whate'er betide us!
(D.)

viii. Firm in Thy Truth retain us, (79)
And ever more sustain us,
To praise Thy Name to all men,
Through Christ our Saviour. Amen.
Ludwig Helmbold (A).

89. NUN LOB', MEIN' SEEL', DEN HERREN

i. My soul, O praise the Lord thy God, (28)
O praise for aye His holy name ;
He crowneth thee with mercies,
His benefits forget thou not.

---

[1] Stanzas vi and viii are a reconstruction of *Hymns Ancient and Modern*, No. 55.

T. B. C.

Thy sin hath He forgiven,
And aided thy distress,
His works the earth have filled.
Green herbs He bringeth forth,
And corn for all man's service,
That they may furnish food.
O praise the Lord of harvest,
Sing praise unto His holy name.
                                        (A.)

iii. Like as a father bendeth   (17, M 1)
In pity o'er his infant race;
So God the Lord befriendeth
The meek and lowly heirs of grace.
That we are frail He knoweth,
Like sheep, we go astray:
Like grass the reaper moweth,
We fall and fade away!
Like wind that ever flieth,
We are but passing breath;
Thus man each moment dieth,
For life must yield to death.
                                        (A.)

v. All laud and praise with honour (28 n., 29, 51, 167)
To Father, Son and Holy Ghost,
Who will fulfil the promise
To give us all that we need most.
In Him, too, firmly trusting,
All evil we have withstood,
Our faith upon Him resting,
With all our heart, mind and mood.
In Him alone believing,
We raise our thankful strain,
Amen, all joy receiving,
If we our faith maintain.
                    Johann Graumann (C).

90. O Ewigkeit, du Donnerwort

i. Eternity, tremendous word, (20, 60)
A soul and body piercing sword,
Beginning without ending!
Eternity, a timeless tide
On which no sorrows e'er may ride,
To thee I'd fain be wending.
My heart affrighted scarce can breathe,
My tongue doth to my palate cleave.

xi. Though God our King from Heaven, His place, (20)
Looks down upon the human race,
Yet Nature's ills assail us.
The thunder's roll, the lightning's flash,
Grim pain and want our bodies lash;
Yet shall they not confound us.
And only may our troubles cease
When God's good time shall give release.

xvi. Eternity, tremendous word, (20)
A soul and body piercing sword,
Beginning without ending!
Eternity, a timeless tide
On which no sorrows e'er may ride,
To thee I'd fain be wending.
Lord Jesus Christ, O grant it me
That Heaven's pure joys one day I see.

Johann Rist (D).

91. O Gott, der du aus Herzensgrund

ix. O let Thy watchful Angel band (D 3)
Defend our Church and nation!
Let peace and quiet on every hand
E'er bless Thy whole creation.
May Satan's realm and evil sway
Be overthrown now and alway
By Thine almighty power.

   x. So, when on brink of death we stand, (D 3)
       Let Satan not deceive us;
       But, drawn by Thy most loving hand,
       Into Thy Halls receive us,
       To where through Heaven's farthest bounds
       The "Holy, Holy, Holy" sounds,
       In praise to Thee unceasing.
                         ? Justus Gesenius (D).

92. O GOTT, DU FROMMER GOTT

   i. O God, Thou faithful God, (24)
       Thou Fountain ever flowing,
       Without Whom nothing is,
       All perfect gifts bestowing;
       A pure and healthy frame
       O give me, and within
       A conscience free from blame,
       A soul unhurt by sin.

  ii. And grant me, Lord, to do, (45)
       With ready heart and willing,
       Whate'er Thou shalt command,
       My calling here fulfilling,
       And do it when I ought,
       With all my strength, and bless
       The work I thus have wrought,
       For Thou must give success.

  vi. And if a longer life (71)
       Be here on earth decreed me,
       And Thou through many a strife
       To age at last will lead me,
       Thy patience on me shed,
       Avert all sin and shame,
       And crown my hoary head
       With pure untarnished fame.
                    Johann Heermann (B, no. 115).

93. O GOTTES GEIST, MEIN TROST UND RATH

ix. God Holy Ghost, to Thee I pray, (175)
O grant me help that so I may
A better, purer life be living,
And win at length my sins' forgiving.
Thy word shines like the Morning Star,
Whose beams enlighten near and far.
So may I now, and e'en alway,
Thy just behests alone obey.

       Johann Rist (D).

94. O GROSSER GOTT VON MACHT

ix. O Lord, Thou God of truth, (46)
Before Whom none may stand,
If Jesus Christ Thy Son
Stay not Thy wrathful hand.
O! to His wounds have Thou regard,
His anguish, pain, and body marred.
For His dear sake O spare us,
And on Thy mercy bear us.

      Balthasar Schnurr (D).

95. O HAUPT VOLL BLUT UND WUNDEN

vi. Here would I stand beside Thee; (159)
Lord, bid me not depart!
From Thee I will not sever,
Though breaks Thy loving heart.
When bitter pain shall hold Thee
In agony opprest,
Then, then will I enfold Thee
Within my loving breast.

       Paul Gerhardt (A).

96. O HERRE GOTT, DEIN GÖTTLICH WORT

viii. O Lord, we pray, (184)
At our last day
In anger do not leave us.
May we who are Thine,
Marked by Thy sign,
Hold fast the Word bequeathed us.
Grant us to be
Eternally,
Of faith and trust possessed,
In certainty
Thy face to see,
Our sins washed white, our souls at rest.
? Anark of Wildenfels (D).

97. O JESU CHRIST, MEIN'S LEBENS LICHT

i. Lord Jesus Christ, my Life, my Light, (118)
My strength by day, my trust by night,
On earth I'm but a passing guest,
And sorely with my sins oppressed.

ii. Far off I see my fatherland, (58)
Where through Thy grace I hope to stand,
But ere I reach that Paradise
A weary way before me lies.
Martin Behm (B, no. 190).

98. O JESU, MEINE LUST

iv. My way is Thine, O God, (128)
For Thou dost guide me truly
With all a Father's love,
And deignest e'en to call me
To join Thee where Thou art
Amid Thy glory throned,
Him evermore to serve
Who hath my sin atoned.
Matthäus Avenarius (D).

APPENDIX II

99. SCHAU', LIEBER GOTT, WIE MEINE FEIND'
   i. How many and how mighty, Lord, (153)
      The foes who press upon me!
      Sore grievously they me assail,
      My spirit faints within me.
      Lord, in their wiles do them enmesh,
      So shall the Devil, World, and Flesh
      Prevail not e'er against me.
                              ? David Denicke (D).

100. SCHMÜCKE DICH, O LIEBE SEELE
   i. Soul, array thyself with gladness, (180)
      Leave the gloomy caves of sadness;
      Come from doubt and dusk terrestrial,
      Gleam with radiant light celestial:
      For the Lord, divine and gracious,
      Full of gifts both rare and precious,
      He of love itself the essence,
      Bids Thee to His sacred Presence.
   iv. Ah, what longing fills my spirit, (180)
      All Thy promise to inherit!
      Now with tears my soul is yearning,
      Now with flames of ardour burning;
      Thirsts for Thee from morn till even,
      Hungers for Thy heavenly leaven;
      Craving only this high pleasure,
      Union with its holiest Treasure.
   ix. Lord of Life, I pray Thee hear me: (180)
      Be Thy Presence ever near me;
      Strength and Will of God uphold me;
      Mighty wings of Love enfold me.
      Through my life, whate'er betide me,
      Thou, O God, defend and guide me;
      And, when Death itself befall me,
      To Thy heavenly Kingdom call me.
                              Johann Franck (C).

101. Schwing' dich auf zu deinem Gott

ii. Shake thy head and sternly say,   (40)
Serpent! hence! avaunt thee!
Why dost torture me alway?
To my trouble haunt me?
Bruised is thy horrid head;
By the pain and sadness
Of my Saviour am I led
To the halls of gladness.

Paul Gerhardt (C).

102. Sei Lob und Ehr' dem höchsten Gut

i. All praise and thanks to God most High,   (117)
The Father, Whose is perfect love;
The God Who doeth wondrously,
The God Who from His Throne above
My soul with richest solace fills,
The God Who every sorrow stills;
Give glory now to Him, our God!

iv. I sought Him in my hour of need,   (117)
I cried,—Lord God, now hear my prayer!
For death He gave me life indeed,
And hope and comfort for despair;
For this my thanks shall endless be,
O thank Him, thank Him too with me;
Give glory now to Him, our God!

(B, no. 2.)

ix. So come ye now into His courts   (117)
With glad and grateful singing,
Nor from His service turn your thoughts,
To Godward set them winging.
He all things hath most wisely planned
And fashioned them in His right hand.
Give glory now to Him, our God!

Johann Jakob Schütz (D).

103. SELIG IST DIE SEELE
  ix. When dark cares oppress me, (87)
      Since my Jesus loves me,
      Vanishes my woe.
      Sweeter than the honey,
      Precious beyond money,
      Jesus' love I know.
      What though pain
      Hath on me lain!
      His love can convert to gladness
      E'en the deepest sadness.
                            Heinrich Müller (D).

104. SINGEN WIR AUS HERZENSGRUND
  iv. Right well hath God the world ordained, (187)
      Good things upon us He hath rained.
      His the valleys and the hills,
      Herbs and pasture-feeding rills.
      His the earth's rich harvest store.
      With smiling plenty earth He wreathes,
      And life into our being breathes.
  vi. We thank Him and we praise Him too (187)
      That He doth our dull sense renew
      To learn His Spirit's bounteous grace,
      In His just laws to run our race,
      And glorify Him here on earth.
      So sing with joy unceasingly
      Loud "gratias" to God on high.
                            Anonymous (D).

105. SO WAHR ICH LEBE, SPRICHT DEIN GOTT
  vi. Amend your ways while yet you may, (102)
      For morrow comes, too late to pray.
      To-day is with us; use it well,
      Lest morning find your soul in Hell.
      Repentant, then, approach your end;
      So shall your soul to God ascend.

vii. O dear Lord Jesu, help Thou me (102)
My footsteps to direct to Thee,
And bring me contrite to Thy throne.
And if Thou summonest me soon,
To-day, to-morrow, home on high,
May I be ready, Lord, to die.
                                  Johann Heermann (D).

106. TREUER GOTT, ICH MUSS DIR KLAGEN

vi. Holy Spirit throned in Heaven, (194)
One with God eternally,
And the Son, for man's sins given,
Source of joy and ecstasy,
All my being is aflame
With the love of Thy great name.
Of Thy grace watch ever o'er me,
Nor withdraw Thy goodness from me.

vii. Send, O send Thy comfort to me, (194)
Shelter deep within my heart.
Lord, fulfil Thy purpose in me,
Make my will of Thine a part.
Kindle in me virtue's glow,
Guide me whither I should go;
Till to join the elect Death calls me,
And the victor's crown befalls me.

xii. All my days, O God, I'll praise Thee, (25)
And Thy mighty arm acclaim.
Care and sorrow flee before Thee,
Captives of Thy glorious name.
Lord, Thy praises will I sound
While there's breath within me found,
And hereafter shall my spirit
Still proclaim Thy glorious merit.
                                  Johann Heermann (D).

APPENDIX II 555

107. TRÖSTET, TRÖSTET, MEINE LIEBEN

   iii. For Elijah's voice is crying (30)
      In the desert far and near,
      Bidding all men to repentance,
      Since the kingdom now is here.
      O that warning cry obey,
      Now prepare for God a way;
      Let the valleys rise to meet Him,
      And the hills bow down to greet Him.
                Johannes Olearius (B, no. 83)[1].

108. VALET WILL ICH DIR GEBEN

   i. Farewell I gladly bid thee, (95)
      False, evil world, farewell!
      Thy life is dark and sinful,
      With thee 1 would not dwell:
      In heaven are joys untroubled,
      I long for that bright sphere
      Where God rewards them doubled
      Who served Him truly here.
                Valerius Herberger (B, no. 137).

109. VERLEIH' UNS FRIEDEN GNÄDIGLICH

   i. Lord, in Thy mercy, grant us peace (42, 126)
      Throughout our generation,
      And make all bloody wars to cease.
      Alone Thou'rt our salvation
      And our availing champion.

[1] The text in Breitkopf & Haertel's English edition of the Cantata is a substitution for, and not a translation of, Olearius' stanza.

ii. Grant to our prince and magistrates (42, 126)
Peace and good regiment:
That under them we may be
Peaceably and quietly governed
In all godliness
And good fellowship. Amen.
                          Martin Luther (D).

110. VERZAGE NICHT, DU HÄUFLEIN KLEIN

i. Fear not, O little flock, the foe (42)
Who madly seeks your overthrow,
Dread not his rage and power:
What though your courage sometimes faints,
His seeming triumph o'er God's saints
Lasts but a little hour.
            Johann Michael Altenburg (E, p. 17).

111. VON GOTT WILL ICH NICHT LASSEN

v. O praise Him, for He never (D 4)
Forgets our daily need;
O blest the hour whenever
To Him our thoughts can speed;
Yea, all the time we spend
Without Him is but wasted,
Till we His joy have tasted,
The joy that hath no end.

ix. For such His will who made us, (73)
The Father seeks our good;
The Son hath grace to aid us,
And save us by His blood;
His Spirit rules our ways,
By faith in us abiding,
To heaven our footsteps guiding;
To Him be thanks and praise.
                  Ludwig Helmbold (B, no. 140).

112. WACH AUF, MEIN HERZ, UND SINGE
    ix. Ah Lord! confirm and guide me, (194)
        And ever stand beside me;
        Throughout life's toilsome journey
        Thy sheltering care be with me!
    x. With Thy dear love direct me, (194)
       And father-like correct me,
       O may Thy Scripture feed me,
       And Heaven at last accept me.
                              Paul Gerhardt (D).

113. WACHET AUF, RUFT UNS DIE STIMME
    i. Sleepers wake! for night is flying, (140)
       The watchmen on thy walls are crying,
       Thou city of Jerusalem!
       Hear ye now ere comes the morning,
       The midnight call of solemn warning:
       Where are ye, O wise virgins, where?
       Behold the Bridegroom comes,
       Arise! and take your lamps,
       Alleluia!
       Yourselves prepare,
       Your Lord draws near,
       He bids you to His marriage-feast.
    ii. Zion hears her watchmen's voices, (140)
       Their gladdening cry her soul rejoices,
       The shadows of her night depart.
       In His might her Lord appeareth,
       His word of grace and truth she heareth,
       The day-star riseth in her heart.
       O come, in splendour bright,
       Lord Jesu, Light of Light!
       Hosianna!
       We follow Thee
       Thy joy to see,
       Where everlasting bliss shall be.

        iii. Glory now to Thee be given, (140)
              On earth as in the highest heaven,
              With lute and harp in sweetest tone.
              All of pearl each dazzling portal,
              Where we shall join the song immortal,
              Of Saints and Angels round Thy throne.
              Beyond all earthly ken
              Those wondrous joys remain,
              That God prepares.
              Our hearts rejoice,
              Io! Io!
              Ever in dulci jubilo.   Philipp Nicolai (A).

114. WÄR' GOTT NICHT MIT UNS DIESE ZEIT
        i.   Were God not with us all the time, (14)
              Israel must loud declare it,
              Were God not with us all the time,
              We should have now despaired ;
              For we are such a little•flock,
              Despised by such a crowd of folk,
              Who all do set upon us !
      iii. Thank God! their throat He did not yet (14)
              Let swallow, though it gaped ;
              As from a snare the bird doth flit,
              So is our soul escaped.
              The snare's in two, and we are through ;
              The name of God it standeth true,
              The God of earth and heaven.
                             Martin Luther (M, p. 68).

115. WARUM BETRÜBST DU DICH, MEIN HERZ?
        i.   Why art thou thus cast down, my heart? (138)
              Why troubled, why dost mourn apart,
              O'er nought but earthly wealth?
              Trust in thy God, be not afraid,
              He is thy Friend, Who all things made.

APPENDIX II

ii. Dost think thy prayers He doth not heed? (138)
He knows full well what thou dost need,
And heaven and earth are His;
My Father and my God, Who still
Is with my soul in every ill.

iii. Since Thou my God and Father art, (138)
I know Thy faithful loving heart
Will ne'er forget Thy child;
See I am poor, I am but dust,
On earth is none whom I can trust.

xi. What here may shine I all resign, (47)
If the eternal crown be mine,
That through Thy bitter death
Thou gainedst, O Lord Christ, for me—
For this, for this, I cry to Thee!

> ? Hans Sachs (B, no. 143).

116. WARUM SOLLT' ICH MICH DENN GRÄMEN

xi. Lord, by Thee am I provided! (M 4)
Thou art mine, I am Thine,
We are undivided;
I am Thine, for Thou didst lave me
When the tide from Thy side
Flowed to cleanse and save me.

xii. Thou art mine, my Shepherd, lead me. (M 4)
Day and night, O my Light!
Shelter, guard, and feed me!
Never, never let us sever;
Holding me, clasping Thee,
Keep me Thine for ever.

> Paul Gerhardt (A).

117. WAS ALLE WEISHEIT IN DER WELT

  viii. So let our voices with accord, (176)
To Heaven's high portals winging,
Acclaim Thy might, O God and Lord,
Thine endless praises singing!
Alone Thou'rt King of Heaven's host,
Of other gods Creator!
God Father, Son, and Holy Ghost,
Our Saviour and Oblationer,
One Godhead, yet three Persons!

                            Paul Gerhardt (D).

118. WAS FRAG ICH NACH DER WELT

  i. What reck I of the world, (64, 94)
Its vain and hollow pleasures?
Jesu, my love for Thee
Contemns its empty treasures.
On Thee, alone on Thee,
All my delight is stayed.
While on Thee I repose
How can I be dismayed?

  iii. To vain and empty show (94)
The world doth give preferment.
How partial is its choice,
How doth it lack discernment!
But not on things below
Are my foundations laid.
If Jesus calls me His,
How can I be dismayed?

  v. How doth the world dismay (94)
Contempt of its allurement,
Or failure to pursue
The joys of its procurement!

APPENDIX II

But Jesus by His Cross
All else pure dross hath made.
And since He loveth me,
How can I be dismayed?

vii. What reck I of the world? (94)
It fadeth in a moment,
Nor 'gainst Death's stern decree
Can gain an hour's postponement.
Its glories must decay,
Their lure in ashes laid.
But Jesu's at my side;
How can I be dismayed?

viii. What reck I of the world! (94)
Lord Jesus doth enrich me.
My treasure great He is,
With love He doth bewitch me.
Mine, mine is Heaven's abode,
The price hath Jesus paid.
Wherefore I proudly cry,
How can I be dismayed?
        Georg Michael Pfefferkorn (D).

119. WAS GOTT THUT, DAS IST WOHLGETHAN

i. Whate'er my God ordains is right, (98, 99, 100, 144)
Holy His will abideth;
I will be still whate'er He doth,
And follow where He guideth.
He is my God,
Though dark my road,
He holds me that I shall not fall,
Wherefore to Him I leave it all.

v. Whate'er my God ordains is right, (75)
Though now this cup in drinking
May bitter seem to my faint heart,
I take it all unshrinking;

>   Tears pass away
>   With dawn of day,
>   Sweet comfort yet shall fill my heart,
>   And pain and sorrow shall depart.
>
>   (B, no. 135.)
>
> vi. What God ordains is best of all,   (12, 69, 99, 100)
>   Therewith will I content me,
>   Though fear of death upon me fall,
>   Though want and pain are sent me.
>   For God my Father tenderly
>   With His right arm will shield me;
>   To Him I gladly yield me.
>
>   Samuel Rodigast (A).

120. WAS MEIN GOTT WILL, DAS G'SCHEH' ALLZEIT

> i. What my God wills be done alway,   (72, 111, 144)
>   His purpose is the best;
>   He still abides my Strength and Stay,
>   The Rock whereon I rest.
>   Faithful indeed,
>   He helps in need;
>   He chastens but in measure.
>   He'll ne'er forsake
>   The souls who make
>   His gracious will their pleasure.
>
>   (P, p. 111.)
>
> iv. Once more, dear Lord, I Thee intreat,   (111)
>   Thine ear incline unto me,
>   And when I Death's last summons meet
>   Encourage and sustain me.
>   O quickly raise
>   My soul to praise
>   Thyself in highest heaven.

         Thou wilt not fail
         Thy creatures frail;
         Wherefore Lord, Amen! Amen!
    Albrecht Margrave of Brandenburg-Culmbach (D).

121. WAS WILLST DU DICH BETRÜBEN
  i. Why art cast down within thee? (107)
     Why dost in doubting dwell?
     Give but thy love, and deeply,
     To our Immanuel.
     In Him alone confide;
     For He will ne'er deny thee,
     Nor fail to stand beside thee;
     He will for thee provide.
                    Johann Heermann (D).

122. WEG, MEIN HERZ, MIT DEN GEDANKEN
  xii. Open wide the gates of mercy, (32)
       Let the living fountains flow.
       Those that taste its healing waters,
       These shall all Thy sweetness know.
       Call me to Thee, Love divine,
       Cleanse this sin stained soul of mine.
       Till at last Thou wilt receive me,
       Nevermore by sin to grieve Thee.
                        Paul Gerhardt (C).

123. WELT, ADE! ICH BIN DEIN MÜDE
  i. World, farewell! of thee I'm weary, (27, 158)
     I will seek the things above.
     There forget my wanderings dreary,
     In the realm of peace and love.
     War and strife we find in thee,
     World, thou hast but vanity;
     While in Heaven abide alway
     Gladness, joy, eternal day.
                    Johann Georg Albinus (A).

124. WENN EINER ALLE DING VERSTÜND
   viii. Thou art Thyself, O Jesu dear,   (77)
   Of purest love the purest ray.
   Give me but strength to persevere
   And follow Thee now and alway;
   That I in word and thought and deed
   May love and succour all in need,
   Therein Thy Word fulfilling.
        ? David Denicke (D).

125. WENN MEIN STÜNDLEIN VORHANDEN IST
   iv. Since Thou didst leave the grave again, (15, 95)
   It cannot be my dwelling;
   Thou art in heaven—this soothes my pain,
   All fear of death dispelling;
   For Thou wilt have me where Thou art,
   And so with joy I can depart
   To be with Thee for ever.
   v. To Thee I now stretch out mine arms, (31)
   And gladly hence betake me;
   I sleep at peace from all alarms,
   No human voice can wake me.
   But Christ is with me through the strife,
   And He will bear me into life,
   And open heaven before me.
       Nicolaus Herman (B, no. 193).

126. WER NUR DEN LIEBEN GOTT LÄSST WALTEN
   i. If thou but sufferest God to guide thee, (93)
   And hopest in Him all thy days,
   He'll give thee strength whate'er betide thee,
   And keep thy feet in all thy ways.
   Who trusts in God's unchanging love
   Hath stronghold that shall ne'er remove.

APPENDIX II

ii. What can these anxious cares avail thee? (93)
    What serve these ceaseless moans and sighs?
    What can it help, if thou bewail thee?
    With groaning from thy sleep arise?
    The heavier grow our grief and pain
    Through craven fears and lamentation.
    We find our soul's salvation
    When we our cross in patience and in faith sustain[1].

ii. Of what avail our bitter sorrow? (21)
    Of what avail our pain and grief?
    Of what avail that each new morrow
    Still finds our woe beyond relief?
    The weight of every cross and care
    We make but greater by despair.

iii. Only be still, wait thou His leisure, (93)
    Take up the cross His wisdom sends.
    Trust thou in God and His good pleasure,
    As with a shield His love defends.
    God, Who His chosen children knows,
    God, from Whose life our being flows,
    He will at last our sorrow lighten,
    Will with glad hope our darkness brighten[1].

iv. Due time for joy He knoweth truly, (93)
    It shall come when He sees it meet;
    When He hath tried and purged us throughly,
    And finds us free from all deceit.
    Then comes God to us unaware,
    And makes us own His love and care.

v. Think not amid the hour of trial (21, 93)
    That God hath cast thee off unheard;
    That he whose hopes meet no denial
    Must surely be of God preferred.
    Time passes and much change doth bring,
    Time sets a bound to everything.

[1] This is a translation of the Bach-Picander text and not of Neumark's stanza.

vi. I have waited for the Lord, (93)
Ever trusting in His word.
He by His mighty arm alone
Thrusts the rich from high estate,
And the humble makes He great—
In all the world His will is done[1].

vii. Sing, pray, and keep His ways unswerving,
So do thine own part faithfully;   (88, 93, 197)
And trust His word, though undeserving,
Thou yet shalt find it true for thee.
God never yet forsook at need
The soul that trusted Him indeed.

        Georg Neumark (A).

127. WER WEISS, WIE NAHE MIR MEIN ENDE

i. O teach me, Lord, my days to number, (27, 166)
For Time flies fast, and Death draws near.
How swiftly comes that last dread slumber,
How nigh that hour of mortal fear!
My God, for Jesu's sake I pray
Thy peace may bless my dying day.
        (A.)

xii. And thus I live in God at peace, (84)
And die without a thought of fear,
Content to take what God decrees,
For through His Son my faith is clear.
His grace shall be in death my stay,
And peace shall bless my dying day.
    Emilie Juliane Countess of Schwarzburg-
       Rudolstadt (B, no. 187).

---

[1] This is a translation of the Bach-Picander text and not of Neumark's stanza.

128. WERDE MUNTER, MEIN GEMÜTHE

vi. Have I e'er from Thee departed, (55)
Now I seek Thy face again,
And Thy Son, the loving-hearted,
Made our peace through bitter pain.
Yes, far greater than our sin,
Though it still be strong within,
Is the Love that fails us never,
Mercy that endures for ever.

Johann Rist (B, no. 167).

129. WIE SCHÖN LEUCHTET DER MORGENSTERN

i. How brightly shines yon Star of Morn, (1)
Of God's great love and wisdom born,
From Jesse's root ascending.
Hail, David's Son, of Jacob's line!
My King and Bridegroom all divine!
Thy reign is never ending!
Gracious, lovely,
Priceless treasure, passing measure!
Rich in blessing!
Every perfect gift possessing!

vii. My chosen Spouse is Christ the Lord, (1, 49, 61)
The First, and Last, Eternal Word,
From God the Father springing.
He will me take, I know full well,
With Him in Paradise to dwell.
Rejoice, my soul, with singing.
Amen! Amen!
Haste Thou, then, my joy, my glory,
Soon to meet me!
All my soul doth long to greet Thee!

(A.)

iv. But if Thou look on me in love, (172)
There straightway falls from God above
A ray of purest pleasure;
Thy word and Spirit, flesh and blood,
Refresh my soul with heavenly food,
Thou art my hidden treasure;
Let Thy grace, Lord,
Warm and cheer me. O draw near me;
Thou hast taught us
Thee to seek since Thou hast sought us!
                    (B, no. 149.)

v. O God, the Champion of our race, (37)
Who from the world's remotest trace
Through Thy dear Son hast bought me!
Jesus hath given me His dear heart,
I am of Him so close a part,
From Heaven He came and sought me.
Eya! Eya!
O the wonder! heaven yonder
Calls me to Him,
Evermore to praise and love Him.
                                    (D.)

vi. Awake the sound of harp and string, (36)
And tuneful hymns of gladness sing,
Pure hearts with voices blending:
But let me sit at Jesu's feet,
My heavenly Bridegroom, passing sweet,
In joyaunce never-ending:
Meetly, featly,
Sing *Cantate, Jubilate*:
Spread the story;
Great is Christ, the King of glory.
            Philipp Nicolai (H, no. 329 A).

130. WIR CHRISTENLEUT'

iii. Sin brings us grief, (40)
Christ brings relief,
Since He came down to give us consolation.
God's on our side
When ills betide.
Then who shall rob the Christian of salvation?
(C.)

v. Yes, let us praise (110, 142)
Our God and raise
Loud hallelujahs to the skies above us.
The bliss bestowed
To-day by God
To ceaseless thankfulness and joy should move us.
Caspar Fuger (B, no. 34).

131. WO GOTT DER HERR NICHT BEI UNS HÄLT

i. If God were not upon our side (178)
When foes around us rage,
Were not Himself our Help and Guide
When bitter war they wage,
Were He not Israel's mighty Shield
To whom their utmost crafts must yield,
We surely must have perished.

ii. But now no human wit or might (178)
Should make us quail for fear,
God sitteth in the highest height,
And makes their counsels clear;
When craftiest snares and nets they lay,
God goes to work another way,
And makes a path before us.

iv. They call us heretics, and lie (178)
In wait to spill our blood;
Yet flaunt their Christian name on high,
And boast they worship God.
Ah God! that precious name of Thine
O'er many a wicked deed must shine,
But Thou wilt once avenge it.

v. They open wide their ravenous jaws (178)
To swallow us indeed,
But thanks to God who rules our cause,
They shall not yet succeed:
Their snares He yet will bring to nought,
And overthrow what they have taught,
God is too mighty for them.

vii. Our foes, O God, are in Thy hand, (178)
Thou knowest every plot;
But only give us strength to stand,
And let us waver not,
Though Reason strive with Faith, and still
She fear to wholly trust Thy will,
And sees not Thy salvation.

viii. But heaven and earth, O Lord, are Thine, (178)
By Thee alone were made,
Then let Thy light upon us shine,
O Thou our only aid!
Kindle our hearts to love and faith
That shall be steadfast e'en to death,
Howe'er the world may murmur!

Justus Jonas (K, p. 117).

132. WO SOLL ICH FLIEHEN HIN

  i. O whither shall I fly? (5)
    To Thee, O Lord, I cry.
    My heavy sins dismay me,
    Whence cometh help to stay me?
    Jesus my soul descrieth
    And on Him firm relieth.

  iii. A heavy load of sin (199)
    To Thee, my Lord, I bring;
    Whate'er the tasks that daunt me,
    The fear and doubts that haunt me,
    From out Thy side love floweth
    And saving grace bestoweth.

  vii. How poor's my life indeed! (89)
    How urgent is my need!
    And yet how rich in blessing
    Through Jesu's love possessing!
    Death vanquished, sin enchainéd,
    Hell and proud Satan taméd.

  ix. Thy Blood's most precious flow (136)
    With might availeth so,
    One drop from out Thy pierc'd side
    Can throughly cleanse the world wide,
    From Satan's jaws can snatch us,
    And to Thyself can match us.

  xi. O guide my heart and will, (5, 148, 163)
    Firm strength in me instil.
    From all my sins deliver
    Which me from Thee still sever;
    Until, from evil parted,
    In Thee I be engrafted.

                            Johann Heermann (D).

133. **WOHL DEM, DER SICH AUF SEINEN GOTT**

  i. How happy he who on His God (139)
     Can place his full reliance!
     He to the world and Hell's dark brood
     May boldly bid defiance.
     How great content he may command
     Who on God's friendship takes his stand.

  v. Of what avail the hosts of Hell? (139)
     Death can no farther fright me.
     The world no longer weaves a spell,
     Its vain things ne'er delight me.
     God is my help, I clasp His hand,
     On His firm friendship do I stand.

                    Johann Christoph Rube (D).

134. **ZEUCH EIN ZU DEINEN THOREN**

  v. O teach our hearts, Spirit divine, (183)
     How rightly we should pray,
     That our prayers may prevail, as Thine,
     Our songs arise alway,
     And mount to Heaven's throne,
     To where the Father reigneth,
     With Whom true prayer availeth;
     On Him we trust alone.

                    Paul Gerhardt (D).

135. **ZION KLAGT MIT ANGST UND SCHMERZEN**

  ii. God Himself hath given His promise (13)
     Our strong helper e'er to be.
     Thence my soul doth find assurance,
     Doubt and sadness from me flee.
     Will He then His grace withhold?
     In just anger will He scold?
     Sure He will have mercy on us,
     He Who died that He might win us.

                    Johann Heermann (D).

APPENDIX III

THE ORIGINAL TEXTS OF BACH'S ORATORIOS, "PASSIONS," MASSES, CANTATAS, AND MOTETTS

Excepting the tunes that he wrote for Schemelli's Hymn book, and the parts of Cantata 71 (Mühlhausen, 1708), not a note of Bach's concerted Church music was printed until after his death. The publication of Forkel's biography in 1802 excited a slowly rising tide of interest. In 1803 Breitkopf & Haertel published Motetts 1, 2, 3, 4, 5. In 1811 Simrock, of Bonn, published (in E flat ma.) the Magnificat, and in 1818 the Mass in A major. In 1830 the Score of the "St Matthew Passion" was published by Schlesinger. Trautwein brought out the "St John Passion" in 1831. In 1833 Nägeli, of Zürich, issued the "Kyrie" and "Gloria" of the B minor Mass, and Simrock printed the remainder of the work in 1845. The first Cantata to be published was "Ein' feste Burg," No. 80, printed by Breitkopf & Haertel in 1821. In 1830 Simrock issued six more: "Nimm von uns, Herr," No. 101; "Herr, deine Augen sehen nach dem Glauben," No. 102; "Ihr werdet weinen und heulen," No. 103;

APPENDIX III

"Du Hirte Israel, höre," No. 104; "Herr, gehe nicht in's Gericht," No. 105; and "Gottes Zeit ist die allerbeste Zeit," No. 106. In 1843 Trautwein published four more: "Nimm, was dein ist, und gehe hin," No. 144; "Himmelskönig, sei willkommen," No. 182; "Barmherziges Herze der ewigen Liebe," No. 185; and "Siehe zu, dass deine Gottesfurcht,". No. 179. Finally, in 1847, Breitkopf & Haertel issued "Warum betrübst du dich," No. 138; "Wachet auf, ruft uns die Stimme," No. 140; and "Also hat Gott die Welt geliebt," No. 68, as a supplement to Winterfeldt's "Evangelischer Kirchengesang," Bd. III. Thus, no more than fourteen Cantatas were in print when the systematic publication of Bach's works began on the foundation of the Bachgesellschaft in July 1850, the centenary of Bach's death. The present note reveals the sources whence, in the half century of its existence, 1850–1900, Bach's Scores were published[1].

In the following list A stands for the Library of St Thomas' School, Leipzig; B for the Royal Library, Berlin; C for the Princess Amalie Library (Amalienbibliothek) in the Joachimsthal Gymnasium, Berlin; D for the collection of Bachiana in the possession of Herr Kämmersinger Joseph Hauser, Carlsruhe, and, before him, of Franz

[1] The parts of Cantata 71 were printed for local use at Mühlhausen in 1708. On the whole subject see Schweitzer, chap. xii.

Hauser (1794-1870), the friend of Mendelssohn and one of the earliest Bach collectors. The italic letters *p* and *s* stand respectively for the Autograph Parts and Autograph Score of the works. In the case of private owners a date in brackets indicates the year when the MS. was in their possession.

THE ORATORIOS, "PASSIONS," MASSES, &c.

"St Matthew Passion." B *p s.*
"St John Passion." B *p s.*
"Christmas Oratorio." B *p s.*
"Easter Oratorio." B *p s.*
"Magnificat." B *s.*
B minor Mass. The Parts of the "Kyrie" and "Gloria" are in the King of Saxony's Privat-Bibliothek, Dresden; the Score and Parts of the "Sanctus" are in B. For the rest of the work early copies by Kirnberger and others, and the Score and Parts of Cantatas in which certain numbers of the Mass are found, have been utilised to present a complete text of the work.
Mass in F major. An early copy of the Score in the handwriting of Bach's son-in-law, Altnikol, is in B.
Mass in A major. Breitkopf & Haertel. *p s.*
Mass in G minor. Two copies of the Score, one in Altnikol's hand, are in B.
Mass in G major. Breitkopf & Haertel. *s.*
"Sanctus" in C. B *p s.*
"Sanctus" in D. B *p s.*
"Sanctus" in D minor. B *s.*
"Sanctus" in G major. B *s.*

THE CANTATAS

Ach Gott, vom Himmel sieh darein. No. 2. Professor Ernst Rudorff, Berlin. *s* [*c.* 1850]. A *p.*
Ach Gott, wie manches Herzeleid. No. 3. D *s.* A *p.*
Ach Gott, wie manches Herzeleid. No. 58. D *s.* A *p.*
Ach Herr, mich armen Sünder. No. 135. Fräulein Marianne Karthaus, Zschepen [1881]. *s.*
Ach, ich sehe, jetzt da ich zur Hochzeit gehe. No. 162. B *p.* Copy Score D.
Ach, lieben Christen, seid getrost. No. 114. A *p.* Professor Ernst Rudorff, Berlin. *s* [1876].
Ach, wie flüchtig. No. 26. B *s.* A *p.*
Ärgre dich, O Seele, nicht. No. 186. B *s.*
Allein zu dir, Herr Jesu Christ. No. 33. A *p.* Pastor Schubring, Dessau. *s* [1857].
Alles nur nach Gottes Willen. No. 72. B *p s.*
Also hat Gott die Welt geliebt. No. 68. A *p.*
Am Abend aber desselbigen Sabbaths. No. 42. B *p s.*
Auf Christi Himmelfahrt allein. No. 128. Hof-Capellmeister Robert Radecke, Berlin. *s* [1878]. D *p.*
Aus der Tiefe rufe ich, Herr, zu dir. No. 131. Wilhelm Rust. *s* [1881].
Aus tiefer Noth schrei ich zu dir. No. 38. A *p.* Copy Score by C. P. E. Bach and J. F. Agricola in C.

Barmherziges Herze der ewigen Liebe. No. 185. B *p s.*
Bereitet die Wege, bereitet die Bahn. No. 132. B *p* (incomplete) *s.*
Bisher habt ihr nichts gebeten in meinem Namen. No. 87. B *p s.*
Bleib' bei uns, denn es will Abend werden. No. 6. B *p* and copy of the Score.
Brich dem Hungrigen dein Brod. No. 39. B *p s.*
Bringet dem Herrn Ehre seines Namens. No. 148. No originals. Copy (*c.* 1754) of the Score in B.

APPENDIX III 577

Christ lag in Todesbanden. No. 4. A *p*.
Christ unser Herr zum Jordan kam. No. 7. A *p*.
Christen, ätzet diesen Tag. No. 63. B *p*.
Christum wir sollen loben schon. No. 121. A *p*. D *s*.
Christus, der ist mein Leben. No. 95. B *p*.
Das ist je gewisslich wahr. No. 141. No originals. Copy Score B.
Das neugebor'ne Kindelein. No. 122. A *p*. D *s*.
Dazu ist erschienen der Sohn Gottes. No. 40. B *p s*.
Dem Gerechten muss das Licht. No. 195. B *p s*.
Denn du wirst meine Seele nicht in der Hölle lassen. No. 15. B *p s*.
Der Friede sei mit dir. No. 158. No originals. Copy (*c.* 1754) Score D.
Der Herr denket an uns. No. 196. No originals. Copy Score C.
Der Herr ist mein getreuer Hirt. No. 112. A *p*. Frau Hoffmeister. *s* [1876].
Der Himmel lacht, die Erde jubiliret. No. 31. B *p*.
Die Elenden sollen essen. No. 75. B *s*.
Die Himmel erzählen die Ehre Gottes. No. 76. B *p s*.
Du Friedefürst, Herr Jesu Christ. No. 116. A *p*. Professor Ernst Rudorff. *s* [1876].
Du Hirte Israel, höre. No. 104. B *p*.
Du sollst Gott, deinen Herren, lieben. No. 77. B *s*.
Du wahrer Gott und Davids Sohn. No. 23. B *p s*.

Ehre sei Gott in der Höhe. No. U 1. Professor J. Epstein, Vienna. *s* [1894].
Ein Herz, das seinen Jesum lebend weiss. No. 134. B *p*. Herr W. Kraukling, Dresden. *s* [1881].
Ein ungefärbt Gemüthe. No. 24. B *p s*.
Ein' feste Burg ist unser Gott. No. 80. No originals. Copies of the Score in the handwriting of Bach's pupils Altnikol and Kirnberger B and C.
Er rufet seinen Schafen mit Namen. No. 175. B *p s*.

578   APPENDIX III

Erforsche mich, Gott, und erfahre mein Herz. No. 136. B *p*.
Erfreut euch, ihr Herzen. No. 66. B *s*.
Erfreute Zeit im neuen Bunde. No. 83. B *p*.
Erhalt' uns, Herr, bei deinem Wort. No. 126. A *p*. Copy of the Score D.
Erhöhtes Fleisch und Blut. No. 173. B *s*.
Erschallet, ihr Lieder. No. 172. B *p* and copy Score.
Erwünschtes Freudenlicht. No. 184. B *p s*.
Es erhub sich ein Streit. No. 19. B *p s*.
Es ist das Heil uns kommen her. No. 9. A *p*.
Es ist dir gesagt, Mensch, was gut ist. No. 45. B *p s*.
Es ist ein trotzig uns verzagt Ding. No. 176. B *s*.
Es ist euch gut, dass ich hingehe. No. 108. B *p s*.
Es ist nichts Gesundes an meinem Leibe. No. 25. B *p*.
Es reifet euch ein schrecklich Ende. No. 90. B *s*.
Es wartet Alles auf dich. No. 187. B *s* and *p* (vocal). Professor Ernst Rudorff. *p* (instrumental) [1891].

Falsche Welt, dir trau ich nicht. No. 52. B *p s*.
Freue dich, erlöste Schaar. No. 30. B *p s*.

Gedenke, Herr, wie es uns gehet. No. D 1. Copy Score C.
Geist und Seele wird verwirret. No. 35. B *p s*.
Gelobet sei der Herr. No. 129. A *p*. Copy of Score D.
Gelobet seist du, Jesu Christ. No. 91. A *p*. Kirnberger's copy of the Score C.
Gleich wie der Regen und Schnee. No. 18. B *p*.
Gloria in excelsis Deo. No. 191. D *s*.
Gott, der Herr, ist Sonn' und Schild. No. 79. B *p s*.
Gott der Hoffnung erfülle euch. No. D 2. Copies of Score B C.
Gott fähret auf mit Jauchzen. No. 43. B *p s*.
Gott ist mein König. No. 71. B *p s*.
Gott ist uns're Zuversicht. No. 197. B *s*.
Gott, man lobet dich in der Stille. No. 120. D *s*.
Gott soll allein mein Herze haben. No. 169. B *p s*.

APPENDIX III 579

Gott, wie dein Name, so ist auch dein Ruhm. No. 171.
Herr Max Jähn, Berlin. *s* [1888].
Gottes Zeit ist die allerbeste Zeit. No. 106. No originals.
Copy Score D.
Gottlob! nun geht das Jahr zu Ende. No. 28. B *p s*.
Halt' im Gedächtniss Jesum Christ. No. 67. B *p s*.
Herr Christ, der ein'ge Gottes-Sohn. No. 96. A *p*. B *s*.
Herr, deine Augen sehen nach dem Glauben. No. 102.
B *p s*.
Herr, gehe nicht in's Gericht. No. 105. B *s*.
Herr Gott, Beherrscher aller Dinge. No. U 3. B *p*.
Herr Gott, dich loben alle wir. No. 130. Professor Woldemar
Bargiel, Berlin. *s* [1878]. Mr Locker, London, Soprano
and Alto vocal parts [1878].
Herr Gott dich loben wir. No. 16. B *p s*.
Herr Jesu Christ, du höchstes Gut. No. 113. Professor
Ernst Rudorff, Berlin. *s* [1876].
Herr Jesu Christ, wahr'r Mensch und Gott. No. 127. A *p*. D *s*.
Herr, wie du willt, so schick's mit mir. No. 73. B *p*.
Herz und Mund und That und Leben. No. 147. B *s*.
Himmelskönig, sei willkommen. No. 182. B *p s*.
Höchsterwünschtes Freudenfest. No. 194. B *s*.

Ich armer Mensch, ich Sündenknecht. No. 55. B *p s*.
Ich bin ein guter Hirt. No. 85. B *p s*.
Ich bin vergnügt mit meinem Glücke. No. 84. B *p s*.
Ich elender Mensch, wer wird mich erlösen. No. 48. B *p s*.
Ich freue mich in dir. No. 133. A and D *p*. Herr Ernst
Mendelssohn. *s* [1881].
Ich geh' und suche mit Verlangen. No. 49. B *p s*.
Ich glaube, lieber Herr. No. 109. B *p s*.
Ich habe genug. No. 82. B *p s*.
Ich hab' in Gottes Herz und Sinn. No. 92. A *p*.
Ich habe meine Zuversicht. No. 188. No originals. Copy
of the Score in the Fischhof Sammlung B.
Ich hatte viel Bekümmerniss. No. 21. B *p*.

580 APPENDIX III

Ich lasse dich nicht, du segnest mich denn. No. 157. No originals. Copy Score (*c.* 1754) D.
Ich liebe den Höchsten von ganzem Gemüthe. No. 174. B *p* (incomplete) *s*.
Ich ruf' zu dir, Herr Jesu Christ. No. 177. A *p*. B *s*.
Ich steh' mit einem Fuss im Grabe. No. 156. A *p*.
Ich weiss, dass mein Erlöser lebt. No. 160. No originals. Early copy of the Score, Wilhelm Rust.
Ich will den Kreuzstab gerne tragen. No. 56. B *p s*.
Ihr, die ihr euch von Christo nennet. No. 164. B *p s*.
Ihr Menschen, rühmet Gottes Liebe. No. 167. B *p* and Kirnberger's copy of Score.
Ihr Pforten zu Zion. No. 193. B *p* (incomplete).
Ihr werdet weinen und heulen. No. 103. B *p s*.
In allen meinen Thaten. No. 97. B *p*. Mr Locker, London *s* [1875].
Jauchzet Gott in allen Landen. No. 51. B *p s*.
Jesu, der du meine Seele. No. 78. A *p*.
Jesu, nun sei gepreiset. No. 41. A *p*. D *s*.
Jesus nahm zu sich die Zwölfe. No. 22. B *s*.
Jesus schläft, was soll ich hoffen? No. 81. B *p s*.

Komm, du süsse Todesstunde. No. 161. No originals. Three copies of Score B.

Leichtgesinnte Flattergeister. No. 181. B *p* and copy *s*.
Liebster Gott, wann werd' ich sterben? No. 8. A *p* and copy *s*.
Liebster Immanuel, Herzog der Frommen. No. 123. A*p*. D*s*.
Liebster Jesu, mein Verlangen. No. 32. B *p s*.
Lobe den Herren, den mächtigen König der Ehren. No. 137. A *p*.
Lobe den Herrn, meine Seele. No. 69. B *p*.
Lobe den Herrn, meine Seele. No. 143. No originals. Copy Score B.
Lobet Gott in seinen Reichen. No. 11. B *p s*.
Lobt ihn mit Herz und Munde. No. D 4. Copies Score B C.

APPENDIX III 581

Mache dich, mein Geist, bereit. No. 115. Professor Ernst
Rudorff. *s* [1876].
Man singet mit Freuden vom Sieg. No. 149. No originals.
Copy Score dated 1756, D.
Mein Gott, wie lang', ach lange. No. 155. B *s*.
Mein Herze schwimmt im Blut. No. 199. Score in Royal
Library, Copenhagen.
Mein liebster Jesus ist verloren. No. 154. B *p* and *s* (incomplete).
Meine Seel' erhebt den Herren. No. 10. Professor Ernst
Rudorff. *s*.
Meine Seele rühmt und preist. No. 189. No originals.
Copy Score (Fischhof Sammlung) B.
Meine Seufzer, meine Thränen. No. 13. B *p s*.
Meinen Jesum lass' ich nicht. No. 124. A *p*. D *s*.
Mit Fried' und Freud' ich fahr' dahin. No. 125. A *p*.
Copy Score D.

Nach dir, Herr, verlanget mich. No. 150. No originals.
Copy Score dated 1753, D.
Nimm von uns, Herr, du treuer Gott. No. 101. A *p*. Copy
Score (perhaps in C. P. E. Bach's hand) C.
Nimm, was dein ist, und gehe hin. No. 144. B *s*.
Nun danket alle Gott. No. 192. B *p*.
Nun ist das Heil und die Kraft. No. 50. No originals.
Copies in B.
Nun komm, der Heiden Heiland. No. 61. B *s*.
Nun komm, der Heiden Heiland. No. 62. A *p*.
Nur Jedem das Seine. No. 163. B *s*.

O ewiges Feuer, O Ursprung der Liebe. No. 34. B *p*. C *s*.
O ewiges Feuer, O Ursprung der Liebe. No. U 2. B *p*.
O Ewigkeit, du Donnerwort. No. 20. A *p*. Professor
Ernst Rudorff. *s*.
O Ewigkeit, du Donnerwort. No. 60. B *p*.
O heil'ges Geist- und Wasserbad. No. 165. No originals.
Copy Score C.

582   APPENDIX III

O Jesu Christ, mein's Lebens Licht. No. 118. Breitkopf
 & Haertel. *s*.
Preise, Jerusalem, den Herrn. No. 119. D *s*.
Schau', lieber Gott, wie meine Feind'. No. 153. B *p*.
Schauet doch und sehet. No. 46. B *p*.
Schlage doch, gewünschte Stunde. No. 53. No originals.
 Copies C.
Schmücke dich, O liebe Seele. No. 180. Mme Pauline
 Viardot-Garcia, Paris. *s* [1888]. Formerly in Felix
 Mendelssohn's possession.
Schwingt freudig euch empor. No. 36. B *p s*.
Sehet, welch' eine Liebe. No. 64. B *p*. Copy Score C.
Sehet, wir geh'n hinauf gen Jerusalem. No. 159. No
 originals. Copy Score (*c.* 1754) D.
Sei Lob und Ehr'. No. 117. Breitkopf & Haertel. *s*.
Selig ist der Mann. No. 57. B *p s*.
Sie werden aus Saba Alle kommen. No. 65. B *s*.
Sie werden euch in den Bann thun. No. 44. B *p s*.
Sie werden euch in den Bann thun. No. 183. B *p s*.
Siehe, es hat überwunden der Löwe. No. D 3. Copy Score B.
Siehe, ich will viel Fischer aussenden. No. 88. B *p s*.
Siehe zu, dass deine Gottesfurcht. No. 179. B *s* and *p*
 (incomplete).
Singet dem Herrn ein neues Lied. No. 190. B *s* (incomplete) and *p* (incomplete).
So du mit deinem Munde bekennest Jesum. No. 145. No
 originals. Copy Score (1816) B.
Süsser Trost, mein Jesus kommt. No. 151. B *p*.
Thue Rechnung! Donnerwort. No. 168. B *p s*.
Trauerode. No. 198. B *s*.
Tritt auf die Glaubensbahn. No. 152. B *s*.
Uns ist ein Kind geboren. No. 142. No originals. Copy
 Score B.
Unser Mund sei voll Lachens. No. 110. B *p s*.
Vergnügte Ruh', beliebte Seelenlust. No. 170. B *p s*.

APPENDIX III 583

Wachet auf, ruft uns die Stimme. No. 140. A *p*.
Wachet, betet, betet, wachet. No. 70. B *p*.
Wär' Gott nicht mit uns diese Zeit. No. 14. D *p s*.
Wahrlich, wahrlich, ich sage euch. No. 86. B *s*.
Warum betrübst du dich, mein Herz. No. 138. B *s*.
Was frag ich nach der Welt. No. 94. A *p*. B *s*.
Was Gott thut, das ist wohlgethan. No. 98. B *p s*.
Was Gott thut, das ist wohlgethan. No. 99. A *p*. B *s*.
Was Gott thut, das ist wohlgethan. No. 100. B *p s*.
Was mein Gott will, das g'scheh' allzeit. No. 111. D *p s*.
Was soll ich aus dir machen, Ephraim? No. 89. B *p*.
Was willst du dich betrüben. No. 107. A *p*.
Weinen, Klagen, Sorgen, Zagen. No. 12. B *p s*.
Wer da glaubet und getauft wird. No. 37. B *p*.
Wer Dank opfert, der preiset mich. No. 17. B *p s*.
Wer mich liebet, der wird mein Wort halten. No. 59. B *p s*.
Wer mich liebet, der wird mein Wort halten. No. 74. B *p*.
Wer nur den lieben Gott lässt walten. No. 93. A *p*.
Wer sich selbst erhöhet. No. 47. B *p s*.
Wer weiss, wie nahe mir mein Ende. No. 27. B *p s*.
Widerstehe doch der Sünde. No. 54. No originals. Copy Score D.
Wie schön leuchtet der Morgenstern. No. 1. A *p*.
Wir danken dir, Gott. No. 29. B *p s*.
Wir müssen durch viel Trübsal in das Reich Gottes eingehen. No. 146. No originals. Copy Score (*c*. 1760) B.
Wo gehest du hin? No. 166. B *p* and copy (Fischhof) Score.
Wo Gott der Herr nicht bei uns hält. No. 178. A *p*. Forkel's copy Score B.
Wo soll ich fliehen hin. No. 5. A *p*. Professor Ernst Rudorff. *s*.
Wohl dem, der sich auf seinen Gott. No. 139. A *p*.

* * * *

Drei Choräle zu Trauungen. B *p s*.

APPENDIX III

THE MOTETTS

The only original MSS. extant are the following[1]:

Der Geist hilft unsrer Schwachheit auf. No. 2. B *s.*
Singet dem Herrn ein neues Lied. No. 1. B *s.*

[1] "Lobet den Herrn," No. 6, was published in 1821 "nach J. S. Bach's Original-handschrift." The other five Motetts were published in 1803.

INDEX

OF FIRST LINES, MELODIES, AUTHORS, COMPOSERS, SOURCES

NOTE. The titles of the Cantatas and Motetts are printed in capitals. Plain numbers stand for the Cantatas; a prefixed M indicates the Motetts; a prefixed U, the unfinished Cantatas; a prefixed D, the Cantatas of doubtful authenticity. Biographical details will be found at the first entry after an author's name. A * prefixed to an author's name indicates that biographical details will be found in Part I of this work. Entries in italic indicate the first line of a Hymn or stanza.

A solis ortus cardine, melody, 121
A STRONGHOLD SURE, 80
A STRONGHOLD SURE IS GOD OUR LORD, 80
Ach bleib' bei uns, Herr Jesu Christ, st. i, 6; st. ii, 6; trans., App. II (1); melody, 6
Ach, dass nicht die letzte Stunde, melody, Introd. p. 74
Ach Gott und Herr, st. iv, 48; trans., App. II (2); melody, 48
ACH GOTT, VOM HIMMEL SIEH DAREIN, 2
Ach Gott, vom Himmel sieh' darein, st. i, 2; st. vi, 2; trans., App. II (3); melody, 2, 77, 153
ACH GOTT, WIE MANCHES HERZELEID, 3, 58
Ach Gott, wie manches Herzeleid, st. i, 3, 44, 58; st. ii, 3; st. xi, 153; st. xii, 3, 153; trans., App. II (4); melody, 3, 44, 58, 118, 153
Ach! Herr Gott, durch die Treue dein, 101
Ach Herr, lass dein' lieb' Engelein, 149
Ach Herr, mein Geist, vergieb mir's doch, 113
ACH HERR, MICH ARMEN SÜNDER, 135
Ach Herr, mich armen Sünder, st. i, 135; st. vi, 135; trans., App. II (5); melody, 25

586   INDEX

Ach Herr, vergieb all' unsre Schuld, 127
Ach, ich habe schon erblicket, 162
ACH, ICH SEHE, JETZT DA ICH ZUR HOCHZEIT GEHE, 162
ACH, LIEBEN CHRISTEN, SEID GETROST, 114
Ach, lieben Christen, seid getrost, st. i, 114; st. iii, 114; st. vi, 114; trans., App. II (6)
ACH WIE FLÜCHTIG, 26
Ach wie flüchtig, st. i, 26; st. xiii, 26; trans., App. II (7); melody, 26
Ach, wie hungert mein Gemüthe, 180
"Actus Tragicus," 106
ÄRGRE DICH, O SEELE, NICHT, 186
Agricola, Johannes (1492-1566), 177, 185
AH GOD, IN MERCY LOOK FROM HEAVEN, 2
Ahle, Johann Rodolph (1625-73), 60, 123
"Ain schöns newes Christlichs lyed" (1530), 74, 86
Ainsi qu'on oit le cerf bruire, melody, 13, 19, 25, 30, 32, 39, 70, 194
*Albert, Heinrich (1604-51), 40, App. I (3)
Albinus, Johann Georg (1624-79), 27, 115, 158, 162
*Albrecht, Margrave of Brandenburg-Culmbach (1522-57), 72, 111, 144
All' solch' dein' Güt' wir preisen, 16, 28
Alle Menschen müssen sterben, st. vii, 162; trans., App. II (8); melody (1652), 162; melody (1715), 162; melody (1678), Introd. p. 70
Allein auf Christi Himmelfahrt, see *Auf Christi*, etc.
Allein Gott in der Hoh' sei Ehr', melody, 85, 104, 112, 128
ALLEIN ZU DIR, HERR JESU CHRIST, 33
Allein zu dir, Herr Jesu Christ, st. i, 33; st. iv, 33; trans., App. II (9); melody, 33
Alleluja, Alleluja, Alleluja! 66
Alleluja! Gelobt sei Gott! 110, 142
"Aller Christen Leib-Stücke" (Leipzig, 1633), 159
Alles ist an Gottes Segen, melody, Introd. p. 68
ALLES NUR NACH GOTTES WILLEN, 72
ALLES WAS VON GOTT GEBOREN, 80 n.
Alsdann so wirst du mich, 128
ALSO HAT GOTT DIE WELT GELIEBT, 68
Also hat Gott die Welt geliebt, st. i, 68; trans., App. II (10); melody, 68; Introd. p. 70
Altenburg, Johann Michael (1584-1640), 42
AM ABEND ABER DESSELBIGEN SABBATHS, 42
Amen! zu aller Stund', 148 n.

INDEX 587

Ammersbach, Heinrich (1673), 128
"Andacht-erweckende Seelen-Cymbeln" (1672), 78
"Andächtig Singender Christen-Mund" (Wesel, 1692), 139
"Andächtige Hertz- und Seelen-Musica" (Nordhausen, c. 1635), 42
"Andächtige Versöhnung mit Gott" (Nürnberg, 1636), 128
"Andächtiger Seelen geistliches Brand- und Gantz-Opfer" (Leipzig, 1697), M 5
"Andachts Zymbeln" (Freiberg, 1655), 48
"Arien oder Melodeyen" (Königsberg, 1642), App. I (3)
Arnold, Gottfried (1666–1714), 133
"As hymnodus sacer" (Leipzig, 1625), 3, 48
Attaignant, Pierre (1529), 65
Auf, auf, die rechte Zeit ist hier, melody, Introd. p. 75
Auf, auf, mein Herz, und du mein ganzer Sinn, melody, Introd. p. 68
AUF CHRISTI HIMMELFAHRT ALLEIN, 128
Auf Christi Himmelfahrt allein, st. i, 128; trans., App. II (11)
Auf dass wir also allzugleich, 176
AUF, MEINE HERZ! DES HERREN TAG, 145
Auf, meine Herz! des Herren Tag, st. i, 145; trans., App. II (12)
Auf meinen lieben Gott, st. i, 188; st. vi, 148 n.; trans., App. II (13); melody, 5, 89, 136, 148, 188
Aufer immensam, Deus, aufer iram, 90
Aufsperen sie den Rachen weit, 178
Augsburg "Gesangbuch" (1530–1), the, 112
AUS DER TIEFE RUFE ICH, HERR, ZU DIR, 131
AUS TIEFER NOTH SCHREI ICH ZU DIR, 38
Aus tiefer Noth schrei ich zu dir, st. i, 38; st. v, 38; trans., App. II (14); melody, 38, 156
Avenarius, Matthäus (1625–92), 128

Babst, Valentin (1545), 33
Bach, Johann Sebastian (1685–1750), his Hymn tunes, Introd. p. 67; the melody, "Ich freue mich in dir," 133; the melody, "Alle Menschen müssen sterben," 162; the melody, "Komm, Jesu, komm," M 5
Barmherzger Vater, höchster Gott, st. ix, 103; trans., App. II (15)
BARMHERZIGES HERZE DER EWIGEN LIEBE, 185
BE NOT AFRAID, M 4
Becker, Cornelius (1561–1604), 85, 104
Befiehl du deine Wege, st. v, 153; trans., App. II (16)

Behm, Martin (1557–1622), 58, 3, 118
BEREITET DIE WEGE, BEREITET DIE BAHN, 132
Beschränkt, ihr Weisen dieser Welt, melody, Introd. p. 76
Beweis' dein Macht, Herr Jesu Christ, 6
Beza, Theodore (1519–1605), 13, 127, 130
BIDE WITH US, 6
Bienemann, Caspar (1540–91), 73, 156
Bin ich gleich von dir gewichen, 55
BISHER HABT IHR NICHTS GEBETEN IN MEINEM NAMEN, 87
BLEIB' BEI UNS, DENN ES WILL ABEND WERDEN, 6
Bleiches Antlitz, sei gegrüsset, melody, 40
BLESSED JESU, PRICELESS TREASURE, 32
Bourgeois, Louis (fl. 1541–61), 13, 19, 25, 30, 32, 39, 70, 127, 130, 194
Brandenburg "Gesang-Buch" (1668), the, 27
BRICH DEM HUNGRIGEN DEIN BROD, 39
BRINGET DEM HERRN EHRE SEINES NAMENS, 148
Burmeister, Franz Joachim (1633?–72), 60

*Calvisius, Seth (1556–1615), 6, 52, 85, 106, 127, App. I (1)
"Cantilenae latinae et germanicae" (Wittenberg, 1591), 41
"Cantional, Oder Gesangbuch Augspurgischer Confession" (Leipzig, 1627), 5, 13, 52
"Cantionale sacrum" (Part II : Gotha, 1648), 46
"Chansons du XVe siècle" (Paris, 1875), 130 n.
Christ ist erstanden, 4, st. iii, 66 ; trans., App. II (17) ; melody, 66
CHRIST LAG IN TODESBANDEN, 4
Christ lag in Todesbanden, st. i–vii, 4 ; st. v, 158 ; trans., App. II (18) ; melody, 4, 158
CHRIST LAY FAST BOUND IN DEATH'S HARSH CHAIN, 4
CHRIST LAY IN DEATH'S DARK PRISON, 4
CHRIST UNSER HERR ZUM JORDAN KAM, 7
Christ unser Herr zum Jordan kam, st. i, 7 ; st. vii, 7 ; trans., App. II (19) ; melody, 7, 69, 176
Christe, du Lamm Gottes, 23 ; trans., App. II (20) ; melody, 23, 127
"Christlich- neuvermehrt und gebessertes Gesangbuch" (Erfurt, 1663), 78
"Christliche Bet-Schule" (Leipzig, 1665), 129
"Christliche Gebet" (1610), 58
"Christliche Kirchen-Ordnung" (Erfurt, 1542), App. I (5)
"Christliche Psalmen, Lieder, und Kirchengesenge" (Leipzig, 1587), 79

INDEX 589

"Christliche und Tröstliche Tischgesenge" (Erfurt, 1572 [1571]), 11, 65
"Christlichen Frauen-Zimmers geistliche Tugend-Spiegel" (Leipzig, 1675), 68
"Christliches Gedenckbüchlein, zu Beförderung eines anfangenden neuen Lebens" (Frankfort a. Main, 1675), 117
CHRISTUM WIR SOLLEN LOBEN SCHON, 121
Christum wir sollen loben schon, st. i, 121; st. viii, 121; trans., App. II (21); melody, 121
CHRISTUS, DER IST MEIN LEBEN, 95
Christus, der ist mein Leben, st. i, 95; trans., App. II (22); melody, 95
Christus, der uns selig macht, melody, App. I (1)
Clauder, Joseph (1630), 3
COME, JESU, COME, M 5
COME, REDEEMER OF OUR RACE, 61
COME REJOICE, YE FAITHFUL, 30
COME, THOU BLESSED SAVIOUR, COME, 61
Cornu, see Roh, Johann
Crespin, Jean (1551), 13
Cruciger, Caspar (1524), 22
Cruciger, Elisabethe (d. 1535), 22, 96, 132, 164
*Crüger, Johann (1598–1662), 11, 20, 26, 40, 56, 60, 64, 65, 67, 74, 78, 79, 81, 87, 103, 139, 145, 159, 162, 176, 180, 183, 192, 194, 195, M 3, M 4, App. I (4)

Da Christus geboren war, melody, 187
Da der Herr Christ zu Tische sass, melody, Introd. p. 70
Da pacem, Domine, 6
Dahero Trotz der Höllen Heer, 139
Dank sei Gott in der Höhe, melody, Introd. p. 69
Danket dem Herrn, heut' und allzeit, melody, 6
Daphnis ging für wenig Tagen, melody, 78
Darmstadt "Cantional" (1687), the, 162; "Gesang-Buch" (1698), 45, 123
Darum wir billig loben dich, 130
Das Aug' allein das Wasser sieht, 7
"Das christlich Kinderlied D. Martini Lutheri" (Wittenberg, 1566), 42
"Das grosse Cantional" (Darmstadt, 1687), 162
Das hat er Alles uns gethan, 64, 91
Das ist des Vaters Wille, 73
Das macht Christus, wahr'r Gottes Sohn, 125

DAS NEUGEBOR'NE KINDELEIN, 122
Das neugebor'ne Kindelein, st. i, 122 ; st. iii, 122 ; st. iv, 122 ; trans., App. II (23) ; melody, 122
Das walt' Gott Vater und Gott Sohn, melody, Introd. p. 69
Das walt mein Gott, Gott Vater, Sohn, melody, Introd. p. 78
Das wollst du, Gott, bewahren rein, 2
Das Wort sie sollen lassen stahn, 80
DAZU IST ERSCHIENEN DER SOHN GOTTES, 40
*Decius, Nicolaus (d. 1541), 85, 104, 112, 128 ; App. I (5)
Dein Blut, der edle Saft, 136
Dein Geist, den Gott vom Himmel giebt, 108
Dein ist allein die Ehre, 41, 171
Deine Hülfe zu mir sende, 194
DEM GERECHTEN MUSS DAS LICHT, 195
Dem wir das Heilig itzt, 129
Demantius, Christopher (1620), 13, 19, 48, 135
Den Glauben mir verleihe, 37
Den Herren meine Seel' erhebt, melody, 74
Den Himmel und auch die Erden, 178
Den Tod Niemand zwingen kunnt, 4
Denicke, David (1603–80), 39, 77, 107, 153, D 3
Denk' nicht in deiner Drangsalshitze, 21, 93
DENN DU WIRST MEINE SEELE NICHT IN DER HÖLLE LASSEN, 15
"Der Bussfertige Sünder" (Nürnberg, 1679), 163
Der du bist dem Vater gleich, 36
DER FRIEDE SEI MIT DIR, 158
DER GEIST HILFT UNSRER SCHWACHHEIT AUF, M 2
Der Gott, der mir hat versprochen, 13
DER HERR IST MEIN GETREUER HIRT, 112
Der Herr ist mein getreuer Hirt (Becker), st. i, 85, 104; trans., App. II (24)
Der Herr ist mein getreuer Hirt (Meusel), st. i, 112 ; st. v, 112 ; trans., App. II (25)
DER HIMMEL LACHT, DIE ERDE JUBILIRET, 31
Der Leib zwar in der Erden, 161
"Der Psalter Dauids Gesangweis" (Leipzig, 1602), 85
Der zeitlichen Ehr' will ich gern entbehr'n, 47
"Des Daphnis aus Cimbrien Galathee" (Hamburg, 1642), 78
Des ew'gen Vaters einig's Kind, 91
"Deutsch Euangelisch Messze" (Altstadt, 1524), 64
"Devoti Musica Cordis" (Leipzig, 1630), 5, 24, 25, 102, 107, 194 ; (2nd edit. Leipzig, 1636), 13
Dich bet ich an, mein höchster Gott, melody, Introd. p. 79
Dicimus grates tibi, summe rerum, 130

INDEX 591

" Die Eitelheit, Falschheit und Unbeständigkeit der Welt"
 (Coburg, 1652), 26
DIE ELENDEN SOLLEN ESSEN, 75
Die Feind' sind all' in deiner Hand, 178
DIE HIMMEL ERZÄHLEN DIE EHRE GOTTES, 76
"Die Historien von der Sindfludt" (Wittenberg, 1562
 [1560]), 15
Die Hoffnung wart't der rechten Zeit, 86
Die Kön'ge aus Saba kamen dar, 65
"Die Sontags Euangelia" (Wittenberg, 1560), 67, 151
Die Sünd' hat uns verderbet sehr, 101
Die Sünd' macht Leid, 40
Die Welt bekümmert sich, 94
Die Welt sucht Ehr' und Ruhm, 94
Die Wollust dieser Welt, melody, 45, 64, 94, 128, 129, U 1
Dies sind die heil'gen zehn Gebot', melody, 77
Dir, dir, Jehovah, will ich singen, melody, Introd. p. 80
Drauf schliess' ich mich in deine Hände, M 5
Dresden "Gesangbuch" (1593), the, 40, 48; (1625), 135 n.
"Drey schöne Newe Geistliche Gesenge" (1592), 40
Drum fahrt nur immerhin, ihr Eitelkeiten, 123
Drum so lasst uns immerdar, 115
Drum will ich, weil ich lebe noch, 153
Drum wir auch billig fröhlich sein, 145
Du bist ein Geist, der lehret, 183
Du bist mein, weil ich dich fasse, M 4
DU FRIEDEFÜRST, HERR JESU CHRIST, 116
Du Friedefürst, Herr Jesu Christ, st. i, 67, 116, 143;
 st. iii, 143; st. vii, 116; trans., App. II (26); melody,
 67, 116, 143
Du geballtes Weltgebäude, 56
Du heilige Brunst, süsser Trost, M 2
DU HIRTE ISRAEL, HÖRE, 104
Du Lebensfürst, Herr Jesu Christ, st. i, 43; st. iv, 11;
 st. xiii, 43; trans., App. II (27)
Du, O schönes Weltgebäude, st. vi, 56; trans., App. II
 (28); melody, 56
DU SOLLST GOTT, DEINEN HERREN, LIEBEN, 77
Du stellst, mein Jesu, selber dich, 77
Du süsse Liebe, schenk' uns deine Gunst, 169, 197
DU WAHRER GOTT UND DAVIDS SOHN, 23
Durch Adams Fall ist ganz verderbt, st. vii, 109; st. viii,
 18; trans., App. II (29); melody, 18, 103, 109

*Ebeling, Johann Georg (1637-76), M 4

Eber, Paul (1511-69), 16, 11, 28, 127, 130
Ebert, Jakob (1549-1614), 67, 116, 143
Ehr' sei Gott in dem höchsten Thron, 33
EHRE SEI GOTT IN DER HÖHE, U 1
Ehr' sei in's Himmels Throne, 135
Ei nun, mein Gott, so fall' ich dir, 65, 92
Eichorn, Johann (1561-69), 16, 130, 187
"Ein Andächtiges Buss-Lied" (Leipzig, 1632), 46
"Ein ander new Opus Geistlicher Deutscher Lieder" (Frankfort, 1605), 3, 5
"Ein ausszug guter alter ūn newer Teutscher liedlein" (Nürnberg, 1539), 13
Ein Kind geborn zu Bethlehem, st. iv, 65; trans., App. II (31); melody, 65
"Ein New Gesengbuchlen" (Jung Bunzlau, 1531), App. I (1)
"Ein Schlesich singebüchlein" (Breslau, 1555), 67
"Ein schön geistlich Gesangbuch" (Jena, 1609), 5, 95, 106, 122, 159
EIN UNGEFÄRBT GEMÜTHE, 24
EIN' FESTE BURG IST UNSER GOTT, 80
Ein' feste Burg ist unser Gott, st. i-iv, 80; trans., App. II (30); melody, 80
Eine Stimme lässt sich hören, 30
Einen guten Kampf hab' ich, melody, 40
Eins ist noth; ach Herr, dies eine, melody, Introd. p. 82
Emilie Juliane Countess of Schwarzburg-Rudolstadt (1637-1706), 27, 84, 166
"Enchiridion Geistliker Leder und Psalmen D. Mar. Luth." (Hamburg, 1565), 127
"Enchiridion Oder eyn Handbuchlein" (Erfurt, 1524), 2, 4, 9, 22, 36, 59, 77, 121, D 2 (Erfurt, 1527), 184
Entlaubt ist uns der Walde, melody, 37
Er ist das Heil und selig Licht, 83, 125.
Er kann und will dich lassen nicht, 138
Er kennt die rechten Freudenstunden, 93
ER RUFET SEINEN SCHAFEN MIT NAMEN, 175
Erbarm' dich mein in solcher Last, 113, 131
ERFORSCHE MICH, GOTT, UND ERFAHRE MEIN HERZ, 136
ERFREUT EUCH, IHR HERZEN, 66
ERFREUTE ZEIT IM NEUEN BUNDE, 83
Erhalt' mein Herz im Glauben rein, 3, 153
ERHALT' UNS, HERR, BEI DEINEM WORT, 126
Erhalt' uns, Herr, bei deinem Wort, st. i, 126; st. ii, 6; st. iii, 126; trans., App. II (32); melody, 6, 42, 126
Erhalt' uns in der Wahrheit, 79

INDEX 593

Erleucht' auch unsern Sinn und Herz, 116
Ermuntre dich, mein schwacher Geist, melody, 11, 43
Ernesti, Johann Heinrich (d. 1729), Introd. p. 46 n.
"Ernewertes Gesangbuch" (Stralsund, 1665), 57
ERSCHALLET, IHR LIEDER, 172
Erschienen ist der herrlich' Tag, st. i, 67; st. xiv, 145; trans., App. II (33); melody, 67
Erstanden ist der heil'ge Christ, melody, 67
Ertödt' uns durch dein' Güte, 22, 96, 132, 164
ERWÜNSCHTES FREUDENLICHT, 184
Es bringt das rechte Jubeljahr, 122
Es danke, Gott, und lobe dich, 69, 76
ES ERHUB SICH EIN STREIT, 19
ES IST DAS HEIL UNS KOMMEN HER, 9
Es ist das Heil uns kommen her, 9, st. i, 9; st. xi, 86; st. xii, 9, 155, 186; trans., App. II (34); melody, 9, 86, 117, 155, 186
ES IST DIR GESAGT, MENSCH, WAS GUT IST, 45
ES IST EIN TROTZIG UND VERZAGT DING, 176
ES IST EUCH GUT, DASS ICH HINGEHE, 108
Es ist genug: Herr, wenn es dir gefällt, 60
Es ist genug; so nimm, Herr, meinen Geist, st. v, 60; trans., App. II (35); melody, 60
Es ist gewisslich an der Zeit, melody, 70
ES IST NICHTS GESUNDES AN MEINEM LEIBE, 25
Es kann mir fehlen nimmermehr, 92
ES REIFET EUCH EIN SCHRECKLICH ENDE, 90
Es sind doch selig alle, melody, App. I (2)
Es sind ja Gott sehr schlechte Sachen, 93
Es war ein wunderlicher Krieg, 4
ES WARTET ALLES AUF DICH, 187
Es woll' uns Gott genädig sein, st. i, 76; st. iii, 69, 76; trans., App. II (36); melody, 7, 69, 76
"Etlich Christlich lider Lobgesang, und Psalm" (Wittenberg, 1524), 2, 9, 38
"Eyn Enchiridion oder Handbuchlein" (Erfurt, 1524), 38, 178, see "Enchiridion"
"Eyn gesang Buchleyn" (Zwickau, 1525), 178

Fabricius, Werner (1633-79), 12, 8
Falck, Georg (1672), 78
FALSCHE WELT, DIR TRAU ICH NICHT, 52
Ferdinand, du grosser Kaiser, melody, 78
"Fest- Bus- und Danck-Lieder" (Zittau, 1659), 70
*Figulus, Wolfgang (c. 1520-91), 11

T. B. C. 38

Flemming, Paul (1609–40), 13, 44, 97
Flora, meine Freude, 64
FOR THE RIGHTEOUS THE LIGHT HATH AWAKENED, 195
" Form und Ordnung Gaystlicher Gesang und Psalmen " (Augsburg, 1533), 52
Forster, Georg (1539), 13
" Fortgepflantzter Musikalisch-Poetischer Lustwald " (Jena, 1657), 21
Franc, Guillaume (d. 1570), 13
*Franck, Johan (1618–77), 56, 64, 81, 180, M 3
Franck, Melchior (d. 1639), 46, 133
Franck, Michael (1609–67), 26
Franck, Salomo (1659–1725), Introd. p. 6 n.
Freu' dich du werthe Christenheit, melody, 9
FREUE DICH, ERLÖSTER SCHAAR, 30
Freu' dich sehr, O meine Seele, st. ix, 19 ; st. x, 70 ; trans., App. II (37) ; melody (see " Ainsi qu'on oit le cerf ")
Freuet euch, ihr Christen alle, st. iv, 40 ; trans., App. II (38) ; melody, 40
" Frewden Spiegel dess ewigen Lebens " (Frankfort, 1599), 1, 140
Freylinghausen, Johann Anastasius (1670–1739), 107
Freystein, Johann Burchard (1671–1718), 115
Frisch auf, mein Geist, sei wohlgemuth, melody, 12
Fritsch, Ahashuerus (1629–1701), 57, 45, 123, 163
Fritzsch, Martin (1593), 40, 110 n.
FROM DEPTHS OF WOE I CALL ON THEE, 38
" Frommer Christen Tägliches Bet-Kämmerlein " (Görlitz, 1661), 147
Führ' auch mein Herz und Sinn, 5, 148, 163
" Fünff Schöne Geistliche Lieder " (Dresden, 1556), 72
Für Freuden lasst uns springen, melody, Introd. p. 71
FÜRCHTE DICH NICHT, ICH BIN BEI DIR, M 4
*Fuger, Caspar (d. *c.* 1592), 40, 110, 142
*Fuger, Caspar (d. 1617), 40, 110, 142
Funcke, Friedrich (1642–99), 40

Gastorius, Severus (1675), 12
Gaudete omnes populi, 80 n.
Gedenk' an deins Sohns bittern Todt, 101
Gedenk' an Jesu bittern Tod, 101
Gedenke doch, mein Geist, zurücke, melody, Introd. p. 83
Gedenk', Herr Jesu, an dein Amt, 143
" Geistliche Andachten " (Berlin, 1666–67), 108, M 4
" Geistliche deutsche Lieder " (Frankfort, 1601), 67

INDEX 595

"Geistliche Kirchen-Melodien" (Leipzig, 1649), 56, 180
"Geistliche Lieder" (Frankfort a. Oder, c. 1580), 16
"Geistliche Lieder" (Wittenberg, 1529-35), 16, 18, 42, 59, 66, 73, 80, 177, 178, D 2
"Geistliche lieder auffs new gebessert und gemehrt" (Leipzig, 1539), 37, 85, 90, App. I (7)
"Geistliche Lieder D. Mart. Lut." (Frankfort a. Oder, 1561), 130; (1569), 187
"Geistliche Lieder, den Gottseligen Christen zugericht" (Mühlhausen, 1575), 79
"Geistliche Lieder und Psalmen" (Berlin, 1653), 20, 79, 145
"Geistliche Lieder und Psalmen" (Erfurt, 1597), 122, 135
"Geistliche Lieder zu Wittemberg" (Wittenberg, 1543), 6, 65
"Geistliche Psalmen" (Nürnberg, 1611), 6
"Geistliche Psalmen, Hymnen, Lieder und Gebet" (Nürnberg, 1607), 188
"Geistliche Seelen Musik" (Rostock, 1659), 87
"Geistliche Singe-Kunst" (Leipzig, 1671), 30
"Geistlicher Harffen-Klang" (Leipzig, 1679), 27
"Geistliches Neu-vermehrtes Gesang-Buch" (Schleusingen, 1672), 27
"Geistreiche Gesang Buch" (Halle, 1697), 133
"Geistreiches Gesang-Buch" (Darmstadt, 1698), 45, 123
GELOBET SEI DER HERR, 129
Gelobet sei der Herr, st. i, 129; st. v, 129; trans., App. II (39)
GELOBET SEIST DU, JESU CHRIST, 91
Gelobet seist du, Jesu Christ, st. i, 91; st. ii, 91; st. vii, 64, 91; trans., App. II (40); melody, 64, 91
Geneva Psalter (1551), the, 13, 127, 130
*Gerhardt, Paul (1607-76), 32, 40, 65, 74, 92, 103, 108, 135, 153, 159, 176, 183, 194, 195, M 4
"Gesangbuch Christlicher Psalmen und Kirchenlieder" (Dresden, 1625), 135 n.
"Gesangbuch. Darinnen Christliche Psalmen unnd Kirchen Lieder" (Dresden, 1593), 40, 48
Gesangbuch der Brüder inn Behemen und Merherrn" (Nürnberg, 1544), 37, 187
Gesenius, Justus (1601-73), D 3, 39
Gesius, Bartholomäus (1555?-1613-4), 67, 3, 5, 116, 143
"Geystliche gesangk Buchleyn" (Wittenberg, 1524), 2, 4, 7, 14, 18, 22, 36, 38, 59, 64, 69, 77, 83, 121, 169
"Geystliche Lieder" (Leipzig, 1545), 33
Gieb, dass ich thu' mit Fleiss, 45

38—2

Gieb dich zufrieden, und sei stille, melodies, Introd. pp. 84, 86
Gieb unsern Fürsten, melody, 42, 126
Gigas, Johannes G. (1514–81), 114
"Glaub- und Liebesübung" (Bremen, 1680), 40, 57, 137
GLEICH WIE DER REGEN UND SCHNEE VOM HIMMEL FÄLLT, 18
Gloria Paschalis, the, melody, 85
Gloria sei dir gesungen, 140
Glorie, Lob, Ehr' und Herrlichkeit, 106
GOD GOETH UP WITH SHOUTING, 43
GOD'S TIME IS BEST, 106
GOD'S TIME IS THE BEST, 106
Görlitz "Gesangbuch" (1611), the, 161
GOTT, DER HERR, IST SONN' UND SCHILD, 79
GOTT DER HOFFNUNG ERFÜLLE EUCH, D 2
Gott des Himmels und der Erden, melody, App. I (3)
Gott fähret auf gen Himmel, st. vii, 11 ; trans., App. II (41)
GOTT FÄHRET AUF MIT JAUCHZEN, 43
Gott hat die Erd' schön zugericht't, 187
Gott heil'ger Geist, du Tröster werth, 126
GOTT IST MEIN KÖNIG, 71
Gott ist mein Schild und Helfersmann, see Ist Gott, etc.
GOTT IST UNS'RE ZUVERSICHT, 197
Gott Lob und Dank, der nicht zugab, 14
GOTT, MAN LOBET DICH IN DER STILLE, 120
Gott, mein Herz dir Dank zusendet, melody, Introd. p. 87
GOTT SEGNE NOCH DIE TREUE SCHAAR, 76 n.
GOTT SOLL ALLEIN MEIN HERZE HABEN, 169
Gott Vater, sende deinen Geist, st. ii, 74 ; st. x, 108 ; trans., App. II (42)
GOTT, WIE DEIN NAME, SO IST AUCH DEIN RUHM, 171
Gott, wie gross ist deine Güte, melody, Introd. p. 88
GOTTES ZEIT IST DIE ALLERBESTE ZEIT, 106
Gottlob, es geht nunmehr zum Ende, melody, Introd. p. 90
GOTTLOB! NUN GEHT DAS JAHR ZU ENDE, 28
Gottsched, Professor J. C., Introd. pp. 12, 24
Goudimel, Claude (1507–72), 130
Graf, Simon, 95
Grates nunc omnes reddamus, melody, 64
Graumann, Johann (1487–1541), 17, 28, 29, 51, 167, M 1
*Greitter, Matthäus (d. c. 1550), 69, App. I (2)
Gross ist, O grosser Gott, melody, 24, 45
Grossgebauer, Philipp (d. 1711), 106 n.
Grüenwald, Georg (d. 1530), 86, 74

INDEX 597

Grummer, Theobald (1642), 78
Gute Nacht, O Wesen, 64
Gutes und die Barmherzigkeit, 112
Gutknecht, Jobst (1531), 80
Halberstadt "Gesangbuch" (1673), the, 128
Halle "Gesangbuch" (1697), the, 133; (1698), 115
HALT' IM GEDÄCHTNISS JESUM CHRIST, 67
Hamburg "Enchiridion" (1565), the, 127
Hammerschmidt, Andreas (1612-75), 40, 70, 124, 154, 157, 163
"Handbüchlein: Geistliche Lieder und Gebetlin" (Frankfort a. Oder, 1586 [1582]), 166
"Hannoverische ordentliche Vollständige Gesangbuch" (Göttingen, 1676), 12; (Lüneburg, 1657), 77
Hanover "Gesang-Buch" (1646), the, 45, 107, D 3; (1657), 77
"Harmonia Cantionum ecclesiasticarum" (Leipzig, 1598), 85, App. I (1)
"Harmoniae sacrae" (Görlitz, 1613), 161
"Harmonischer Lieder-Schatz, oder Allgemeines Evangelisches Choral-Buch" (Frankfort, 1738), 133
Harsdörffer, Georg Philipp (1607-58), 78
*Hassler, Hans Leo (1564-1612), 135, 153, 159, 161
Hast du denn, Jesu, dein Angesicht gäntzlich verborgen, st. vi, 57; trans., App. II (43); melody, 57
Hast du denn, Liebster, dein Angesicht gäntzlich verborgen, 57
"M. Joh. Heinrich Hävecker's...Kirchen-Echo" (Leipzig, 1695), 27
*Heermann, Johann (1585-1647), 5, 13, 24, 25, 45, 71, 89, 107, 136, 148, 163, 194, 199, App. I (4)
Heil'ger Geist in's Himmels Throne, 194
Helbig, Johann F. (1720), Introd. p. 6 n.
Helft mir Gott's Güte preisen, st. vi, 16, 28; trans., App. II (44); melody, 11, 16, 28, 183
Helmbold, Ludwig (1532-98), 73, 11, 79, 165, D 4
Henrici, Christian Friedrich (1700-64), Introd. pp. 6 n., 19 n., 31
Henssberg, Paul von (d. 1652), 162
*Herberger, Valerius (1562-1627), 95
Herbert, Petrus (d. 1571), 159
Herman, Nicolaus (d. 1561), 15, 6, 31, 67, 95, 145, 151, 195
Hermann, Johann (fl. 1548-63), 41, 171, 190
HERR CHRIST, DER EIN'GE GOTTES-SOHN, 96

Herr Christ, der einig' Gotts Sohn, st. i, 96 ; st. v, 22, 96, 132, 164 ; trans., App. II (45) ; melody, 22, 96, 132, 164
HERR, DEINE AUGEN SEHEN NACH DEM GLAUBEN, 102
HERR, GEHE NICHT IN'S GERICHT, 105
Herr, gieb das ich dein' Ehre, 107
HERR GOTT, BEHERRSCHER ALLER DINGE, U 3
HERR GOTT, DICH LOBEN ALLE WIR, 130
Herr Gott, dich loben alle wir, st. i, 130 ; st. xi, xii, 130 ; trans., App. II (46) ; melody, 130
HERR GOTT DICH LOBEN WIR, 16
Herr Gott dich loben wir, 16, 119, 120, 190 ; trans., App. II (47) ; melody, 16, 119, 120, 190
Herr Gott Vater, mein starker Held, 37
Herr! ich glaube, hilf mir Schwachen, 78
Herr, ich habe missgehandelt, melody, 162
Herr, ich hoff' je, 184
Herr Jesu Christ, du hast bereit, melody, Introd. p. 71
HERR JESU CHRIST, DU HÖCHSTES GUT, 113
Herr Jesu Christ, du höchstes Gut, st. i, 113 ; st. ii, 113, 131 ; st. iv, 113 ; st. v, 131 ; st. vii, 113 ; st. viii, 113, 168 ; trans., App. II (48) ; melody, 48, 113, 131, 166, 168
Herr Jesu Christ, einiger Trost, 48
Herr Jesu Christ, ich schrei zu dir, st. xii, 48 ; trans., App. II (49) ; melody, 48, 113, 131, 166, 168
Herr Jesu Christ, ich weiss gar wohl, st. iii, 166 ; trans., App. II (50)
Herr Jesus Christ, mein's Lebens Licht, see *O Jesu Christ*, etc.
HERR JESU CHRIST, WAHR'R MENSCH UND GOTT, 127
Herr Jesu Christ, wahr'r Mensch und Gott, st. i, 127 ; st. viii, 127 ; trans., App. II (51); melody, 127
Herr, mein Hirt, Brunn aller Freuden, M 4
Herr, nun lass' in Friede, melody, Introd. p. 69
HERR, WIE DU WILLT, SO SCHICK'S MIT MIR, 73
Herr, wie du willt, so schick's mit mir, st. i, 73, 156 trans., App. II (52) ; melody, 156
Herrscher über Tod und Leben, 8
HERZ UND MUND UND THAT UND LEBEN, 147
Herzlich lieb hab' ich dich, O Herr, st. i, 174 ; st. iii, 149 ; trans., App. II (53); melody, 149, 174
Herzlich thut mich verlangen, st. iv, 161 ; trans., App. II (54); melody, 25, 135, 153, 159, 161
Herzliebster Jesu, was hast du verbrochen, melody, App. I (4)
Hesse, Johann (1490–1547), 13
Heut' lebst du, heut' bekehre dich, 102

INDEX 599

Heut' schleusst er wieder auf die Thür, 151
Hier ist das rechte Osterlamm, 4, 158
Hier lieg ich nun, O Vater aller Gnaden, melody, Introd. p. 91
Hilf deinem Volk, Herr Jesu Christ, 119
Hilf, Herr Jesu, lass' gelingen, melody, Introd. p. 73
Hilf mir, Herr Jesu, weil ich leb', melody, 3
Hilf mir mein' Sach' recht greifen an, 153
Hilf, O Herr Jesu, hilf du mir, 102
"Himlischer Lieder mit...Melodeien" (Lüneburg, 1641–42), 11, 20, 55, 78
HIMMELSKÖNIG, SEI WILLKOMMEN, 182
"Himmels-Lust und Welt-Unlust" (Jena, 1679), 45, 123
"Himmlische Harpffe Davids" (Nürnberg, 1581), 52
Hinunter ist der Sonnenschein, melody, 6
HÖCHSTERWÜNSCHTES FREUDENFEST, 194
Hojer, Conrad, 3
HOLD IN REMEMBRANCE JESUS CHRIST, 67
Homburg, E. C. (1605–81), "Geistlicher Lieder" (Naumburg, 1659 [1658]), 85, 12
Horn, Johann, see Roh, Johann
HOW BRIGHTLY SHINES, 1
"Hundert ahnmuthig- und sonderbahr geistlicher Arien" (Dresden, 1694), 85, 115; (1714), 139
"Hundert Christenliche Haussgesang" (Frankfort a. Oder, 1569), 187
"Hymni sacri Latini et germanici" (Erfurt, 1594), 6, 127

I HAD GREAT HEAVINESS OF HEART, 21
I WITH MY CROSS-STAFF GLADLY WANDER, 56
Ich armer Mensch, ich armer Sünder, st. i, 179; trans., App. II (55)
ICH ARMER MENSCH, ICH SÜNDENKNECHT, 55
ICH BIN EIN GUTER HIRT, 85
Ich bin, ja, Herr, in deiner Macht, melody, Introd. p. 93
ICH BIN VERGNÜGT MIT MEINEM GLÜCKE, 84
Ich bitte dich, Herr Jesu Christ, 166
Ich bitt' O Herr, aus Herzens Grund, 18
Ich dank' dir, lieber Herre, st. iv, 37; trans., App. II (56); melody, 37
Ich Dein betrubtes Kind, 199
ICH ELENDER MENSCH, 48
ICH FREUE MICH IN DIR, 133
Ich freue mich in dir, st. i, 133; st. iv, 133, U 1; trans., App. II (57); melody, 133, Introd. p. 71

INDEX

ICH GEH' UND SUCHE MIT VERLANGEN, 49
Ich ging einmal spazieren, melody, 11
ICH GLAUBE, LIEBER HERR, HILF MEINEM UNGLAUBEN, 109
Ich gnüge mich an meinem Stande, melody, Introd. p. 94
Ich hab' dich einen Augenblick, 103
ICH HAB' IN GOTTES HERZ UND SINN, 92
Ich hab' in Gottes Herz und Sinn, st. i, ii, 92; st. v, 92; st. x, 65, 92; st. xii, 92; trans., App. II (58)
Ich hab' mein Sach' Gott heimgestellt, melody, 106
ICH HABE MEINE ZUVERSICHT, 188
Ich hab' vor mir ein' schwere Reis', 58
Ich halte treulich still, melody, Introd. p. 96
ICH HATTE VIEL BEKÜMMERNISS, 21
Ich hört ein Fräulein klagen, melody, 22
Ich lass' dich nicht, melody, Introd. p. 68 n.
ICH LASSE DICH NICHT, DU SEGNEST MICH DENN, 157
Ich leb' indess in dir vergnüget, 84
ICH LIEBE DEN HÖCHSTEN VON GANZEM GEMÜTHE, 174
Ich liebe Jesum alle Stund, melody, Introd. p. 97
Ich lieg' im Streit und widerstreb', 177
Ich rief dem Herrn in meiner Noth, 117
ICH RUF' ZU DIR, HERR JESU CHRIST, 177
Ich ruf' zu dir, Herr Jesu Christ, st. i, 177, 185; st. v, 177; trans., App. II (59); melody, 177, 185
Ich steh' an deiner Krippen hier, melody, Introd. p. 98
ICH STEH' MIT EINEM FUSS IM GRABE, 156
Ich weiss mir ein Röslein hübsch und fein, melody, 106
Ich will alle meine Tage, 25
Ich will auf den Herren schau'n, 93
ICH WILL DEN KREUZSTAB GERNE TRAGEN, 56
Ich will des Herren Zorn, melody, 133
Ich will hier bei dir stehen, 159
Ich will zu aller Stunde, st. xiv, 107; trans., App. II (60)
IHR, DIE IHR EUCH VON CHRISTO NENNET, 164
IHR MENSCHEN, RÜHMET GOTTES LIEBE, 167
IHR WERDET WEINEN UND HEULEN, 103
Il me souffit de tous mes maulx, melody, 65
Il n'y a icy celluy, melody, 130
IN ALLEN MEINEN THATEN, 97
In allen meinen Thaten, st. i, 97; st. xv, 13, 44, 97; trans., App. II (61)
In dich hab' ich gehoffet, Herr, st. i, 52; st. vii, 106; trans., App. II (62); melody, 52, 106

INDEX 601

In dieser letzt betrübten Zeit, 6
In Gottes Namen fahren wir, melody, 77
In natali Domini, melody, 187
Innspruck, ich muss dich lassen, melody, 13
*Isaak, Heinrich (b. *c.* 1440), 13, 44, 97
Ist Gott mein Schild und Helfersmann, st. iv, 85 ; trans., App. II (63) ; melody, 85, Introd. p. 69
Ist Gott mein Schutz und treuer Hirt, 85
Ist Gott versöhnt und unser Freund, 122

Jahn, Martin, see Janus, Martin
Jakob, F., and Richter, E., "Allgemeines vierstimmiges Kirchen- und Haus-Choralbuch" (Berlin, [1873]), M 5
Janus, Martin (*c.* 1620–82), 147, 154
JAUCHZET DEM HERRN ALLE WELT, 28 n.
JAUCHZET GOTT IN ALLEN LANDEN, 51
Jedoch dein heilsam Wort, das macht, 113
Jesu, deine Liebeswunden, melody, Introd. p. 99
Jesu, deine Passion, 159, 182
JESU, DER DU MEINE SEELE, 78
Jesu, der du meine Seele, st. i, 78 ; st. xi, 105 ; st. xii, 78 ; trans., App. II (64); melody (1662), 78, 105 ; (1641), 162
Jesu, du mein liebstes Leben, Introd. p. 73
Jesu dulcis memoria, 3
Jesu, Jesu, du bist mein, melody, Introd. p. 100
Jesu Kreuz, Leiden und Pein, melody, 159, 182
Jesu Leiden, Pein und Tod, st. xxxiii, 159, 182 ; trans., App. II (65) ; melody, 159, 182
Jesu, mein Hort und Erretter, 154
JESU, MEINE FREUDE, M 3
Jesu, meine Freude, st. i, M 3 ; st. ii, 81, M 3 ; st. iv, M 3 ; st. v, 64 ; st. vi, M 3 ; trans., App. II (66) ; melody, 64, 81, 87, M 3
Jesu, meiner Seelen Wonne, st. ii, 154 ; st. vi, 147 ; st. xvii, 147 ; trans., App. II (67)
Jesu, nimm dich deiner Glieder, 40
JESU, NUN SEI GEPREISET, 41
Jesu, nun sei gepreiset, st. i, 41 ; st. ii, 190 ; st. iii, 41, 171 ; trans., App. II (68) ; melody, 41, 171, 190
JESU, PRICELESS TREASURE, M 3
Jesu, wahres Brod des Lebens, 180
Jesum lass' ich nicht von mir, 124
Jesus bleibet meine Freude, 147
Jesus Christus, Gottes Sohn, 4

Jesus, meine Zuversicht, melody, 145
JESUS NAHM ZU SICH DIE ZWÖLFE, 22
Jesus nimmt die Sünder an, 113 n.
JESUS SCHLÄFT, WAS SOLL ICH HOFFEN? 81
JESUS SLEEPS, VAIN ALL MY HOPING, 81
JESUS SLEEPS, WHAT HOPE REMAINETH? 81
Jonas, Justus (1493-1555), 178, 73

Keimann, Christian (1607-62), 40, 70, 124, 154, 157
Kein Menschenkind hier auf der Erd', 74
Kein' Frucht das Weizen-Körnlein bringt, 114
"Kirchen Gesäng" (Frankfort, 1584), 15
"Kirchē gesenge, mit vil schönen Psalmen unnd Melodey" (Nürnberg, 1531), 42, 80
"Kirchēampt mit lobgsengen" (Strassburg, 1525), 69, 156; App. I (2)
"Kirchenordnung" (Nürnberg, 1557), 23
Klug, Joseph (fl. 1529-43), 6, 7, 16, 18, 42, 59, 65, 66, 70, 73, 80, 177, 178, D 2
Knoll, Christoph (1563-1650), 161, 135
Knox, John, *Psalter* (1561), 130
König, Johann Balthasar (1691-1758), 133
Kolross, Johann (d. 1558?), 37
KOMM, DU SÜSSE TODESSTUNDE, 161
Komm, Gott Schöpfer, heiliger Geist, st. i, D 2; trans., App. II (69); melody, D 2
Komm, heiliger Geist, Herre Gott, st. i, 59; st. iii, M 2; trans., App. II (70); melody, 59, 172, 175, M 2
KOMM, JESU, KOMM, M 5
Komm, Jesu, komm, mein Leib ist müde, st. xi, M 5; trans., App. II (71); melody, M 5
Komm, O Tod, du Schlafes Bruder, 56
Komm, süsser Tod, melody, Introd. p. 102
Kommst du nun, Jesu, vom Himmel herunter, melody, 57
Kommt her, ihr lieben Schwesterlein, 151
Kommt her zu mir, spricht [sagt] Gottes Sohn, st. xvi, 86; trans., App. II (72); melody, 74, 86, 108
Kommt, lasst euch den Herren lehren, st. vi, 39; trans., App. II (73)
Kommt, Seelen, dieser Tag, melody, Introd. p. 104
Kommt wieder aus der finstern Gruft, melody, Introd. p. 105
Kradenthaller, Hieronymus (1675), 24
Krebs, Johann Ludwig, Introd. p. 73
Kugelmann, Johann (d. 1542), 17, 28, 29, 167, M 1

INDEX 603

Lass' dein' Engel mit mir fahren, 19
Lass' deine Kirch' und unser Land, D 3
Lass' uns das Jahr vollbringen, 190
Leit' uns mit deiner rechten Hand, 90, 101
LET SONGS OF REJOICING BE RAISED, 149
LIEBSTER GOTT, WANN WERD' ICH STERBEN? 8
Liebster Gott, wann werd' ich sterben? st. i, 8 ; st. v, 8 ;
    trans., App. II (74) ; melody, 8
Liebster Herr Jesu, wo bleibst du so lange, melody, Introd.
    p. 106
LIEBSTER IMMANUEL, HERZOG DER FROMMEN, 123
Liebster Immanuel, Herzog der Frommen, st. i, 123; st. v,
    123 ; trans., App. II (75) ; melody, 123
LIEBSTER JESU, MEIN VERLANGEN, 32
Lob, Ehr' und Dank sei dir gesagt, 121
Lob, Ehr' und Preis sei Gott, 192
Lob sei Gott dem Vater g'thon, 36, 62
Lob und Preis sei Gott dem Vater, 10
LOBE DEN HERREN, DEN MÄCHTIGEN KÖNIG DER
    EHREN, 137
Lobe den Herren, den mächtigen König der Ehren, st. i, ii, 137 ;
    st. iv, v, 137, U 3 ; trans., App. II (76) ; melody, 57, 137,
    U 3
Lobe den Herren, der Alles so herrlich regieret, 137
Lobe den Herren, der deinen Stand sichtbar gesegnet, 137, U 3
Lobe den Herren, was in mir ist, lobe den Namen, 137, U 3
LOBE DEN HERRN, MEINE SEELE, 69, 143
Lob' Gott getrost mit Singen, melody, 37
LOBET GOTT IN SEINEN REICHEN, 11
Lobt Gott, ihr Christen alle gleich, st. viii, 151 ; trans.,
    App. II (77) ; melody, 151, 195
LOBT IHN MIT HERZ UND MUNDE, D 4
Lobt ihn mit Herz und Munde, D 4
Lossius, Lucas (1553), 65
Louise Henriette, Electress of Brandenburg (1627-67), 145
Lüneburg "Gesangbuch" (1661), the, 128 ; (1686), 40
Luppius, Andreas (1692), 139
"Lust- und Artzneigarten des Königlichen Propheten
    Davids" (Regensburg, 1675), 24
"Lustgarten Neuer Teutscher Gesäng" (Nürnberg, 1601),
    135
Luther, Martin (1483-1546), 2, 4, 6, 14, 16, 22, 36, 38, 42,
    59, 61, 62, 64, 69, 70, 76, 77, 80, 83, 90, 91, 95, 106,
    119, 120, 121, 125, 126, 153, 156, 158, 169, 190, 197,
    D 2, M 2 ; App. I (6)

MACHE DICH, MEIN GEIST, BEREIT, 115
Mache dich, mein Geist, bereit, st. i, 115; st. x, 115;
  trans., App. II (78); melody, 115
Mach's mit mir, Gott, nach deiner Güt', st. i, 156; trans.,
  App. II (79); melody, 139, 156
*Magdeburg, Joachim (*c.* 1525–83), 11, 65
Major, Johann (1564–1654), 48
Man halte nur ein wenig stille, 93
MAN SINGET MIT FREUDEN VOM SIEG, 149
Manebit verbum Domini, 80 n.
Marenzio, Luca (d. 1598), 79
"Meditationes Sanctorum Patrum" (Görlitz, 1584, 1587),
  3, 90
Mein Gott, öffne mir die Pforten, 32
MEIN GOTT, WIE LANG', ACH LANGE, 155
MEIN HERZE SCHWIMMT IM BLUT, 199
Mein Jesu, was vor Seelenweh, melody, Introd. p. 108
MEIN LIEBSTER JESUS IST VERLOREN, 154
Meine Hoffnung stehet feste, melody, 40
MEINE SEEL' ERHEBT DEN HERREN, 10
Meine Seel' erhebt den Herren, melody, 10; trans., App. II
  (80)
Meine Seele, lass' es gehen, melody, Introd. p. 109
MEINE SEUFZER, MEINE THRÄNEN, 13
MEINEN JESUM LASS' ICH NICHT, 124
Meinen Jesum lass' ich nicht, st. i, 124; st. v, 70; st. vi,
  124, 154, 157; trans., App. II (81); melody, 70, 124,
  154, 157, 163, Introd. p. 69
Meines Lebens letzte Zeit, melody, Introd. p. 71
Melanchthon, Philipp (1497–1560), 130
Melissander, see Bienemann, Caspar
Meusel, Wolfgang (1497–1563), 112
Meyfart, Johann Matthäus (1590–1642), 46
Mir mangelt zwar sehr viel, 89
MIT FRIED' UND FREUD' ICH FAHR' DAHIN, 125
Mit Fried' und Freud' ich fahr' dahin, st. i, 95, 106,
  125; st. ii, 125; st. iv, 83, 125; trans., App. II (82);
  melody, 83, 95, 106, 125
Mit Segen mich beschütte, 194
Mit unsrer Macht ist nichts gethan, 80
Moller, Martin (1547–1606), 3, 44, 58, 90, 101, 153
Monoetius, Bartholomäus (1565), 47
Müller, Heinrich (1631–75), 87
Muntzer, Thomas (1524), 64
Musculus, see Meusel, Wolfgang

INDEX   605

"Musicalische Kirch- und Hauss-Ergötzlichkeit" (Leipzig, 1713), 8, 40, 78, M 4
"Musicalischer Andachten Geistlicher Moteten undt Concerten" (Freiberg, 1646), 40
Muss ich sein betrübet, 87
MY SOUL DOTH MAGNIFY THE LORD, 10
MY SPIRIT WAS IN HEAVINESS, 21

Neander, Joachim (1650-80), 137, 40, 57, U 3
"Neu Leipziger Gesangbuch" (Leipzig, 1682 [1681]), 1, 27, 68, 159
"Neuer geistlicher Arien" (Mühlhausen, 1660-64), 60
Neumann, Caspar (1648-1715), 8, 145
Neumark, Georg (1621-81), 21, 84, 88, 93, 166, 179, 197
Neumeister, Erdmann (1671-1756), Introd. p. 6 n.
"Neu-vermehrtes...Meiningisches Gesangbuch" (Meiningen, 1693), 24
"Neuvermehrtes vollständiges Gesangbuch" (Brunswick, 1661), 26
"Neu-Vollständigers Marggräfl. Brandenburgisches Gesang-Buch" (Bayreuth, 1668), 27
"New Leipziger Gesangbuch" (Leipzig, 1682 [1681]), 1, 159
"New Ordentlich Gesangbuch" (Brunswick, 1648), 39
"New Ordentlich Gesang-Buch" (Hanover, 1646), 45, 107, D 3
"Newe Symbola etlicher Fürsten" (Nürnberg, 1571), 149
"Newes vollkömliches Gesangbuch" (Berlin, 1640), App. I (4)
"News Gesanng, mit Dreyen stymmen" (Augsburg, 1540), 17
Nicht nach Welt, nach Himmel nicht, 70
Nicht so traurig, nicht so sehr, melody, Introd. p. 110
Nicolai, Philipp (1556-1608), 1, 36, 37, 49, 61, 140, 172
NIMM VON UNS, HERR, DU TREUER GOTT, 101
Nimm von uns, Herr, du treuer Gott, st. i, iii, iv, v, vi, 101; st. vii, 90, 101; trans., App. II (83)
NIMM, WAS DEIN IST, UND GEHE HIN, 144
Noch eins, Herr, will ich bitten dich, 111
Nun bitten wir den heiligen Geist, st. iii, 169, 197; trans., App. II (84); melody, 169, 197
NUN DANKET ALLE GOTT, 192
Nun danket alle Gott, st. i, 79, 192; st. iii, 192; trans., App. II (85); melody, 79, 192
Nun danket all' und bringet Ehr', st. i, 195; trans., App. II (86)

606   INDEX

Nun freut euch, lieben Christen g'mein, melody, 70
Nun hilf uns, Herr, den Dienern dein, 120
Nun, ich weiss, du wirst mir stillen, 105
NUN KOMM, DER HEIDEN HEILAND, 61, 62
Nun komm, der Heiden Heiland, st. i, 36, 61, 62; st. vi, 36; st. viii, 36, 62; trans., App. II (87); melody, 36, 61, 62
Nun lasst uns Gott dem Herren, st. v, 165; st. viii, 79; trans., App. II (88); melody, 79, 165, 194
Nun lieget alles unter dir, 11
Nun lob', mein Seel', den Herren, st. i, 28; st. iii, 17, M 1; st. v, 28 n., 29, 51, 167; trans., App. II (89); melody, 17, 28, 29, 51, 167, M 1
Nun werther Geist, ich folg' dir, 175
Nunc Dimittis, 83
NUR JEDEM DAS SEINE, 163
" Nürnbergisches Gesang-Buch " (Nürnberg, 1690), 12

O EWIGKEIT, DU DONNERWORT, 20, 60
O Ewigkeit, du Donnerwort, st. i, 20, 60; st. xi, 20; st. xvi, 20; trans., App. II (90); melody, 20, 60
O finstre Nacht, melody, Introd. p. 111
O GOD, HOW MANY PAINS OF HEART, 3
O Gott, der du aus Herzensgrund, st. ix, x, D 3; trans., App. II (91)
O Gott, du frommer Gott, st. i, 24; st. ii, 45; st. vi, 71; trans., App. II (92); melody (1646), 24, 45; melody (1679), 45, 64, 94, 128, 129, U 1; melody (1693), 24, 71, 133, 164
O Gottes Geist, mein Trost und Rath, st. ix, 175; trans., App. II (93)
O grosser Gott der Treu', 46
O grosser Gott von Macht, st. ix, 46; trans., App. II (94); melody, 46, 133
O Haupt voll Blut, st. vi, 159; trans., App. II (95); melody, see *Herzlich thut mich verlangen*
O HEIL'GES GEIST- UND WASSERBAD, 165
O Herr, vergib, vergib mir's doch, 113
O Herre Gott, dein göttlich Wort, st. viii, 184; trans., App. II (96); melody, 184
O Herzensangst, O Bangigkeit und Zagen, melody, Introd. p. 113
O JESU CHRIST, MEIN'S LEBENS LICHT, 118
O Jesu Christ, mein's Lebens Licht, st. i, 118; st. ii, 58; trans., App. II (97); melody, 3, 44, 118, 153

INDEX 607

O JESU CHRIST, THOU PRINCE OF PEACE, 116
O Jesu, du mein Bräutigam, melody, Introd. p. 69
O Jesu, meine Lust, st. iv, 128; trans., App. II (98)
O Lamm Gottes unschuldig, melody, App. I (5)
O liebe Seele, zieh die Sinnen, melody, Introd. p. 115
O Mensch, bewein' dein Sünde gross, melody, App. I (2)
O Mensch, schau Jesum Christum an, melody, Introd. p. 70
O PRAISE THE LORD FOR ALL HIS MERCIES, 28
O stilles Gottes Lamm, melody, 133
O Welt, ich muss dich lassen, melody, 13, 44, 97
Ob bei uns ist der Sünden viel, 38
Ob sich's anliess, als wollt' er nicht, 9, 155, 186
Oemler, Georg Aemilius, 47 n.
"Old Hundredth," the, 130
Olearius, Johannes (1611–84), 30, 129
On a beau son maison bastir, melody, 127
Or sus, serviteurs du Seigneur, melody, 130
"Ordnung des Herren Nachtmal" (Strassburg, 1525), 69, 156
Otto, Stephen (*c.* 1622), 40

Pachelbel, Johann (1653–1706), 12, 5, 163
"Pavia Tone," the, 18
Peter, Christoph (1655), 48
Pfefferkorn, Georg Michael (1645–1732), 64, 27, 94
Picander, see Henrici, Christian Friedrich
Poliander, see Graumann, Johann
PRAISE JEHOVAH IN HIS SPLENDOUR, 11
PRAISE GOD! THE YEAR DRAWS TO ITS CLOSING, 28
PRAISE OUR GOD WHO REIGNS IN HEAVEN, 11
PRAISE THOU THE LORD, JERUSALEM, 119
"Praxis Pietatis Melica" (Berlin, 1647), 32, 65, 194, 195;
  (Berlin, 1648), 11, 79; (Berlin, 1653), 20, 40, 56, 64, 74, 103, 145, 153, 176, 180, 183, M 4; (Frankfort, 1656), 159; (Berlin, 1661), 26; (Frankfort, 1662), 37, 78, 95; (Berlin, 1709), 73, 139, 179
PREISE, JERUSALEM, DEN HERRN, 119
"Psalmen und geystliche Lieder" (Strassburg, 1537), 121
"Psalmodia, hoc est, Cantica sacra veteris ecclesiae selecta" (Nürnberg, 1553 [1550]), 65
"Psalmodia nova" (Leipzig, 1630), 3
"Psalmodia sacra" (Gotha, 1715), 24
"Pseaumes octante trois de David" (Geneva, 1551), 13, 127, 130
Puer natus in Bethlehem, melody, 65

Quirsfeld, Johann (1679), 27 n.

Reese, Frau (d. 1723), Introd. p. 46 n.
"Reformatorisches Choralbuch für Kirche, Schule und Haus" (Berlin, [1873]), M 5
*Reissner, Adam (1496–c. 1575), 52, 106
Resonet in laudibus, melody, 1
Reusner, Adam, see Reissner, Adam
Rhau, Johann (1589), 106
Rhodanthracius, see Kolross, Johann
Richte dich, Liebste, nach meinem Gefallen und gläube, 57
Richter, E. (1873), M 5
Ringwaldt, Bartholomäus (1532–c. 1600), 113, 48, 70, 131, 166, 168
Rinkart, Martin (1586–1649), 79, 192
*Rist, Johann (1607–67), 11, 20, 40, 43, 55, 60, 78, 105, 175
Rodigast, Samuel (1649–1708), 12, 69, 75, 98, 99, 100, 144
Roh, Johann (d. 1547), 37, 187
Rosenmüller, Johann (1619–84), 27, 158, 162
Rube, Johann Christoph (1665–1746), 139
*Runge, Christoph (1619–81), 20, 79, 145
Rutilius, Martin (1550–1618), 48

"Sabbahtische Seelenlust...von Johann Rist" (Lüneburg, 1651), 175
*Sacer, Gottfried Wilhelm (1635–99), 11
Sachs, Hans (1494–1576), 47, 138
Schaffs mit mir, Gott, nach deinem Willen, melody, Introd. p. 116
*Schalling, Martin (1532–1608), 149, 174
SCHAU', LIEBER GOTT, WIE MEINE FEIND', 153
Schau', lieber Gott, wie meine Feind', st. i, 153 ; trans., App. II (99)
SCHAUET DOCH UND SEHET, 46
Scheffler, Johann (1624–77), 147
*Schein, Johann Hermann (1586–1630), 5, 13, 52, 139, 156
Schemelli, Georg Christian, " Musicalisches Gesang-Buch" (Leipzig, 1736), 8, 123 ; Introd. pp. 56, 72
Schmidt, Bernhard (1577), 149
SCHMÜCKE DICH, O LIEBE SEELE, 180
Schmücke dich, O liebe Seele, st. i, 180 ; st. iv, 180 ; st. ix, 180 ; trans., App. II (100); melody, 180
Schneegass, Cyriacus (1546–97), 122, 135

Schneesing, Johannes (d. 1567), 33
Schnurr, Balthasar (1572–1644), 46
Schönster Immanuel etc., see *Liebster Immanuel*
*Schop, Johann (d. c. 1665), 11, 20, 43, 55, 60, 146, 147, 154, 162
Schüttle deinen Kopf und sprich, 40
Schütz, Johann Jakob (1640–90), 117, 45
Schumann, Valentin S. (d. 1545), 37, 85, 90, App. I (6)
Schwedler, Johann Christoph (1672–1730), M 5
Schwing' dich auf zu deinem Gott, st. ii, 40; trans., App. II (101); melody, 40, Introd. p. 70
SCHWINGT FREUDIG EUCH EMPOR, 36
Sedulius, Coelius, 121
SEHET, WELCH' EINE LIEBE HAT UNS DER VATER ERZEIGET, 64
SEHET, WIR GEH'N HINAUF GEN JERUSALEM, 159
SEI LOB UND EHR' DEM HÖCHSTEN GUT, 117
Sei Lob und Ehr' dem höchsten Gut, st. i, 117; st. iv, 117; st. ix, 117; trans., App. II (102)
Sei Lob und Preis mit Ehren, 28 n., 29, 51, 167; Introd. p. 47 n.
Sein Wort, sein' Taufe, sein Nachtmahl, 165
Seklucyan, Pastor (1559), 47
SELIG IST DER MANN, 57
Selig ist die Seele, st. ix, 87; trans., App. II (103)
Selig sind, die aus Erbarmen, 39
Selig, wer an Jesum denkt, melody, Introd. p. 118
Selnecker, Nicolaus (1532–92), 6, 79
Sie stellen uns wie Ketzern nach, 178
SIE WERDEN AUS SABA ALLE KOMMEN, 65
SIE WERDEN EUCH IN DEN BANN THUN, 44, 183
SIEHE, ES HAT ÜBERWUNDEN DER LÖWE, D 3
SIEHE, ICH WILL VIEL FISCHER AUSSENDEN, 88
SIEHE ZU, DASS DEINE GOTTESFURCHT NICHT HEUCHELEI SEI, 179
SING TO THE LORD A GLAD NEW SONG, 190
SING YE TO THE LORD, M 1
Sing', bet' und geh' auf Gottes Wegen, 88, 93, 197 n.
Singen wir aus Herzensgrund, st. iv, 187; st. vi, 187; trans., App. II (104); melody, 187
SINGET DEM HERRN EIN NEUES LIED, 190, M 1
Singt dem Herren, singet, melody, Introd. p. 119
SLEEPERS WAKE! FOR NIGHT IS FLYING, 140
SLEEPERS WAKE, LOUD SOUNDS THE WARNING, 140
Sneider, see Agricola, Johannes

INDEX

So du mit deinem Munde bekennest Jesum, 145
So fahr' ich hin zu Jesu Christ, 31
So feiern wir das hohe Fest, 4
So giebst du nun, mein Jesu, gute Nacht, melody, Introd. p. 71
So kommet vor sein Angesicht, 117
So lang ein Gott im Himmel lebt, 20
So sei nun, Seele, deine, 13, 44, 97
So wahr ich lebe, spricht dein Gott, st. vi, vii, 102; trans., App. II (105)
So wandelt froh auf Gottes Wegen, 197
So wünsch ich mir zu guter letzt, melody, Introd. p. 119
Sömeren, Theodor von (1609), 188 n.
Söhren, Peter (1676), 70
Solls ja so sein, 48
Soll ich auf dieser Welt, 71
Soll ich denn auch des Todes Weg, 92
Soul, array thyself with gladness, 180
Spangenberg, Johann (1545), 85
Spengler, Lazarus (1479-1534), 18, 109
Speratus, Paul (1484-1551), 9, 86, 155, 186
Sprich Ja zu meinen Thaten, 194
Stärk mich mit deinem Freudengeist, 113, 168
Stay with us, the evening approaches, 6
Stenger, Nicolaus (1663), 78
Sternhold, Thomas, and Hopkins, John, "The whole Book of Psalmes" (1562), 130
Stieler, Caspar (1679), 163, 199
*Stockmann, Paul (1602?-36), 159, 182
Stolberg, Anna Countess of, 95
Straf mich nicht in deinem Zorn, melody, 115
Stralsund "Gesangbuch" (1665), the, 17
"Sünden-Schmertzen, Trost im Hertzen, Todten Kertzen" (Nürnberg, 1663), 179
Süsser Trost, mein Jesus kommt, 151
Sunderreitter, Gregorius (1581), 52

Tate, Nahum, and Brady, Nicolas, " New Version of the Psalms" (1696), 130
Teller, Abraham (1649), 27
The Lord is my Shepherd, 112
The sages of Sheba, 65
The Spirit also helpeth us, M 2
There is nought of soundness in my body, 25
Thou very God and David's Son, 23

"Threnodiae" (Freiberg, 1620), 13, 18, 48, 135
THUE RECHNUNG! DONNERWORT, 168
Tietze, Christoph (1641-1703), 179
Titius, see Tietze, Christoph
Tonus Peregrinus, 10
"Trente et quatre chansons musicales" (Paris, [1529]), 65
Treuer Gott, ich muss dir klagen, st. vi, 194; st. vii, 194; st. xii, 25; trans., App. II (106)
Tröstet, tröstet, meine Lieben, st. iii, 30; trans., App. II (107)

Und bitten dich: wollst allezeit, 130
Und obgleich alle Teufel, 153
Und was der ewig güt'ge Gott, 86
Und weil ich denn in meinem Sinn, 131
Und wenn die Welt voll Teufel wär', 80
UNS IST EIN KIND GEBOREN, 142
UNSER MUND SEI VOLL LACHENS, 110
Unter deinen Schirmen, 81, M 3

Valet will ich dir geben, st. i, 95; trans., App. II (108); melody, 95
Vater unser im Himmelreich, melody, 90, 101, 102
Veni Creator Spiritus, D 2
Veni Redemptor gentium, melody, 36
Veni Sancte Spiritus, 59
Venus du und dein Kind, melody, 5
Vergiss mein nicht, mein allerliebster Gott, melody, Introd. p. 121
Verleih' uns Frieden gnädiglich, st. i, 42, 126; trans., App. II (109); melody, 6, 42, 126
"Vermehrtes Gesang-Büchlein" (Halberstadt, 1673), 128
Verzage nicht, O Häuflein klein, st. i, 42; trans., App. II (110)
Vespera jam venit, nobiscum Christe maneto, 6
Vetter, Daniel (d. 1721), 8, 40, 78, M 4
Victimae paschali, 4
"Vollständige Kirchen- und Haus-Music" (Breslau, c. 1700), 8
"Vollständiges Gesang-Buch" (Lüneburg, 1661), 128
Vom Himmel hoch da komm ich her, melody, App. I (6)
Vom Himmel kam der Engel Schaar, melody, 65
Von Adam her so lange Zeit, melody, 36 n.
Von Gott kommt mir ein Freudenschein, 172

612   INDEX

Von Gott will ich nicht lassen, st. v, D 4 ; st. ix, 73 ; trans.,
    App. II (111); melody, 11, 73, 107, D 4
Vopelius, Gottfried (1645–1715), 1, 27, 68, 159
*Vulpius, Melchior (1560?–1615), 5, 95, 106, 122, 159, 182

Wach auf, mein Geist, erhebe dich, melody, 20, 60
Wach auf, mein Herz, und singe, st. ix, 194; st. x, 194;
    trans., App. II (112); melody, 79, 165, 194
WACHET AUF, RUFT UNS DIE STIMME, 140
Wachet auf, ruft uns die Stimme, st. i–iii, 140; trans., App.
    II (113); melody, 140
WACHET, BETET, BETET, WACHET, 70
Wachet doch, erwacht, ihr Schläfer, melody, 78, 105
WÄR' GOTT NICHT MIT UNS DIESE ZEIT, 14
Wär' Gott nicht mit uns diese Zeit, st. i, iii, 14 ; trans.,
    App. II (114); melody, 14
Wagner, Paul, "Andächtiger Seelen geistliches Brand- und
    Gantz-Opfer" (Leipzig, 1697), 11, 128, 129
WAHRLICH, WAHRLICH, ICH SAGE EUCH, 86
WAILING, CRYING, MOURNING, SIGHING, 12
*Walther, Johann (1496–1570), 2, 4, 7, 14, 18, 22, 36, 38, 59,
    64, 69, 77, 83, 121, 169, 176
Wann soll es doch geschehen, 11
WARUM BETRÜBST DU DICH, MEIN HERZ, 138
Warum betrübst du dich, mein Herz, st. i, ii, iii, 138; st. xi,
    47 ; trans., App. II (115) ; melody, 47, 106, 138
Warum betrübst du dich und beugest dich zu Erden, melody,
    Introd. p. 122
Warum sollt' ich mich denn grämen, st. xi, M 4 ; st. xii, M 4 ;
    trans., App. II (116); melody, M 4
Warum willst du so zornig sein? 101
Was alle Weisheit in der Welt, st. viii, 176 ; trans., App. II
    (117)
Was betrübst du dich, mein Herze, melody, Introd. p. 123
WAS FRAG ICH NACH DER WELT, 94
Was frag ich nach der Welt, st. i, 64, 94; st. iii, 94 ; st. v,
    94 ; st. vii, viii, 94 ; trans., App. II (118)
WAS GOTT THUT, DAS IST WOHLGETHAN, 98, 99, 100
Was Gott thut, das ist wohlgethan, st. i, 98, 99, 100, 144 ;
    st. v, 75 ; st. vi, 12, 69, 99, 100 ; trans., App. II (119);
    melody, 12, 69, 75, 98, 99, 100, 144
Was helfen uns die schweren Sorgen, 21, 93
WAS HILFT DES PURPURS MAJESTÄT, 75 n.
WAS MEIN GOTT WILL, DAS G'SCHEH' ALLZEIT, 111

INDEX 613

Was mein Gott will, st. i, 72, 111, 144 ; st. iv, 111 ; trans., App. II (120) ; melody, 65, 72, 92, 103, 111, 144
Was Menschen Kraft und Witz ansäht, 178
WAS SOLL ICH AUS DIR MACHEN, EPHRAIM? 89
WAS WILLST DU DICH BETRÜBEN, 107
Was willst du dich betrüben, st. i, 107; trans., App. II (121); melody, 107
Was wöll wir aber heben an, melody, 18
WATCH YE, PRAY YE, 70
Weber, Jeremias, " Gesangbuch" (Leipzig, 1638), 46
WEEPING, WAILING, MOURNING, FEARING, 12
Weg, mein Herz, mit den Gedanken, st. xii, 32 ; trans., App. II (122)
Weg mit allen Schätzen, M 3
Wegelin, Josua (1604-40), 128
Weicht, ihr Trauergeister, M 3
"Weihenacht und New Jahrs-Gesäng" (Erfurt, 1595), 122
Weil du mein Gott und Vater bist, 138
Weil du vom Tod' erstanden bist, 15, 95
WEINEN, KLAGEN, SORGEN, ZAGEN, 12
Weingärtner, Sigismund (1607), 188, 148 n.
*Weisse, Michael (1480?-1534), 36 n., App. I (1)
Welt, ade! ich bin dein müde, st. i, 27, 158 ; trans., App. II (123) ; melody, 27, 158
Wenn einer alle Ding verstünd, st. viii, 77 ; trans., App. II (124)
Wenn mein Stündlein vorhanden ist, st. iv, 15, 95 ; st. v, 31 ; trans., App. II (125) ; melody, 15, 31, 95
WER DA GLAUBET UND GETAUFT WIRD, 37
WER DANK OPFERT, DER PREISET MICH, 17
Wer hofft in Gott und dem vertraut, 109
WER MICH LIEBET, DER WIRD MEIN WORT HALTEN, 59, 74
WER NUR DEN LIEBEN GOTT LÄSST WALTEN, 93
Wer nur den lieben Gott lässt walten, st. i, 93 ; st. ii, 21, 93; st. iii, iv, 93; st. v, 21, 93; st. vi, 93; st. vii, 88, 93, 197 ; trans., App. II (126); melody, 21, 27, 84, 88, 93, 166, 179, 197
WER SICH SELBST ERHÖHET, 47
WER WEISS, WIE NAHE MIR MEIN ENDE, 27
Wer weiss, wie nahe mir mein Ende? st. i, 27, 166 ; st. xii, 84 ; trans., App. II (127)
Werde munter, mein Gemüthe, st. vi, 55 ; trans., App. II (128); melody, 55, 146, 147, 154
Werner, Margarita (d. 1628), 156
"Weynacht Liedlein" (Frankfort, 1575 [1569]), 11

WHEN WILL GOD RECALL MY SPIRIT? 8
Wie bin ich doch so herzlich froh, 1, 49
Wie schön leuchten die Aeugelein, 1
WIE SCHÖN LEUCHTET DER MORGENSTERN, 1
Wie schön leuchtet der Morgenstern, st. i, 1; st. iv, 172;
  st. v, 37; st. vi, 36; st. vii, 1, 49, 61; trans., App. II
  (129); melody, 1, 36, 37, 49, 61
Wie schwerlich lässt sich Fleisch und Blut, 3
Wie sich ein Vat'r erbarmet, 17, M 1
Wie wohl ist mir, O Freund der Seelen, melody, Introd.
  p. 125
Wildenfels, Anark Herr zu (d. 1539), 184
Wilisius, Jakob (d. 1695), 8
Wir Christenleut', st. iii, 40; st. v, 110, 142; trans., App. II
  (130); melody, 40, 110, 142
WIR DANKEN DIR, GOTT, WIR DANKEN DIR, 29
Wir danken dir, O frommer Gott, melody, 6
Wir danken sehr und bitten ihn, 187
Wir essen und leben wohl, 4
WIR MÜSSEN DURCH VIEL TRÜBSAL IN DAS REICH
  GOTTES EINGEHEN, 146
Wir wachen oder schlafen ein, 114
Witt, Christian Friedrich (d. 1716), 24
WO GEHEST DU HIN? 166
WO GOTT DER HERR NICHT BEI UNS HÄLT, 178
Wo Gott der Herr nicht bei uns hält, st. i, 178; st. ii, 178;
  st. iv, 178; st. v, 178; st. vii, 178; st. viii, 178; trans.,
  App. II (131); melody, 73, 114, 178, D 3
WO SOLL ICH FLIEHEN HIN, 5
Wo soll ich fliehen hin, st. i, 5; st. iii, 199; st. vii, 89; st.
  ix, 136; st. xi, 5, 148, 163; trans., App. II (132);
  melody (1609), 5, 89, 136, 188; (1679), 163, 199
WOHL DEM, DER SICH AUF SEINEN GOTT, 139
Wohl dem, der sich auf seinen Gott, st. i, 139; st. v, 139;
  trans., App. II (133)
Wohl mir, das ich Jesum habe, 147
Wohlan! so will ich mich, 133, U 1

YE MORTALS EXTOL THE LOVE OF THE FATHER, 167
YOU WILL THEY PUT UNDER BAN, 44

"Zehen Sterbegebet Reimweise zugerichtet" (Wittenberg,
  1611), 58
Zeuch ein zu deinen Thoren, st. v, 183; trans., App. II (134)
Ziegler, Caspar (1621–90), 133, U 1

Ziegler, Marianne von (1728), Introd. p. 12 n.
Zieh' uns dir nach, so laufen wir, 43
Zinckeisen, M. Eucharius (1584), 15
Zion hört die Wächter singen, 140
Zion klagt mit Angst und Schmerzen, st. ii, 13 ; trans., App. ii (135) ; melody, 32
Zu dem ist Weisheit und Verstand, 92
Zuletzt lass sie an unserm End', D 3
" Zwey Bücher Einer Neuen Kunstlichen Tabulatur auf Orgel und Instrument " (Strassburg, 1577), 149
" Zwey schöne newe geistliche Lieder " (Nürnberg, c. 1560), 47
Zwingt die Saiten in Cythara, 36

Cambridge:
PRINTED BY J. B. PEACE, M.A.,
AT THE UNIVERSITY PRESS

CPSIA information can be obtained
at www.ICGtesting.com
Printed in the USA
BVHW051641030822
643690BV00002B/276

9 789353 897208